T0234949

Lecture Notes in Computer Science　　12835

More information about this subseries at http://www.springer.com/series/7410

Toru Nakanishi · Ryo Nojima (Eds.)

Advances in Information and Computer Security

16th International Workshop on Security, IWSEC 2021
Virtual Event, September 8–10, 2021
Proceedings

 Springer

Editors
Toru Nakanishi
Hiroshima University
Hiroshima, Japan

Ryo Nojima
National Institute of Information
and Communications Technology
Tokyo, Japan

ISSN 0302-9743 ISSN 1611-3349 (electronic)
Lecture Notes in Computer Science
ISBN 978-3-030-85986-2 ISBN 978-3-030-85987-9 (eBook)
https://doi.org/10.1007/978-3-030-85987-9

LNCS Sublibrary: SL4 – Security and Cryptology

This Springer imprint is published by the registered company Springer Nature Switzerland AG
The registered company address is: Gewerbestrasse 11, 6330 Cham, Switzerland

Preface

The 16th International Workshop on Security, IWSEC 2021, was held online (originally scheduled to be held in Tokyo, Japan), during September 8–10, 2021. The workshop was co-organized by ISEC (the Technical Committee on Information Security in Engineering Sciences Society of IEICE) and CSEC (the Special Interest Group on Computer Security of IPSJ).

This year, we categorized topics of interests into two tracks, namely, Cryptography Track (Track A) and Cybersecurity and Privacy Track (Track B); each track was formed by separate Program Committee members. We received 37 submissions, 21 in Track A and 16 in Track B. After extensive reviews and shepherding, we accepted 11 regular papers (7 from Track A and 4 from Track B) and 3 short papers (2 from Track A and 1 from Track B). Each submission was anonymously reviewed by four reviewers on average. These proceedings contain revised versions of the accepted papers. Track A consists of the sessions on lattice-based cryptography, multiparty computation, post-quantum cryptography, and symmetric-key cryptography. Track B consists of the sessions on system security, machine learning and security, and game theory and security.

The Best Paper Awards were given to "Solving the Problem of Blockwise Isomorphism of Polynomials with Circulant Matrices" by Yasufumi Hashimoto and to "KPRM: Kernel Page Restriction Mechanism to Prevent Kernel Memory Corruption" by Hiroki Kuzuno and Toshihiro Yamauchi. The Best Student Paper Award was given to "Evolving Homomorphic Secret Sharing for Hierarchical Access Structures" by Kittiphop Phalakarn, Vorapong Suppakitpaisarn, Nuttapong Attrapadung, and Kanta Matsuura.

Under the COVID-19 pandemic circumstances, a number of people contributed to the success of IWSEC 2021. We would like to thank all authors for submitting their papers to the workshop, and we are also deeply grateful to the members of the Program Committee and to the external reviewers for their in-depth reviews and detailed discussions. Last but not least, we would like to thank the general co-chairs, Tetsuya Izu and Yuji Suga, for leading the Organizing Committee, and we would also like to thank the members of the Organizing Committee for ensuring the smooth running of the workshop.

September 2021

Toru Nakanishi
Ryo Nojima

IWSEC 2021
16th International Workshop on Security
Organization

Online, September 8–10, 2021

co-organized by

ISEC in ESS of IEICE

(Technical Committee on Information Security in Engineering Sciences Society of the Institute of Electronics, Information and Communication Engineers)

and

CSEC of IPSJ

(Special Interest Group on Computer Security of Information Processing Society of Japan)

General Co-chairs

Tetsuya Izu   Fujitsu Laboratories Ltd., Japan
Yuji Suga   Internet Initiative Japan Inc., Japan

Program Co-chairs

Toru Nakanishi   Hiroshima University, Japan
Ryo Nojima   NICT, Japan

Poster Chair

Mitsuaki Akiyama   NTT, Japan

Publication Chair

Chen-Mou Cheng   Kanazawa University, Japan

Local Organizing Committee

Mitsuaki Akiyama   NTT, Japan
Chen-Mou Cheng   Kanazawa University, Japan
Xuping Huang   Advanced Institute of Industrial Technology, Japan
Yasuhiko Ikematsu   Kyushu University, Japan
Satoru Izumi   National Institute of Technology, Sendai College, Japan
Kaisei Kajita   Japan Broadcasting Corporation, Japan
Kazuya Kakizaki   NEC, Japan
Noboru Kunihiro   University of Tsukuba, Japan
Minako Ogawa   Toshiba Corporation, Japan
Toshiya Shimizu   Fujitsu Laboratories Ltd., Japan
Yuta Takata   Deloitte Tohmatsu Cyber LLC, Japan
Atsushi Takayasu   NICT, Japan
Hiroshi Tsunoda   Tohoku Institute of Technology, Japan
Sven Wohlgemuth   SECOM Co., Ltd., Japan
Masaya Yasuda   Rikkyo University, Japan

Program Committee

Track A: Cryptography Track

Chen-Mou Cheng   Kanazawa University, Japan
Sherman S.M. Chow   The Chinese University of Hong Kong, Hong Kong
Geoffroy Couteau   CNRS, IRIF, Université de Paris, France
Bernardo David   IT University of Copenhagen, Denmark
Antonio Faonio   EURECOM, France
Akinori Hosoyamada   NTT, Japan
Yuichi Komano   Toshiba Corporation, Japan
Florian Mendel   Infineon Technologies, Germany
Kazuhiko Minematsu   NEC, Japan
Khoa Nguyen   Nanyang Technological University, Singapore
Koji Nuida   Kyushu University, Japan
Jae Hong Seo   Hanyang University, Republic of Korea
Yannick Seurin   Agence Nationale de la Securite des Systemes d'Information,
                          France
Daniel Slamanig   AIT Austrian Institute of Technology, Austria
Willy Susilo   University of Wollongong, Australia
Katsuyuki Takashima   Waseda University, Japan
Atsushi Takayasu   NICT, Japan
Mehdi Tibouchi   NTT, Japan
Damien Vergnaud   Sorbonne Université/Institut Universitaire de France, France
Yuyu Wang   University of Electronic Science and Technology of China,
                          China
Yohei Watanabe   The University of Electro-Communications, Japan
Bo-Yin Yang   Academia Sinica, Taiwan
Kazuki Yoneyama   Ibaraki University, Japan

Track B: Cybersecurity and Privacy Track

Mitsuaki Akiyama	NTT, Japan
Josep Balasch	KU Leuven, Belgium
Gregory Blanc	Telecom SudParis, France
Herve Debar	Telecom SudParis, France
Josep Domingo-Ferrer	Universitat Rovira i Virgili, Catalonia
Koki Hamada	NTT, Japan
Yuichi Hayashi	Nara Institute of Science and Technology, Japan
Hiroaki Kikuchi	Meiji University, Japan
Frederic Majorczyk	DGA-MI/CentraleSupelec, France
Yuji Suga	Internet Initiative Japan Inc., Japan
Giorgos Vasiliadis	Qatar Computing Research Institute HBKU, Greece
Takeshi Yagi	NTT Security (Japan) KK, Japan
Akira Yamada	KDDI Research, Inc., Japan
Takumi Yamamoto	Mitsubishi Electric Corporation, Japan

External Reviewers

Behzad Abdolmaleki
Yusuke Aikawa
Ming-Shing Chen
Nariyoshi Chida
Heewon Chung
Valerio Cini
Reo Eriguchi
Daisuke Fujimoto
Jingnan He
Jingwei Hu
Yasuhiko Ikematsu
Toshiyuki Isshiki
Tezuka Masayuki
William H.Y. Mui

Yuto Otsuki
Sebastian Ramacher
Bagus Santoso
Martin Schläffer
Kazumasa Shinagawa
Chuanjie Su
Xiangyu Su
Erkan Tairi
Junko Takahashi
Xiuhua Wang
Takuya Watanabe
Huangting Wu
Takanori Yasuda
Quan Yuan

Contents

Lattice-Based Cryptography

A Trace Map Attack Against Special Ring-LWE Samples 3
  Yasuhiko Ikematsu, Satoshi Nakamura, and Masaya Yasuda

Shortest Vectors in Lattices of Bai-Galbraith's Embedding Attack
on the LWR Problem 23
  Shusaku Uemura, Kazuhide Fukushima, Shinsaku Kiyomoto,
  Momonari Kudo, and Tsuyoshi Takagi

System Security

KPRM: Kernel Page Restriction Mechanism to Prevent Kernel Memory
Corruption 45
  Hiroki Kuzuno and Toshihiro Yamauchi

(Short Paper) Evidence Collection and Preservation System with Virtual
Machine Monitoring 64
  Toru Nakamura, Hiroshi Ito, Shinsaku Kiyomoto, and Toshihiro Yamauchi

Multiparty Computation

Evolving Homomorphic Secret Sharing for Hierarchical Access Structures 77
  Kittiphop Phalakarn, Vorapong Suppakitpaisarn,
  Nuttapong Attrapadung, and Kanta Matsuura

Machine Learning and Security

Understanding Update of Machine-Learning-Based Malware Detection
by Clustering Changes in Feature Attributions 99
  Yun Fan, Toshiki Shibahara, Yuichi Ohsita, Daiki Chiba,
  Mitsuaki Akiyama, and Masayuki Murata

Proposal of Jawi CAPTCHA Using Digraphia Feature of the Malay
Language 119
  Hisaaki Yamaba, Ahmad Saiful Aqmal Bin Ahmad Sohaimi,
  Shotaro Usuzaki, Kentaro Aburada, Masayuki Mukunoki, Mirang Park,
  and Naonobu Okazaki

Post-Quantum Cryptography (1)

Solving the Problem of Blockwise Isomorphism of Polynomials
with Circulant Matrices 137
  Yasufumi Hashimoto

FFT Program Generation for Ring LWE-Based Cryptography 151
  Masahiro Masuda and Yukiyoshi Kameyama

Symmetric-Key Cryptography

Optimum Attack on 3-Round Feistel-2 Structure 175
  Takanori Daiza and Kaoru Kurosawa

Post-Quantum Cryptography (2)

An Intermediate Secret-Guessing Attack on Hash-Based Signatures 195
  Roland Booth, Yanhong Xu, Sabyasachi Karati, and Reihaneh Safavi-Naini

(Short Paper) Analysis of a Strong Fault Attack on Static/Ephemeral CSIDH ... 216
  Jason T. LeGrow and Aaron Hutchinson

(Short Paper) Simple Matrix Signature Scheme 227
  Changze Yin, Yacheng Wang, and Tsuyoshi Takagi

Game Theory and Security

Moving Target Defense for the CloudControl Game 241
  Koji Hamasaki and Hitoshi Hohjo

Author Index 253

Lattice-Based Cryptography

A Trace Map Attack Against Special Ring-LWE Samples

Yasuhiko Ikematsu[1], Satoshi Nakamura[2], and Masaya Yasuda[3(⊠)]

[1] Institute of Mathematics for Industry, Kyushu University, Fukuoka, Japan
ikematsu@imi.kyushu-u.ac.jp
[2] NTT Secure Platform Laboratories, Tokyo, Japan
satoshi.nakamura.xn@hco.ntt.co.jp
[3] Department of Mathematics, Rikkyo University, Tokyo, Japan
myasuda@rikkyo.ac.jp

Abstract. The learning with errors (LWE) problem is one of the hard problems supporting the security of modern lattice-based cryptography. Ring-LWE is the analog of LWE over the ring of integers of a cyclotomic field, and it has provided efficient cryptosystems. In this paper, we give cryptanalysis against ring-LWE using the trace map over the ring of integers of a cyclotomic field, without using any reduction to other structured lattice problems. Since it maps to a ring of a smaller degree, a trace map attack is expected to be able to decrease the hardness of ring-LWE. However, the trace map does not necessarily transform ring-LWE samples to samples over the smaller ring with a common secret. We give a sufficient and necessary condition on a pair of ring-LWE samples for which the trace map attack is applicable. We call such a pair of samples *special*. We demonstrate how efficiently the trace map attack can solve ring-LWE when a special pair of samples is given. Specifically, we compare blocksizes of the Blockwise Korkine-Zolotarev (BKZ) algorithm required for solving ring-LWE in the trace map attack and a standard attack. Moreover, we discuss the (in)feasibility of the trace map attack for random ring-LWE samples to evaluate how the trace map attack can give a threat against ring-LWE-based cryptosystems on a practical side.

Keywords: Ring-LWE · Trace map · Lattices · Lattice basis reduction

1 Introduction

Recently, lattice-based cryptography has been studied to construct various cryptosystems, including post-quantum cryptography (PQC) and high-functional encryption such as fully homomorphic encryption. In particular, the National Institute of Standards and Technology (NIST) has proceeded with a PQC standardization since 2015 [33]. At the second-round submission in 2019, 26 proposals were accepted, including 12 lattice-based cryptosystems. In July 2020, NIST selected 15 of the second-round candidates to move onto the third round of the standardization process [27]. Of 15 advancing candidates, 7 proposals have

© Springer Nature Switzerland AG 2021
T. Nakanishi and R. Nojima (Eds.): IWSEC 2021, LNCS 12835, pp. 3–22, 2021.
https://doi.org/10.1007/978-3-030-85987-9_1

been selected as finalists, and 8 as alternate candidates. Regarding lattice-based cryptosystems, 5 proposals are included in finalists, and 2 in alternate candidates. The security of the lattice-based proposals relies on the hardness of either LWE or NTRU problem (e.g., see [3] for details). Precisely, 3 module-LWE and 2 NTRU proposals have been selected as finalists. (Module-LWE [11,21] is the analog of LWE over a module lattice that addresses shortcomings in both LWE and ring-LWE.) Module-LWE and NTRU are both structured lattice problems, and they are a central target of algebraic cryptanalysis in lattice-based cryptography.

The NTRU problem is the hard problem underlying the NTRU cryptosystem [18]. NTRU and FALCON are the NTRU-based finalists in NIST's PQC standardization process. The problem can be reduced to the shortest vector problem (SVP) in the NTRU lattice, associated with an ideal of the ring $\mathbb{Z}_q[x]/(x^n-1)$ for two integers n and q. Lattice basis reduction such as LLL [22] and BKZ [32] is a strong tool to solve lattice problems, and its hybrid with the meet-in-the-middle, proposed in [19], is the best-known attack to solve the NTRU problem in practice. For a 2-power integer n, let $R = \mathbb{Z}[x]/(x^n + 1)$ denote the ring of integers of the $2n$-th cyclotomic field $L = \mathbb{Q}[x]/(x^n + 1)$. The overstretched NTRU problem is a variant of NTRU that uses the quotient ring $R_q := R/qR$ with a large modulus q, and it is available to construct fully homomorphic encryption [23]. In algebraic cryptanalysis, Cheon et $al.$ in [15] made use of the trace map to reduce the overstretched NTRU problem to lattice problems in smaller dimensions. Albrecht et $al.$ in [2] proposed a subfield attack by using the norm map to break the overstretched NTRU problem with a huge modulus q. The LWE problem is the hard problem proposed by Regev [31] that asks to find a solution from a system of linear equations over $\mathbb{Z}_q$ with errors for a modulus q. The ring-LWE problem is the ring-based analog of LWE [24] that uses the same base ring R as in the overstretched NTRU. Informally, given ring-LWE samples $(a_i, b_i) \in R_q^2$ with $b_i = s \cdot a_i + e_i$, it asks to find its secret $s \in R_q$ for a modulus q. Advantages of ring-LWE are its compactness and efficiency since each ring element yields an n-dimensional information in its coefficients. In particular, qTesla, NewHope, and LAC had been ring-LWE-based candidates in the second round of NIST's PQC standardization process [33]. In contrast, module-LWE is less algebraically structured than ring-LWE, and it is at least as hard as ring-LWE. In NIST's PQC standardization process, SABER, CRYSTALS-KYBER, and CRYSTALS-DILITHIUM are based on module-LWE (precisely, SABER is based on module-LWR, learning with rounding), and they are selected as the third-round finalists [27]. There are several recent works on reductions between ring-LWE and module-LWE [4,10,30,34]. However, both ring-LWE and module-LWE are generally reduced to standard LWE by expressing every ring element as its coefficient vector in an estimate of security level.

In this paper, we consider cryptanalysis using the trace map against ring-LWE rather than module-LWE since ring-LWE is more algebraically structured and it can be regarded as module-LWE with a module of rank 1. For a 2-power integer n, let $R = \mathbb{Z}[x]/(x^n+1)$ denote the ring of integers of the $2n$-th cyclotomic field $L = \mathbb{Q}[x]/(x^n + 1) \simeq \mathbb{Q}(\zeta_{2n})$, where ζ_{2n} is a primitive $2n$-th root of unity in $\mathbb{C}$. Let K denote the maximal real subfield in L, and R' its ring of integers. The trace map $\mathrm{Tr} : R \longrightarrow R'$ is defined by mapping every element $f(x) \in R$ to $f(x) + f(x^{-1})$. Since the ranks of R and R' as $\mathbb{Z}$-modules are respectively equal to n and $\frac{n}{2}$, we expect that the trace map could decrease the degree of ring-LWE. However, unlike the case of NTRU, it has difficulty to use the trace map for solving ring-LWE due to that the trace map is linear but not multiplicative over R. Precisely, given a ring-LWE sample (a_i, b_i) over R_q with $b_i = s \cdot a_i + e_i$, a ring-LWE relation $\mathrm{Tr}(b_i) = \mathrm{Tr}(s) \cdot \mathrm{Tr}(a_i) + \mathrm{Tr}(e_i)$ does not hold over R'_q, except for the case where the secret $s \in R'_q$. In this paper, we give a sufficient and necessary condition on a pair of ring-LWE samples for which a trace map attack is applicable. We call such a typical sufficient condition *special*. We also demonstrate how efficiently the trace map attack can solve ring-LWE when a special pair of samples is given. Specifically, we compare blocksizes of BKZ required in both the trace map and the standard attack for success to recover the secret of ring-LWE. (Here the standard attack means the canonical reduction of ring-LWE to standard LWE by coefficient representation. The success probability and the complexity of both the trace map and the standard attacks depend on blocksizes of BKZ.) Moreover, we discuss the (in)feasibility of the trace map attack for randomly chosen ring-LWE samples. Specifically, we estimate the probability that a special pair of ring-LWE samples is included among randomly chosen samples, to evaluate the practical impact of the trace map attack.

Notation. The symbols $\mathbb{Z}$, $\mathbb{Q}$, $\mathbb{R}$, and $\mathbb{C}$ denote the ring of integers, the field of rational numbers, the field of real numbers, and the field of complex numbers, respectively. For an odd prime q, let $\mathbb{Z}_q$ denote a set of representatives of integers modulo q as $\mathbb{Z}_q = \mathbb{Z} \cap \left[-\frac{q}{2}, \frac{q}{2}\right)$. We represent all vectors in *row* format. For $\mathbf{v} = (v_1, \ldots, v_d)$, $\mathbf{w} = (w_1, \ldots, w_d) \in \mathbb{R}^d$, let $\langle \mathbf{v}, \mathbf{w} \rangle$ denote the inner product $\sum_{i=1}^d v_i w_i$. We also let $\|\mathbf{v}\|$ denote the Euclidean norm defined as $\|\mathbf{v}\| = \sqrt{\langle \mathbf{v}, \mathbf{v} \rangle}$. We write by $\mathbf{A}^\top$ the transpose of a matrix $\mathbf{A}$.

2 Preliminaries from Lattices to LWE Problems

In this section, we shall present mathematical and algorithmic background on lattices, and then recall the LWE and the ring-LWE problems.

2.1 Mathematical and Algorithmic Background on Lattices

In this subsection, we present basic definitions and properties on lattices and computational lattice problems, which shall be used later for reduction of the LWE problem and its variants. We also recall lattice basis reduction algorithms, which are strong tools to solve lattice problems (e.g., see [12, 28, 36] for details).

Lattices and Their Bases. Let d be a positive integer. For linearly independent vectors $\mathbf{b}_1, \ldots, \mathbf{b}_d$ in the d-dimensional Euclidean space $\mathbb{R}^d$, the set of all their *integral* combinations

$$L = \mathcal{L}(\mathbf{b}_1, \ldots, \mathbf{b}_d) := \left\{ \sum_{i=1}^{d} v_i \mathbf{b}_i \in \mathbb{R}^d \,\middle|\, v_i \in \mathbb{Z}, \ 1 \leq i \leq d \right\}$$

is called a (full-rank) lattice in $\mathbb{R}^d$ of dimension d. The set $\{\mathbf{b}_1, \ldots, \mathbf{b}_d\}$ is called a *basis* of L, and the matrix $\mathbf{B}$ whose i-th row is $\mathbf{b}_i$ is called a *basis matrix*. (We simply write $L = \mathcal{L}(\mathbf{B})$, the lattice spanned by the rows of $\mathbf{B}$.) Two matrix bases $\mathbf{B}_1$ and $\mathbf{B}_2$ span the same lattice if and only if there exists a unimodular matrix $\mathbf{T}$ satisfying $\mathbf{B}_2 = \mathbf{T}\mathbf{B}_1$. The *volume* of L is defined as $\mathrm{Vol}(L) := |\det \mathbf{B}|$ for a basis matrix $\mathbf{B}$ of L. It is independent of the choice of matrix bases. For each i, the i-th successive minimum of L, denoted by $\lambda_i(L)$, is the minimum of $\max_{1 \leq j \leq i} \|\mathbf{v}_j\|$ over all i linearly independent vectors $\mathbf{v}_1, \ldots, \mathbf{v}_i$ in L. In particular, the first minimum $\lambda_1(L)$ means the norm of a non-zero shortest vector in L.

The *Gram-Schmidt orthogonalization* for an ordered basis $\{\mathbf{b}_1, \ldots, \mathbf{b}_d\}$ is the orthogonal vectors $\mathbf{b}_1^*, \ldots, \mathbf{b}_d^*$, recursively defined as $\mathbf{b}_1^* := \mathbf{b}_1$ and for $i \geq 2$

$$\mathbf{b}_i^* := \mathbf{b}_i - \sum_{j=1}^{i-1} \mu_{i,j} \mathbf{b}_j^*, \quad \mu_{i,j} := \frac{\langle \mathbf{b}_i, \mathbf{b}_j^* \rangle}{\|\mathbf{b}_j^*\|^2} \quad (1 \leq j < i \leq d).$$

We expand the Gram-Schmidt coefficients as a square matrix $\mu = (\mu_{i,j})$, where let $\mu_{i,j} = 0$ for all $i < j$ and $\mu_{k,k} = 1$ for all k. Let $\mathbf{B}^*$ denote the matrix whose i-th row is $\mathbf{b}_i^*$ for $1 \leq i \leq d$. Then it is clear that $\mathbf{B} = \mu \mathbf{B}^*$ and hence $\mathrm{Vol}(L) = \prod_{i=1}^{d} \|\mathbf{b}_i^*\|$ by the orthogonality of Gram-Schmidt vectors for the lattice $L = \mathcal{L}(\mathbf{B})$. For each $1 \leq k \leq d$, let π_k denote the orthogonal projection from $\mathbb{R}^d$ onto the orthogonal supplement of the $\mathbb{R}$-vector space $V_k := \langle \mathbf{b}_1, \ldots, \mathbf{b}_{k-1} \rangle_{\mathbb{R}}$ as

$$\pi_k : \mathbb{R}^d \longrightarrow V_k^{\perp} = \langle \mathbf{b}_k^*, \ldots, \mathbf{b}_d^* \rangle_{\mathbb{R}}, \quad \pi_k(\mathbf{v}) = \sum_{i=k}^{d} \frac{\langle \mathbf{v}, \mathbf{b}_i^* \rangle}{\|\mathbf{b}_i^*\|^2} \mathbf{b}_i^*.$$

Main Lattice Problems. Here we introduce main computational problems for lattices. The most famous lattice problem is the *shortest vector problem (SVP)*; "Given a basis $\{\mathbf{b}_1, \ldots, \mathbf{b}_d\}$ of a lattice L, find a shortest non-zero vector in L, that is, a vector $\mathbf{s} \in L$ such that $\|\mathbf{s}\| = \lambda_1(L)$." Ajtai [1] proved that SVP is NP-hard under randomized reductions. It can be relaxed by an approximate factor; "Given a basis of a lattice L and an approximation factor $f \geq 1$, find a non-zero vector $\mathbf{v}$ in L such that $\|\mathbf{v}\| \leq f \lambda_1(L)$." Approximate-SVP is exactly SVP when $f = 1$. For a lattice L of dimension d and a measurable set C in $\mathbb{R}^d$, the *Gaussian Heuristic* predicts that the number of lattice vectors in C is roughly equal to $\mathrm{Vol}(C)/\mathrm{Vol}(L)$. In particular, if we take C as the ball of radius $\lambda_1(L)$ centered at the origin in $\mathbb{R}^d$, then we can expect $\mathrm{Vol}(C)/\mathrm{Vol}(L) \approx \#(L \cap C) \approx 1$. Denote by ω_d the volume of the unit ball in $\mathbb{R}^d$, thus $\mathrm{Vol}(C) = \omega_d \lambda_1(L)^d$. Therefore the norm of a non-zero shortest vector in L is roughly expected as

$$\lambda_1(L) \approx \left(\frac{\text{Vol}(L)}{\omega_d} \right)^{1/d} \sim \text{GH}(L) := \sqrt{\frac{d}{2\pi e}} \text{Vol}(L)^{1/d} \tag{1}$$

by using Stirling's formula for ω_d.

Another famous lattice problem is the *closest vector problem (CVP)*; "Given a basis $\{\mathbf{b}_1, \ldots, \mathbf{b}_d\}$ of a lattice L and a target vector $\mathbf{t}$, find a vector in L closest to $\mathbf{t}$, that is, a vector $\mathbf{v} \in L$ such that the distance $\|\mathbf{t} - \mathbf{v}\|$ is minimized." It is known that CVP is at least as hard as SVP. (See the textbook [25].) As in the case of SVP, we can relax CVP by an approximate factor. Approximate-CVP is at least as hard as approximate-SVP with the same factor. From a practical point of view, both problems considered equally hard, due to Kannan's embedding technique [20], transforming approximate-CVP into approximate-SVP. (See Subsect. 2.2 below for the embedding for solving the LWE problem.)

The security of modern lattice-based cryptosystems is based on the hardness of cryptographic problems, such as LWE and NTRU problems. Such problems are reduced to approximate-SVP or approximate-CVP (e.g., see [3] for details).

Lattice Basis Reduction. Given arbitrary basis of a lattice, *lattice basis reduction* aims to find a new basis of the same lattice with short and nearly-orthogonal vectors. (Such basis is called to be *reduced* or *good*.) It is a mandatory tool in solving lattice problems.

Reduction Algorithms. Below we introduce two typical algorithms. These algorithms output short lattice vectors, not necessarily the shortest ones.

LLL (Lenstra-Lenstra-Lovász). It is the celebrated algorithm by Lenstra, Lenstra and Lovász [22]. For a reduction parameter $\frac{1}{4} < \eta < 1$, an ordered basis $\{\mathbf{b}_1, \ldots, \mathbf{b}_d\}$ is called η-*LLL-reduced* if it satisfies two conditions; (i) Size-reduction condition: The Gram-Schmidt coefficients satisfy $|\mu_{i,j}| \leq \frac{1}{2}$ for all $1 \leq j < i \leq d$. (ii) Lovász' condition: It holds $\eta \|\mathbf{b}_{k-1}^*\|^2 \leq \|\pi_{k-1}(\mathbf{b}_k)\|^2$ for all $2 \leq k \leq d$. The LLL algorithm [22] finds an LLL-reduced basis by swapping adjacent basis vectors $(\mathbf{b}_{k-1}, \mathbf{b}_k)$ when they do not satisfy Lovász' condition. Its complexity is polynomial in dimension d. Moreover, LLL is applicable also for linearly dependent vectors to remove the linear dependency.

BKZ (Blockwise Korkine-Zolotarev). It is a blockwise generalization of LLL. For an ordered basis $\{\mathbf{b}_1, \ldots, \mathbf{b}_d\}$ of a lattice L and two indexes $j < k$, let $L_{[j,k]}$ denote the lattice spanned by the local projected block basis

$$\{\pi_j(\mathbf{b}_j), \pi_j(\mathbf{b}_{j+1}), \ldots, \pi_j(\mathbf{b}_k)\}.$$

(The projected block lattice depends on the choice of a basis and its order.) For a blocksize $2 \leq \beta \leq d$, an ordered basis $\{\mathbf{b}_1, \ldots, \mathbf{b}_d\}$ of a lattice L is called β-*BKZ-reduced* if it is size-reduced and it satisfies $\|\mathbf{b}_j^*\| = \lambda_1(L_{[j,k]})$ for $1 \leq j < d$ with $k = \min(j + \beta - 1, d)$. The BKZ algorithm [32] finds an almost

β-BKZ-reduced basis, and it calls LLL to reduce every local block lattice $L_{[j,k]}$ before finding a shortest vector in the block lattice. Since larger β decreases $\gamma_\beta^{1/(\beta-1)}$, it can find a shorter lattice vector. However, the computational cost is more expensive as β increases, since it is dominant to find a shortest vector in every block lattice of dimension β. Specifically, the running time of BKZ depends on algorithms of SVP subroutine (such as ENUM and Sieve), and hence the complexity of BKZ is at least exponential in β.

The Hermite Factor. It is a good index to measure the *practical* output quality of a reduction algorithm. The *Hermite factor* is defined by $\delta := \frac{\|\mathbf{b}_1\|}{\text{Vol}(L)^{1/d}}$, where $\mathbf{b}_1$ is a shortest basis vector output by a reduction algorithm for a lattice L of dimension d. (The first vector of a reduced basis is shorter than other vectors in general.) Smaller δ means that it can find a shorter lattice vector. It was shown in [17] by exhaustive experiments that for practical reduction algorithms such as LLL and BKZ, their root factor $\delta^{1/d}$ converges to a constant for high dimensions $d \geq 100$. For example, it achieves around 1.0219 by LLL and 1.0128 by BKZ with blocksize $\beta = 20$ for random lattices, respectively. Moreover, under the Gaussian Heuristic and some heuristic assumptions, a limiting value of the root Hermite factor of BKZ (or BKZ 2.0 [14], an improved BKZ) with large blocksize β is predicted in [13] as

$$\lim_{d \to \infty} \delta_{\text{BKZ}}^{1/d} = \left(\omega_\beta^{-\frac{1}{\beta}} \right)^{\frac{1}{\beta-1}} \sim \left(\frac{\beta}{2\pi e} (\pi\beta)^{\frac{1}{\beta}} \right)^{\frac{1}{2(\beta-1)}}. \tag{2}$$

(Recall that ω_β is the volume of the β-dimensional unit ball.) There are experimental evidences supporting this prediction for $\beta > 50$. More precisely, in a simple form based on the Gaussian Heuristic, the Gram-Schmidt norms of a β-BKZ-reduced basis $\{\mathbf{b}_1, \ldots, \mathbf{b}_d\}$ of volume 1 is predicted as

$$\|\mathbf{b}_i^*\| \approx \alpha_\beta^{\frac{d-1}{2} - i}, \quad \alpha_\beta = \left(\frac{\beta}{2\pi e} \right)^{\frac{1}{\beta}}. \tag{3}$$

This is reasonably accurate in practice for $\beta > 50$ and $\beta \ll d$ (see [13,14,37]).

2.2   LWE and Ring-LWE Problems

In this subsection, we recall the LWE problem and also describe how to reduce it to main lattice problems such as SVP and CVP. We then recall the ring-LWE problem, the ring-based analog of LWE.

The LWE Problem. We let $[a]_q \in \mathbb{Z}_q$ denote the reduction of an integer a by modulo q.

Question 1 (LWE). Let n be a dimension parameter, q a modulus parameter, and χ an error distribution over $\mathbb{Z}$. (The distribution is often taken the discrete

Gaussian distribution.) Let $\mathbf{s} \in \mathbb{Z}_q^n$ denote a secret with entries chosen uniformly at random from $\mathbb{Z}_q$. Given d samples with $d > n$

$$(\mathbf{a}_i, t_i) \in \mathbb{Z}_q^n \times \mathbb{Z}_q, \quad t_i = [\langle \mathbf{a}_i, \mathbf{s} \rangle + e_i]_q, \quad i = 1, 2, \ldots, d, \tag{4}$$

where $\mathbf{a}_i$'s are uniformly chosen at random from $\mathbb{Z}_q^n$ and e_i's are sampled from χ. Then two questions are asked; (i) *Decision-LWE* is to distinguish whether a given vector $\mathbf{t} = (t_1, \ldots, t_d) \in \mathbb{Z}_q^d$ is obtained from (4) for some $\mathbf{a}_i$, or uniformly at random. (ii) *Search-LWE* is to recover the secret $\mathbf{s}$ from LWE samples (4).

It was shown in [31] that Decision- and Search-LWE are equivalent when the prime modulus q is bounded by some polynomial in n. We focus on Search-LWE for a practical cryptanalysis, and we do not restrict the number of samples d for simplicity. From d samples (4), we set an error vector $\mathbf{e} = (e_1, \ldots, e_d)$ and a target vector $\mathbf{t} = (t_1, \ldots, t_d)$. We set $\mathbf{A}$ as the matrix whose i-th row is $\mathbf{a}_i$ for $1 \le i \le d$. Then samples (4) are written as a pair $(\mathbf{A}, \mathbf{t}) \in \mathbb{Z}_q^{d \times n} \times \mathbb{Z}_q^d$ satisfying

$$\mathbf{t} \equiv \mathbf{s}\mathbf{A}^\top + \mathbf{e} \pmod{q}. \tag{5}$$

In other words, Search-LWE asks us to recover the secret $\mathbf{s}$ or equivalently the error vector $\mathbf{e}$ from an LWE instance $(\mathbf{A}, \mathbf{t})$ satisfying (5).

Reduction to Lattice Problems. There are a number of strategies for solving Search-LWE. (See the survey work [7].) Here we recall how to reduce Search-LWE to lattice problems. Given an LWE instance $(\mathbf{A}, \mathbf{t})$, we let

$$\Lambda_q(\mathbf{A}) := \left\{ \mathbf{x} \in \mathbb{Z}^d \mid \mathbf{x} \equiv \mathbf{z}\mathbf{A}^\top \pmod{q}, \ \exists \mathbf{z} \in \mathbb{Z}_q^n \right\}$$

denote a q-ary lattice of dimension d. (See [26] for q-ary lattices.) The rows of the $(d + n) \times d$ matrix

$$\mathbf{C} = \begin{pmatrix} \mathbf{A}^\top \\ q\mathbf{I}_d \end{pmatrix}$$

form a system of generators of the lattice, where $\mathbf{I}_d$ denotes the $d \times d$ identity matrix. A basis matrix $\mathbf{B}$ of the lattice is obtained by computing LLL (or Hermite normal form) for the rows of $\mathbf{C}$. Then we can regard the target vector $\mathbf{t}$ as a vector bounded in distance from $\mathbf{s}\mathbf{A}^\top \in \Lambda_q(\mathbf{A})$. The minimum distance between $\mathbf{t}$ and $\mathbf{s}\mathbf{A}^\top$ over $\Lambda_q(\mathbf{A})$ is equal to the norm of the error vector $\|\mathbf{e}\|$ by (5) if it is sufficiently short. (In general setting, the error vector is considerably shorter than the modulus prime q.) Technically speaking, this is a reduction of Search-LWE to the *bounded distance decoding (BDD)* problem, a particular case of CVP.

There are several methods such as Kannan's embedding [20] to reduce BDD to *unique-SVP*, a particular case of SVP finding a non-zero shortest vector in a lattice L under $\lambda_2(L) > \gamma \lambda_1(L)$ for some factor $\gamma \ge 1$. The basic procedure of Kannan's embedding for an LWE instance $(\mathbf{A}, \mathbf{t})$ is as follows; With a $d \times d$ basis matrix $\mathbf{B}$ of the q-ary lattice $\Lambda_q(\mathbf{A})$, we construct the $(d + 1) \times (d + 1)$ matrix

$$\mathbf{B}' = \begin{pmatrix} \mathbf{B} & 0 \\ \mathbf{t} & 1 \end{pmatrix}. \tag{6}$$

Set $L' := \mathcal{L}(\mathbf{B}')$. Its dimension is $d+1$ and volume is equal to $\mathrm{Vol}(\Lambda_q(\mathbf{A})) = q^{d-n}$ for almost $\mathbf{A}$. Then the lattice L' includes a very short vector $\mathbf{e}' := (\mathbf{e}, 1)$, since it satisfies $\mathbf{e}' \equiv (\mathbf{t}, 1) - (\mathbf{s}\mathbf{A}^\top, 0) \pmod{q}$ by the condition (5). In general setting, embedding vectors $\pm\mathbf{e}'$ are shortest in L'. By reducing $\mathbf{B}'$ *enough* by lattice reduction, we can recover $\mathbf{e}'$, from which the error vector $\mathbf{e}$ is obtained.

Known Estimates for Reduction Algorithms. As described above, a suitable reduction algorithm is required to find the vector $\mathbf{e}'$ in L'. Below we recall two known estimates which algorithm is required for succeeding to recover $\mathbf{e}'$.

2008 Estimate. It is the estimate for solving unique-SVP by Gama and Nguyen [17]. They showed that a reduction algorithm with Hermite factor δ can recover the shortest vector in unique-SVP with gap factor $\gamma \geq 1$ if $\gamma \geq \tau \cdot \delta$ for some empirical constant τ. We apply it to Search-LWE. Assume that the vector $\mathbf{e}'$ is the shortest in the lattice L'. We simply predict that the second successive minimum of L' equals to $\mathrm{GH}(L')$ (see Eq. (1) for $\mathrm{GH}(L')$). Then the gap factor in unique-SVP over L' is larger than

$$\frac{\lambda_2(L')}{\lambda_1(L')} \approx \frac{\mathrm{GH}(L')}{\|\mathbf{e}'\|}.$$

Therefore, in order to recover $\mathbf{e}'$, the Hermite factor δ is required to satisfy

$$\delta \leq \frac{\mathrm{GH}(L')}{\|\mathbf{e}'\| \cdot \tau} \approx \sqrt{\frac{d}{2\pi e}} \cdot \frac{q^{\frac{d-n}{d}}}{\|\mathbf{e}\| \cdot \tau}. \tag{7}$$

It has been investigated in [5,6] by experiments that the constant τ lies in between 0.3 and 0.4 in using BKZ. In most cases, an optimal number of samples d is around $2n$ or $3n$ to maximize the right-hand side in (7). (See also [26].) On the other hand, Search-LWE becomes harder as d approaches n.

2016 Estimate. It is another estimate discussed in [8], in which the evolution of the Gram-Schmidt lengths is investigated in processing of BKZ. More precisely, it compares the expected length of the projected shortest vector $\pi_k(\mathbf{e}')$ with the Gram-Schmidt lengths simulation (3) of BKZ. A recent comparison [9] showed that this improves the 2008 estimate for high LWE dimensions such as $n \geq 400$.

The Ring-LWE Problem. It is parametrized by a ring R over $\mathbb{Z}$ of degree n, a prime modulus q defining the quotient ring $R_q := R/qR$, and an error distribution χ over R outputting "small" ring elements. The ring R is often taken as the ring of integers in the cyclotomic field $L = \mathbb{Q}(\zeta_{2n})$ of 2-power degree n where ζ_{2n} denotes a primitive $2n$-th root of unity (that is, $R = \mathbb{Z}[x]/(x^n + 1)$), and χ some kind of discretized Gaussian distribution in the canonical embedding $L \longrightarrow \mathbb{C}^n$, mapping each element $z \in L$ to the vector $\left(z(\zeta_{2n}^i)\right)_i \in \mathbb{C}^n$ for odd $1 \leq i \leq 2n$. We stress that the canonical embedding and complex numbers are used mainly for security proofs (e.g., see [29]), and they never need to be computed explicitly for construction.

Question 2 (Ring-LWE). For a secret $s(x) \in R_q$, the ring-LWE distribution $A_{s,\chi}$ over $R_q \times R_q$ is sampled by choosing $a(x) \in R_q$ uniformly at random, choosing $e(x) \leftarrow \chi$, and outputting the pair $(a(x), b(x)) \in R_q \times R_q$ satisfying

$$b(x) = s(x) \cdot a(x) + e(x) \in R_q. \tag{8}$$

Then two questions are asked like standard LWE; decision and search versions. We only introduce the search version; "Given independent samples from $A_{s,\chi}$ for a uniformly random $s(x) \in R_q$, find the secret $s(x)$."

The number of samples can be considered as an additional parameter of ring-LWE, but we here do not restrict it for simplicity. Sample generators of LWE and ring-LWE are implemented in the Sage mathematics software SageMath [16].

Reduction to LWE. We describe how to reduce ring-LWE samples to LWE samples. We express every polynomial $f(x) = f_0 + f_1 x + \cdots + f_{n-1} x^{n-1}$ of R_q as its coefficient vector $\mathbf{f} = (f_0, f_1, \ldots, f_{n-1}) \in \mathbb{Z}_q^n$. Let $(a(x), b(x))$ be a ring-LWE sample satisfying (8). For the coefficient vector $\mathbf{a} = (a_0, a_1, \ldots, a_{n-1})$ of $a(x)$, we put the $n \times n$ matrix

$$\mathbf{A} = \begin{pmatrix} a_0 & -a_{n-1} & \cdots & -a_1 \\ a_1 & a_0 & \cdots & -a_2 \\ \vdots & \vdots & \ddots & \vdots \\ a_{n-1} & a_{n-2} & \cdots & a_0 \end{pmatrix}.$$

Then the condition (8) is expressed as $\mathbf{b} \equiv \mathbf{s}\mathbf{A}^\top + \mathbf{e} \pmod{q}$ in the coefficient representation, since the i-th row of $\mathbf{A}^\top$ corresponds to $x^{i-1} a(x)$ for every i. Namely, one ring-LWE sample corresponds to n LWE samples $(\mathbf{A}, \mathbf{b})$.

We consider multiple ring-LWE samples. For example, let $(a_1(x), b_1(x))$ and $(a_2(x), b_2(x))$ be two ring-LWE samples with $b_i(x) = s(x) \cdot a_i(x) + e_i(x)$ for $i = 1, 2$. As above, we obtain LWE condition $\mathbf{b}_i \equiv \mathbf{s}\mathbf{A}_i^\top + \mathbf{e}_i$ from each $(a_i(x), b_i(x))$. By combining them, we get the condition

$$(\mathbf{b}_1 \mid \mathbf{b}_2) \equiv \mathbf{s} \left(\frac{\mathbf{A}_1}{\mathbf{A}_2} \right)^\top + (\mathbf{e}_1 \mid \mathbf{e}_2) \pmod{q}.$$

This condition implies that we have $2n$ LWE samples from two ring-LWE samples. To solve ring-LWE, we basically reduce multiple ring-LWE samples to (standard) LWE samples, from which we recover the coefficient vector $\mathbf{s}$ of the secret. (In general, it is hard to solve ring-LWE from only one sample by lattice attacks.)

Recent Works on Cryptanalysis of Ring-LWE. There are a number of recent works on reductions among ring-LWE and other structured LWE problems. In 2017, Albrecht and Deo [4] gave a reduction from module-LWE of rank d with modulus q to ring-LWE with modulus q^d over a 2-power cyclotomic field. This gives a conclusion that module-LWE is polynomial-time equivalent to ring-LWE over a 2-power cyclotomic field. In 2019, Wang and Wang improved the reduction of [4] to obtain a reduction from worst-case decision module-LWE to average-case decision ring-LWE over any cyclotomic field [34]. (See also the recent work [10] for reductions of module-LWE to lattice problems.) Recently, Peikert and Pepin [30] unified and simplified various reductions among algebraically structured LWE variants, including ring-LWE and module-LWE. Different from these works, the aim of this paper is to give a *direct* attack against ring-LWE without using any reduction to other structured LWE problems.

3   A Trace Map Attack Against the Ring-LWE Problem

For a 2-power integer n, we consider $R = \mathbb{Z}[x]/(x^n+1)$, the basic ring defining the ring-LWE problem. We regard R as the ring of integers of the $2n$-th cyclotomic field $L = \mathbb{Q}(x)/(x^n + 1) \simeq \mathbb{Q}(\zeta_{2n})$. (Recall that ζ_{2n} denotes a primitive $2n$-th root of unity.) Let K denote the subfield in L generated by $x + x^{-1}$ over $\mathbb{Q}$. Then K is the maximal real subfield of L and its ring of integers R' is the subring of R generated by $x + x^{-1}$ (e.g., see [35] for a proof). We now define trace maps as

$$
\begin{array}{ccc}
L & \xrightarrow{\mathrm{Tr}_{L/K}} & K \\
\cup & & \cup \\
R & \xrightarrow[\mathrm{Tr}]{} & R'
\end{array}
\quad, \quad \mathrm{Tr}_{L/K} : f(x) \longmapsto f(x) + f(x^{-1}),
$$

where 'Tr' is the restriction map of $\mathrm{Tr}_{L/K}$ to the integer ring R. In this section, we shall make use of the trace map to solve the ring-LWE problem efficiently. In particular, since the set

$$
\{1, x + x^{-1}, x^2 + x^{-2}, \dots, x^{m-1} + x^{1-m}\} \tag{9}
$$

gives a $\mathbb{Z}$-basis of the ring R' with $m = \frac{n}{2}$, the trace map enables us to reduce the degree of the ring-LWE problem over R from n to m (cf., the set $\{1, x, x^2, \dots, x^{n-1}\}$ is a $\mathbb{Z}$-basis of the ring R).

3.1   Special Pairs of Ring-LWE Samples

For a prime q, let Tr_q denote the map from $R_q = R/qR$ to $R'_q = R'/qR'$ induced by the trace map $\mathrm{Tr} : R \longrightarrow R'$. Our basic strategy for attack is to reduce the ring-LWE problem over R_q to that over R'_q via the trace map. Consider two ring-LWE samples over R_q

$$
(a_1(x), b_1(x)), \quad (a_2(x), b_2(x)) \tag{10}
$$

with $b_i(x) = a_i(x) \cdot s(x) + e_i(x)$ for $i = 1, 2$, where $s(x)$ is a secret and $e_i(x)$ an error polynomial. We now apply the trace map for these samples to obtain

$$
\begin{cases}
\mathrm{Tr}_q(b_1(x)) = \mathrm{Tr}_q(a_1(x)s(x)) + \mathrm{Tr}_q(e_1(x)) \\
\mathrm{Tr}_q(b_2(x)) = \mathrm{Tr}_q(a_2(x)s(x)) + \mathrm{Tr}_q(e_2(x))
\end{cases} \tag{11}
$$

by the linearity of the trace map. If the secret $s(x)$ is an element of R'_q, it holds $\mathrm{Tr}_q(a(x)s(x)) = \mathrm{Tr}_q(a(x))s(x)$ for any element $a(x)$ of R_q. Therefore, in this case, we obtain ring-LWE samples over R'_q from the condition (11) with secret $s(x) \in R'_q$. However, we cannot obtain such samples over R'_q in general, since the trace map is not multiplicative.

For general $s(x) \in R_q \setminus R'_q$, we shall give a condition on (11) so that we can obtain ring-LWE samples over R'_q having a common secret. We regard the first equation in (11) as the basic ring-LWE sample $(1, \mathrm{Tr}_q(b_1(x)))$ on R'_q associated with a secret $\mathrm{Tr}_q(a_1(x)s(x))$. We assume that the secret is invertible in R'_q. (The probability that the secret is invertible is overwhelmingly high for a large prime q. See Sect. 4 below.) Then we express the second equation in (11) as

$$\begin{cases} \mathrm{Tr}_q(b_2(x)) = \theta \cdot \mathrm{Tr}_q(a_1(x)s(x)) + \mathrm{Tr}_q(e_2(x)), \\ \theta = \dfrac{\mathrm{Tr}_q(a_2(x)s(x))}{\mathrm{Tr}_q(a_1(x)s(x))} \in R'_q. \end{cases} \tag{12}$$

The element θ must be public to publish the pair $(\theta, \mathrm{Tr}_q(b_2(x)))$ as a ring-LWE sample over R'_q associated with the secret $\mathrm{Tr}_q(a_1(x)s(x))$, which is common with the basic sample $(1, \mathrm{Tr}_q(b_1(x)))$. For example, if the condition $a_2(x) = \theta' a_1(x)$ is satisfied for some $\theta' \in R'_q$, then it satisfies

$$\theta = \frac{\mathrm{Tr}_q(\theta' a_1(x)s(x))}{\mathrm{Tr}_q(a_1(x)s(x))} = \frac{\theta' \cdot \mathrm{Tr}_q(a_1(x)s(x))}{\mathrm{Tr}_q(a_1(x)s(x))} = \theta',$$

and hence the element θ can be computed from public ring-LWE samples (10). Below we summarize the above discussion:

Proposition 1. *We consider two ring-LWE samples* (10) *over* R_q.

- *We assume that the secret* $s(x)$ *is an element of* R'_q. *Then the two pairs transformed by the trace map*

$$(\mathrm{Tr}_q(a_1(x)), \mathrm{Tr}_q(b_1(x))), \quad (\mathrm{Tr}_q(a_2(x)), \mathrm{Tr}_q(b_2(x)))$$

can be regarded as two ring-LWE samples over R'_q *associated with common secret* $s(x)$ *and error polynomials* $\mathrm{Tr}_q(e_1(x))$ *and* $\mathrm{Tr}_q(e_2(x))$, *respectively.*
- *For a general secret* $s(x) \in R_q \setminus R'_q$, *we consider*

$$(1, \mathrm{Tr}_q(b_1(x))), \quad \mathrm{Tr}_q(b_1(x)) = 1 \cdot \mathrm{Tr}_q(a_1(x)s(x)) + \mathrm{Tr}_q(e_1(x))$$

as a ring-LWE sample over R_q *associated with a secret* $\mathrm{Tr}_q(a_1(x)s(x))$ *and an error polynomial* $\mathrm{Tr}_q(e_1(x))$. *Assume that the secret is invertible in* R'_q, *and let*

$$\theta = \frac{\mathrm{Tr}_q(a_2(x)s(x))}{\mathrm{Tr}_q(a_1(x)s(x))} \in R'_q. \tag{13}$$

Then the pair $(\theta, \mathrm{Tr}_q(b_2(x)))$ *satisfying* (12) *can be regarded as a ring-LWE sample with the same secret* $\mathrm{Tr}_q(a_1(x)s(x))$ *and error* $\mathrm{Tr}_q(e_2(x))$ *if and only if the element* θ *is public. In particular, if* $a_2(x) = \theta' a_1(x)$ *for some* $\theta' \in R'_q$, *then* $\theta' = \theta$ *and it can be recovered from public information* $a_1(x)$ *and* $a_2(x)$. *We say such pairs of ring-LWE samples* "special".

3.2   A Trace Map Attack Against Special Pairs of Ring-LWE Samples

As described in Proposition 1, special pairs of ring-LWE samples over R_q can be reduced to certain ring-LWE samples over R'_q with a common secret via the trace map. Here we shall describe the procedure of a trace map attack. We consider a special pair of ring-LWE samples (10) over R_q, satisfying $a_2(x) = \theta a_1(x)$ for some $\theta \in R'_q$. (The element θ is public and it is expressed as (13).) To recover the secret $s(x)$ of ring-LWE samples (10), we perform the below procedure:

Step 1. From Proposition 1, we first consider two ring-LWE samples over R'_q

$$\begin{cases} (1, \mathrm{Tr}_q(b_1(x))), & \mathrm{Tr}_q(b_1(x)) = 1 \cdot \mathrm{Tr}_q(a_1(x)s(x)) + \mathrm{Tr}_q(e_1(x)) \\ (\theta, \mathrm{Tr}_q(b_2(x))), & \mathrm{Tr}_q(b_2(x)) = \theta \cdot \mathrm{Tr}_q(a_1(x)s(x)) + \mathrm{Tr}_q(e_2(x)) \end{cases} \quad (14)$$

with common secret $\mathrm{Tr}_q(a_1(x)s(x))$ and two error polynomials $\mathrm{Tr}_q(e_1(x))$ and $\mathrm{Tr}_q(e_2(x))$. In this step, we recover the error polynomials by reducing the ring-LWE problem to BDD and then to unique-SVP, as described in the previous section. The main advantage of this attack is that the dimension of the reduced lattice is $m = \frac{n}{2}$, the half size of the standard reduction described in the previous section. (In general, a lattice problem is much easier as its dimension decreases.) More precisely, since the set (9) gives a basis of the ring R'_q, every element α of R'_q is uniquely expressed as

$$\alpha = \alpha_0 + \alpha_1(x + x^{-1}) + \alpha_2(x^2 + x^{-2}) + \cdots + \alpha_{m-1}(x^{m-1} + x^{1-m})$$

with $\alpha_i \in \mathbb{Z}_q$, and we then define an isomorphism map

$$\phi : R'_q \longrightarrow \mathbb{Z}_q^m, \quad \phi(\alpha) = (\alpha_0, \alpha_1, \ldots, \alpha_{m-1}).$$

We also denote by ψ the composition map of ϕ with Tr_q. We clearly have

$$\psi(f) = (2f_0, f_1 - f_{n-1}, \ldots, f_{m-1} - f_{m+1})$$

for any element $f(x) = f_0 + f_1 x + \cdots + f_{n-1} x^{n-1}$ in R_q. Moreover, we define a map from the ring R'_q to the set of $m \times m$ matrices with entries in $\mathbb{Z}_q$ as

$$\Phi : R'_q \longrightarrow \mathbb{Z}_q^{m \times m}, \quad \Phi(\alpha) = \begin{pmatrix} \phi(\alpha) \\ \phi(\alpha(x + x^{-1})) \\ \vdots \\ \phi(\alpha(x^{m-1} + x^{1-m})) \end{pmatrix}.$$

Then we reduce two ring-LWE samples (14) over R'_q to $2m$ LWE samples of dimension m associated with the secret $\psi(a_1 s)$, which satisfies

$$(\psi(b_1) \mid \psi(b_2)) \equiv \psi(a_1 s) \cdot (\Phi(1) \mid \Phi(\theta)) + (\psi(e_1) \mid \psi(e_2)) \pmod{q}. \quad (15)$$

Step 2. We next take an integer i with $1 \le i < n$ to consider a new pair of ring-LWE samples $(x^i a_1(x), x^i b_1(x))$ and $(x^i a_2(x), x^i b_2(x))$, which clearly satisfy the special condition $x^i a_2(x) = \theta \cdot x^i a_1(x)$. Thus we apply the first step to this pair in order to recover the error polynomials $\mathrm{Tr}_q(x^i e_j(x))$ for $j = 1, 2$. (Note that the norm of the coefficient vector of $x^i e_j(x)$ is the same as that of $e_j(x)$.) Since for each $j = 1, 2$ it satisfies

$$\begin{cases} \mathrm{Tr}_q(e_j(x)) = e_j(x) + e_j(x^{-1}) \\ \mathrm{Tr}_q(x^i e_j(x)) = x^i e_j(x) + x^{-i} e_j(x^{-1}), \end{cases}$$

we can recover each error $e_j(x)$ from $\mathrm{Tr}_q(e_j(x))$ and $\mathrm{Tr}_q(x^i e_j(x))$ as

$$e_j(x) = \frac{\mathrm{Tr}_q(x^i e_j(x)) - x^{-i}\mathrm{Tr}_q(e_j(x))}{x^i - x^{-i}}.$$

Then the secret $s(x)$ can be easily recovered from either $e_1(x)$ or $e_2(x)$.

As described above, the trace map attack requires twice lattice attacks against different pairs of ring-LWE samples. But the attack reduces samples over rings from R_q to R'_q via the trace map. It enables us to halve the dimension of reduced lattices, which would make lattice problems much easier to be solved.

Remark 1. Given any sample $(a_1(x), b_1(x))$ with $b_1(x) = s(x) \cdot a_1(x) + e_1(x)$, we select an element $\theta \in R'_q$ and make a new sample $(a_2(x), b_2(x)) = (\theta a_1(x), \theta b_1(x))$ to obtain a special pair. However, since $b_2(x) = s(x) \cdot a_2(x) + \theta e_1(x)$, the coefficients of the new error polynomial $e_2(x) = \theta e_1(x)$ are large for almost elements θ, and it is very hard to solve ring-LWE with large errors. On the other hand, the error polynomial $e_2(x)$ still has small norm for simple elements $\theta \in R'_q$ such as $\theta = x + x^{-1}$. But in this case, since coefficient vectors of $a_1(x)$ and $a_2(x)$ are almost linearly dependent over R_q, it is also hard to solve ring-LWE with such samples by lattice reduction attacks. That is, the trace map attack is applicable *in practice* for a special pair of samples with linearly *independent* $a_1(x)$ and $a_2(x)$ over R_q.

Remark 2. As mentioned in Sect. 1, both the trace and the norm maps have been considered in cryptanalysis against the NTRU problem. Since the norm map is multiplicative but not additive, it is not straightforward to apply it to ring-LWE. Specifically, a ring-LWE relation

$$\mathrm{Nm}(b(x)) = \mathrm{Nm}(s(x)) \cdot \mathrm{Nm}(a(x)) + \mathrm{Nm}(e(x))$$

does not hold in general for any ring-LWE sample $(a(x), b(x))$ with $b(x) = s(x) \cdot a(x) + e(x)$, where 'Nm' denotes the norm map. In particular, the small ring element $\mathrm{Nm}(e(x))$ cannot be extracted from the element $\mathrm{Nm}(b(x))$.

3.3 Comparison with the Standard Attack

In this section, we compare the trace map attack with a standard attack for concrete ring-LWE parameters. Specifically, we compare required blocksizes for

BKZ to succeed to solve ring-LWE by the trace map and standard attacks against a special pair of samples (10). Here the standard attack means the canonical reduction of ring-LWE to standard LWE, which is also reduced to BDD and then to unique-SVP, as described in Sect. 2.2.

Verification for Small Parameters by Experiments. We verified by experiments the effect of the trace map attack for small parameters. For our experiments, we chose $n = 64$ and 128 as the degree parameter of ring-LWE, and fixed $q = 257$ the prime modulus parameter. We generated a special pair of ring-LWE samples (10) over R_q as follows; We randomly chose a secret $s \in R_q$, and two error polynomials $e_1(x)$ and $e_2(x)$ in $R = \mathbb{Z}[x]/(x^n + 1)$ with binary coefficients. (That is, we consider binary ring-LWE in our experiments.) Then we chose $a_1(x)$ randomly from R_q, generated the other polynomial $a_2(x) = \theta a_1(x)$ for randomly chosen $\theta \in R'_q$, and computed $b_i(x) = s(x) \cdot a_i(x) + e_i(x)$ over R_q to obtain $(a_i(x), b_i(x))$ for $i = 1, 2$.

All experiments were performed using SageMath [16] on 1.3 GHz Intel core i5. We also used two reduction algorithms LLL and BKZ with blocksize $\beta = 20$ for solving ring-LWE with a special pair of samples. We had experimented 20 times for every parameter set. For the case $n = 64$ (resp., $n = 128$), LLL (resp., BKZ with $\beta = 20$) was sufficient to solve ring-LWE by the trace map attack. On the other hand, the standard attack could solve the case $n = 64$ by not LLL but BKZ with $\beta = 20$. With regard to the running time for $n = 64$, the trace map attack and the standard attack took about 0.74 and 12.31 seconds on average, respectively. Furthermore, the standard attack could neither solve the case $n = 128$ by LLL nor BKZ with $\beta = 20$. We estimate that the standard attack requires at least $\beta = 60$ for BKZ to solve the case $n = 128$.

Comparison for Large Parameters. The success probability and the complexity of both the trace map and the standard attacks depend on blocksizes of BKZ (see [3] for estimates of the complexity of BKZ). Here we compare two attacks on which blocksizes of BKZ are required for solving large ring-LWE parameters.

In order to succeed to solve ring-LWE, we estimate from (7) that the standard attack requires the root Hermite factor at most

$$\delta^{1/d} = \left(\frac{1}{\|\mathbf{e}\| \tau} \sqrt{\frac{nq}{\pi e}} \right)^{\frac{1}{2n}}, \tag{16}$$

for which we take $d = 2n$ as the number of LWE samples in the right-hand side of (7). Recall that $\mathbf{e} = (\mathbf{e}_1 \mid \mathbf{e}_2)$ is the combined vector of coefficient vectors of two error polynomials $e_1(x)$ and $e_2(x)$. For binary ring-LWE with the above case $(n, q) = (128, 257)$, the Eq. (16) implies that it requires $\delta^{1/d} \approx 1.01142$, for which we set $\|\mathbf{e}\| \approx \sqrt{n}$ and $\tau = 0.3$ for simplicity. (Recall that the empirical constant τ lies bewteen 0.3 and 0.4.) Furthermore, we estimate from (2) that around $\beta = 60$ is required for BKZ to achieve such $\delta^{1/d}$. In contrast, the trace map attack reduces ring-LWE over R_q to that over R'_q. Thus it requires the root Hermite factor at most

$$\delta^{1/d} = \left(\frac{1}{\|\mathrm{Tr}(\mathbf{e})\|\tau} \sqrt{\frac{mq}{\pi e}} \right)^{\frac{1}{2m}} = \left(\frac{1}{\|\mathrm{Tr}(\mathbf{e})\|\tau} \sqrt{\frac{nq}{2\pi e}} \right)^{\frac{1}{n}}, \qquad (17)$$

where $\mathrm{Tr}(\mathbf{e})$ denotes the combined vector $(\psi(e_1) \mid \psi(e_2))$ in (15) and we take $d = 2m$ as the number of LWE samples. (Recall that $m = \frac{n}{2}$, the degree of polynomial defining R'_q.) We simply estimate $\|\mathrm{Tr}(\mathbf{e})\| \approx \sqrt{2}\|\mathbf{e}\|$ with an enough merge. For binary ring-LWE with the above case $(n, q) = (128, 257)$, the trace map attack requires $\delta^{1/d} \approx 1.01744$. It is sufficient for BKZ with blocksize $\beta = 20$ to achieve such $\delta^{1/d}$, as shown in above experiments. (Recall that the root Hermite factor of BKZ with $\beta = 20$ is around 1.0128, as mentioned in Subsect. 2.1.)

Table 1. Comparison of required blocksizes of BKZ in standard and trace map attacks (The standard attack means the canonical reduction from ring-LWE to standard LWE. Required root Hermite factors $\delta^{1/d}$ are estimated from (16) and (17), respectively.)

Ring-LWE parameters			Required blocksizes β of BKZ	
n	$\log_2(q)$	σ	Standard attack	Trace map attack
128	11	4	$\beta \approx 115$ $(\delta^{1/d} = 1.00868)$	$\beta \approx 50$ $(\delta^{1/d} = 1.01193)$
		8	$\beta \approx 220$ $(\delta^{1/d} = 1.00595)$	$\beta \approx 190$ $(\delta^{1/d} = 1.00647)$
	12	4	$\beta \approx 85$ $(\delta^{1/d} = 1.01004)$	$\beta \approx 20$ $(\delta^{1/d} = 1.01468)$
		8	$\beta \approx 155$ $(\delta^{1/d} = 1.00731)$	$\beta \approx 100$ $(\delta^{1/d} = 1.00920)$
256	13	4	$\beta \approx 235$ $(\delta^{1/d} = 1.00569)$	$\beta \approx 115$ $(\delta^{1/d} = 1.00868)$
		8	$\beta \approx 355$ $(\delta^{1/d} = 1.00433)$	$\beta \approx 220$ $(\delta^{1/d} = 1.00595)$
	14	4	$\beta \approx 195$ $(\delta^{1/d} = 1.00637)$	$\beta \approx 80$ $(\delta^{1/d} = 1.01004)$
		8	$\beta \approx 285$ $(\delta^{1/d} = 1.00501)$	$\beta \approx 155$ $(\delta^{1/d} = 1.00731)$
512	15	4	$\beta \approx 475$ $(\delta^{1/d} = 1.00352)$	$\beta \approx 235$ $(\delta^{1/d} = 1.00569)$
		8	$\beta \approx 640$ $(\delta^{1/d} = 1.00284)$	$\beta \approx 355$ $(\delta^{1/d} = 1.00432)$
	16	4	$\beta \approx 420$ $(\delta^{1/d} = 1.00386)$	$\beta \approx 195$ $(\delta^{1/d} = 1.00637)$
		8	$\beta \approx 550$ $(\delta^{1/d} = 1.00318)$	$\beta \approx 285$ $(\delta^{1/d} = 1.00500)$

In Table 1, we give a comparison of required blocksizes β of BKZ in the standard and the trace map attacks for solving several ring-LWE instances (n, q, σ). We estimate required root Hermite factors $\delta^{1/d}$ in both attacks from (16) and (17), respectively, and we also estimate required blocksizes β of BKZ to achieve target $\delta^{1/d}$ from the Eq. (2). For the sake of simplicity, we consider that every coefficient of error polynomials in R is sampled from the discrete Gaussian distribution with standard deviation σ. (We can apply our discussion to other kinds of distributions.) We roughly estimate $\|\mathbf{e}\| \approx \sigma\sqrt{2n}$ and $\|\mathrm{Tr}(\mathbf{e})\| \approx 2\sigma\sqrt{n}$.

We see from Table 1 that the trace map attack requires considerably smaller blocksizes β than the standard attack. We also see that the difference of required blocksizes between both attacks increases as the degree parameter n increases. In particular, the difference of blocksizes is larger than at least 100 for cases $n \geq 256$. Since the complexity of BKZ is at least exponential in β as described in Subsect. 2.1, the trace map attack is much faster than the standard attack, and it becomes more efficient for larger n. For example, in the case $(n, \log_2(q), \sigma) = (256, 14, 8)$, the difference of blocksizes is 130 from Table 1, and thus the trace map attack is at least 2^{130} times faster than the standard attack.

4   (In)feasibility of Trace Map Attack for Random Samples

As mentioned in Proposition 1, the trace map attack requires a strong condition between two ring-LWE samples over R_q. (We recall that such the typical condition is called *special* in Proposition 1.) In this section, we discuss the (in)feasibility of the trace map attack for random ring-LWE samples. Specifically, we investigate the probability that randomly chosen ring-LWE samples includes a special pair.

Let $R_q^\times$ denote the group of invertible elements in R_q. Since $\#R_q \approx \#R_q^\times$ for a large prime q, we assume that any elements are randomly chosen from $R_q^\times$ for a simple discussion.

Lemma 1. *Let a_1, a_2 be two randomly chosen elements in $R_q^\times$. Then the probability that there exists an element $\theta \in R_q'$ satisfying $a_2 = \theta a_1$ or $a_1 = \theta a_2$ is around q^{-m} with $m = \frac{n}{2}$.*

Proof. Since $a_1, a_2 \in R_q^\times$, the following two conditions are equivalent: (1) There exists $\theta \in R_q'$ satisfying $a_2 = \theta a_1$. (2) Conversely, there exists $\theta \in R_q'$ satisfying $a_1 = \theta a_2$. In particular, such an element θ is in $R_q'^\times$. Thus the probability of the lemma is equal to the probability that $a_2 \in R_q^\times$ is contained in the set $R_q'^\times \cdot a_1$. Therefore it is equal to

$$\#R_q'^\times / \#R_q^\times = (q^m - 1)/(q^n - 1) = 1/(q^m + 1) \approx q^{-m}.$$

This completes a proof of this lemma.   □

For a small parameter set $(n, q) = (64, 257)$, the probability that two ring-LWE samples satisfy the special condition is roughly equal to $257^{-32} \approx 2^{-256}$. Thus, it is considered that given two ring-LWE samples of cryptographic size hardly meet the special condition.

Below we consider how many samples are necessary to find a special pair.

Lemma 2. *Given ℓ elements $a_1, \ldots, a_\ell \in R_q^\times$ with $\ell = q^{m/2}$, the probability that there exists a pair (a_i, a_j) satisfying the special condition is around $\frac{1}{2}$.*

Proof. Let $\Psi : R_q^\times \longrightarrow R_q^\times / R_q'^\times$ be the canonical homomorphism. It is clear that two elements $a, a' \in R_q^\times$ satisfy the special condition if and only if $\Psi(a) = \Psi(a')$. Thus, we would like to find a collision under the map Ψ. Since the number of $R_q^\times / R_q'^\times$ roughly equals to q^m, we see from the birthday paradox that $q^{m/2}$ elements are necessary to find such a collision with the probability around $\frac{1}{2}$. □

Remark 3. A trace map can be defined for a finite extension L/K. Therefore a trace map attack can be constructed for such an extension. However, as the extension degree $d = [L : K]$ increases, the probability that special ring-LWE samples are met becomes much less. Throughout this paper, we have considered the minimum degree case $d = 2$ for $L = \mathbb{Q}(\zeta_{2n})$ and $K = \mathbb{Q}(\zeta_{2n} + \zeta_{2n}^{-1})$. We see from the discussion in this section that we rarely meet special ring-LWE samples even in the minimum degree case $d = 2$.

Remark 4. Module-LWE is the analogue of LWE over modules, introduced in [11, 21], which is between LWE and ring-LWE. Specifically, module-LWE uses a free R_q-module of rank d for a positive integer d. Like in the case of standard LWE, a module-LWE sample is a pair of $(\mathbf{a}, b) \in R_q^d \times R_q$ with $\mathbf{a} = (a_1, \ldots, a_d)$ satisfying

$$b = \sum_{i=1}^{d} a_i s_i + e$$

over the ring R_q, where $\mathbf{s} = (s_1, \ldots, s_d) \in R_q^d$ is a secret and $e \in R_q$ is an error (cf., Eq. (4)). The particular case $d = 1$ corresponds to ring-LWE. For two module-LWE samples $(\mathbf{a}, b)$ and $(\mathbf{a}', b')$ with $\mathbf{a} = (a_1, \ldots, a_d)$ and $\mathbf{a}' = (a_1', \ldots, a_d')$, a trace map attack is applicable if there exist elements $\theta_1, \ldots, \theta_d \in R_q'$ satisfying $a_i = \theta_i a_i'$ for all $1 \le i \le d$. The probability that such condition is met becomes much less as the rank d increases.

5   Conclusion

We discussed a cryptanalysis for ring-LWE using the trace map over the integer ring $R = \mathbb{Z}[x]/(x^n + 1)$ of the $2n$-th cyclotomic field for a 2-power integer n. Specifically, we gave a sufficient and necessary condition on a pair of ring-LWE samples for which the trace map attack is applicable (Proposition 1). As a typical case, the trace map attack can efficiently solve ring-LWE with a *special* pair of samples. We see from Table 1 that the trace map attack requires much smaller blocksizes of BKZ than the standard attack for success to recover the secret. This shows that the trace map attack drastically decreases the hardness of ring-LWE when a special pair of samples is given. (Note that the complexities of both the trace map and the standard attacks depend on BKZ, and the complexity of BKZ is at least exponential in an input blocksize.) However, since a special pair of samples is rarely included among randomly chosen samples, the trace map attack is not a threat against ring-LWE-based cryptosystems on a practical side. On another point of view, this work would be an alert that any ring-LWE sampler should never generate any special pair of samples for security.

Acknowledgments. This work was supported by JSPS KAKENHI Grant Numbers JP19K20266 and JP20H04142, Japan.

References

1. Ajtai, M.: Generating hard instances of lattice problems. In: Symposium on Theory of Computing (STOC 1996), pp. 99–108. ACM (1996)
2. Albrecht, M., Bai, S., Ducas, L.: A subfield lattice attack on overstretched NTRU assumptions. In: Robshaw, M., Katz, J. (eds.) CRYPTO 2016. LNCS, vol. 9814, pp. 153–178. Springer, Heidelberg (2016). https://doi.org/10.1007/978-3-662-53018-4_6
3. Albrecht, M.R.: Estimate all the LWE, NTRU schemes!. In: Catalano, D., De Prisco, R. (eds.) SCN 2018. LNCS, vol. 11035, pp. 351–367. Springer, Cham (2018). https://doi.org/10.1007/978-3-319-98113-0_19
4. Albrecht, M.R., Deo, A.: Large modulus ring-LWE $\geq$ module-LWE. In: Takagi, T., Peyrin, T. (eds.) ASIACRYPT 2017. LNCS, vol. 10624, pp. 267–296. Springer, Cham (2017). https://doi.org/10.1007/978-3-319-70694-8_10
5. Albrecht, M.R., Fitzpatrick, R., Göpfert, F.: On the efficacy of solving LWE by reduction to unique-SVP. In: Lee, H.-S., Han, D.-G. (eds.) ICISC 2013. LNCS, vol. 8565, pp. 293–310. Springer, Cham (2014). https://doi.org/10.1007/978-3-319-12160-4_18
6. Albrecht, M.R., Göpfert, F., Virdia, F., Wunderer, T.: Revisiting the expected cost of solving uSVP and applications to LWE. In: Takagi, T., Peyrin, T. (eds.) ASIACRYPT 2017. LNCS, vol. 10624, pp. 297–322. Springer, Cham (2017). https://doi.org/10.1007/978-3-319-70694-8_11
7. Albrecht, M.R., Player, R., Scott, S.: On the concrete hardness of learning with errors. J. Math. Cryptol. **9**(3), 169–203 (2015)
8. Alkim, E., Ducas, L., Pöppelmann, T., Schwabe, P.: Post-quantum key exchange: a new hope. In: 25th USENIX Security Symposium, pp. 327–343 (2016)
9. Bai, S., Miller, S., Wen, W.: A refined analysis of the cost for solving LWE via uSVP. In: Buchmann, J., Nitaj, A., Rachidi, T. (eds.) AFRICACRYPT 2019. LNCS, vol. 11627, pp. 181–205. Springer, Cham (2019). https://doi.org/10.1007/978-3-030-23696-0_10
10. Boudgoust, K., Jeudy, C., Roux-Langlois, A., Wen, W.: Towards classical hardness of module-LWE: The linear rank case. IACR ePrint Archive: Report 2020/1020 (2020)
11. Brakerski, Z., Gentry, C., Vaikuntanathan, V.: (Leveled) fully homomorphic encryption without bootstrapping. ACM Trans. Comput. Theor. (TOCT) **6**(3), 1–36 (2014)
12. Bremner, M.R.: Lattice Basis Reduction: An Introduction to the LLL Algorithm and Its Applications. CRC Press, Boca Raton (2011)
13. Chen, Y.: Réduction de réseau et sécurité concrete du chiffrement completement homomorphe. Ph.D. thesis, Paris 7 (2013)
14. Chen, Y., Nguyen, P.Q.: BKZ 2.0: better lattice security estimates. In: Lee, D.H., Wang, X. (eds.) ASIACRYPT 2011. LNCS, vol. 7073, pp. 1–20. Springer, Heidelberg (2011). https://doi.org/10.1007/978-3-642-25385-0_1
15. Cheon, J.H., Jeong, J., Lee, C.: An algorithm for NTRU problems and cryptanalysis of the GGH multilinear map without a low-level encoding of zero. LMS J. Comput. Math. **19**(A), 255–266 (2016)
16. Developers, T.S.: Sagemath (2016). https://www.sagemath.org/
17. Gama, N., Nguyen, P.Q.: Predicting lattice reduction. In: Smart, N. (ed.) EURO-CRYPT 2008. LNCS, vol. 4965, pp. 31–51. Springer, Heidelberg (2008). https://doi.org/10.1007/978-3-540-78967-3_3

18. Hoffstein, J., Pipher, J., Silverman, J.H.: NTRU: a ring-based public key cryptosystem. In: Buhler, J.P. (ed.) ANTS 1998. LNCS, vol. 1423, pp. 267–288. Springer, Heidelberg (1998). https://doi.org/10.1007/BFb0054868

19. Howgrave-Graham, N.: A hybrid lattice-reduction and meet-in-the-middle attack against NTRU. In: Menezes, A. (ed.) CRYPTO 2007. LNCS, vol. 4622, pp. 150–169. Springer, Heidelberg (2007). https://doi.org/10.1007/978-3-540-74143-5_9

20. Kannan, R.: Minkowski's convex body theorem and integer programming. Math. Oper. Res. **12**(3), 415–440 (1987)

21. Langlois, A., Stehlé, D.: Worst-case to average-case reductions for module lattices. Des. Codes Crypt. **75**(3), 565–599 (2014). https://doi.org/10.1007/s10623-014-9938-4

22. Lenstra, A.K., Lenstra, H.W., Lovász, L.: Factoring polynomials with rational coefficients. Math. Ann. **261**(4), 515–534 (1982)

23. López-Alt, A., Tromer, E., Vaikuntanathan, V.: On-the-fly multiparty computation on the cloud via multikey fully homomorphic encryption. In: Symposium on Theory of Computing (STOC 2012), pp. 1219–1234. ACM (2012)

24. Lyubashevsky, V., Peikert, C., Regev, O.: On ideal lattices and learning with errors over rings. In: Gilbert, H. (ed.) EUROCRYPT 2010. LNCS, vol. 6110, pp. 1–23. Springer, Heidelberg (2010). https://doi.org/10.1007/978-3-642-13190-5_1

25. Micciancio, D., Goldwasser, S.: Complexity of lattice problems: A cryptographic perspective, vol. 671. Springer Science & Business Media (2012)

26. Micciancio, D., Regev, O.: Lattice-based cryptography. In: Post-Quantum Cryptography, pp. 147–191 (2009)

27. Moody, D., et al.: NISTIR 8309: Status report on the second round of the NIST Post-Quantum Cryptography standardization process (2020). https://nvlpubs.nist.gov/nistpubs/ir/2020/NIST.IR.8309.pdf

28. Nguyen, P.Q.: Hermite's constant and lattice algorithms. In: The LLL Algorithm, pp. 19–69. Springer (2009). https://doi.org/10.1007/978-3-642-02295-1_2

29. Peikert, C.: How (Not) to instantiate ring-LWE. In: Zikas, V., De Prisco, R. (eds.) SCN 2016. LNCS, vol. 9841, pp. 411–430. Springer, Cham (2016). https://doi.org/10.1007/978-3-319-44618-9_22

30. Peikert, C., Pepin, Z.: Algebraically structured LWE, revisited. In: Hofheinz, D., Rosen, A. (eds.) TCC 2019. LNCS, vol. 11891, pp. 1–23. Springer, Cham (2019). https://doi.org/10.1007/978-3-030-36030-6_1

31. Regev, O.: On lattices, learning with errors, random linear codes, and cryptography. In: Symposium on Theory of Computing (STOC 2005), pp. 84–93. ACM (2005)

32. Schnorr, C.P., Euchner, M.: Lattice basis reduction: improved practical algorithms and solving subset sum problems. Math. Program. **66**, 181–199 (1994)

33. The National Institute of Standards and Technology (NIST): Post-quantum cryptography. https://csrc.nist.gov/projects/post-quantum-cryptography/post-quantum-cryptography-standardization

34. Wang, Y., Wang, M.: Module-LWE versus ring-LWE, revisited. IACR ePrint Archive: Report 2019/930 (2019)

35. Washington, L.C.: Introduction to cyclotomic fields, vol. 83. Springer Science & Business Media (1997). https://doi.org/10.1007/978-1-4612-1934-7

36. Yasuda, M.: A survey of solving SVP algorithms and recent strategies for solving the SVP challenge. In: Takagi, T., Wakayama, M., Tanaka, K., Kunihiro, N., Kimoto, K., Ikematsu, Y. (eds.) International Symposium on Mathematics, Quantum Theory, and Cryptography. MI, vol. 33, pp. 189–207. Springer, Singapore (2021). https://doi.org/10.1007/978-981-15-5191-8_15
37. Yu, Y., Ducas, L.: Second order statistical behavior of LLL and BKZ. In: Adams, C., Camenisch, J. (eds.) SAC 2017. LNCS, vol. 10719, pp. 3–22. Springer, Cham (2018). https://doi.org/10.1007/978-3-319-72565-9_1

Shortest Vectors in Lattices of Bai-Galbraith's Embedding Attack on the LWR Problem

Shusaku Uemura[1]($\boxtimes$), Kazuhide Fukushima[2], Shinsaku Kiyomoto[2], Momonari Kudo[1], and Tsuyoshi Takagi[1]

[1] Graduate School of Information Science and Technology, The University of Tokyo, Tokyo, Japan
shusaku_uemura@mist.i.u-tokyo.ac.jp
[2] KDDI Research, Inc., Saitama, Japan

Abstract. The Learning With Rounding (LWR) problem has attracted increasing attention as a foundation for post-quantum cryptosystems. It is known to be a variant of the Learning With Errors (LWE) problem, and so far the computational hardness of the LWE problem has been analyzed through various types of attacks using the structure of lattices. Bai-Galbraith's embedding attack is one of the most effective attacks against the LWE problem. Their embedding attack is also applicable to the LWR problem - through the transformation from the LWR problem to the LWE problem - and its effect on the LWR problem has been directly analyzed with the structure of a certain lattice (referred to as a BG-lattice in this paper) constructed in the LWE problem. However, the structure of a BG-lattice in the LWR problem is not the same as that in the LWE problem with this transformation; thus, it requires more concrete investigation for the security analysis of LWR-based cryptosystems. In this paper, we study the structure of a BG-lattice constructed in the LWR problem through the transformation from the LWR problem to the LWE problem. Specifically, we explicitly find a certain vector in the lattice that can be the shortest, and formulate the condition where such a vector is surely the shortest one. The existence of such a shortest vector causes a situation that the second shortest vector linearly independent of the shortest vector in a BG-lattice is different from the expected. We also study the probability that this situation occurs, and obtain a relation between the probability and parameters of the LWR problem. Our experimental results confirm the existence of this shortest vector and the aforementioned relation. Note that the focus of this paper is a theoretical analysis, and applying it to the security analysis of LWR-based cryptosystems will be conducted in future work.

Keywords: Post-quantum cryptography · Lattice-based cryptography · Learning With Rounding · Bai-Galbraith's embedding attack

© Springer Nature Switzerland AG 2021
T. Nakanishi and R. Nojima (Eds.): IWSEC 2021, LNCS 12835, pp. 23–41, 2021.
https://doi.org/10.1007/978-3-030-85987-9_2

1   Introduction

In 2016, the National Institute of Standards and Technology (NIST) initiated a project called PQC Standardization to determine the post-quantum cryptography standards [22]. Among various kinds of post-quantum cryptosystems, four public-key cryptosystems were selected as the finalists of NIST-PQC Standardization with five as alternative candidates. Three cryptosystems (NTRU [15], CRYSTALS-KYBER [7], SABER [12]) out of the four finalists and two cryptosystems (FrodoKEM [4], NTRU Prime [13]) out of the five alternative candidates are lattice-based. Their security base is the hardness of computational problems in lattice theory, such as the Learning With Errors (LWE) and the Learning With Rounding (LWR) problems. In particular, the security of CRYSTALS-KYBER and FrodoKEM (resp. SABER) are based on the LWE (resp. LWR) problem. An LWE-based cryptosystem was first introduced by Regev [23,24] in 2005, and the LWE problem is parameterized by a triple (m, n, q) of three positive integers and a pair (χ_e, χ_s) of two discrete probability distributions. The LWE problem requires to solve a system of linear equations over $\mathbb{Z}_q := \mathbb{Z}/q\mathbb{Z}$ in the presence of noise. More specifically, for an $(m \times n)$-matrix A whose entries are uniformly sampled from $\mathbb{Z}_q$, and for two vectors $\mathbf{s} \in \mathbb{Z}_q^n$ and $\mathbf{e} \in \mathbb{Z}_q^m$, the LWE problem is to find $\mathbf{s}$ if A and $\mathbf{s}A^\top + \mathbf{e}$ are given (see Definition 3 below). Each entry s (resp. e) of $\mathbf{s}$ (resp. $\mathbf{e}$) is sampled from χ_s (resp. χ_e), where $|e|$ is much smaller than q. On the other hand, Banerjee et al. [11] introduced the LWR problem, which is parameterized by a quadruple (m, n, q, p) and one discrete probability distribution χ_s. Given A and $\left\lfloor \frac{p}{q}\mathbf{s}A^\top \right\rceil$, the LWR problem is to determine $\mathbf{s}$ (see Definition 4 below). The parameters m, n, q, and χ_s play the same roles as in the LWE problem, whereas the parameter p is regarded as an alternative to χ_e for the following reason: While the LWE problem transforms $\mathbf{s}A^\top$ into $\mathbf{s}A^\top + \mathbf{e}$ with the error vector $\mathbf{e}$ generated by χ_e, the LWR problem does it to $\left\lfloor \frac{p}{q}\mathbf{s}A^\top \right\rceil$ via a rounding operation with p/q scaling.

The computational hardness of the LWE problem has been analyzed through many attacks, such as Arora-Ge's algebraic algorithm [6], a combinatorial method that uses the BKW algorithm [14] and methods transforming the LWE problem to other known lattice-related problems. Arora-Ge's algorithm solves the LWE problem via linearization, and requires the sample number m to be sufficiently large to solve the LWE problem correctly. The method using the BKW algorithm also requires a large sample number to solve the LWE problem properly. On the other hand, two major embedding methods (Kannan's embedding attack [18] and Bai-Galbraith's embedding attack [9]), which transform the LWE problem to the Shortest Vector Problem (SVP), require relatively fewer samples. More specifically, in Bai-Galbraith's embedding attack, an $(n + m + 1)$-dimensional lattice denoted by $\mathcal{L}_{\mathrm{BG}}$ (which we call a BG-lattice) is constructed and a vector of the form $(\mathbf{s}\ \mathbf{e}\ 1)$ can be obtained as the shortest vector in $\mathcal{L}_{\mathrm{BG}}$ (see Subsect. 3.2 below). Bai-Galbraith's embedding attack has been regarded as one of the most efficient attacks on LWE-based cryptosystems (thus, this is often called the primal attack). Since the LWR problem can be transformed into the LWE problem for given A and $sA^\top + e$ with $e := \left\lfloor \frac{q}{p} \left\lfloor \frac{p}{q} sA^\top \right\rceil \right\rceil - sA^\top$ (see Subsect. 2.4 for details), the analysis of this attack against the LWR problem has been conducted in a manner similar to that for the LWE case. However, the LWE problem transformed from the LWR problem is a special case of the LWE problem, and therefore, a specific analysis of the lattice $\mathcal{L}_{BG}$, constructed in Bai-Galbraith's embedding attack against the LWR problem, should be provided.

1.1 Contribution

We provide a theoretical analysis of the structure of the lattice $\mathcal{L}_{BG}$ constructed in Bai-Galbraith's embedding attack against the LWR problem of the parameter set (m, n, q, p). We shall prove the existence of a certain short vector in $\mathcal{L}_{BG}$ of the form $(\mathbf{0} \quad \mathbf{c} \quad p)$ with $\mathbf{0} \in \mathbb{Z}^n$, $\mathbf{c} \in \mathbb{Z}^m$ and $p \in \mathbb{Z}$, where the absolute value of each entry of $\mathbf{c}$ is bounded by $p/2$. Thus, the vector of the form $(\mathbf{0} \quad \mathbf{c} \quad p)$ is shorter than $(\mathbf{s} \quad \mathbf{e} \quad 1)$ for some small p, where $\mathbf{s}$ (resp. $\mathbf{e}$) is a secret (resp. error) vector in the LWE problem transformed from the LWR problem. This short vector exists because the error vector $\mathbf{e}$ is generated by rounding through the transformation from the LWR problem to the LWE problem. We determine the condition in which $(\mathbf{0} \quad \mathbf{c} \quad p)$ is the shortest vector in $\mathcal{L}_{BG}$ with high probability.

In the case where $(\mathbf{0} \quad \mathbf{c} \quad p)$ is the shortest vector in $\mathcal{L}_{BG}$, the vector $(\mathbf{s} \quad \mathbf{e} \quad 1)$ is expected to be the second shortest vector that is linearly independent of $(\mathbf{0} \quad \mathbf{c} \quad p)$. Contrary to this expectation, we show that the second shortest vector in $\mathcal{L}_{BG}$ can be $(\mathbf{s} \quad \mathbf{e} \quad 1) \pm (\mathbf{0} \quad \mathbf{c} \quad p)$ instead of $(\mathbf{s} \quad \mathbf{e} \quad 1)$ if $p \nmid q$. We also discuss the probability distribution of the norm $\|(\mathbf{s} \quad \mathbf{e} \quad 1) \pm (\mathbf{0} \quad \mathbf{c} \quad p)\|$, and determine the lower bound of the probability of $\|(\mathbf{s} \quad \mathbf{e} \quad 1) \pm (\mathbf{0} \quad \mathbf{c} \quad p)\| < \|(\mathbf{s} \quad \mathbf{e} \quad 1)\|$. Our lower bound written with the parameters m, q and p implies a deduction; it becomes more probable that $(\mathbf{s} \quad \mathbf{e} \quad 1) \pm (\mathbf{0} \quad \mathbf{c} \quad p)$ is shorter than $(\mathbf{s} \quad \mathbf{e} \quad 1)$ when q becomes larger than p^2.

Finally, we conduct experiments with small n in order to examine our theoretical analysis above. Our experimental results confirm that a vector of the form $(\mathbf{0} \quad \mathbf{c} \quad p)$ is the shortest vector in $\mathcal{L}_{BG}$, and we examine the deduction on $(\mathbf{s} \quad \mathbf{e} \quad 1) \pm (\mathbf{0} \quad \mathbf{c} \quad p)$ described above.

Although we only discuss the case of Bai-Galbraith's embedding attack, almost the same discussion can be applied to that of Kannan's embedding attack. We also note that this paper focuses only on a theoretical observation of the LWR problem, and our future work is to analyze realistic attacks against LWR-based cryptosystems via our observation.

1.2 Organization

In Sect. 2, we recall the definition of lattices, and describe the LWE and LWR problems. Section 3 provides a brief explanation of how two embedding attacks (Kannan's embedding attack [18] and Bai-Galbraith's embedding attack [9]) work on the LWE problem. In Sect. 4, we prove the existence of an unexpected short vector in a BG-lattice for the LWR problem, and provide the condition where it is the shortest with high probability. In Sect. 5, we discuss the second shortest vector in a BG-lattice and a probability related to the second shortest vector. Section 6 is the conclusion.

2   Preliminaries

In this section, we define the notation that will be used in the rest of this paper, and recall the definitions of the LWE and LWR problems.

2.1   Notation

We denote by $\mathbb{Z}$ and $\mathbb{R}$ the set of integers and that of real numbers respectively. For a positive integer q, the quotient ring of integers modulo q is denoted by $\mathbb{Z}_q$. For positive integers m and n, the set of m-dimensional vectors over $\mathbb{Z}_q$ (resp. the set of $(m \times n)$-matrices over $\mathbb{Z}_q$) is denoted by $\mathbb{Z}_q^m$ (resp. $\mathbb{Z}_q^{m \times n}$). Bold lower cases (e.g., $\mathbf{s}$) denote vectors, whereas upper cases (e.g., A) indicate matrices. We regard vectors as row vectors, and write $\mathbf{v}^\top$ as the transposed vector of a vector $\mathbf{v}$ (matrices as well). For a positive integer m, we denote by I_m the $(m \times m)$ identity matrix. For a real number x, the largest integer less than or equal to x is denoted by $\lfloor x \rfloor$, and the closest integer to x is $\lceil x \rfloor = \lfloor x + 1/2 \rfloor$. For an m-dimensional vector $\mathbf{v} = (v_1, \ldots, v_m) \in \mathbb{R}^m$, we denote by $\lfloor \mathbf{v} \rceil$ the vector whose i-th entry is $\lfloor v_i \rceil$ for each $1 \le i \le m$. For a random variable X, its expected value and variance are denoted by $\mathrm{E}[X]$ and $\mathrm{Var}(X)$, respectively.

2.2   Lattices

In this subsection, we recall the definition and some fundamental properties of lattices. Next, we also describe the LWE and LWR problems in the following two subsections.

Definition 1 (Lattices). *Let $\mathbf{b}_1, \ldots, \mathbf{b}_m \in \mathbb{R}^n$ be linearly independent vectors. We define a subset $\mathcal{L}$ of $\mathbb{R}^n$ as*

$$\mathcal{L} := \{x_1 \mathbf{b}_1 + \cdots + x_m \mathbf{b}_m \mid x_1, \ldots, x_m \in \mathbb{Z}\}.$$

We call the set $\mathcal{L}$ a lattice, and $\{\mathbf{b}_1, \ldots, \mathbf{b}_m\}$ a basis of the lattice $\mathcal{L}$. The cardinality m does not depend on the choice of a basis of $\mathcal{L}$, and it is called the dimension of the lattice $\mathcal{L}$.

With the same notation as in Definition 1, let B be the matrix whose i-th row is $\mathbf{b}_i$ for each $1 \le i \le m$. In this case, we denote by $\mathcal{L}(B)$ the lattice $\mathcal{L}$ defined by $\{\mathbf{b}_1, \ldots, \mathbf{b}_m\}$ as a basis, and call B a basis matrix of $\mathcal{L}(B)$. The volume of the lattice $\mathcal{L}(B)$ is defined as follows:

$$\mathrm{Vol}(\mathcal{L}(B)) := \sqrt{|\det(BB^\top)|}. \tag{2.1}$$

If two matrices B_1 and B_2 define the same lattice $\mathcal{L}$, then the right-hand side of (2.1) for B_1 is equal to that for B_2.

Definition 2 (Successive minima). *For each* $1 \leq i \leq m$, *the i-th successive minimum* $\lambda_i(\mathcal{L})$ *is defined as*

$$\lambda_i(\mathcal{L}) := \min_{\mathbf{b}_1,\ldots,\mathbf{b}_i \in \mathcal{L}} \max\{\|\mathbf{b}_1\|,\ldots,\|\mathbf{b}_i\|\},$$

where $\mathbf{b}_1,\ldots,\mathbf{b}_i$ *run through linearly independent non-zero vectors in* $\mathcal{L}$. *We call a vector* $\mathbf{v}$ *in* $\mathcal{L}$ *with* $\|\mathbf{v}\| = \lambda_1(\mathcal{L})$ *the shortest vector in* $\mathcal{L}$. *A vector* $\mathbf{v}$ *in* $\mathcal{L}$ *with* $\|\mathbf{v}\| = \lambda_2(\mathcal{L})$ *linearly independent of the shortest vector in* $\mathcal{L}$ *is called the second shortest vector in* $\mathcal{L}$; *generally, the i-th shortest vector can be defined similarly.*

The first successive minimum $\lambda_1(\mathcal{L})$ is estimated by the Gaussian heuristic. Specifically, the value $\lambda_1(\mathcal{L})$ is estimated as

$$\lambda_1(\mathcal{L}) \approx \sqrt{\frac{m}{2\pi e}} \mathrm{Vol}(\mathcal{L})^{1/m}.$$

There exist some computational problems related to lattices such as the Shortest Vector Problem (SVP), which requires to find the shortest vector in $\mathcal{L}$ for a given basis matrix B defining the lattice $\mathcal{L}$. A typical method for solving SVP is the *lattice basis reduction* such as the BKZ (Block Korkin-Zolotarev) [16,25] algorithm.

Remark 1. The ratio of the norms of the shortest and the second shortest vectors deeply affects the solvability of the SVP. Specifically, Gama and Nguyen [19] estimated that the (unique-)SVP for an m-dimensional lattice $\mathcal{L}(B)$ can be solved if

$$\frac{\lambda_2(\mathcal{L})}{\lambda_1(\mathcal{L})} \geq \tau \delta^m \qquad (2.2)$$

holds, where τ is a constant less than 1, and where δ is a positive real number with $\delta^m = \|\mathbf{b}_1\|/\mathrm{Vol}(\mathcal{L}(B)^{1/m}$. The value of δ depends upon a basis of $\mathcal{L}$, and it is often used as a parameter to measure the quality of the basis returned by a basis reduction algorithm. In the case of the BKZ algorithm, Chen (cf. the formula (4.8) on page 95 of [17]) estimated the value of δ for the output basis as

$$\delta(\beta) \approx \left(\frac{\beta}{2\pi e} (\pi \beta)^{1/\beta} \right)^{\frac{1}{2(\beta-1)}},$$

where β is an input parameter (called the *block size*) of the BKZ algorithm. If the left-hand side of (2.2) is larger, the range of values of β satisfying (2.2) with $\delta = \delta(\beta)$ can become wider. In this case β can take smaller values, which implies that the BKZ algorithm might solve SVP more efficiently.

2.3   Search-LWE and Search-LWR Problems

The LWE problems are lattice-related problems, which have two types: the Decision-LWE problem and the Search-LWE problem. The Search-LWE problem is defined in Definition 3 below, and it is a problem parameterized by a triple

(m, n, q) of three positive integers and a pair (χ_e, χ_s) of two discrete probability distributions over $\mathbb{Z}_q$. The distributions χ_e and χ_s both have mean values of 0, with standard deviations being σ_e and σ_s respectively.

Definition 3 (Search-LWE). *Let $A \in \mathbb{Z}_q^{m \times n}$ be a matrix whose entries are uniformly sampled over $\mathbb{Z}_q$. Let $\mathbf{s} \in \mathbb{Z}_q^n$ and $\mathbf{e} \in \mathbb{Z}_q^m$ be vectors whose entries are sampled from χ_s and χ_e respectively. Given a pair $(A, \mathbf{b} := \mathbf{s}A^\top + \mathbf{e})$, the Search-LWE problem requires to find $\mathbf{s}$.*

In the Search-LWE problem, the integers m, q, the vectors $\mathbf{e}$ and $\mathbf{s}$ are referred to as the number of samples, a modulo, an error vector and a secret vector respectively.

Similar to the LWE problems, the LWR problems are lattice-related problems with two types: the Decision-LWR problem and the Search-LWR problem. The Search-LWR problem (Definition 4 below) is a variant of the Search-LWE problem (Definition 3). It is parameterized by a quadruple (m, n, q, p) of four positive integers and one discrete probability distribution χ_s over $\mathbb{Z}_q$. Unlike the LWE problem, the LWR problem does not use a probability distribution χ_e as a parameter, but instead employs a positive integer p as an alternative.

Definition 4 (Search-LWR). *Let $A \in \mathbb{Z}_q^{m \times n}$ be a matrix whose entries are uniformly sampled over $\mathbb{Z}_q$. Let $\mathbf{s} \in \mathbb{Z}_q^n$ be a vector whose entries are sampled from χ_s. Given a pair $(A, \mathbf{b} := \left\lfloor \frac{p}{q} \mathbf{s} A^\top \right\rceil \mod p)$, the Search-LWR problem requires to find the secret $\mathbf{s}$.*

In the rest of this paper, we call the Search-LWE problem (resp. the Search-LWR problem) the LWE problem (resp. the LWR problem) for simplicity.

2.4   Transformation of LWR to LWE

To solve the LWR problem, the most efficient existing method is to solve it as the LWE problem after the following transformation: Let $(A, \mathbf{b}) \in \mathbb{Z}_q^{m \times n} \times \mathbb{Z}_p^m$ be an instance of the LWR problem parameterized by m, n, q, p and χ_s. Then, we define a vector $\mathbf{b}' \in \mathbb{Z}_q^m$ as

$$\mathbf{b}' := \left\lfloor \frac{q}{p} \mathbf{b} \right\rceil = \left\lfloor \frac{q}{p} \left\lfloor \frac{p}{q} \mathbf{s} A^\top \right\rceil \right\rceil.$$

Putting $\mathbf{e} := \mathbf{b}' - \mathbf{s}A^\top$, we have $\mathbf{b}' = \mathbf{s}A^\top + \mathbf{e}$. Therefore the pair $(A, \mathbf{b}')$ can be viewed as an instance of the LWE problem with the parameter set $(m, n, q, \chi_s, \chi_e)$, where χ_e is expected to be the uniform distribution over the set

$$\left\{ -\left\lfloor \frac{\lfloor q/2 \rfloor}{p} \right\rceil, \dots, \left\lfloor \frac{\lfloor q/2 \rfloor}{p} \right\rceil \right\}, \tag{2.3}$$

see [20, Theorem 1]. The standard deviation σ_e is approximately calculated by

$$\sigma_e \approx \sqrt{\frac{q^2 + 2pq}{12p^2}}. \tag{2.4}$$

By this approximate equality, we can also estimate the squared norm of $\mathbf{e}$: It follows from the law of large number that

$$\|\mathbf{e}\|^2 = \sum_{i=1}^{m} e_i^2 \approx m\mathrm{E}[e_i^2] = m\sigma_e^2 \approx m \cdot \frac{q^2 + 2pq}{12p^2}. \tag{2.5}$$

where we used $\mathrm{E}[e_i] \approx 0$.

We remark from [21] that if $q = 2up$ for some $u \in \mathbb{Z}$ (this is the case of SABER [12] and Round5 [8]), the distribution χ_e is expected to be the uniform distribution over the set $\{-u + 1, \ldots, u\}$, which is slightly different from (2.3), and moreover

$$\sigma_e \approx \sqrt{\frac{q^2 - p^2}{12p^2}}. \tag{2.6}$$

The estimation (2.5) of $\|\mathbf{e}\|^2$ should also be modified, see Appendix for details.
In order to discuss general cases, we use (2.4) in the rest of this paper.

3   Embedding Attacks Against LWE

In this section, we outline the embedding attacks on the LWE problem. In particular, we describe in detail the two embedding attacks suggested respectively in [9] and [18]. Both these two attacks transform the LWE problem to SVP.

3.1   Kannan's Embedding Attack

Kannan's embedding attack [18] constructs a lattice ($\mathcal{L}_{\mathrm{Kan}}$ below) from an LWE instance so that an error vector $\mathbf{e}$ can be embedded in the shortest vector in $\mathcal{L}_{\mathrm{Kan}}$. For an LWE instance $(A, \mathbf{b}) \in \mathbb{Z}_q^{m \times n} \times \mathbb{Z}_q^m$, we define a matrix B_{Kan} as

$$B_{\mathrm{Kan}} = \begin{pmatrix} I_n & A' & \mathbf{0}^\top \\ O & qI_{m-n} & \mathbf{0}^\top \\ & \mathbf{b} & M \end{pmatrix} \in \mathbb{Z}^{(m+1)\times(m+1)},$$

where M is a constant and $\begin{pmatrix} I_n & A' \\ O & qI_{m-n} \end{pmatrix} \in \mathbb{Z}^{m \times m}$ with $A' \in \mathbb{Z}^{n \times (m-n)}$ is the Hermite normal form of $\begin{pmatrix} A^\top \\ qI_m \end{pmatrix} \in \mathbb{Z}^{(n+m)\times m}$. A typical choice of M for analyzing the hardness of the LWE problem is $M = 1$, see e.g., [1,2,10]. From this and for simplicity, we take M to be 1 here. We denote by $\mathcal{L}_{\mathrm{Kan}}$ the lattice defined by the basis matrix B_{Kan}. Note that the lattice $\mathcal{L}_{\mathrm{Kan}}$ contains the vector $(\mathbf{e} \ 1) \in \mathbb{Z}^{m+1}$ as its element. It follows from the law of large numbers that

$$\|(\mathbf{e} \ 1)\| = \sqrt{\sum_{i=1}^{m} e_i^2 + 1} \approx \sqrt{m\mathrm{E}[e_i^2] + 1} = \sqrt{m\sigma_e^2 + 1}$$

where e_i denotes the i-th entry of $\mathbf{e}$ for each $1 \le i \le m$. On the other hand, by the Gaussian heuristic, the norm of the shortest vector in $\mathcal{L}_{\mathrm{Kan}}$ is estimated as

$$\min\left\{q, \sqrt{\frac{m+1}{2\pi e}}q^{(m-n)/(m+1)}\right\}.$$

Therefore, if the inequality

$$\sqrt{m\sigma_e^2 + 1} < \min\left\{q, \sqrt{\frac{m+1}{2\pi e}}q^{(m-n)/(m+1)}\right\}$$

holds, the vector $(\mathbf{e}\ 1)$ is expected to be the shortest. In this case, once we find $(\mathbf{e}\ 1)$ as the shortest vector in $\mathcal{L}_{\mathrm{Kan}}$, we can obtain the secret $\mathbf{s}$ by solving the equation $\mathbf{b} = \mathbf{s}A^\top + \mathbf{e}$.

3.2   Bai-Galbraith's Embedding Attack

Unlike Kannan's embedding attack, Bai-Galbraith's embedding attack [9] constructs a lattice ($\mathcal{L}_{\mathrm{BG}}$ below) containing $(\mathbf{s}\ \mathbf{e}\ 1)$ as its element. For the secret $\mathbf{s}$ with a small norm, the vector $(\mathbf{s}\ \mathbf{e}\ 1)$ can be the shortest one in $\mathcal{L}_{\mathrm{BG}}$. In the following, we describe this attack in detail.

For an LWE instance $(A, \mathbf{b}) \in \mathbb{Z}_q^{m\times n} \times \mathbb{Z}_q^m$, we define a matrix B_{BG} as

$$B_{\mathrm{BG}} = \begin{pmatrix} \nu I_n & -A^\top & \mathbf{0}^\top \\ O & qI_m & \mathbf{0}^\top \\ \mathbf{0} & \mathbf{b} & M \end{pmatrix} \in \mathbb{Z}^{(n+m+1)\times(n+m+1)}, \qquad (3.1)$$

where $\nu = \sigma_e/\sigma_s$ and $M \in \mathbb{Z}$ is a constant. For the same reason as in the case of Kannan's embedding attack described in Subsect. 3.1, we set $M = 1$ (cf. [3,5,10]). Note that for any other choice of M, a discussion similar to that in the rest of this paper can be conducted. In the following, we set $\nu = 1$ because many LWE-based protocols set σ_s almost equal to σ_e [4,5,7]. Note that even if $\nu \ne 1$, the following discussion can be applied by replacing σ_s and $\mathbf{s}$ with $\nu\sigma_s$ and $\nu\mathbf{s}$, respectively.

Definition 5 (BG-lattices). *Using the notation as above, we denote by $\mathcal{L}_{\mathrm{BG}}$ the lattice with the basis matrix $B_{\mathrm{BG}} \in \mathbb{Z}^{(m+n+1)\times(m+n+1)}$, and we refer to $\mathcal{L}_{\mathrm{BG}}$ as a BG-lattice.*

From the definition of the LWE problem (see Definition 3), we have $\mathbf{b} = \mathbf{s}A^\top + \mathbf{e}$ mod q, and hence there exists a vector $\mathbf{u} \in \mathbb{Z}^m$ that satisfies

$$\mathbf{b} = \mathbf{s}A^\top + \mathbf{e} + q\mathbf{u}.$$

Therefore, we have

$$(\mathbf{s}\ -\mathbf{u}\ 1)B_{\mathrm{BG}} = (\mathbf{s}\ -\mathbf{s}A^\top - q\mathbf{u} + \mathbf{b}\ 1) = (\mathbf{s}\ \mathbf{e}\ 1),$$

which implies that the lattice $\mathcal{L}_{\mathrm{BG}}$ contains $(\mathbf{s}\ \mathbf{e}\ 1)$. As in Kannan's embedding attack, it follows from the law of large numbers that

$$\|(\mathbf{s}\ \mathbf{e}\ 1)\| \approx \sqrt{n\sigma_s^2 + m\sigma_e^2 + 1},$$

and the norm of the shortest vector in $\mathcal{L}_{\mathrm{BG}}$ is expected to be

$$\min\left\{q, \sqrt{\frac{n+m+1}{2\pi e}}q^{m/(n+m+1)}\right\}.$$

Therefore, if the inequality

$$\sqrt{n\sigma_s^2 + m\sigma_e^2 + 1} < \min\left\{q, \sqrt{\frac{n+m+1}{2\pi e}}q^{m/(n+m+1)}\right\} \tag{3.2}$$

holds, the vector $(\mathbf{s}\ \mathbf{e}\ 1)$ is expected to be the shortest vector in $\mathcal{L}_{\mathrm{BG}}$. Hence, under the inequality (3.2), we can find the secret $\mathbf{s}$ (with high probability) by obtaining the shortest vector in $\mathcal{L}_{\mathrm{BG}}$.

4   Our Analysis of Shortest Vectors in BG-Lattices

In this section, we show the existence of a certain short vector in a lattice constructed in Bai-Galbraith's embedding attack against the LWR problem of the parameter set (m, n, q, p). We use the same notation as in Sect. 3. Recall from Subsect. 3.2 that the BG-lattice $\mathcal{L}_{\mathrm{BG}}$ (see Definition 5) constructed in the LWE problem has the shortest vector of the form $(\mathbf{s}\ \mathbf{e}\ 1)$ with high probability if (3.2) holds, where $\mathbf{s} \in \mathbb{Z}^n$ (resp. $\mathbf{e} \in \mathbb{Z}^m$) is a secret (resp. an error) vector in the LWE problem transformed from the LWR problem. Unlike the LWE problem, we will prove in Theorem 1 below that the BG-lattice $\mathcal{L}_{\mathrm{BG}}$ constructed in the LWR problem contains a vector of the form $(\mathbf{0}\ \mathbf{c}\ p)$ which can be shorter than $(\mathbf{s}\ \mathbf{e}\ 1)$, where $\mathbf{0} \in \mathbb{Z}^n$ and $\mathbf{c} \in \mathbb{Z}^m$. After proving Theorem 1, we will also determine the condition in which $(\mathbf{0}\ \mathbf{c}\ p)$ is shorter than $(\mathbf{s}\ \mathbf{e}\ 1)$ with high probability. Note that in the rest of this paper, we only discuss Bai-Galbraith's embedding attack, but the same discussion can be applied to the case of Kannan's embedding attack. For details, see Remark 2 at the end of this section.

Here, we prove Theorem 1 which shows the existence of a certain short vector described above.

Theorem 1. *Let $(A, \mathbf{b}) \in \mathbb{Z}_q^{m \times n} \times \mathbb{Z}_p^m$ be an instance of the LWR problem. We set $\mathbf{b}' := \lfloor (q/p)\mathbf{b} \rceil \subset \mathbb{Z}_q^m$, and*

$$\mathbf{c} := p\mathbf{b}' - q\mathbf{b} \in \mathbb{Z}^m.$$

Denoting by c_i the i-th entry of $\mathbf{c}$ for each $1 \leq i \leq m$, we then have

$$-\frac{p}{2} < c_i \leq \frac{p}{2}.$$

We also have that the vector $(\mathbf{0}\ \mathbf{c}\ p) \in \mathbb{Z}^{n+m+1}$ is contained in the BG-lattice $\mathcal{L}_{\mathrm{BG}}$ constructed from $(A, \mathbf{b}')$. If p divides q, we can take $\mathbf{c} = \mathbf{0} \in \mathbb{Z}^m$.

Proof. The vector $\mathbf{c}$ can be written as

$$\mathbf{c} = p \left\lfloor \frac{q}{p} \mathbf{b} \right\rceil - q\mathbf{b} = p \left(\left\lfloor \frac{q}{p} \mathbf{b} \right\rceil - \frac{q}{p} \mathbf{b} \right).$$

Since the absolute value of each entry of the vector $\left\lfloor \frac{q}{p} \mathbf{b} \right\rceil - \frac{q}{p} \mathbf{b}$ is bounded by $1/2$, we have

$$-\frac{p}{2} < c_i \le \frac{p}{2}$$

for each $1 \le i \le m$.

Assume that p divides q, i.e., $q = kp$ for some integer k. In this case, we have

$$\mathbf{c} = p \left\lfloor \frac{q}{p} \mathbf{b} \right\rceil - q\mathbf{b} = p(\lfloor k\mathbf{b} \rceil - k\mathbf{b}) = p(k\mathbf{b} - k\mathbf{b}) = \mathbf{0}.$$

Let B_{BG} be the matrix defined in (3.1) constructed from the LWE instance $(A, \mathbf{b}')$. Then one has

$$(\mathbf{0} \ \ -\mathbf{b} \ \ p) B_{\mathrm{BG}} = (\mathbf{0} \ \ p\mathbf{b}' - q\mathbf{b} \ \ p) = (\mathbf{0} \ \ \mathbf{c} \ \ p) \in \mathcal{L}_{\mathrm{BG}}.$$

∎

Next, we discuss the condition under which the vector $(\mathbf{0} \ \ \mathbf{c} \ \ p)$ constructed in Theorem 1 is the shortest vector in the BG-lattice $\mathcal{L}_{\mathrm{BG}}$. Note that each entry of $\mathbf{c}$ is expected to be uniformly distributed over the set of all integers in the interval $(-\frac{p}{2}, \frac{p}{2}]$. It follows from the law of large numbers that

$$\|\mathbf{c}\|^2 \approx \frac{\left(2 \lfloor \frac{p}{2} \rfloor + 1\right)^2 - 1}{2} m \approx \frac{p^2 + 2p}{12} m. \tag{4.1}$$

If the inequality

$$\|(\mathbf{0} \ \ \mathbf{c} \ \ p)\| < \|(\mathbf{s} \ \ \mathbf{e} \ \ 1)\|$$

holds, the shortest vector in $\mathcal{L}_{\mathrm{BG}}$ has the form $(\mathbf{0} \ \ \mathbf{c} \ \ p)$ with high probability. From the law of large numbers together with (4.1), this inequality can be written as

$$\frac{p^2 + 2p}{12} m + p^2 < \sigma_s^2 n + \sigma_e^2 m + 1.$$

By approximating the value σ_e by (2.4), we have

$$\frac{p^2 + 2p}{12} m + p^2 < \sigma_s^2 n + \frac{q^2 + 2pq}{12p^2} m + 1. \tag{4.2}$$

Thus, if (4.2) holds, the vector of the form $(\mathbf{0} \ \ \mathbf{c} \ \ p)$ is the shortest vector in $\mathcal{L}_{\mathrm{BG}}$ with high probability.

Remark 2. Recall from Subsect. 3.1 that Kannan's embedding attack can be applied to the LWE problem, and that we can obtain the vector of the form (**e** 1) as the shortest vector in the lattice $\mathcal{L}_{\mathrm{Kan}}$. However, for the LWE problem which is transformed from the LWR problem, Kannan's embedding attack might find a vector of the form (**c** p) instead of (**e** 1).

Similar to the derivation of the inequality (4.2), the condition in which (**c** p) is the shortest vector in $\mathcal{L}_{\mathrm{Kan}}$ is obtained as

$$\frac{p^2 + 2p}{12}m + p^2 < \frac{q^2 + 2pq}{12p^2}m + 1. \tag{4.3}$$

This inequality is stricter than the inequality (4.2) because the first term on the right-hand side of (4.2) does not appear in that of (4.3).

5   Second Shortest Vectors in BG-lattices

In this section, we explain that the second shortest vector in the BG-lattice for the LWR problem of the parameter set (m, n, q, p, χ_s) can be (**s** **e** $\pm$ **c** 1 $\pm$ p) instead of (**s** **e** 1), where $\mathbf{s} \in \mathbb{Z}^n$, $\mathbf{e} \in \mathbb{Z}^m$ and $\mathbf{c} \in \mathbb{Z}^m$ will be described below. This implies that there exists a vector in the BG-lattice with the information of the secret vector which is shorter than expected. We use the same notation as in Sects. 3 and 4. In Theorem 1 of Sect. 4, we prove the existence of a vector in the BG-lattice $\mathcal{L}_{\mathrm{BG}}$ of the form (**0** **c** p) with $0 \le |c_i| \le p/2$ for each $1 \le i \le m$. Recall also from Subsect. 3.2 that $\mathcal{L}_{\mathrm{BG}}$ contains a vector of the form (**s** **e** 1), where **s** (resp. **e**) is the secret (resp. error) vector in the LWE problem transformed from the LWR problem. Even if (**0** **c** p) is the shortest vector in $\mathcal{L}_{\mathrm{BG}}$, the vector (**s** **e** 1) is still a short vector, provided that (3.2) holds. Since the vectors (**s** **e** 1) and (**0** **c** p) are linearly independent, the vector (**s** **e** 1) can be the second shortest vector (Definition 2) in $\mathcal{L}_{\mathrm{BG}}$. Furthermore, (**s** **e** 1) as well as a vector in $\mathcal{L}_{\mathrm{BG}}$ of the form

$$(\mathbf{s} \ \ \mathbf{e} \ \ 1) + k\,(\mathbf{0} \ \ \mathbf{c} \ \ p) \tag{5.1}$$

for some integer $k \in \mathbb{Z} \setminus \{0\}$ can be the second shortest vector, since both (**s** **e** 1) and (**0** **c** p) are short vectors.

The aim of this section is to discuss the probability that

$$\| (\mathbf{s} \ \ \mathbf{e} + k\mathbf{c} \ \ 1 + kp) \| < \| (\mathbf{s} \ \ \mathbf{e} \ \ 1) \| \tag{5.2}$$

holds. For simplicity, we consider only the case of $k = \pm 1$, that is,

$$\| (\mathbf{s} \ \ \mathbf{e} \pm \mathbf{c} \ \ 1 \pm p) \| < \| (\mathbf{s} \ \ \mathbf{e} \ \ 1) \| \tag{5.3}$$

which is equivalent to $\|\mathbf{e} \pm \mathbf{c}\|^2 + (1 \pm p)^2 < \|\mathbf{e}\|^2 + 1$. Since p is constant, in the following two subsections, we focus on the relation between $\|\mathbf{e} \pm \mathbf{c}\|^2$ and $\|\mathbf{e}\|^2$, and estimate the probability of (5.3) by that of

$$\|\mathbf{e} \pm \mathbf{c}\| < \|\mathbf{e}\|. \tag{5.4}$$

In the rest of this section, we assume that p does not divide q since otherwise we can take $\mathbf{c} = \mathbf{0}$, as stated in Theorem 1. This means that (5.2) does not hold for any integer k.

If the inequality (5.2) holds, then the second shortest vector in $\mathcal{L}_{BG}$ is shorter than expected. Owing to the existence of such an unexpected vector, the ratio of the norms of the second shortest vector and the *third* shortest vector is expected to become large, compared to the case where $(\mathbf{s} \ \mathbf{e} \ 1)$ is the second shortest vector. This might affect the solvability of the SVP of BG-lattices for the LWR problem if a discussion similar to that in Remark 1 is applicable.

5.1   Probability Distribution of $\|\mathbf{e} \pm \mathbf{c}\|^2$

To simplify the notation, we first set $\frac{r}{2} := \left\lfloor \frac{\lfloor q/2 \rfloor}{p} \right\rfloor$. Note that for each $1 \leq i \leq m$, the i-th entry e_i of $\mathbf{e}$ follows the uniform distribution over $\{-r/2, \ldots, r/2\}$, and c_i follows that over $\{-\lfloor p/2 \rfloor, \ldots, \lfloor p/2 \rfloor\}$. Thus we have $0 \leq |e_i + c_i| \leq \frac{r+p}{2}$.

To estimate the probability of (5.4), we calculate the probability distribution of $\|\mathbf{e} \pm \mathbf{c}\|^2$ by assuming that $q > p^2$ (for the case of $q < p^2$, see Remark 3 below). The reason why we mainly consider the case of $q > p^2$ is the following: It follows from $\{-\lfloor p/2 \rfloor, \ldots, \lfloor p/2 \rfloor\} \subset \{-r/2, \ldots, r/2\}$ that $\|\mathbf{c}\| < \|\mathbf{e}\|$ holds with high probability, by which we expect that the probability of (5.4) would be much higher compared to the case of $q < p^2$.

Since the distribution of each entry of $\mathbf{c}$ is symmetrical to the origin, the distribution of $\|\mathbf{e} + \mathbf{c}\|^2$ is the same as that of $\|\mathbf{e} - \mathbf{c}\|^2$. Hence it suffices to consider the distribution of $\|\mathbf{e} + \mathbf{c}\|^2$. Moreover, the probability distribution of $\|\mathbf{e} + \mathbf{c}\|^2$ is calculated as the product of the probabilities of the entries of $\mathbf{e} + \mathbf{c}$ since the i-th entries e_i and c_i are independently and identically distributed respectively for each $1 \leq i \leq m$. In the following, we calculate the probability of $e_i + c_i = k$ for each integer k, by considering two cases of $|k|$.

First, for the case of $0 \leq |k| \leq \frac{r-p}{2}$, the probability of $e_i + c_i = k$ coincides with that of $e_i = k - c_i$ because $-r/2 \leq k - c_i \leq r/2$ for any c_i. Therefore we have

$$\text{Prob}(e_i + c_i = k) = \sum_{d=-\lfloor p/2 \rfloor}^{\lfloor p/2 \rfloor} \text{Prob}(e_i = k - d)\text{Prob}(c_i = d)$$

$$\approx \sum_{d=-\lfloor p/2 \rfloor}^{\lfloor p/2 \rfloor} \frac{1}{r+1} \cdot \frac{1}{p+1} \approx \frac{1}{r+1}.$$

Second, in the case of $\frac{r-p}{2} < |k| \leq \frac{r+p}{2}$, the probability of $e_i + c_i = k$ coincides with that of $|k - c_i| \leq \frac{r}{2}$ and $e_i = k - c_i$. The conditions $|k - c_i| \leq r/2$ and $e_i = k - c_i$ imply that

$$k - \frac{p}{2} \leq k - c_i \leq k + \frac{p}{2}. \tag{5.5}$$

If k is positive, the left-hand side of (5.5) is larger than $-\frac{r}{2}$ because of our assumption that $q > p^2$, whereas the right-hand side is larger than $\frac{r}{2}$ because

$k > \frac{r-p}{2}$. Therefore the number of integers d in $\{-\lfloor p/2 \rfloor, \ldots, \lfloor p/2 \rfloor\}$ which satisfy $|k - d| \le \frac{r}{2}$ is approximately $\frac{r}{2} - (k - \frac{p}{2}) = \frac{r+p}{2} - k$. Similarly, if k is negative, the number is approximately $\frac{r+p}{2} + k$. Hence, the probability of $e_i + c_i = k$ for each integer k with $\frac{r-p}{2} < |k| \le \frac{r+p}{2}$ is

$$\text{Prob}(e_i + c_i = k) = \frac{\frac{r+p}{2} - |k|}{(r+1)(p+1)} = \frac{r + p - 2|k|}{2(r+1)(p+1)}.$$

Combining the above two cases for $|k|$, we have

$$\text{Prob}(e_i + c_i = k) \approx \begin{cases} \dfrac{1}{r+1} & \text{if } 0 \le |k| \le \frac{r-p}{2}, \\ \dfrac{r + p - 2|k|}{2(r+1)(p+1)} & \text{if } \frac{r-p}{2} < |k| \le \frac{r+p}{2}, \\ 0 & \text{otherwise.} \end{cases}$$

We finally have

$$\text{Prob}(\|\mathbf{e} + \mathbf{c}\|^2 = k) = \sum_{(k_1, \ldots, k_m) \in S(k)} \prod_{i=1}^{m} \text{Prob}(e_i + c_i = k), \tag{5.6}$$

where

$$S(k) := \left\{ (k_1, k_2, \ldots, k_m) \in \mathbb{Z}^m \mid |k_i| < \tfrac{r+p}{2}, \ \sum_{i=1}^{m} k_i^2 = k \right\}.$$

Note that the right-hand side of (5.6) is not an analytical expression because of the appearance of the set $S(k)$.

Remark 3. If p^2 is larger than q, we have the same discussion as above with p and r swapped. This is because c_i and e_i are symmetric in the above discussion, and they are uniformly distributed over $\{-\lfloor p/2 \rfloor, \ldots, \lfloor p/2 \rfloor\}$ and $\{-r/2, \ldots, r/2\}$, respectively.

5.2 Lower Bound of Probability

In this subsection, we investigate the lower bound of the probability of (5.4). For the lower bound of this probability, we have the following:

Theorem 2. *Let a pair* $(A, \mathbf{b}) \in \mathbb{Z}_q^{m \times n} \times \mathbb{Z}_p^m$ *be an instance of the LWR problem. Set* $\mathbf{e} := \left\lfloor \frac{q}{p} \mathbf{b} \right\rfloor - \mathbf{s}A^\top$. *Let* $\mathbf{c} \in \mathbb{Z}^m$ *be the vector as in Theorem 1. Then, we have*

$$\text{Prob} \begin{pmatrix} \|\mathbf{e} + \mathbf{c}\| < \|\mathbf{e}\| \\ \text{or} \\ \|\mathbf{e} - \mathbf{c}\| < \|\mathbf{e}\| \end{pmatrix} \ge 2 \left(\frac{1}{2} - \frac{p^2}{8(q+p)} \right)^m. \tag{5.7}$$

Proof. For each $1 \leq i \leq m$, we denote by e_i and c_i the i-th entry of $\mathbf{e}$ and $\mathbf{c}$, respectively. To obtain the lower bound, we first calculate the probability of $|e_i + c_i| < |e_i|$. Putting $\frac{r}{2} := \left\lfloor \frac{\lfloor q/2 \rfloor}{p} \right\rfloor$, we have

$$\mathrm{Prob}(|e_i + c_i| < |e_i|) = \mathrm{Prob}(-2e_i < c_i < 0, \ e_i < 0)$$
$$+ \mathrm{Prob}(0 < c_i < -2e_i, \ e_i < 0)$$

$$= \frac{1}{r+1} \sum_{e_i = -r/2}^{r/2} \min\left\{\frac{2|e_i|}{p+1}, \frac{1}{2}\right\}$$

$$= \frac{1}{r+1} \left\{ \sum_{e_i = -\lfloor p/4 \rfloor}^{\lfloor p/4 \rfloor} \frac{2|e_i|}{p+1} + \sum_{\lfloor p/4 \rfloor < |e_i| < |r/2|} \frac{1}{2} \right\}$$

$$\approx \frac{p+4}{8(r+1)} + \frac{2r - p}{4(r+1)} = \frac{1}{2} - \frac{p}{8(r+1)}$$

$$\approx \frac{1}{2} - \frac{p^2}{8(q+p)}.$$

Since the values e_i and c_i are independently and identically distributed respectively, we have

$$\mathrm{Prob}(\|\mathbf{e} + \mathbf{c}\| < \|\mathbf{e}\|) \geq \prod_{i=1}^{m} \mathrm{Prob}(|e_i + c_i| < |e_i|)$$

$$\approx \prod_{i=1}^{m} \left(\frac{1}{2} - \frac{p^2}{8(q+p)}\right) = \left(\frac{1}{2} - \frac{p^2}{8(q+p)}\right)^m.$$

Similarly, we also have

$$\mathrm{Prob}(\|\mathbf{e} - \mathbf{c}\| < \|\mathbf{e}\|) \geq \left(\frac{1}{2} - \frac{p^2}{8(q+p)}\right)^m.$$

As $\|\mathbf{e} + \mathbf{c}\| < \|\mathbf{e}\|$ and $\|\mathbf{e} - \mathbf{c}\| < \|\mathbf{e}\|$ do not hold simultaneously, we finally have (5.7). ∎

This theorem implies that when the ratio p^2/q becomes smaller, it becomes more likely that $\|\mathbf{e} \pm \mathbf{c}\|^2 < \|\mathbf{e}\|^2$.

Remark 4. If the sample number m is larger, the lower bound—the right-hand side of the inequality (5.7)—becomes smaller. This implies that the second shortest vector in $\mathcal{L}_{\mathrm{BG}}$ is $(\mathbf{s} \ \mathbf{e} \ 1)$ with high probability if m is sufficiently large; it follows from the law of large numbers that

$$\|\mathbf{e} \pm \mathbf{c}\|^2 \approx m\mathrm{E}[e_i^2] + m\mathrm{E}[c_i^2] \geq m\mathrm{E}[e_i^2] \approx \|\mathbf{e}\|^2$$

holds asymptotically. Therefore, (5.3) does not hold for $m \gg 0$.

5.3 Experimental Results

We conducted experiments to obtain the probability that the second shortest vector in $\mathcal{L}_{BG}$ is $(\mathbf{s} \quad \mathbf{e} \pm k\mathbf{c} \quad 1 \pm kp)$ for some non-zero integer k. In this case, (5.2) definitely holds.

Our experiments was set as follows. We set $n = 20$, $q = 401$ and χ_s a rounded Gaussian distribution with $\sigma_s = \sqrt{(q^2 + 2pq)/12p^2}$, and generated LWR instances for several values of m and p. To obtain the shortest vectors, we applied the BKZ algorithm [16] with the parameter $\beta = 30$ as a lattice basis reduction. We also obtained the second shortest vectors in the BG-lattices for the LWR problem. We conducted this experiment 1000 times for each parameter set (m, p). We used Python 3.7.6 to generate LWR instances and fpylll (version 0.4.0) for the BKZ algorithm on a computer with macOS Catalina 10.15.7. whose CPU is 2.3GHz Intel Core i7 (quad core) CPU with the 32GB of RAM. The source codes are available at our GitHub repository [26].

Table 1. The number that vectors of the form $(\mathbf{s} \quad \mathbf{e} + k\mathbf{c} \quad 1 + kp)$ for some non-zero integer k are obtained as the second shortest vectors in BG-lattices for the LWR problem with the parameters $(n, q) = (20, 401)$, where we take the rounded Gaussian distribution with $\sigma_s = \sqrt{(q^2 + 2pq)/12p^2}$ as χ_s.

m	p	$(\mathbf{0} \quad \pm\mathbf{c} \quad \pm p)$ is the shortest	$(\mathbf{s} \quad \mathbf{e} + k\mathbf{c} \quad 1 + kp)$ is the 2nd shortest
	9	1000	72 (7.2%)
40	12	1000	66 (6.6%)
	15	1000	9 (0.9%)
	9	1000	142 (14.2%)
45	12	1000	58 (5.8%)
	15	1000	8 (0.8%)

In Table 1, we summarize our experimental results. Table 1 illustrates that the shortest vectors in BG-lattices are $(\mathbf{0} \quad \pm\mathbf{c} \quad \pm p)$ in all the cases we experimented. We also confirmed from Table 1 that when the ratio p^2/q becomes smaller, it becomes more likely that the second shortest vector is $(\mathbf{s} \quad \mathbf{e} + k\mathbf{c} \quad 1 + kp)$ for some non-zero integer k as expected from Theorem 2. This shows that a BG-lattice for the LWR problem with $p^2 \ll q$ contains (with high probability) a shorter vector with the information of the secret vector $\mathbf{s}$ than expected.

6 Conclusion

In this paper, we presented a theoretical analysis of the structure of lattices (referred to as BG-lattices) that appear in Bai-Galbraith's embedding attack applied to the LWR problem. In particular, we proved the existence of a certain vector of the form $(\mathbf{0} \quad \mathbf{c} \quad p)$ which can be the shortest in a BG-lattice. We also determined the condition of the parameters of the LWR problem under which such a vector is the shortest one in the BG-lattice with high probability. The second shortest vector in the BG-lattice for the LWR problem is expected to be a vector of the form $(\mathbf{s} \ \mathbf{e} \ 1)$ with the secret vector $\mathbf{s}$ and the error vector $\mathbf{e}$. However, because of the existence of the shorter vector of the form $(\mathbf{0} \ \mathbf{c} \ p)$, a vector of the form $(\mathbf{s} \ \mathbf{e} \ 1) + k(\mathbf{0} \ \mathbf{c} \ p)$ for some non-zero integer k can be the second shortest vector in the BG-lattice instead. We determined the lower bound of the probability that this occurs. In addition, we confirmed from our experimental results that $(\mathbf{0} \ \mathbf{c} \ p)$ are exactly the shortest ones in BG-lattices. The experimental results also show a relation between the ratio p^2/q (q and p are parameters of the LWR problem) and the probability that $(\mathbf{s} \ \mathbf{e} \ 1) + k(\mathbf{0} \ \mathbf{c} \ p)$ is obtained as the second shortest vector in a BG-lattice.

From the results in this study, we show that the LWR problem of a parameter set with the condition $p \nmid q$ and $p^2 \ll q$ have vectors shorter than those expected in BG-lattices. Since the parameter sets of SABER and Round5 do not satisfy the above condition, the analysis of these cryptosystems is not affected by our findings.

While this work focuses on a theoretical observation, our future work is to precisely analyze how our results in this paper influence the security of LWR-based cryptosystems. For this, we need to obtain an analytical expression of the probability distribution of the second successive minimum of a BG-lattice, or to find a stricter lower bound of the probability.

Appendix: Expected Norm of Error Vector

Let $\mathbf{e}$ be an error vector of the LWE problem transformed from the LWR problem of the parameter set (m, n, q, p, χ_s) (see Subsect. 2.4 for details). In this appendix, we shall modify the estimation (2.5) of $\|\mathbf{e}\|^2$ in general case to that in the case where $q = 2up$ for some $u \in \mathbb{Z}$, as pointed out in Subsect. 2.4.

Assume that $q = 2up$ for some $u \in \mathbb{Z}$. Recall from Subsect. 2.4 that for each $1 \leq i \leq m$, the i-th entry of the vector $\mathbf{e}$ approximately follows a uniform distribution over the set $\{-u+1, \ldots, u\}$, and thus we have the approximate equality (2.6): $\mathrm{Var}(e_i) = \sigma_e^2 \approx \frac{q^2-p^2}{12p^2}$. Since $\mathrm{E}[e_i] \approx \frac{1}{2}$, we can estimate the value of $\|\mathbf{e}\|^2$ as follows:

$$\|\mathbf{e}\|^2 = \sum_{i=1}^{m} e_i^2 \approx m\mathrm{E}[e_i^2] = m\left(\mathrm{Var}(e_i) + \mathrm{E}[e_i]^2\right) = m\left(\sigma_e^2 + \frac{1}{4}\right)$$
$$= m \cdot \frac{q^2 + 2p^2}{12p^2}.$$

We conducted an experiment to confirm this by the following method: We generated one million LWR instances with $m = 768$, $n = 256$, $q = 2^{13} = 8192$ and $p = 2^{10} = 1024$. The distribution χ_s is a centered binomial distribution with $\mu = 8$. This is the parameter set of SABER-KEM; as SABER-KEM is Module-LWR based, this is the parameter set of the LWR problem transformed from the Module-LWR problem. We obtained error vectors $\mathbf{e}$ by transforming the generated LWR instances to LWE instances. We create a histogram of the value $\|\mathbf{e}\|^2$, and depict it in Fig. 1. Our experimental results show that the expected value of $\|\mathbf{e}\|^2$ is close to $m \cdot \frac{q^2 + 2p^2}{12p^2}$.

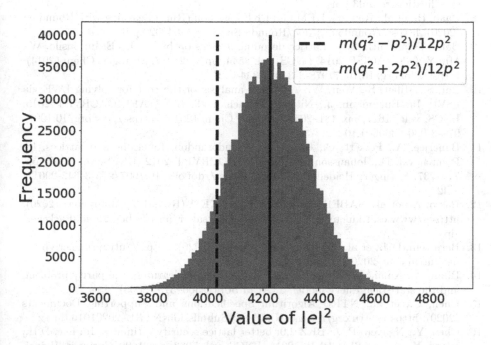

Fig. 1. Histogram of the value of $\|\mathbf{e}\|^2$

References

1. Albrecht, M.R., Fitzpatrick, R., Göpfert, F.: On the efficacy of solving LWE by reduction to unique-SVP. In: Lee, H.-S., Han, D.-G. (eds.) ICISC 2013. LNCS, vol. 8565, pp. 293–310. Springer, Cham (2014). https://doi.org/10.1007/978-3-319-12160-4_18
2. Albrecht, M.R., Player, R., Scott, S.: On the concrete hardness of learning with errors. J. Math. Cryptol. **9**(3), 169–203 (2015)
3. Albrecht, M.R., Göpfert, F., Virdia, F., Wunderer, T.: Revisiting the expected cost of solving uSVP and applications to LWE. In: Takagi, T., Peyrin, T. (eds.) ASIACRYPT 2017. LNCS, vol. 10624, pp. 297–322. Springer, Cham (2017). https://doi.org/10.1007/978-3-319-70694-8_11
4. Alkim, E., et al.: FrodoKEM Learning With Errors Key Encapsulation Algorithm Specifications and Supporting Documentation (2020). https://frodokem.org/files/FrodoKEM-specification-20200930.pdf
5. Alkim, E., et al.: NewHope Algorithm Specifications and Supporting Documentation (2020). https://newhopecrypto.org/data/NewHope_2019_07_10.pdf

6. Arora, S., Ge, R.: New algorithms for learning in presence of errors. In: Aceto, L., Henzinger, M., Sgall, J. (eds.) ICALP 2011. LNCS, vol. 6755, pp. 403–415. Springer, Heidelberg (2011). https://doi.org/10.1007/978-3-642-22006-7_34

7. Avanzi, R., et al.: CRYSTALS-KYBER Algorithm Specifications and Supporting Documents (version 3.0) (2020). https://pq-crystals.org/kyber/data/kyber-specification-round3.pdf

8. Baan, H., et al.: Round5: KEM and PKE based on (Ring) Learning with Rounding (2020). https://round5.org/doc/Round5_Submission042020.pdf

9. Bai, S., Galbraith, S.D.: Lattice decoding attacks on binary LWE. In: Susilo, W., Mu, Y. (eds.) ACISP 2014. LNCS, vol. 8544, pp. 322–337. Springer, Cham (2014). https://doi.org/10.1007/978-3-319-08344-5_21

10. Bai, S., Miller, S., Wen, W.: A refined analysis of the cost for solving LWE via uSVP. In: Buchmann, J., Nitaj, A., Rachidi, T. (eds.) AFRICACRYPT 2019. LNCS, vol. 11627, pp. 181–205. Springer, Cham (2019). https://doi.org/10.1007/978-3-030-23696-0_10

11. Banerjee, A., Peikert, C., Rosen, A.: Pseudorandom functions and lattices. In: Pointcheval, D., Johansson, T. (eds.) EUROCRYPT 2012. LNCS, vol. 7237, pp. 719–737. Springer, Heidelberg (2012). https://doi.org/10.1007/978-3-642-29011-4_42

12. Basso, A., et al.: SABER: Mod-LWR based KEM (Round 3 Submission) (2020). https://www.esat.kuleuven.be/cosic/pqcrypto/saber/files/SaberRound3Package.zip

13. Bernstein, D.J., et al.: NTRU Prime: round 3 (2020). https://ntruprime.cr.yp.to/nist/ntruprime-20201007.pdf

14. Blum, A., Kalai, A., Wasserman, H.: Noise-tolerant learning, the parity problem, and the statistical query model. J. ACM **50**(4), 506–519 (2003)

15. Chen, C., et al.: NTRU Algorithm Specifications and Supporting Documents (2020). https://ntru.org/release/NIST-PQ-Submission-NTRU-20201016.tar.gz

16. Chen, Y., Nguyen, P.Q.: BKZ 2.0: better lattice security estimates. In: Lee, D.H., Wang, X. (eds.) ASIACRYPT 2011. LNCS, vol. 7073, pp. 1–20. Springer, Heidelberg (2011). https://doi.org/10.1007/978-3-642-25385-0_1

17. Chen, Y.: Réduction de Réseau Et Sécurité Concrète Du Chiffrement Complètement Homomorphe, Dissertation for Ph.D. Degree. Ecole Normale Supérieure, Paris (2013)

18. Kannan, R.: Minkowski's convex body theorem and integer programming. Math. Oper. Res. **12**(3), 415–440 (1987)

19. Gama, N., Nguyen, P.Q.: Predicting lattice reduction. In: Smart, N. (ed.) EUROCRYPT 2008. LNCS, vol. 4965, pp. 31–51. Springer, Heidelberg (2008). https://doi.org/10.1007/978-3-540-78967-3_3

20. Le, H.Q., Mishra, P.K., Duong, D.H., Yasuda, M.: Solving LWR via BDD strategy: modulus switching approach. In: Camenisch, J., Papadimitratos, P. (eds.) CANS 2018. LNCS, vol. 11124, pp. 357–376. Springer, Cham (2018). https://doi.org/10.1007/978-3-030-00434-7_18

21. Nguyen, P.: Comment on PQC forum (2018). https://groups.google.com/a/list.nist.gov/g/pqc-forum/c/nZBIBvYmmUI/m/J0pug16CBgAJ. Accessed 16 June 2021

22. NIST: Post-Quantum Cryptography. https://csrc.nist.gov/projects/post-quantum-cryptography. Accessed 16 June 2021

23. Regev, O.: On lattices, learning with errors, random linear codes, and cryptography. In: Proceedings of the Thirty-Seventh Annual ACM Symposium on Theory of Computing (STOC 2005), pp. 84–93 (2005)

24. Regev, O.: On lattices, learning with errors, random linear codes, and cryptography. J. ACM **56**(6) Article 34 (2009)

25. Schnorr, C.P., Euchner, M.: Lattice basis reduction: improved practical algorithms and solving subset sum problems. Math. Program. **66**, 181–199 (1994). https://doi.org/10.1007/BF01581144

26. https://github.com/shusakuU/analysis_of_BG_lattice_IWSEC_2021

System Security

KPRM: Kernel Page Restriction Mechanism to Prevent Kernel Memory Corruption

Hiroki Kuzuno[1]([✉])(iD) and Toshihiro Yamauchi[2](iD)

[1] Intelligent Systems Laboratory, SECOM Co., Ltd., Tokyo, Japan
kuzuno@s.okayama-u.ac.jp
[2] Graduate School of Natural Science and Technology, Okayama University,
Okayama, Japan
yamauchi@cs.okayama-u.ac.jp

Abstract. An operating system (OS) comprises a mechanism for sharing the kernel address space with each user process. An adversary's user process compromises the OS kernel through memory corruption, exploiting the kernel vulnerability. It overwrites the kernel code related to security features or the kernel data containing privilege information.

Process-local memory and system call isolation divide one kernel address space into multiple kernel address spaces. While user processes create their own kernel address space, these methods leave the kernel code vulnerable. Further, an adversary's user process can involve malicious code that elevates from user mode to kernel mode.

Herein, we propose the kernel page restriction mechanism (KPRM), which is a novel security design that prohibits vulnerable kernel code execution and prevents writing to the kernel data from an adversary's user process. The KPRM dynamically unmaps the kernel page of vulnerable kernel code and attack target kernel data from the kernel address space. This removes the reference of the unmapped kernel page from the kernel page table at the system call invocation. The KPRM achieves that an adversary's user process can not employ the reference of unmapped kernel page to exploit the kernel through vulnerable kernel code on the running kernel. We implemented KPRM on the latest Linux kernel and showed that it successfully thwarts actual proof-of-concept kernel vulnerability attacks that may cause kernel memory corruption. In addition, the KPRM performance results indicated limited kernel processing overhead in software benchmarks and a low impact on user applications.

1 Introduction

The operating system (OS) thwarts kernel vulnerability attacks that aim to subvert the kernel security features and then modify privilege information to compromise computer devices. Kernel vulnerability attacks rely on the user processes that share the kernel address space in the kernel mode; then, an adversary's user process can execute the kernel memory corruption available kernel code (vulnerable kernel code).

© Springer Nature Switzerland AG 2021
T. Nakanishi and R. Nojima (Eds.): IWSEC 2021, LNCS 12835, pp. 45–63, 2021.
https://doi.org/10.1007/978-3-030-85987-9_3

To prevent kernel memory corruption, the kernel adopts a verification of kernel control flow integrity (CFI) [1], the kernel uses kernel address randomization (KASLR) [2], or a CPU privilege mechanism for accessing and execution permission between the user mode and the kernel mode [3]. Additionally, process-local memory (Proclocal) allocates a specific kernel address space for a user process [4], and system call isolation (SCI) creates a dedicated kernel address space for the processing system call's routines [5].

While these approaches can effectively prevent the kernel memory corruption, they leave two issues remain unaddressed. First, the OS kernel still requires full kernel page mapping of kernel code, where vulnerable kernel code and attack targeted kernel code or remaining kernel data are potentially share the same kernel address space. Second, Proclocal can protect kernel data of specific kernel components without user process-related information, and SCI creates a statically duplicated kernel address space for each user process owing to stable behavior for kernel processing. These follow the idea that the vulnerable kernel code can be invoked to escalate privileges and evade security features [6,7].

In this paper, we propose the kernel page restriction mechanism (KPRM), which is a novel security capability that mitigates memory corruption through kernel vulnerabilities. The design of KPRM can extend the controlling of vulnerable kernel code execution and kernel data access of an adversary's user process on the running kernel. KPRM uses two types of kernel pages, namely, normal kernel pages and restricted kernel pages, to run the kernel and user processes. KPRM assigns vulnerable kernel code and protected kernel data (e.g., user identifiers) to a restricted kernel page; then, KPRM stores the remaining kernel code and kernel data in normal kernel pages. KPRM can manually employ the already known kernel vulnerability (e.g., common vulnerabilities and exposures (CVE) information or online available proof-of-concept code) to identify the vulnerable kernel code. KPRM achieves two objectives. First, the kernel page handling assures that the adversary's user process can not access restricted kernel page references in their own kernel address space to mitigate memory corruption. Second, KPRM dynamically unmaps restricted kernel page references for the adversary's user process at the system call invocation. KPRM applies this mechanism to all user processes without benign identification are manually registered to the benign user process list on the running kernel. KPRM ensures that kernel can reduce instances where the kernel address space is shared by both vulnerable kernel code and attack target kernel code or kernel data.

We implemented two types of KPRM prototypes on the latest Linux kernel. The first implementation aims to adopt a security capability that requires an additional kernel address space. It reserves vulnerable kernel code and protected kernel data for restricted kernel pages for the adversary's user process. KPRM prepares process-context identifiers (PCID) of the translation lookaside buffer (TLB) for switching page tables of kernel address spaces to reduce the TLB flushing cost. The second implementation aims to lower the overhead. It is possible to reserve protected kernel data for restricted kernel pages owing to user processes sharing kernel address space. KPRM only handles kernel page references of kernel code related to the adversary's user process and related information for reducing kernel misuse during interruption processing.

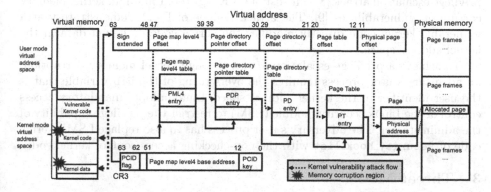

Fig. 1. Page table management of virtual address and physical address with attack regions

The primary contributions of this study are summarized as follows:

1. The proposed KPRM is a novel approach for kernel memory corruption mitigation for an adversary's user process in the kernel layer. We consider the key requirements for restricting the execution of vulnerable kernel code and access to kernel data on KPRM implementations. The threat model, capability, limitations, portability, and hardware consideration are also discussed.
2. We evaluate the efficacy of the implemented KPRM based on how well it prevents the vulnerable kernel code invocation and illegal modification of the kernel data through PoC user processes. We measure KPRM's performance using software benchmarks and actual applications such as the Apache web server and compiler. The results of our experiment indicate that KPRM implementations have low latency overhead effects for the kernel and acceptable cost for user application processing.

2   Background

2.1   Address Space and Page Table

Modern kernels support the virtual memory mechanism that provides a virtual address space that is larger than the physical memory for each user process. Linux x86_64 stores the virtual address of the page table in the CR3 register. As depicted in Fig. 1, the virtual address space is separated into two regions for the user and kernel modes.

Linux has a multiple-page table structure that creates virtual address spaces. It can be used to change a virtual address (48 bits on x86_64) to a physical address on the page table. The smallest set is a page (4 KB on x86_64). The kernel page stores the kernel code and kernel data in the specific virtual address space for the kernel mode.

2.2   Kernel Memory Corruption Vulnerability

Kernel memory corruption is a type of kernel vulnerability that leads to the privilege escalation attack [8]. The list of CVE registers 130 Linux kernel memory corruption vulnerabilities [9]. The attack regions of Fig. 1 demonstrate that a vulnerable kernel code directly modifies the kernel code or kernel data in the kernel address space.

To achieve a privilege escalation attack through kernel memory corruption, an adversary's user process requires the overwriting of the UID variable that is the user identifier in the kernel address space. Linux adopts mandatory access control of the Linux security module (LSM) to restrict the privilege capability of the administrator. The adversary's user process has to also replace LSM's kernel code of security_hook_list with the non-checking access control kernel code.

3   Threat Model

We postulate that a threat model of the kernel that contains an adversary's environment and kernel vulnerability is as follows:

- **Adversary**: An adversary takes normal user privileges and controls the shell command with the PoC kernel vulnerability code.
- **Kernel**: It provides the sharing of the kernel address space for every user process. The kernel address space contains the vulnerable kernel code, attack target kernel code, and kernel data.
- **Kernel vulnerability**: This is identified as a known piece of vulnerable kernel code. The adversary's user process executes the vulnerable kernel code to modify any kernel code or kernel data that is present in the kernel address space.
- **Attack target**: It contains the security feature of the kernel code (i.e., mandatory access control) and privilege information of kernel data (i.e., user identifier). These are the key points of the administrator's privilege restriction on the kernel.

From this point, to achieve kernel memory corruption, the adversary's user process must access and execute the kernel vulnerability code at the attack's starting point. The adversary's process can access any kernel virtual address from the vulnerable kernel code in the same kernel address space. Therefore, the adversary's user process alters the security features of the kernel code. Subsequently, it forcibly invokes the kernel code that modifies the privilege information of the kernel data for privilege escalation.

Building the KPRM's resilience requires the protection of security features and privilege information from the adversary's environment. KPRM has prepared a list of vulnerable kernel code, attack target of kernel code and kernel data at the KPRM kernel booting. Additionally, KPRM covers all user processes that contain the adversary's user process. To reduce the performance overhead, KPRM manages a benign user process list. It manually registers the flag of benign to avoid the restriction of KPRM for each user process on the running kernel.

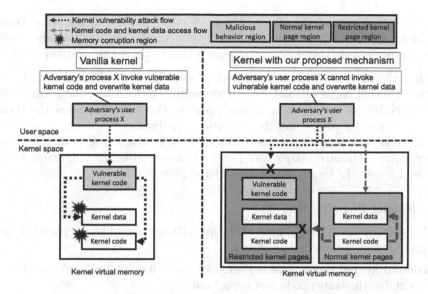

Fig. 2. Comparison of kernel page restriction mechanism

4   Design and Implementation

4.1   Design Requirements of the KPRM

We designed KPRM to achieve the primary requirements of preventing the invocation of the vulnerable kernel code and the illegal modification of kernel data.

- **Requirement for restriction of kernel page reference**
  User processes share the kernel address space as the kernel page table, which manages all the kernel code and data. User processes employ kernel features and store privilege information in the kernel address space (e.g., mandatory access control, user identifiers). The requirement is to prevent vulnerable kernel code invocation, followed by illegal kernel data modification. It prevents malicious behavior from the adversary's user process on the running kernel.

4.2   Design Overview

To satisfy the requirements of KPRM to enhance the kernel capability, the following design requirements must be fulfilled:

- **Dynamic kernel page reference management**
  The KPRM design provides normal and restricted kernel pages. KPRM relies on two types of pages and assigns vulnerable kernel code and privilege information of kernel data to restricted kernel pages for controlling the kernel address space. KPRM unmaps the restricted page references before the adversary's user process can execute vulnerable kernel code. This mechanism

ensures that restricted pages and normal pages are not in the same kernel address space. KPRM maintains kernel resilience by keeping the adversary's user process from causing memory corruption in the kernel address space.

Figure 2 depicts the adversary's user process X on the KPRM kernel. The restricted kernel pages are assigned to vulnerable kernel code, the kernel code, and kernel data of the adversary's user process. The KPRM handles the kernel page references for controlling the execution privilege and data access privilege on the restricted kernel page using unmapping management from the kernel address space. The adversary's user process cannot invoke the vulnerable kernel code and access the kernel data on restricted pages.

4.3 Kernel Page Types

KPRM provides two types of page structures, the restricted kernel page list, and benign user process list for the kernel.

- **Normal kernel page**: This is shared by every user process and kernel task. It contains the kernel code and kernel data.
- **Restricted kernel page**: This is assigned to an adversary's user process. KPRM unmaps restricted kernel page references during kernel execution.

To create a restricted kernel page list, KPRM can automatically calculate a valid page frame number from the virtual address of kernel code and kernel data. KPRM specifies restricted kernel pages when all the vulnerable kernel code and kernel data are identified at the kernel booting. Additionally, KPRM manages the restricted kernel page list that stores and deletes a restricted kernel page and the benign user process list that manually contains benign user process identifiers to avoid the restricted kernel page management at the running kernel.

4.4 Restricted Kernel Page Object

KPRM supports the following kernel code and kernel data for protection with a restricted kernel page.

- **Kernel code**: It is a component of the kernel features
- **Kernel data**: It is a variable of privilege information

Specifically, KPRM assumes that kernel code is already known, and that the kernel vulnerability and kernel data are credential variables of the running user process.

4.5 Timing of Restricted Kernel Page Management

The KPRM requires handling of the user process and kernel for accessible kernel pages. The timing of the KPRM in the kernel layer assumes that KPRM interrupts the user process behavior to handle a kernel page reference before the system call invocation. Moreover, the KPRM manages all the page table entries of the page table to check whether a kernel page matches with the restricted kernel page.

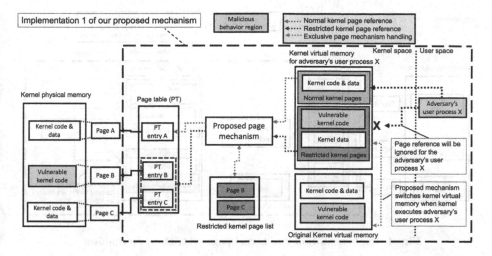

Fig. 3. Implementation 1 of kernel page restriction mechanism

4.6 Attack Situations

KPRM manages vulnerable kernel code to protect the kernel from memory corruption in the following attack situations.

- **Situation 1**: The vulnerable kernel code and attack target kernel code or kernel data are on a normal kernel page. The adversary's user process can execute the vulnerable kernel code that can override any kernel code or data on the normal kernel page.
- **Situation 2**: The vulnerable kernel code is on a restricted kernel page. The adversary's user process cannot access any restricted kernel page. If the adversary's user process attempts to execute the vulnerable kernel code, the kernel issues a page fault; KPRM does not allow execution of the vulnerable kernel code for the adversary's user process, which is killed after completion of the page fault handler.
- **Situation 3**: The vulnerable kernel code is on a normal kernel page and the attack target kernel code or kernel data is on a restricted kernel page. If the adversary's user process executes the vulnerable kernel code that tries to override the target kernel code or kernel data, the kernel issues a page fault; KPRM catches this page fault, and then kills the adversary's user process owing to access of the restricted kernel page.

4.7 Implementation

We implemented KPRM on a Linux kernel with x86_64 CPU architecture. Linux with KPRM manages the kernel page table that controls the visible kernel pages for an adversary's user process.

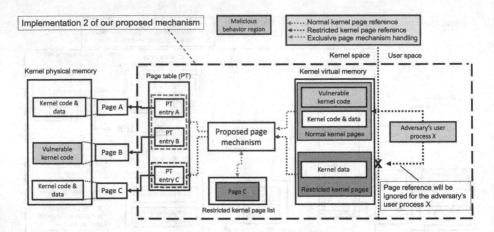

Fig. 4. Implementation 2 of kernel page restriction mechanism

Table 1. Implementations of KPRM (○: covered; ●: non-covered;).

Item	Implementation 1	Implementation 2
Kernel data protection	○	○
Kernel code restriction	○	●
Stability effect	Low	High
Performance effect	High	Low

Table 1 illustrates the KPRM implementations, comparing their different characteristics and effects. Figure 3 shows that KPRM implementation 1 can prevent invocation of vulnerable kernel code and protect kernel data with restricted kernel pages on the additional kernel address space of kernel page table for the adversary's user process. Figure 4 shows that KPRM implementation 2 can prevent kernel data memory corruption. It requires complex restricted kernel page handling on the shared kernel address space of one kernel page table.

Restricted Kernel Page Management. Linux with KPRM handles benign identification **benign** flag on the struct **task_struct** to user process. KPRM enables **benign** flag to refer application binary's absolute path within the benign user process list **benign_user_process_list**. This list is manually created in the kernel source code. Linux with KPRM also manages the restricted kernel page list **restricted_page_list** that stores the restricted kernel page information including the virtual address. A virtual address is related to the kernel code or kernel data.

Implementation 1. It adopts an additional kernel page table with the Linux kernel page table structure (Fig. 3). The KPRM kernel creates the kernel address

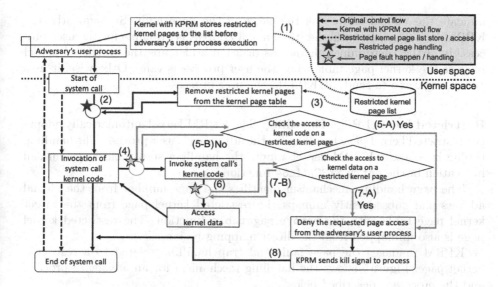

Fig. 5. KPRM for the adversary's user process

space of the page table for the kernel and it is restricted to system calls. The additional kernel page table is the variable kprm of mm_strct on the struct task_struct.

The additional kernel page table duplicates the initial value pgd of init_mm to kprm for the user process creation. During the running of the kernel, the KPRM kernel prepares the PCID of TLB and then writes kprm in current to the CR3 register for system call invocation. KPRM also applies the timing of restricted kernel page handling.

The Linux kernel executes a task under the kernel address space constructed from variable pgd of current when the kernel receives an asynchronous interruption. To overcome the issue of interruption, implementation 1 of KPRM kernel switches to the kernel address space from the additional kernel address space. This requires the writing of the CR3 register with the kernel page tables as the variable pgd of current with PCID of TLB.

Implementation 2. It adopts the directory management of the Linux kernel page table (Fig. 4). The KPRM kernel uses the variable pgd of current at the system call invocation for the timing of restricted kernel page handling.

The KPRM kernel directory modifies the original kernel page table, which leads to unstable behavior during interruption processing. For handling an interruption, implementation 2 of KPRM kernel affixes the restricted kernel page references to the original kernel page table.

Page Fault. Both the implementations of the KPRM kernels catch the page fault with the do_page_fault or the do_double_fault function. These functions indicate the virtual address of the cause of the page fault. Subsequently, the KPRM kernel inspects whether the virtual address is available for the user process. It further determines the access decision and maps the restricted kernel page to the kernel page table when the user process is valid. Otherwise, it uses force_sig_info to send SIGKILL to the user process.

Restricted Kernel Page Handling. The KPRM kernel automatically adopts the restricted kernel page handling for the adversary's user process. The handling timing is that the KPRM kernel adopts the handling steps before system call invocation in the entry_SYSCALL_64 function.

The page handling mechanism identifies the page number from the virtual address and subsequently unmaps the restricted kernel page from the target kernel page table with the remove_pagetable function. The restricted kernel page is also unmapped from the direct mapping region.

KPRM manages the page fault and trap handling related to a restricted kernel page. Figure 5 shows the handling mechanism for an adversary process, and the process is described below.

1. KPRM creates and stores restricted kernel pages to the restricted kernel page list and the benign user process list at kernel booting.
2. An adversary's user process starts the system call execution, following which the KPRM traps the system call routing and moves to KPRM processing.
3. KPRM determines adversary's user process identifies with benign flag is off, and then KPRM restores the restricted kernel pages from the restricted kernel page list and subsequently unmaps all of them in the kernel page table.
4. The system call is invoked along with access to the kernel code of the system call routine, following which the kernel issues the page fault and KPRM traps the page fault.
5. KPRM identifies the virtual address of the page fault that indicates the virtual address of kernel code is on the restricted kernel page.
   (a) In case of an invalid accesses of the restricted kernel page, KPRM denies access from the user process.
   (b) If the access is valid, KPRM maps the restricted kernel page of the kernel code to the kernel page table for the user process to continue.
6. The system call routine's kernel code accesses kernel data; then, the kernel also issues the page fault, and KPRM traps the page fault.
7. KPRM identifies the virtual address of the page fault that indicates the virtual address of kernel data is on the restricted kernel page.
   (a) In case of an invalid access of kernel data on the restricted kernel page, KPRM denies access from the user process.
   (b) If the access is valid, KPRM maps the restricted kernel page of kernel data to the kernel page table for the user process to continue.
8. If KPRM determines an adversary's process, access is not allowed on the restricted kernel page, and KPRM sends a signal to the user process.

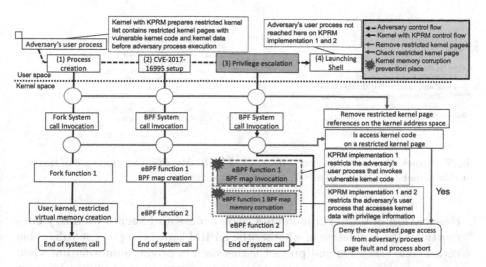

Fig. 6. Handling of restricted kernel page reference for the actual kernel vulnerability

4.8 Case Study

Vulnerable Kernel Code Invocation and Memory Corruption: As a case study of actual kernel memory corruption vulnerability, Fig. 6 shows that CVE-2017-16995 [10] PoC code invokes the vulnerable kernel code at the eBPF system call. The vulnerable kernel code is the `map_update_elem` function of `kernel/bpf/syscall.c`. The adversary's user process tries to modify the virtual address of the privilege information of kernel data on the kernel address space to execute the shell with administrator privileges.

To prevent such attacks, both implementations of the KPRM kernel specify privilege information to the restricted kernel page. The adversary's user process of the PoC code cannot modify the restricted kernel page. Additionally, implementation 1 of the KPRM kernel specifies the vulnerable kernel code as `map_update_elem` function to the restricted kernel page. Then, the adversary's user process cannot invoke the vulnerable kernel code. Next, a page fault of the restricted kernel pages occurs. Both the implementations of the KPRM kernel can catch this page fault to determine whether to send SIGKILL to the attack process in the page fault handler.

5   Evaluation

5.1   Purpose and Environment

The evaluation objectives are to identify security capabilities and overhead measurements for the user process and KPRM with the kernel. The evaluation topics are as follows:

```
// PoC code running, process id is 1642
1. www-data$ ./cve-2017-16995
2. [*] creating bpf map
3. Killed

// Kernel log message
4. [ 91.425545] target system call, pid : 1642
5. [ 91.425884] sysnum: 0000000000000141
// ffffffff81131e00 is the virtual address of map_update_elem
6. [ 91.426586] remove_exclusive_pages() : ffffffff81131e00
// 0x30 is page fault error code
7. [ 91.426925] error_handling() pid: 1642,
8. [ 91.426966] killing target pid: 1642
```

```
1. www-data$ ./cve-2017-16995
2. [*] creating bpf map
3. [*] sneaking evil bpf past the verifier
4. [*] creating socketpair()
5. [*] attaching bpf backdoor to socket
6. [*] skbuff => ffff88001d3c8b00
7. [*] Leaking sock struct from ffff88001d1b6f00
8. [*] Sock->sk_rcvtimeo at offset 472
9. [*] Cred structure at ffff88001c46df00
10.[*] UID from cred structure: -33686019,
    matches the current: -33686019
11.[*] hammering cred structure at ffff88001c46df00
12.[*] credentials patched, launching shell...
13.$ id
14.uid=4261281277 gid=4261281277 groups=4261281277, 33(www-data)
```

Fig. 7. Attack prevention case of vulnerable kernel code invocation

Fig. 8. Attack prevention case of kernel data access

1. **Prevention of vulnerable kernel code access and kernel memory corruption:** The evaluation of whether the KPRM kernel can prevent vulnerable kernel code execution and protect kernel data of privilege information when an adversary's user process tries to exploit an actual kernel vulnerability at system call invocation.
2. **Measurement of system call overhead:** To measure the implementation effect for kernel feasibility, a benchmark software was used to calculate the overhead of system call invocation latency.
3. **Measurement of application overhead:** The performance overhead for the application was measured using a web benchmark software and kernel compilation of Linux kernel on the KPRM kernel.

The KPRM was evaluated on the Linux kernel 4.4.114 with CVE-2017-16995 kernel vulnerability in terms of practical security capability and the Linux kernel 5.0.0 for performance measurement. The performance overhead is not different between Linux kernel 4.4.114 and 5.0.0. The evaluation environment for the system performance and a web server was executed on a physical machine equipped with an Intel (R) Core (TM) i7-7700HQ (2.80 GHz, x86_64) processor with 16 GB memory. The web client machine was equipped with an Intel (R) Core (TM) i5 4200U (1.6 GHz) processor with 8 GB of memory, running Windows 10. The Linux distribution used was Debian 9.0; the CVE-2017-16995 PoC code [10] was modified to handle any kernel address space. The KPRM implementation required 40 source files and 1,832 lines in the Linux kernels.

5.2 Prevention of Vulnerable Kernel Code Access and Kernel Memory Corruption

The prevention of vulnerable kernel code invocation and the protection of privilege kernel data on the KPRM kernel is achieved through the eBPF kernel attack with CVE-2017-16995 [10]. The PoC code invokes the `map_update_elem` function to execute the malicious code to try to modify the `cred` variable of the privilege kernel data of the running user process at the `sys_bpf` system call. The KPRM kernel prepares the restricted kernel page containing the vulnerable kernel code and targeted privilege kernel data.

Table 2. One time system call invocation overhead of KPRM kernel (μs)

System call	Vanilla kernel	Implementation 1	Implementation 2
open/close	0.532	1.187 (0.655)	1.119 (0.587)
read	0.276	0.896 (0.620)	0.838 (0.562)
write	0.238	0.856 (0.617)	0.796 (0.557)
stat	0.547	1.251 (0.703)	1.173 (0.626)
fstat	0.291	0.938 (0.647)	0.873 (0.582)

Figure 7 shows that the adversary's user process tries to invoke the map_update_elem function during the sys_bpf system call processing at line 5. The KPRM kernel proceeds with the restricted kernel page handling at line 6; thereafter, it can catch the page fault that contains the virtual address of the vulnerable kernel code. In this situation, the KPRM kernel determines the running process that requests invalid access to the restricted kernel page and then sends SIGKILL to stop the adversary's user process.

Figure 8 shows the prevention success case of memory corruption. The user www-data with user id 33 also executes the PoC code at line 1. The adversary's user process tries to modify the cred struct of the privilege kernel data to the root with user id 0 at lines 9 to 11. The KPRM kernel automatically restricts the access of the adversary's user process to the privilege kernel data on the restricted kernel page. Finally, the adversary's user process runs the shell program without administrator privilege at line 14.

From the results, the KPRM kernel can prohibit vulnerable kernel code invocation and protect the privilege kernel data to prevent memory corruption from an actual kernel vulnerability attack with the stable behavior for running the kernel and user process.

5.3   Measurement of System Call Overhead

For the measurement of the performance overhead, we compare the Linux kernel using the KPRM measurement with a vanilla kernel. The benchmark software LMbench was executed 10 times to determine the average system call overhead. The result was the overhead time of kernel with KPRM that incurs a page handling cost for each system call invocation.

Table 2 summarizes the lmbench result for each system call invocation. Implementation 1 and 2 had the highest overhead is for stat (0.703 μs and 0.626 μs), whereas the lowest overhead was for write (0.617 μs and 0.557 μs).

Table 3. ApacheBench overhead of KPRM kernel (μs).

File size (KB)	Vanilla kernel	Implementation 1	Implementation 2
1	599.143	623.667 (4.093%)	617.167 (3.008%)
10	764.250	784.250 (2.617%)	773.333 (1.188%)
100	2,443.714	2,509.167 (2.678%)	2502.667 (2.412%)

Table 4. Kernel building overhead of KPRM kernel (s)

Vanilla kernel	Implementation 1	Implementation 2
5926.644 (s)	6072.413 (2.459%)	6056.629 (2.193%)

5.4 Measurement of Application Overhead

We measured the web application process overhead and kernel compiling overhead for the vanilla kernel and KPRM kernel. The web application process used was an Apache 2.4.25 web server. The benchmark software was ApacheBench 2.4 for the web client. The network environment was 1 Gbps. The benchmark environment of ApacheBench was a download request average of 100,000 HTTP accesses to file sizes of 1 KB, 10 KB, and 100 KB in one connection.

Table 3 indicates that implementation 1 of the KPRM kernel has an average overhead of 2.617%–4.093% and the implementation 2 of the KPRM kernel has an average overhead of 1.188%–3.008% for each file download access.

The kernel compiling overhead measures the processing time of specific applications (i.e., compiler and linker). The compile target was Linux kernel 5.0.0 source code with Debian 9.0 kernel configuration (e.g., default .config file) that was compiled five times to determine the average kernel processing time.

Table 4 indicates that implementation 1 and 2 of the KPRM kernel had kernel compiling overhead of 2.459% and 2.193%, respectively.

6   Discussion

6.1   Kernel Resilience

During the evaluation, the KPRM kernel successfully prevented access to the restricted kernel page from the PoC of the eBPF kernel vulnerability attack. The KPRM kernel can protect the kernel data and disable invocation of the vulnerable kernel code by the malicious program. Therefore, the KPRM realizes kernel resilience such that the kernel address space isolates the vulnerable kernel code from the attack target kernel code or kernel data for the execution of the adversary's user process. It addresses actual kernel vulnerabilities to maintains kernel integrity before the occurrence of memory corruption by kernel subverting.

6.2   Performance Evaluation

From the performance cost, the benchmark measurement results indicate that the KPRM implementations require additional processing in the kernel layer. We consider that LMbench, ApacheBench, and kernel compile correctly calculate the cost of the overhead. KPRM implementations search restricted kernel pages of the kernel page table while page table walk and unmapping require additional processing time for the kernel mode. Moreover, the performance cost depends on the page table size, the number of restricted kernel pages, and the system call invocation count. We are continuing to inspect property of multiple points of KPRM for better performance.

In addition, the page table switching requires the CR3 register update and TLB flush cost. KPRM implementation 1 adopts the PCID of TLB for the overhead reducing, which only requires the CR3 update without TLB flush. We consider that the improvement of implementations removes restricted kernel pages from the kernel page table at a process creation to avoid the page table walk at the time of the system call invocation timing.

6.3   Limitation

We consider two limitations of KPRM. The first limitation is that the KPRM kernel delivers the already known kernel vulnerability prevention that requires a specific vulnerable kernel code to be registered as a restricted kernel page for the adversary's user processes. The second limitation is the benign user process list is statically managed in the kernel code. It requires the modification of the kernel for the updating of the benign user process list. The KPRM adopts the registering capability of vulnerable kernel code and the dynamically controlling of the benign user process that is in progress. These deliver to quick response for the kernel vulnerability disclosure.

For KPRM implementations, the implementation 1 requires the performance overhead by adopting an additional kernel address space with page table switching for restricted kernel page handling. Additionally, PCID covers 4,096 IDs for the performance improvement owing to hardware limitation. We apply the least recently used algorithms for the user process creation. The implementation 2 might cause misbehavior in terms of kernel stability with page access restriction when the kernel manages interruption. The benchmark software cannot cover all the kernel features. It is necessary to verify the kernel feasibility when the kernel code and kernel data are protected on the KPRM kernel.

6.4   Portability

Here, we consider the applicability of the KPRM to other OSs. The Linux implementation of KPRM ported to the kernel of another OS adopts the page table approach to manage virtual memory. Moreover, FreeBSD manages the page table entries and page table combination for handling the user and kernel virtual memory region [11].

7   Related Work

Memory Isolation at Hardware. The CPU features support a memory isolation mechanism. A trusted execution environment executes the kernel in the secure memory region to mitigate kernel attacks from a non-secure memory region [12–14]. IskiOS adopts a memory protection key that restricts a specific memory region related to the kernel virtual memory [15]. In addition, hardware virtualization is available for the separation of the kernel virtual memory [16].

Memory Isolation at Software. Memory isolation is also supported in the kernel layer. KPTI provides dedicated page tables for the user and kernel modes to mitigate meltdown side-channel attacks [17]. XPFO protects the kernel to manage the page attribution distinction between the user and the kernel modes through direct mapping region attacks [18]. Moreover, Proclocal allocates dedicated pages of the kernel data for each user process [4] and SCI creates an isolated page table to execute system calls during kernel processing [5].

Kernel Memory Protection. Kernel memory protection is another aspect of a kernel resilience approach that realizes mitigation of memory corruption. The randomization of the kernel page table position protects the entire page table structure from malicious activity in the kernel layer [19]. kRˆX provides the exclusive mechanism between access and execution of the kernel code and kernel data [20]. Moreover, KHide restricts the granularity of software diversity techniques for kernel code and kernel data with hardware virtualization [21]. xMP provides switching of the visible virtual memory region between the user and the kernel modes for the guest OS with the hypervisor [22].

Reducing Kernel Attack Surface. Reducing the kernel attack surface restricts the visible virtual memory region for user processes. PerspicuOS allows minimum privilege assignment for kernel isolation mechanism [23]. kRazor and KASR prepare a set of kernel code and kernel data for each user program execution [24,25]. Moreover, Multik profiles the necessary kernel code generated for a customized kernel image for each application [26].

7.1   Comparison with Related Work

We compare the security features of the KPRM kernel with those of four kernel memory protection mechanisms (Table 5) [4,5,20–23]. KPRM supports a majority of security features for the running kernel.

PerspicuOS [23] provides a privilege deduction design to ensure isolation between trusted and untrusted kernels. KHide [21] enforces the granularity of diversification for kernel code and kernel data at kernel deployment with hardware virtualization. Moreover, kRˆX [20] provides an exclusive privilege management method that directly protects the kernel code and kernel data. These approaches provide static customized kernel page tables, whereas KPRM dynamically manages the kernel page reference to isolate the vulnerable kernel code and attack target kernel code or kernel data for the adversary's user processes.

Table 5. Granularity of kernel memory protection comparison (✓: supported; △: partially supported).

Feature	PerspicuOS [23]	KHide [21]	kR^X [20]	xMP [22]	Proclocal [4]	SCI [5]	KPRM
Kernel data protection	△	△	✓	✓	✓		✓
Kernel code restriction	△	✓	✓			✓	✓
Page reference management		△			✓	△	✓
Access restriction for user process			✓	✓	△	✓	✓

Another approach, xMP [22] provides dynamic switching of the customized visible virtual memory region between the user mode and the kernel mode for the guest OS with hypervisor. KPRM provides more granularity for a region of kernel address space for the adversary's user processes as well as easy porting to other OSs in the kernel layer.

Proclocal [4] reserves the kernel page to allocate the dedicated kernel memory region at the kernel layer and SCI [5] prepares additional page tables to execute the kernel code during system call processing. The combination of Proclocal and SCI is similar to the supporting capabilities of KPRM. Proclocal can protect kernel features' variable of kernel data and despite SCI's memory isolation, full kernel page mapping is required. We believe that the design and architecture of KPRM provide more granularity for the control of the kernel address space. It is possible to focus on completely isolating kernel page mapping of vulnerable kernel code from attack target kernel code or kernel data at the starting point of the kernel attacking flow to the adversary's user process.

8   Conclusion

The OS kernel focuses on mitigating the effect of kernel memory corruption that leads to privilege escalation or defeats security features. The kernel adopts several countermeasures, including stack monitoring, CFI, KASLR, KPTI, Proclocal, and SCI, for attack surface reduction and prevention. However, vulnerable kernel code, and kernel code or kernel data still share the kernel address space.

The novel security design of KPRM presents the restriction of kernel code and kernel data for an adversary's user process. The KPRM assigns vulnerable kernel code and attack target kernel code to the restricted kernel pages, and then dynamically unmap restricted kernel pages from the kernel page table for the adversary's user process. This ensures that vulnerable kernel code and remaining kernel code or kernel data are isolated in the kernel address space to reduce the kernel attack surface. An evaluation of the latest Linux kernel showed that KPRM can prevent vulnerable kernel code invocation and protect privilege data from memory corruption. The maximum overhead was 0.703 μs in terms of each system call invocation; the overhead of the web client program was 1.188%–4.093 % for HTTP download sessions. Moreover, the implementations of KPRM indicate 2.459% and 2.193% as the kernel compiling time overhead.

Acknowledgment. This work was partially supported by Japan Society for the Promotion of Science (JSPS) KAKENHI Grant Number JP19H04109.

References

1. Abadi, M., Budiu, M., Erlingsson, U., Ligatti, J.: Control-flow integrity principles, implementations, and applications. In: Proceedings of the 12th ACM Conference on Computer and Communications Security, pp. 340–353. ACM (2005). https://doi.org/10.1145/1609956.1609960
2. Shacham, H., Page, M., Pfaff, B., Goh, E., Modadugu, N., Boneh, D.: On the effectiveness of address-space randomization. In: Proceedings of the 11th ACM Conference on Computer and Communications Security, pp. 298–307. ACM (2004). https://doi.org/10.1145/1030083.1030124
3. Intel: 8th and 9th Generation Intel®Core™Processor Families and Intel® Xeon®E Processor Families Datasheet. Volume 1 of 2. Revision 006 (2020). https://www.intel.com/content/dam/www/public/us/en/documents/datasheets/8th-gen-core-family-datasheet-vol-1.pdf. Accessed 8 Dec 2020
4. Hillenbrand, M.: Process-local memory allocations for hiding KVM secrets (2019). https://lwn.net/Articles/791069/. Accessed 8 Aug 2019
5. Rapoport, M.: x86: introduce system calls address space isolation (2019). https://lwn.net/Articles/786894/. Accessed 8 Aug 2019
6. Exploit Database, Nexus 5 Android 5.0 - Privilege Escalation. https://www.exploit-db.com/exploits/35711/. Accessed 21 May 2019
7. grsecurity: super fun 2.6.30+/RHEL5 2.6.18 local kernel exploit. https://grsecurity.net/~spender/exploits/exploit2.txt. Accessed 21 May 2019
8. Chen, H., Mao, Y., Wang, X., Zhow, D., Zeldovich, N., Kaashoek, F.M.: Linux kernel vulnerabilities - state-of-the-art defenses and open problems. In: Proceedings of the Second Asia-Pacific Workshop on Systems, pp. 1–5. ACM (2011). https://doi.org/10.1145/2103799.2103805
9. Linux Vulnerability Statistics. https://www.cvedetails.com/vendor/33/Linux.html. Accessed 8 Dec 2020
10. CVE-2017-16995. https://cve.mitre.org/cgi-bin/cvename.cgi?name=CVE-2017-16995. Accessed 10 June 2019
11. The FreeBSD documentation project.: FreeBSD architecture handbook (2006). https://www.freebsd.org/doc/en_US.ISO8859-1/books/arch-handbook/. Accessed 8 Aug 2019
12. Ge, X., Vijayakumar, H., Jaeger, T.: Sprobes: enforcing kernel code integrity on the trustzone architecture. In: Proceedings of the Third Workshop on Mobile Security Technologies. ACM (2014)
13. Lee, D., Kohlbrenner, D., Shinde, S., Asanović, K., Song, D.: Keystone: an open framework for architecting trusted execution environments. In: Proceedings of the Fifteenth European Conference on Computer Systems, pp. 1–16. ACM (2020). https://doi.org/10.1145/3342195.3387532
14. Marcela, S.M., Michael, J.F., Mic, B.: EnclaveDom: privilege separation for large-TCB applications in trusted execution environments. https://arxiv.org/abs/1907.13245. Accessed 8 Dec 2020

15. Gravani, S., Mohammad, H., Criswell, J., Scott, L.M.: IskiOS: lightweight defense against kernel-level code-reuse attacks. https://arxiv.org/abs/1903.04654. Accessed 8 Dec 2020
16. Hua, Z., Du, D., Xia, Y., Chen, H., Zang, B.: EPTI: efficient defence against meltdown attack for unpatched VMs. In: Proceedings of the 2018 USENIX Annual Technical Conference, pp. 255–266. USENIX (2018). https://dl.acm.org/doi/10.5555/3277355.3277380
17. Gruss, D., Lipp, M., Schwarz, M., Fellner, R., Maurice, C., Mangard, S.: KASLR is dead: long live KASLR. In: Bodden, E., Payer, M., Athanasopoulos, E. (eds.) ESSoS 2017. LNCS, vol. 10379, pp. 161–176. Springer, Cham (2017). https://doi.org/10.1007/978-3-319-62105-0_11
18. Kemerlis, P.V., Polychronakis, M., Kemerlis, D.A.: ret2dir: rethinking kernel isolation. In: Proceedings of the 23rd USENIX Conference on Security Symposium, pp. 957–972. USENIX (2014). https://dl.acm.org/doi/10.5555/2671225.2671286
19. Davi, L., Gens, D., Liebchen, C., Sadeghi, A.-R.: PT-Rand: practical mitigation of data-only attacks against page tables. In: Proceedings of the 23rd Network and Distributed System Security Symposium. Internet Society (2016)
20. Pomonis, M., Petsios, T.: kRˆX: comprehensive kernel protection against just-in-time code reuse. In: Proceedings of the Twelfth European Conference on Computer Systems, pp. 420–436. ACM (2017). https://doi.org/10.1145/3064176.3064216
21. Gionta, J., Enck, W., Larsen, P.: Preventing kernel code-reuse attacks through disclosure resistant code diversification. In: Proceedings of the 2016 IEEE Conference on Communications and Network Security, pp. 189–197. IEEE (2016). https://doi.org/10.1109/CNS.2016.7860485
22. Sergej, P., Marius, M., Seyedhamed, G., Vasileios, P.K., Michalis, P.: xMP: selective memory protection for kernel and user space. In: Proceedings of the 41st IEEE Symposium on Security and Privacy, pp. 563–577. IEEE (2020). https://doi.ieeecomputersociety.org/10.1109/SP40000.2020.00041
23. Dautenhahn, N., Kasampalis, T., Dietz, W., Criswell, J., Adve, V.: Nested kernel: an operating system architecture for intra-kernel privilege separation. In: Proceedings of the 20th International Conference on Architectural Support for Programming Languages and Operating Systems, pp. 191–206. ACM (2015). https://doi.org/10.1145/2694344.2694386
24. Kurmus, A., Dechand, S., Kapitza, R.: Quantifiable run-time kernel attack surface reduction. In: Dietrich, S. (ed.) DIMVA 2014. LNCS, vol. 8550, pp. 212–234. Springer, Cham (2014). https://doi.org/10.1007/978-3-319-08509-8_12
25. Zhang, Z., Cheng, Y., Nepal, S., Liu, D., Shen, Q., Rabhi, F.: KASR: a reliable and practical approach to attack surface reduction of commodity OS kernels. In: Bailey, M., Holz, T., Stamatogiannakis, M., Ioannidis, S. (eds.) RAID 2018. LNCS, vol. 11050, pp. 691–710. Springer, Cham (2018). https://doi.org/10.1007/978-3-030-00470-5_32
26. Kuo, H.C., et al.: MultiK: a framework for orchestrating multiple specialized kernels. https://arxiv.org/abs/1903.06889v1. Accessed 16 May 2019

(Short Paper) Evidence Collection and Preservation System with Virtual Machine Monitoring

Toru Nakamura[1,3]([⊠]) [iD], Hiroshi Ito[2], Shinsaku Kiyomoto[1],
and Toshihiro Yamauchi[2,3] [iD]

[1] KDDI Research, Inc., 2-1-15 Ohara, Fujimino-shi, Saitama 356-8502, Japan
{tr-nakamura,kiyomoto}@kddi-research.jp
[2] Graduate School of Natural Science and Technology, Okayama University,
3-1-1 Tsushima-naka, Kita-ku, Okayama 700-8530, Japan
ito-hiroshi@s.okayama-u.ac.jp, yamauchi@cs.okayama-u.ac.jp
[3] Advanced Telecommunications Research Institute International, 2-2-2 Hikaridai,
Seika-cho, Soraku-gun, Kyoto 619-0288, Japan

Abstract. In a system audit and verification, it is important to securely collect and preserve evidence of execution environments, execution processes, and program execution results. Evidence-based verification of program processes ensures their authenticity; for example, the processes include no altered/infected program library. This paper proposes a solution for collection of evidence on program libraries based on Virtual Machine Monitor (VMM). The solution can solve semantic gap by obtaining library file path names. This paper also shows a way to obtain hash values of library files from a guest OS. Furthermore, this paper provides examples of evidence on program execution and the overhead of the solution.

Keywords: Virtual Machine Introspection · Forensics · OS security

1 Introduction

1.1 Background

Audit and verification based on log files as digital evidence of program execution environments, execution processes, and execution results are important for trustworthiness. In particular, a secure collection and preservation mechanism for the evidence should be implemented on the system in order to ensure the validity of the evidence. There are two types of logs for verifying execution; logs of application programs (APs) such as a web server program and "system level" logs such as those of operating systems. Sufficient logs for verification might not be always collected due to the design of the APs. Thus, collection of system level logs of execution processes is required for amending evidence as well.

© Springer Nature Switzerland AG 2021
T. Nakanishi and R. Nojima (Eds.): IWSEC 2021, LNCS 12835, pp. 64–73, 2021.
https://doi.org/10.1007/978-3-030-85987-9_4

1.2 Attack Model

Our target is a system based on virtual machine (VM). The threat considered in this paper is defined as executing illegal processing while concealing the wrongdoing. Our assumed adversary is a user of a guest OS, who has neither an administrator account of the guest OS nor any account of the host OS, while we assume that an administrator of host OS is trusted. One example of an attack scenario is to run a program with malicious and different library files from those usually used by employing an illegal and malicious method. For example, it is possible for a user by modifying LD_PRELOAD. In this case, we subsequently need to obtain the path names of the library files and the hash values for proof that such attack has occurred. From existing studies, it is not clear if this is possible.

1.3 Related Work

Linux Audit [1] is a mechanism for collecting system level logs in the Linux system. In Linux Audit, a collection mechanism in kernel space collects information about events occurring on a system based on a preliminary set of rules, and an audit daemon process in the user space stores the information in log files [2,3]. Pfoh et al. [4] proposed a hardware-based system call tracing function for VMs. The function on the virtual hardware of the guest VM obtains information from the guest VM using Virtual Machine Monitor (VMM) and monitors system calls. Yan et al. [5] presented a method for recording events on the VM and reproducing in order to analyze malware behaviors. The method records the initial state and processes of state changes in an environment, reproducing them in another environment. The method includes both hardware virtualization support technology and software emulation technology. In addition, the initial state is recorded and changing states are processed by an instruction unit of the CPU and a program function unit. Hassan et al. [6] proposed a method of generating provenance graphs based on logs by APs and an operating system. The graphs are useful for analyzing malicious behaviors perpetrated by an attacker.

1.4 Our Contribution

The goal of our study is to realize a system, called an Evidence Collection and Preservation System (ECoPS), for collecting and preserving evidence without any restrictions of information on collecting evidence for program execution. In this paper, we focus on collection of evidence on program libraries as a first step of our study. From the viewpoint of security, it is more desirable to obtain the evidence from a VMM than from a guest OS. To obtain evidence from a VMM the issue of semantic gap needs to be solved. We show a solution to this issue by obtaining the library file path names. We also show how to obtain the hash values of library files from a guest OS. We evaluate the solution by performing an implementation, and provide examples of evidence on program execution for proof of concept. We also evaluate the overhead of system calls incurred by the solution.

2   Issues on Existing Evidence Collection Systems

Pfoh *et al.* [4] proposed a method whereby information on system call can be obtained via Virtual Machine Introspection (VMI) [7]. VMI is a monitoring mechanism for the guest OS that works by obtaining a memory statement on virtual hardware through VMM. In their scheme, the information related to the guest OS is not stored in the guest OS, but in the host OS, and no adversary can gain influence over VMM at all from the guest OS. Their scheme suffers from the semantic gap issue [8]; VMM does not interpret data on memory in the virtual hardware of the guest OS due to the lack of information on data structure in the guest OS. Pfoh *et al.* considered a solution only on standard inputs/outputs and command line arguments; it does not include the path name of executable files, or executed library files because it is not for auditing.

In this paper, we propose an effective method to fill semantic gaps not only on standard inputs/outputs and command line arguments, but also on path name of executed files, environment variables, and OS type and its version for collecting evidence for auditing. Furthermore, our method calculates hash values in guest OS, after that they are stored to host OS, in order to collect hash values of executable files, executed library files, and accessed files.

3   Evidence Collection and Preservation System (ECoPS)

3.1   Requirements

The requirements for ECoPS are shown as follows.

System requirement 1: *prevents alteration of evidence.*
System requirement 2: *prevents attacks from infiltrating monitoring functions.*
System requirement 3: *collects appropriate information related to program execution.*

For system requirements 1 and 2, we adopt a VMM based architecture for ECoPS. Regarding system requirement 3, we need to identify the type of program execution for extracting the list of information related to program execution for use as evidence. We show the assumed program process flow in Fig. 1. We assume that a program is executed in a shell. The user first inputs a path name and arguments of the execution file to a shell. A shell process creates a duplicate process of itself via a `fork` system call. A child process issues an `execve` system call, loads the specified program, and initializes the state of the process. Next, it runs the program process. In addition, program libraries are mapped to a virtual memory space before the process begin in the case of a dynamically linked program. In this paper, we regard program processes as processes with a file, standard input and output, and standard error output.

For the assumed program processes previously shown, an evidence collection system should obtain the following information.

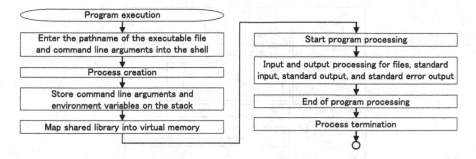

Fig. 1. Program process flow

- Information to identify the executable files
  1. Path name of an executable file
  2. Hash value of an executable file
- Information to identify the executed library files
  3. Path names of executed library files
  4. Hash values of executed library files
- Information to identify the user's inputs and outputs
  5. Contents of standard input, standard output and standard error output
- Information to identify used files
  6. Path names of used files
  7. Hash values of used files
- Information to identify the execution environment
  8. Command line arguments
  9. Environment variables
  10. OS type and its version

3.2 Design Criteria for ECoPS

An overview of ECoPS is shown in Fig. 2. In ECoPS, we assume that the monitored OS is a guest OS on the VM. We adopt a Kernel-based Virtual Machine (KVM) that supports full virtualization as the VMM because if using full virtualization VMM, the source codes of the guest OS do not need to be modified. Note that we assume that the VMM is secure and the administrator of the VMM does not perform any illegal actions.

In ECoPS, both the monitoring function in the guest OS and that in the KVM of the host OS obtain information by executing a hooking system call from a user process in the guest OS. The reason for using two different monitoring functions is due to the issue of semantic gap. It is comparatively easy to obtain OS information from the monitoring function in the guest OS. However, the monitoring function is not so tolerant. The processes involved in obtaining information from the KVM can also obtain OS information by referring virtual hardware such as the memory of the guest OS directly. The monitoring function

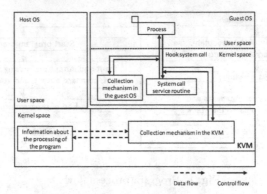

Fig. 2. Overview of ECoPS

in the KVM is tolerant to attacks against the OS because they are isolated from the guest OS. However, the data structure of the guest OS needs to be analyzed to solve the semantic gap. Therefore, to minimize the security risk, we decided that the only information for which it is difficult to solve the semantic gap should be obtained from guest OS.

The monitoring function in the guest OS is realized by implementing a kernel module. The monitoring function in the KVM obtains information by executing a hooking system call and tracing variables on the memory in the guest OS and members of structures. We use a system call hook method described in [9] for the hooking system call in the guest OS with the KVM. This method uses a hardware breakpoint. ECoPS can obtain information about the guest OS by setting a hardware breakpoint and executing a hooking system call. In the case of x86-64 architecture, we use hardware debug registers for setting the breakpoint. ECoPS can set the breakpoint to an instruction which is run just before the system call process by setting the address of the instruction into the hardware debug register. If the instruction, which exists in the breakpoint address, is executed, a debug exception occurs. Therefore, a system call in the guest OS can be hooked because the KVM can capture the occurrence of VMexit by the debug exception.

The following design criteria were considered in the design of ECoPS.

Criterion 1: Specific methods to obtain information on a system call with taking semantic gap into consideration
Criterion 2: Specific methods for securely transferring information obtained from the guest OS to the KVM
Criterion 3: Specific methods for securely storing the information in the KVM

In the later sections, we focus on only the Criterion 1 and regard the Criteria 2 and 3 as outside the scope. We provide the specific method for obtaining the information in the case of identifying executed libraries as an example in the next section. In particular, we present a method for obtaining the path name and the hash values of libraries.

4   Evidence Collection Mechanism

In this section, we describe the method for obtaining the information on executed library files. The following information are required for auditing;

(a) Library file path name
(b) Hash values of library files

In many Linux distributions, the mechanism of dynamic link is widely used because it contributes to reducing the amount of memory. In using dynamic links, linked libraries are mapped on a virtual memory space for program execution. Storing the path names of linked libraries is not sufficient to regard them as evidence of program execution because we cannot determine whether the linked libraries have replaced with illegal ones. Therefore, we need not only the path names of library files, but also the hash values of the files. openat and mmap are system calls for dynamically linked libraries. The openat system call opens a library file that is dynamically linked. The mmap system call maps the library file on a virtual memory space. We adopt the use of the openat system call for hooking because this system call is used earlier than mmap. It helps to reduce the possibility of statements on memory being altered by adversaries. We show methods for identifying the path names and the hash values of libraries. We assume that both the guest OS and host OS are Linux 4.15.18 and a KVM is used as the virtualization environment.

4.1   Library File Path Names

We use the dentry structure for obtaining the library file path names because although the arguments of the openat system call include the file path names, they may be a relative path or symbolic links by which it is difficult to identify the absolute path. The dentry structure is a data structure holding file names, directory names and the address of the parent dentry structure in virtual file systems. The relationships among structures related to file path names are shown in Fig. 3. To obtain a path name of the target library, we need to refer to the d_name in the dentry structure. Though the d_name stores a file name or directory name, we need to trace the parents' dentry structures recursively in order to obtain the absolute path of the target.

First, we explain the method used to identify a dentry structure of the target library. We assume that a CPU based on the x80-04 architecture is used. We obtain the contents of IA32 GS BASE register, which is an MSR (Model Specific Register) in the architecture. MSR is a group of registers for CPU control. The register stores the initial addresses of CPU variables, including the current_task variable. The current_task variable stores the initial address of the task_struct structure which stores the files variable. The files variable stores the initial address of the files_struct structure which stores the fdt variable. The fdt variable stores the initial address of the fdtable structure which stores the fd variable. The fd variable stores the initial address of

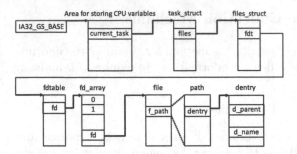

Fig. 3. Relations of structures from MSR to **dentry** structure

the **fd_array**. The **fd_array** stores the initial addresses of the **file** structures which stores the **f_path** variable. In **openat** system call, the file descriptor is received as the return value. The file descriptor is the index of the **fd_array** for the target library. Therefore, we identify the initial address of the **file** structure of the target library by the file descriptor. The **f_path** variable is the **path** structure, which stores the initial **dentry** address. We identify the **dentry** structure of the target from the address.

Next, the method used to obtain the absolute path of a target library will be explained. By the above method, we identify the **dentry** structure of the target library. The **dentry** structure stores the **d_name** variable and **d_parent** variable. The **d_parent** variable stores the address of the **dentry** structure of the parent directory. We repeatedly refer to the **dentry** structure of the parent and obtain the directory name until the root directory is reached. Finally, we construct the absolute path of the target library from the file name and directory names.

4.2   Hash Values of Library Files

In this paper, we show a way to obtain the hash values of libraries not in KVM, but in the guest OS. As mentioned in Sect. 3, it is desirable to obtain the hash values in KVM if this is possible. However, we need to append additional routines to analyze the file system of the guest OS to solve the semantic gap. We must implement different routines for each file system. This is not practical because it causes an increase in the cost for the modification as well as an increased risk of vulnerabilities. Therefore, we install a module into the guest OS to obtain the hash values of libraries.

The module is installed into a guest Linux kernel as a Linux Kernel Modules (LKM). It also hooks into **openat** system calls to obtain the hash value of a library file specified with the argument of **openat**. It uses Integrity Measurement Architecture (hereinafter called IMA) [10], which is one of the integrity verification frameworks that are adopted in the Linux kernel, to calculate the hash values of libraries. IMA has the **ima_calc_file_hash** function to calculate file hash values. We can also use Linux Kernel Crypto API [11] instead of IMA.

```
[ 1527.161376] i_ino = 136731
[ 1527.161377] full_path = /lib/x86_64 linux gnu/libc-2.27.so
```

Fig. 4. Logs of processes of getting a path-name of a file

4.3   Consideration of Ways to Collect Other Information

We discuss mechanisms to obtain other information as follows;

Standard inputs, standard outputs, and standard error outputs. These are obtained by hooking `write/read` system call and referring to the argument of the system call storing the address of the buffer storing the contents. In a similar way, we may also be able to obtain evidence on command line arguments and environment variables with `execve` system call.

Path names of files and OS types. These are obtained using the same approach described in Sect. 4.1, to trace `dentry` structures. For the hash values of executable files and executed files, these may be obtainable using the way described in Sect. 4.2, to calculate hash values.

Path names of executable files. Though not difficult to obtain from a guest OS, it is desirable to obtain these from KVM for reasons of security. A candidate of system call for obtaining path names of executable files is `execve` system call. However, the returned variable is different from `openat`; hence we cannot directly apply the concept proposed in this paper. This is still an open issue.

5   Evaluation

The evaluation environment consists of Intel(R) Core(TM) i5-6500 @ 3.20 GHz, 4 GB memory for the Guest OS, 32 GB memory for the Host OS, and Ubuntu 18.04 LTS (Linux 4.15.18, 64bit) for both the Guest OS and Host OS. In the implementations, we assigned one vCPU to a monitored guest OS. We show a part of the kernel logs in the host OS related to the process of obtaining the path name of a library in Fig. 4. We can find that an `inode` number of a target library and the corresponding path name of the target library. Figure 5 shows the kernel logs in the guest OS related to the processes of obtaining the hash value of a library. We used SHA-256 as the hash algorithm. We can find that an `inode` number of a target library, the corresponding path name, and the corresponding hash value of the target library. We used the Linux `sha256sum` command for validating the operation, and confirmed that the hash value obtained from our implementation matched the hash value with the Linux `sha256sum`.

We evaluated the overhead of system calls incurred by the collection mechanism for path names. We measured the number of clock cycles for repeating `openat` system calls and `getpid` system calls 100 times, and repeated this trial 10 times. Table 1 shows the result. From this result, the overhead for `openat` system call was 121,880 clock cycles per system call and that in another system

[1562.289421] filename = /lib/x86_64-linux-gnu/libc-2.27.so
[1562.305725] i_ino = 136731
[1527.161377] digest = f0ad9639b2530741046e06c96270b25da2339b6c15a7ae46de8fb021b3c4f529

Fig. 5. Logs of processes of getting a hash value of a file

Table 1. Result of evaluating `openat` and `getpid` system calls (clock)

	openat				getpid			
	Max.	Min.	Ave.	Med.	Max.	Min.	Ave.	Med.
Normal	310,976	3,688	9,756	9,313	3,632	1,312	2,348	2,504
Ours	13,409,152	66,596	131,636	67,438	9,445,120	34,324	69,583	34,528

call such as `getpid` was 67,235 clock cycles. The substance between these over-heads of 54,645 clock cycles is a result of obtaining the path names in the `openat` system call. If it is assumed that a 3.0 GHz processor is used, the overhead of system calls without `openat` is about 22.4 μs. The overhead of an applications is increased in proportion to the number of system calls which the application issues. Therefore, the influence on performance from the overhead caused by the collection mechanism is acceptable unless the application issues system calls too frequently. Note that the overhead is not included the calculations of hash values, hence it remains as future work.

Table 2 shows a comparison with our perspective of ECoPS and other existing techniques. Note that it is just our perspective as described in Sect. 4.3, we have not implemented and evaluated all collection functions. While existing techniques did not provide any way to collect the path names and hash values of executed libraries. In our perspective, ECoPS is capable of collecting all the information required for evidence of program executions as shown in Sect. 3.

Table 2. Comparison with our perspective of ECoPS and existing work

Collected evidence	ECoPS (this paper)	Linux Audit [1]	Pfoh *et al.* [4]
Path names of executable files	✓(Guest OS)	✓	
Hash values of executable files	✓ (Guest OS)		
Path names of executed libraries	✓		
Hash values of executed libraries	✓ (Guest OS)		
Standard I/O and error output	✓	✓	✓
Path names of used files	✓		
Hash values of used files	✓ (Guest OS)		
Command line arguments	✓	✓	✓
Environment variables	✓	✓	
OS Type and its version	✓		

6   Conclusion

In this paper, we showed a solution to solve the semantic gap in obtaining the library file path names as a first step of realizing ECoPS. We also showed a way to obtain hash values of library files from a guest OS. We evaluated the solution by performing an implementation, and provided examples of evidence on program execution for proof of concept. We also evaluated the overhead of system calls incurred by the solution and showed that the overhead can be acceptable. In future work, we will try to find a way of obtaining the path names of executable files in VMM. Though the Criteria 2 and 3 shown in Sect. 3 are regarded as outside the scope, we will discuss and attempt to realize a method capable of securely transferring evidence from the guest OS to KVM and a method to securely store evidence in KVM.

Acknowledgements. This work was partially supported by JSPS KAKENHI Grant Numbers 19H04109 and 19H05579.

References

1. Linux Audit. https://people.redhat.com/sgrubb/audit/. Accessed 02 Dec 2020
2. Latzo, T., Freiling, F.: Characterizing the limitations of forensic event reconstruction based on log files. In: Proceedings of 2019 18th IEEE International Conference on Trust, Security and Privacy in Computing and Communications/13th IEEE International Conference on Big Data Science and Engineering (TrustCom/BigDataSE), pp. 466–475 (2019)
3. Ma, S., Zhai, J., Kwon, Y., et al.: Kernel-supported cost-effective audit logging for causality tracking. In: Proceedings of 2018 USENIX Annual Technical Conference (USENIX ATC 2018), pp. 241–253 (2018)
4. Pfoh, J., Schneider, C., Eckert, C.: Nitro: hardware-based system call tracing for virtual machines. In: Proceedings of 6th International conference on Advances in Information and Computer Security, pp. 96–112 (2011)
5. Yan, L.K., Jayachandra, M., Zhang, M., Yin, H.: V2E: combining hardware virtualization and softwareemulation for transparent and extensible malware analysis. In: Proceedings of 8th ACM SIGPLAN/SIGOPS International Conference on Virtual Execution Environments (VEE 2012), pp. 227–237 (2012)
6. Hassan, W.U., Noureddine, M.A., Datta, P., Bates, A.: OmegaLog: high-fidelity attack investigation via transparent multi-layer log analysis. In: Proceedings of the Network and Distributed System Security Symposium (NDSS 2020), pp. 1–16 (2020)
7. Garfinkel, T., Rosenblum, M.: A virtual machine introspection based architecture for intrusion detection. In: Proceedings of Network and Distributed Systems Security Symposium (NDSS 2003) (2003)
8. Chen, P.M., Noble, B.D.: When virtual is better than real. In: Proceedings of 8th Workshop on Hot Topics in Operating Systems, pp. 133–138 (2001)
9. Fujii, S., Sato, M., Yamauchi, T., Taniguchi, H.: Evaluation and design of function for tracing diffusion of classified information for file operations with KVM. J. Supercomput. **72**(5), 1841–1861 (2016)
10. Linux Integrity Subsystem. http://linux-ima.sourceforge.net/. Accessed 04 Dec 2020
11. Linux Kernel Crypto API. https://www.kernel.org/doc/html/v4.15/crypto/index. html. Accessed 04 Dec 2020

Multiparty Computation

Evolving Homomorphic Secret Sharing for Hierarchical Access Structures

Kittiphop Phalakarn[1]([✉]), Vorapong Suppakitpaisarn[1],
Nuttapong Attrapadung[2], and Kanta Matsuura[1]

[1] The University of Tokyo, Tokyo, Japan
{kittipop,kanta}@iis.u-tokyo.ac.jp, vorapong@is.s.u-tokyo.ac.jp
[2] National Institute of Advanced Industrial Science and Technology, Tokyo, Japan
n.attrapadung@aist.go.jp

Abstract. Secret sharing is a cryptographic primitive that divides a secret into several shares, and allows only some combinations of shares to recover the secret. As it can also be used in secure multi-party computation protocol with outsourcing servers, several variations of secret sharing are devised for this purpose. Most of the existing protocols require the number of computing servers to be determined in advance. However, in some situations we may want the system to be "evolving". We may want to increase the number of servers and strengthen the security guarantee later in order to improve availability and security of the system. Although evolving secret sharing schemes are available, they do not support computing on shares. On the other hand, "homomorphic" secret sharing allows computing on shares with small communication, but they are not evolving. As the contribution of our work, we give the definition of "evolving homomorphic" secret sharing supporting both properties. We propose two schemes, one with hierarchical access structure supporting multiplication, and the other with partially hierarchical access structure supporting computation of low degree polynomials. Comparing to the work with similar functionality of Choudhuri et al. (IACR ePrint 2020), our schemes have smaller communication costs.

Keywords: Secure multi-party computation · Evolving secret sharing · Homomorphic secret sharing · Hierarchical secret sharing

1 Introduction

Secret sharing is a cryptographic primitive that divides a secret into several shares, and different shares will be given to different parties. The authorized sets of parties can recover the secret from their shares, while the unauthorized sets cannot. A collection of authorized sets is called as an access structure. In one type of the access structures, called as threshold structures, a set of parties is in the collection if the size of the set is larger than a particular number.

This basic primitive can be used as a building block to construct secure multi-party computation protocols [3,13]. We will consider the model of outsourcing

© Springer Nature Switzerland AG 2021
T. Nakanishi and R. Nojima (Eds.): IWSEC 2021, LNCS 12835, pp. 77–96, 2021.
https://doi.org/10.1007/978-3-030-85987-9_5

servers [10,15]. In this model, there are three roles, namely, several input clients (dealers), several computing servers, and one output client. We have several secrets from several input clients. Each input client divides its secret into shares, and distributes them to computing servers. The goal of the scheme is to let only the output client know some functions of the secret inputs. We want to use multiple servers to calculate a function of those secrets without having them know the secrets. To achieve the goal, the computing servers calculate some functions on the shares, may communicate to other servers, and send their results to the output client. The output client then reconstructs the final result using partial results from participating servers. We note again that the protocol may require several communications back and forth between computing servers.

To achieve a smaller communication cost, a variation of secret sharing called as "homomorphic" secret sharing is introduced by Boyle et al. in [6]. Functions can be calculated on shares homomorphically without any communication between computing servers. Homomorphic secret sharing has been widely studied recently with multiple constructions from different assumptions, such as decisional Diffie–Hellman assumption (DDH) [7] and learning with errors (LWE) [8]. Furthermore, evaluation of low-degree polynomials in homomorphic secret sharing setting was also considered in [22,24]. Homomorphic secret sharing is shown in [7] to imply a useful related primitive called server-aided secure multi-party computation [16,17].

In most of the existing multi-party computation protocols from secret sharing, including homomorphic secret sharing, number of outsourcing servers must be determined in advance, and the access structure has to be fixed. This prevents us from adding more servers in order to improve availability of the system, or changing the access structure in order to improve security. Some recent works [4,9,14] allow new servers to join during the protocol, but they use resharing which requires interactions and communications. In addition, these works only support threshold structures.

There are some cryptographic schemes that allow us to add more servers without resharing. We call such schemes as "evolving" schemes. Those include evolving secret sharing proposed by Komargodski et al. [20]. Some improvements in this research area were proposed in [1,2,21]. Although we can construct secure multi-party computation protocols for outsourcing servers from secret sharing, it is not trivial to construct an evolving version from the evolving secret sharing. The construction is stated as a future work in [20], and is still an open problem.

1.1 Our Contributions

To provide a solution for the open problem, we give the definition of "evolving homomorphic" secret sharing. For "evolving", the schemes allow us to increase the number of outsourcing servers without resharing, and for "homomorphic", the schemes support computing on shares without any communications between servers. Thus, our schemes provide protocols for evolving outsourcing servers with smaller communication cost than previous works.

Table 1. Our contributions compared to evolving secret sharing schemes

	Homomorphic	Correctness	Security	Access structure
Evolving secret sharing [1,2,20,21]	✗	Perfect	Perfect	(Dynamic) threshold or ramp
Our warm-up scheme	✓ Degree-d	Almost perfect	Perfect	Fixed threshold
Our scheme 1	✓ Multiplication	Almost perfect	Perfect	Dynamic threshold
Our scheme 2	✓ Degree-d	Perfect	Computational	Partially dynamic threshold

Our proposed evolving homomorphic secret sharing schemes focus on hierarchical access structures, where threshold values can be changed for different number of servers. These "hierarchical access structures" allow us to adjust the security level when new servers are added.

We construct our schemes from combinations of homomorphic secret sharing and cryptographic primitives, namely hash functions and pseudo-random functions. This work focuses on the schemes that support low degree polynomial computation. Our two proposed schemes support hierarchical structure and partially hierarchical structure. We relax some constraints in order to get simple schemes. The first scheme is perfectly secure, but almost perfectly correct. This scheme is quite simple, uses only one share per secret, and has flexible access structure. However, the supported function here is just multiplication. In the second scheme, the supported function is improved to degree-d polynomials, but the access structure is a little more restricted, and it requires a few more shares per secret. This scheme is perfectly correct, but computationally secure. Table 1 compares our work to the existing evolving secret sharing schemes.

There exists a concurrent and independent work by Choudhuri et al. [9], who consider a secret sharing scheme that involves dynamic sets of servers and can securely compute on shares. However, their scheme requires interactions among servers, and thus, is different from our evolving secret sharing setting, which does not require interaction among servers. We will compare their scheme with our work in Sect. 1.3.

1.2 Our Approach

As a warm-up, we introduce our idea here. If we allow the secret sharing scheme to be almost perfectly correct, the scheme can be simpler than the existing evolving secret sharing scheme. From the homomorphic property of the Shamir's secret sharing [25], we would like to extend it to evolving homomorphic secret sharing. Normally, each input client in the Shamir's scheme generates a polynomial over a specified prime field. However, the degree of the polynomial has to be fixed. This means the security threshold of the scheme cannot be change without resharing. In addition, the number of computing servers is limited due to the size of the underlying field.

Our idea is that, it is possible to use a collision-resistant hash function to map the ID of each server, which can be infinite, to an element in the finite prime field. Informally, the share of the original Shamir's scheme is the polynomial P of the ID of each server, $P(ID)$, while our idea uses $P(h(ID))$ where h is the hash function. Using this technique, the scheme can support infinite number of servers, with negligible collision probability from the hash function. The reconstructions and homomorphic property immediately follow from the Shamir's scheme. The overview of the warm-up scheme can be shown as in Fig. 1.

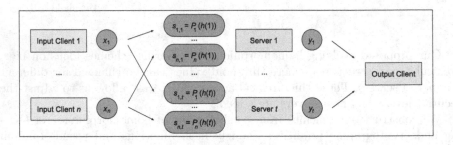

Fig. 1. The overview of our warm-up evolving homomorphic secret sharing scheme.

Shamir's scheme supports only one fixed threshold value k, i.e., any combinations with more than k servers can reconstruct the secrets. We may want to change the threshold when we add new servers to the system. To address this issue in the first proposed scheme, we elaborate the hash function idea into the hierarchical secret sharing of [26]. However, it is not straightforward to see which polynomials will be used in this case. Originally, the work of [26] used derivatives of polynomials. To realize evolving hierarchical access structure, which is equivalent to dynamic threshold structure in [21], our proposed scheme will use integrals. This scheme is correct with overwhelming probability. As shown in Table 2, share size of this scheme is $poly(\lambda)$ where λ is the security parameter.

To improve the scheme to be perfectly correct and support more general functions, we trade-off the share size, the security, and the generality of the access structure in the second proposed scheme. Based on the Shamir's scheme, instead of using only one fixed prime field, we try to expand the field during the sharing phase. We change the tool to pseudo-random function in order to maintain the consistency between several shares of different prime fields. Each computing server will get two or three values as its shares instead of one. In our second scheme, we can divide the protocol into two phases. In the setup phase, random values with size $O(\lambda)$ can be distributed in advance before secret inputs are determined. And in the online phase, when the secret inputs are ready, the t-th party that join the protocol will get a share with size $O(\log t)$. Share size of each phase is also shown in Table 2.

Table 2. Quantitative comparison of evolving secret sharing schemes

Scheme	|Unauth. Set|	|Auth. Set|	Share size
Komargodski et al. [20]	k	$k+1$	$O(k \log t)$
Komargodski et al. [21]	$f(t)$	$f(t)+1$	$O(t^4 \log t)$
Beimel and Othman [1]	αt	βt	$O(1)$
Beimel and Othman [2]	$\gamma t - t^\beta$	γt	$O(t^{4-\log^{-2}(1/\beta)} \log t)$
Our warm-up scheme	k	$k+1$	$O(\lambda)$
Our scheme 1	$f(t)$	$f(t)+1$	$poly(\lambda)$
Our scheme 2	See Sect. 5		$O(\lambda)$ for setup phase $O(\log t)$ for online phase

1.3 Related Works

We consider two types of secret sharing that involve dynamic sets of servers.

Schemes that only Support Storage and Retrieval of Secrets. Evolving secret sharing is a secret sharing scheme that supports infinite number of parties. The input clients will secretly share their inputs to the computing servers, and only authorized subsets of servers can reconstruct the secrets. The idea was firstly proposed by Komargodski et al. in [20]. Their scheme has one fixed threshold value k, i.e., subsets with more than k servers can reconstruct the secrets. The scheme is improved to dynamic threshold by Komargodski et al. in [21]. In this case, when the t-th party arrives, the threshold is changed to $f(t)$, which can be any non-decreasing function of t.

The next two schemes are based on ramp access structure. For some integers x and y, subsets with at most x parties will not be able to reconstruct the secret, and subsets with at least y parties will be able to reconstruct the secret. The key of the ramp schemes is that x and y do not have to be adjacent in order to reduce the share size, and there is no condition for subsets with size between x and y. In the work of Beimel and Othman [1], $x = \alpha t$ and $y = \beta t$ for some value $0 \le \alpha < \beta \le 1$. The same authors proposed closer bounds in [2], with $x = \gamma t$ and $y = \gamma t - t^\beta$ for some value $0 \le \gamma, \beta \le 1$. Table 2 shows the maximum size of unauthorized sets, the minimum size of authorized sets, and the share sizes.

None of the previous works claimed an application to multi-party computation. In these works, several generations of secret sharing are used, and some are additive secret sharing. If we build multi-party computation protocol from these schemes, the multiplication operation will require a lot of communication. Thus, we want to construct a better protocol which has no communication between computing servers at all.

For our proposed scheme, with security parameter λ, the access structure of the warm-up scheme is equivalent to [20], and that of the first scheme is equivalent to [21]. The access structure of the second scheme is less general, and details will be presented in the later section.

Schemes that also Support Computation on Shares. Apart from evolving secret sharing, there exist some other works that achieve a somewhat similar evolving functionality by using blockchain. These works allow a set of participating servers to change during the protocol. The work of Goyal et al. [14] used a technique called "dynamic proactive secret sharing", and the work of Benhamouda et al. [4] used a similar idea called "evolving-committee proactive secret sharing". Although the main objective of both works is to store and retrieve secrets on blockchain, an application to MPC is also suggested. A notable work that directly focuses on MPC in the setting where dynamic sets of servers securely computing functions on shares is a recent protocol called "Fluid MPC" by Choudhuri et al. [9], which can be considered as a "fluid" version of the classic BGW protocol [3].

In these three papers, a set of participating servers is changed during the protocol by resharing the secrets from one set of servers to the other set. This point increases the numbers of communication and interaction in the protocol, and is obviously different from our work. In addition, these works only support threshold access structures, and hence all computing servers have the same role. On the other hand, our schemes support hierarchical access structures [26], where some parties can be assigned with different roles and powers in accessing the shared secret, and thus can be more flexible.

1.4 Organization

In Sect. 2, we review the background on secret sharing and some cryptographic primitives. Combining these definitions, we propose the definition of the evolving homomorphic secret sharing in Sect. 3. The first evolving protocol with hierarchical access structure is proposed in Sect. 4. The second proposed scheme, which improve the first one with some trade-offs, is proposed in Sect. 5. We compare our schemes to the work with similar functionality [9] in Sect. 6. Finally, Sect. 7 concludes the papers.

2 Preliminaries

In this section, we review the definitions of secret sharing, homomorphic secret sharing, and evolving secret sharing. We then review two cryptographic primitives, including collision-resistant hash function and pseudo-random function.

2.1 Secret Sharing

Our setting includes n input clients, t computing servers, and one output client (see Fig. 1). For now, t will be fixed. In the next subsection, t can be "evolving" or increased during the protocol.

For the i-th input client, who has secret input x_i, a pack of t shares will be generated as $s_{i,1}, \ldots, s_{i,t}$, and the share $s_{i,j}$ is forwarded to the j-th computing server. To reconstruct the secret, the authorized subset of servers will send the given shares to the output client. The output client then reconstructs the desired value from these shares. We refer to the definitions on access structure and secret sharing from [20]. Let $\mathcal{P} = \{1, \ldots, t\} = [t]$ be the set of t computing servers.

Definition 1. *An access structure $\mathcal{A} \subseteq 2^{\mathcal{P}}$ contains all subsets of computing servers that can reconstruct the secret. The set $\mathcal{A}$ must be monotone, i.e., if $A \in \mathcal{A}$ and $A \subseteq A' \subseteq \mathcal{P}$, then $A' \in \mathcal{A}$. Subsets in $\mathcal{A}$ are called authorized, while subsets not in $\mathcal{A}$ are called unauthorized.*

Definition 2. *Secret sharing scheme for an access structure $\mathcal{A}$ consists of two probabilistic algorithms* Share *and* Recon. *The properties are:*

1. **Secret Sharing.** *As in the earlier description, the i-th input client uses* Share$(x_i) = (s_{i,1}, \ldots, s_{i,t})$ *to randomly generate shares of x_i. The share $s_{i,j}$ is given to the j-th computing server.*
2. **Correctness.** *For every authorized set $A \in \mathcal{A}$ and every secret x_i in the domain, we have $Pr[\mathsf{Recon}((s_{i,j})_{j \in A}) = x_i] = 1$.*
3. **Security.** *Consider the following game.*
   - *The adversary chooses two different secrets $x_i^{(0)}$ and $x_i^{(1)}$, and sends to the challenger.*
   - *The challenger randomly chooses $b \in \{0, 1\}$, and generates shares from* Share$(x_i^{(b)}) = (s_{i,1}^{(b)}, \ldots, s_{i,t}^{(b)})$.
   - *The adversary chooses an unauthorized subset $B \in 2^{\mathcal{P}} \setminus \mathcal{A}$, and sends to the challenger.*
   - *The adversary receives $(s_{i,j}^{(b)})_{j \in B}$, and outputs b'.*
   We say that the scheme is secure if $b' = b$ with probability $\frac{1}{2}$.

There exists several well-known secret sharing schemes. Here, we introduce the work of Shamir [25] and Tassa [26]. Shamir's secret sharing supports threshold access structures. The definition and the scheme are as follows.

Definition 3. *The access structure $\mathcal{A} = \{A \in 2^{\mathcal{P}} : |A| > k\}$ of $\mathcal{P} = [t]$ is called (k, t)-threshold access structure.*

Let the desired access structure be (k, t)-threshold. To share the secret input x_i using the Shamir's scheme, the i-th input client generates degree-k polynomial P_i over a prime field with size larger than t such that $P_i(0) = x_i$. Then, $s_{i,j} = P_i(j)$ is distributed to the j-th computing server. From Lagrange interpolation, secrets can be reconstructed by using a system of linear equations $s_{i,j} = P_i(j)$ where j is the server in the authorized set $A \in \mathcal{A}$.

Tassa's secret sharing supports hierarchical access structures. (In this paper, we only focus on disjunctive type.) The definition and the scheme are as follows.

Definition 4. *In disjunctive hierarchical access structure, the computing servers are divided into disjoint partitions $\mathcal{P}_1 \cup \ldots \cup \mathcal{P}_\ell = \mathcal{P} = [t]$. Let $k_1 \leq \ldots \leq k_\ell$ be threshold for each hierarchical level. The $(k_1, \ldots, k_\ell, \mathcal{P}_1, \ldots, \mathcal{P}_\ell)$-hierarchical access structure is defined as*

$$\mathcal{A} = \left\{ A \in 2^{\mathcal{P}} : \exists j \in [\ell], \left| A \cap \bigcup_{m=1}^{j} \mathcal{P}_m \right| > k_j \right\}.$$

In other words, the hierarchical access structure can be viewed as a disjunction of several threshold structures, namely, $(k_1, |\mathcal{P}_1|)$-threshold, $(k_2, |\mathcal{P}_1 \cup \mathcal{P}_2|)$-threshold, ..., and $(k_\ell, |\bigcup_{m=1}^{\ell} \mathcal{P}_m|)$-threshold.

Let $\mathcal{P} = [t]$, and the desired access structure be $(k_1, \ldots, k_\ell, \mathcal{P}_1, \ldots, \mathcal{P}_\ell)$-hierarchical. To share the secret input x_i, the i-th input client generates degree-k_ℓ polynomial P_i over a prime field with size $p > t$ such that the coefficient of the term with the highest degree is x_i. Then, $s_{i,j} = P_i(j)$ is distributed to the j-th computing server in $\mathcal{P}_\ell$. For the j-th computing server in $\mathcal{P}_m$ where $m < \ell$, the share $s_{i,j} = P_i^{(k_\ell - k_m)}(j)$ is given, where $P_i^{(k_\ell - k_m)}$ is the $(k_\ell - k_m)$-th derivative of P_i. Note that $P_i^{(k_\ell - k_m)}$ has degree k_m, and the coefficient of the term with the highest degree includes x_i. From Birkhoff interpolation, secrets can be reconstructed by using a system of linear equations $s_{i,j} = P_i^{(k_\ell - k_m)}(j)$ where $j \in \mathcal{P}_m$ is the server in the authorized set. Although the equations may not have a unique solution in some settings, it is unique with overwhelming probability, as stated in the following theorem.

Proposition 1. [18,26]. *For random allocation of participant identities, the above scheme from [26] realized the access structure in Definition 4 with probability at least $1 - \varepsilon'$ where*

$$\varepsilon' \leq \frac{\binom{t+1}{k_\ell+1} k_\ell (k_\ell - 1)}{2(p - k_\ell - 1)}.$$

2.2 Homomorphic Secret Sharing

We continue considering the same setting as in the previous subsection. In multi-party computation, we want to do more than reconstructing the secrets. The goal of multi-party computation is to let the output client learns the result of a function of secret inputs. Unauthorized subsets of servers must not learn the secret inputs or the results. Multi-party protocols can be constructed from garbled circuits [28], homomorphic encryption [11], secret sharing [13], etc.

In this paper, we focus on multi-party computation protocols that are based on homomorphic secret sharing. Each server can locally calculate some functions of the shares, but communication with other servers is not allowed. We refer to the definition of homomorphic secret sharing from [7] as follows.

Definition 5. *A degree-d homomorphic secret sharing is a secret sharing scheme with one additional algorithm Eval. The property for Eval is that, for* *every degree-d polynomial f of secret inputs, every secret inputs $x_1, \ldots, x_n$, and some authorized subset $A \in \mathcal{A}' \subseteq \mathcal{A}$, the j-th computing server which $j \in A$ can locally compute $y_j = \mathsf{Eval}(A, f, j, (s_{i,j})_{i \in [n]})$ such that $\mathsf{Recon}((y_j)_{j \in A}) = f(x_1, \ldots, x_n)$.*

In addition to the previous subsection, Shamir's scheme has the following homomorphic property.

Proposition 2. [3]. *Shamir's scheme with (k, t)-threshold is degree-d homomorphic when $\mathcal{A}' = \{A \in 2^{\mathcal{P}} : |A| > d \cdot k\}$. The value $f(x_1, \ldots, x_n)$ where f is a degree-d polynomial can be reconstructed from $f(s_{1,j}, \ldots, s_{n,j})$ for the j-th server in an authorized set with at least $d \cdot k + 1$ servers.*

It is also proved in [18] that Tassa's scheme is 2-multiplicative for some specified settings, i.e., value $f(x_i, x_{i'}) = x_i x_{i'}$ can be reconstructed from $s_{i,j} s_{i',j}$ for the j-th server in some authorized subsets. The scheme can also be strongly 2-multiplicative in some stronger settings, i.e., value $f(x_i, x_{i'}) = x_i x_{i'}$ can be reconstructed from $s_{i,j} s_{i',j}$ where j comes from "any" authorized subsets.

2.3 Evolving Secret Sharing

In contrast to the previous subsections, evolving secret sharing allows infinite number of participated servers. We then have $\mathcal{P} = \mathbb{Z}^+$. The following definitions for evolving access structure and evolving secret sharing are from [20].

Definition 6. *An evolving access structure $\mathcal{A} \subseteq 2^{\mathcal{P}}$ is defined in the same way as Definition 1, except that $\mathcal{P}$ is infinite and $\mathcal{A}$ can be infinite. $\mathcal{A}_t = \mathcal{A} \cap 2^{[t]}$ is a finite access structure of the first t servers.*

Definition 7. *Let $\mathcal{A} = \{\mathcal{A}_t\}_{t \in \mathcal{P}}$ be an evolving access structure. An evolving secret sharing scheme for $\mathcal{A}$ contains two algorithms Share and Recon such that*

1. **Secret Sharing.** *To share the secret input x_i, the share $s_{i,t}$ randomly generated from $\mathsf{Share}(x_i, s_{i,1}, \ldots, s_{i,t-1})$ is given to the t-th computing server when it arrives. This share cannot be modified later after it is given.*
2. **Correctness.** *For every secret input x_i and $t \in \mathcal{P}$, an authorized subset $A \in \mathcal{A}_t$ can reconstruct the secret. That is $Pr[\mathsf{Recon}((s_{i,j})_{j \in A}) = x_i] = 1$.*
3. **Security.** *Consider the following game.*
   - *The adversary chooses two different secrets $x_i^{(0)}$ and $x_i^{(1)}$, and sends to the challenger.*
   - *The challenger randomly chooses $b \in \{0, 1\}$, and generates $s_{i,j}^{(b)}$ from $x_i^{(b)}$ using Share algorithm.*
   - *The adversary chooses $t \in \mathcal{P}$ and an unauthorized subset $B \in 2^{[t]} \setminus \mathcal{A}_t$, and sends to the challenger.*
   - *The adversary receives $(s_{i,j}^{(b)})_{j \in B}$, and outputs b'.*
   We say that the scheme is secure if $b' = b$ with probability $\frac{1}{2}$.

2.4   Cryptographic Primitives

We refer to the definition of collision-resistant hash function from [5, Chapter 8].

Definition 8. *Let λ be the security parameter. A collision-resistant hash function $h : S_1 \to S_2$ is a function such that for all probabilistic polynomial time algorithm Λ, the following probability is negligible in λ.*

$$Pr[x_1, x_2 \leftarrow \Lambda(h); x_1 \neq x_2 : h(x_1) = h(x_2)]$$

In the real-world implementation, one normally uses the current standard hash function, namely, SHA-3 [23]. Heuristically, it can be said that outputs from SHA-3 look almost uniformly distributed [5, Chapter 8]. We will use this latter property to attain the random allocation, as required by Proposition 1 in our first construction.[1]

The other tool that we review is pseudo-random function [12].

Definition 9. *Let λ be the security parameter, and S_1, S_2, and S_3 be collections of sets indexed by λ. A pseudo-random function $g : S_1 \times S_2 \to S_3$ is a function such that for all probabilistic polynomial time algorithm Λ, the following probability is negligible in λ.*

$$| \, Pr[s \leftarrow S_1 : \Lambda(g(s, \cdot)) = 1] - Pr[a \text{ random map } g \text{ from } S_2 \text{ to } S_3 : \Lambda(g(\cdot)) = 1] \, |$$

3   Evolving Homomorphic Secret Sharing

In this section, we propose the definition of evolving homomorphic secret sharing. We combine Definition 5 and Definition 7 as follows. We also allow the scheme to be almost perfectly correct and computationally secure.

Definition 10. *An evolving degree-d homomorphic secret sharing is an evolving secret sharing scheme with three algorithms* Share, Recon, *and* Eval. *Security parameter λ can be used as necessary. Properties of the three algorithms include:*

1. **Secret Sharing.** *This is the same as in Definition 7.*
2. **Correctness.** $Pr[\mathsf{Recon}((s_{i,j})_{j \in A}) = x_i]$ *equals to 1 for perfect correctness, or equals to $1 - \varepsilon$ for almost perfect correctness where ε is negligible in λ.*
3. **Security.** *Consider the following game.*
   - *The adversary chooses two different secrets $x_i^{(0)}$ and $x_i^{(1)}$, and sends to the challenger.*
   - *The challenger randomly chooses $b \in \{0, 1\}$, and generates $s_{i,j}^{(b)}$ from $x_i^{(b)}$ using* Share *algorithm.*

---

[1] We could also go all the way by using the random oracle model. However, the random oracle model usually allows us to do more: a reduction algorithm can simulate an output of any queried input to the hash function. We do not use this property, and hence do not directly assume the random oracle.

- *The adversary chooses $t \in \mathcal{P}$ and an unauthorized subset $B \in 2^{[t]} \setminus \mathcal{A}_t$, and sends to the challenger.*
- *The adversary receives $(s_{i,j}^{(b)})_{j \in B}$, and outputs b'.*

We say that the scheme is perfectly secure if $b' = b$ with probability $\frac{1}{2}$, and is computationally secure if $b' = b$ with probability $\frac{1}{2} + \varepsilon$, where the advantage ε is negligible in λ.

4. **Homomorphism.** *For every degree-d polynomial f, every secret inputs $x_1, \ldots, x_n$, every $t \in \mathcal{P}$, and some authorized subset of servers $A \in \mathcal{A}'_t \subseteq \mathcal{A}_t$, the j-th computing server which $j \in A$ can locally compute $y_j = \mathsf{Eval}(A, f, j, (s_{i,j})_{i \in [n]})$ such that $\mathsf{Recon}((y_j)_{j \in A}) = f(x_1, \ldots, x_n)$.*

This definition will be applied for our first scheme in Sect. 4 and our second scheme in Sect. 5.

4   Our Scheme 1: From Hierarchical Secret Sharing

In the first proposed scheme, we combine the hierarchical secret sharing from [26] and [18] with a collision-resistant hash function. The purpose of hash function here is similar to the warm-up scheme in Sect. 1.2.

4.1   Access Structure

The evolving disjunctive hierarchical access structure is similar to the disjunctive hierarchical access structure in Definition 4. In addition, the computing servers may be infinite, and the partition of servers may also be infinite.

Definition 11. *In evolving disjunctive hierarchical access structure, the computing servers are divided into disjoint partitions $(\mathcal{P}_m)_{m \in \mathbb{Z}^+}$ such that $\bigcup_{m \in \mathbb{Z}^+} \mathcal{P}_m = \mathcal{P} = \mathbb{Z}^+$. Let $(k_m)_{m \in \mathbb{Z}^+}$ be threshold for each hierarchical level where $k_m \leq k_{m+1}$ for all $m \in \mathbb{Z}^+$. The evolving $((k_m)_{m \in \mathbb{Z}^+}, (\mathcal{P}_m)_{m \in \mathbb{Z}^+})$-hierarchical access structure is defined as*

$$\mathcal{A} = \left\{ A \in 2^{\mathcal{P}} : \exists j \in \mathcal{P}, \left| A \cap \bigcup_{m=1}^{j} \mathcal{P}_m \right| > k_j \right\}.$$

Note that the number of partitions and number of thresholds are unbounded. This evolving disjunctive hierarchical access structure is equivalent to the dynamic threshold structure in [21]. We have dynamic threshold $f(t) = k_m$ for $t \in \mathcal{P}_m$. Here, the computing servers in $\mathcal{P}_m$ must come before those in $\mathcal{P}_{m+1}$.

4.2   Construction

Secret Sharing. We propose the first scheme based on the idea of hierarchical secret sharing. In [26], the work realized the access structure by using the idea of derivatives. Our work will use the idea of integrals, since the number of servers can not be determined in advance. In this way, our scheme can support the evolving setting while preserving the properties of [18].

1. All input clients agree on a collision-resistant hash function h with uniformly distributed output. The domain and range of h are $\{0,1\}^*$ and $\mathbb{Z}_p\backslash\{0\}$ where p (will be specified later) is a prime number greater than 2^λ, and λ is the security parameter. We also assume that each t-th computing server has a unique random identity, ID_t, over $\{0,1\}^*$.[2]

2. To share the secret input x_i to the computing servers in $\mathcal{P}_1$, the i-th input client generates a degree-k_1 polynomial $P_{i,1}(\chi) = \sum_{j=0}^{k_1} a_j\chi^j$ over $\mathbb{Z}_p$ with random coefficients a_j, and the coefficient $a_{k_1} = x_i$. When the t-th computing server in $\mathcal{P}_1$ arrives, it gets its share as $s_{i,t} = P_{i,1}(h(ID_t))$. It can be seen that the hash function h is used in order to map from infinite set of IDs ($\{0,1\}^*$) to the finite prime field $\mathbb{Z}_p$.

3. For $m \geq 2$, when the first server in $\mathcal{P}_m$ arrives, the input client generates a degree-k_m polynomial

$$P_{i,m}(\chi) = P_{i,m-1}^{[k_m-k_{m-1}]}(\chi) + \sum_{j=0}^{k_m-k_{(m-1)}-1} a_j\chi^j$$

with random coefficients a_j, where the term $P_{i,m-1}^{[k_m-k_{m-1}]}(\chi)$ is defined as the $(k_m - k_{m-1})$-th integral of $P_{i,m-1}(\chi)$. For $t \in \mathcal{P}_m$, when the t-th computing server arrives, it gets its share as $s_{i,t} = P_{i,m}(h(ID_t))$.

Reconstruction. Assume that a subset $A \in \mathcal{A}_t$ for some t is going to reconstruct the secret. The linear system described in Sect. 2.1 can be constructed from the equations $s_{i,t} = P_{i,m}(h(ID_t))$ for all $t \in A$. According to Proposition 1, the secret can be reconstructed by using Birkhoff interpolation. Recall that the coefficient of the term with the highest degree of $P_{i,m}(\chi)$ is a_{k_m}. Then, the secret is $a_{k_m} \times (k_m!/k_1!)$.

Evaluation. From the multiplicative property shown in [18], to calculate the multiplication of two secret inputs x_i and $x_{i'}$, each j-th computing server can locally compute its partial result $y_j = s_{i,j}s_{i',j}$. Suppose that we share the secrets using polynomials $P_{i,m}(\chi)$ and $P_{i',m}(\chi)$, and the coefficients of the terms with the highest degree are a_{k_m} and a'_{k_m}. We will obtain $a_{k_m}a'_{k_m}$ from the reconstruction. To obtain the multiplication result, which is $(a_{k_m}k_m!/k_1!)(a'_{k_m}k_m!/k_1!)$, we multiply the value from the reconstruction with $(k_m!/k_1!)^2$.

Example 1. Assume that the thresholds are $k_1 = 1$, $k_2 = 2$, and $k_3 = 3$. (The setting for other levels are omitted.) To share a value 12, the i-th input client randomly chooses a polynomial $P_{i,1}(\chi) = 12\chi + 2$, and uses it to generate shares for servers in the first level.

To generate shares for other levels, we calculate the integration result of $P_{i,1}(\chi)$ as $6\chi^2 + 2\chi$. We add the result with a random constant to obtain $P_{i,2}(\chi)$. Suppose that the constant is 3. We then have $P_{i,2}(\chi) = 6\chi^2 + 2\chi + 3$. Similarly, we have $P_{i,3}(\chi) = 2\chi^3 + \chi^2 + 3\chi + 4$.

---

[2] A public bulletin board can be used for keeping the record and checking the uniqueness of all IDs.

In reconstruction process, after recovering $P_{i,3}(\chi)$ from Birkhoff interpolation, we know that the coefficient of the term with the highest degree (a_3) is 2. The secret is then $a_3 \times (k_3!/k_1!) = 12$.

Compare to [26], there exists a scheme using the same sequence of polynomials. To share a value 2, the input client randomly chooses $P_{i,3}(\chi) = 2\chi^3 + \chi^2 + 3\chi + 4$ for the third level. From derivatives, the polynomials for the second and the first levels are $P_{i,2}(\chi) = 6\chi^2 + 2\chi + 3$ and $P_{i,1}(\chi) = 12\chi + 2$. Thus, the correctness from [26] and [18] can be applied to ours.

4.3 Properties

In this subsection, we are interested in correctness, security, and share size of the scheme. We summarize the properties of the first scheme in the following theorem, and give a brief explanation.

Theorem 1. *If $k_m \leq poly(\lambda)$, there exists p with $poly(\lambda)$ bits such that the evolving homomorphic secret sharing scheme over $\mathbb{Z}_p$ proposed in Sect. 4.2 is almost perfectly correct and perfectly secure.*

Correctness. From the construction in Sect. 4.2, the sequence of polynomials $(P_{i,1}(\chi), P_{i,2}(\chi), \ldots, P_{i,m}(\chi))$ from integrals is the same as $(P_{i,m}(\chi), \ldots, P_{i,m}^{(k_m-k_2)}(\chi), P_{i,m}^{(k_m-k_1)}(\chi))$ from derivatives, but the order is reversed. Using the correctness of [26] and [18], the combinations according to the access structure $\mathcal{A}$ in Definition 11 can reconstruct the secret by using Birkhoff interpolation.

Although we have k_m+1 servers from the first m levels, we cannot reconstruct the polynomial only when 1) the solution of Birkhoff interpolation is not unique, or 2) some of the parties holds the same point in the polynomial.

Since ID_t is random and the output of h is uniformly distributed, Proposition 1 can be applied. The probability that the interpolation solution is not unique is no more than ε'. And because h is collision-resistant, $h(ID_t)$ and $h(ID_{t'})$ from two servers are equal with negligible probability ε''. The probability that there is at least one collision in $k_m + 1$ servers is at most $\binom{k_m+1}{2}\varepsilon''$. Therefore, the probability that we cannot have the polynomial is no more than $\varepsilon' + \binom{k_m+1}{2}\varepsilon''$.

There is p with $poly(\lambda)$ bits that makes ε' in Proposition 1 negligible. Also, if we assume that $k_m \leq poly(\lambda)$, the value of $\binom{k_m+1}{2}\varepsilon''$ will be also negligible.[3] Thus, the probability that we cannot have the polynomial is negligible.

From [18], if there exists $m \in \mathcal{P}$ such that $|\mathcal{P}_m| > 2k_m$, then the scheme is 2-multiplicative, i.e., all the servers together can calculate multiplication of two inputs. If $|\mathcal{P}_m| > 3k_m$ for some m, then the scheme is strongly 2-multiplicative, any authorized subsets can calculate multiplication of two inputs. (See Sect. 7

---

[3] It is important to note that the correctness of our protocol does not depend on the number of all parties, but the minimum number of parties involving in the reconstruction, denoted by k_m. Therefore, although k_m must be polynomial of the security parameter, our protocol can support infinite number of parties.

for more discussion.) The scheme that can calculate more general functions will be proposed in the next section.

Security. From Proposition 1, our scheme realizes evolving disjunctive hierarchical access structure, and is perfectly secure with overwhelming probability. We know from [26] and [18] that, even when the adversary knows exactly k_j pieces of different $P_{i,m}(h(ID_t))$ for any $m \leq j$, they cannot recover the secrets from those values. When the adversary can collect shares from at most k_j servers from $\bigcup_{m=1}^{j} \mathcal{P}_m$, they will know at most k_j pieces of different $P_{i,m}(h(ID_t))$. Therefore, they cannot recover the secrets from those values.

Share Size. From the description, the t-th computing server in $\mathcal{P}_m$ will get only one share $s_{i,t} = P_{i,m}(h(ID_t))$ for each secret input x_i, which is an element in $\mathbb{Z}_p$. In this scheme, we can trade-off the share size with correctness. If we increase λ, the share size will be larger, but the probability that the hashed values will be collided is reduced.

5   Our Scheme 2: Multi-generation of Shamir's Scheme

From the previous section, it can be seen that the first proposed scheme has negligible error probability from the hash function, so it is not perfectly correct. The computable function is also limited. We will address these issues in this section. Here, we combine the Shamir's secret sharing [25] with pseudo-random functions, and allow the computing servers to store more than one shares. A variant of this scheme is also proposed.

5.1   Access Structure

We describe the partially hierarchical structure as follows. This structure is similar to, but less general than the hierarchical one introduced in the previous section. Parameters for the access structure are $(k_m)_{m \in \mathbb{N}}$ where each k_m is a non-negative integer. The authorized sets that can reconstruct the secret are the combination of $k_m + 1$ servers from the first k_{m+2} servers, or (k_m, k_{m+2})-threshold, for any $m \in \mathbb{N}$. The authorized sets that can compute degree-d polynomials are the combination of $d \cdot k_m + 1$ servers from the first k_{m+2} servers, or $(d \cdot k_m, k_{m+2})$-threshold, for any $m \in \mathbb{N}$. We call the set of all servers $1 \leq j \leq k_1$ as the 1st generation, and the set of all servers $k_{m-1} < j \leq k_m$ as the m-th generation for $m \geq 2$. Note that the number of thresholds here is also unbounded.

5.2   Construction

Secret Sharing. In this scheme, we use pseudo-random functions with security parameter λ. The usage is different from hash functions in the previous section.

1. When the first server arrives, the i-th input client generates a degree-k_0 polynomial $P_{i,1}$ of prime field $p_1 > k_2$, where $P_{i,1}(0) = x_i$.

2. For $1 \leq t \leq k_2$, the share $s_{i,t}$, which includes $P_{i,1}(t)$ and a random bit string $r_{i,t}$ of size λ, is given to the t-th computing server in the 1st and 2nd generations when it arrives. Note that the random value $r_{i,t}$ can be distributed in the setup phase before the value of x_i is known.
3. For all $j \geq 2$, when the $(k_{j-1} + 1)$-th server (which is the first server of the j-th generation) arrives, the input clients agree on a pseudo-random function $g_j : \{0,1\}^\lambda \times \mathbb{Z}_{p_{j-1}} \to \mathbb{Z}_{p_j}$, where $p_j > k_{j+1}$ is a prime number. Then, generate a degree-k_{j-1} polynomial $P_{i,j}$ of prime field p_j, where $P_{i,j}(0) = x_i$ and $P_{i,j}(t) = g_j(r_{i,t}, P_{i,j-1}(t))$ for all $1 \leq t \leq k_{j-1}$.
4. For all $j \geq 2$ and $k_{j-1} + 1 \leq t \leq k_{j+1}$, the share $s_{i,t}$ which includes $P_{i,j}(t)$ and a random bit string $r_{i,t}$ of size λ is given to each server in the j-th and the $(j + 1)$-th generations when it arrives. Intuitively, the pseudo-random functions in this second scheme are used to maintain the consistency of the shares from different prime fields.

Table 3 summarizes the share values related to the i-th input client. In addition to $r_{i,t}$, each server will get only bold values in the corresponding row which is at most two elements per secret input. Other values that are not given can be generated from $r_{i,t}$, $P_{i,j}(t)$, and the pseudo-random functions.

Table 3. Values need for reconstruction in the second scheme.

	Polynomial	$P_{i,1}$	$P_{i,2}$	$P_{i,3}$	$P_{i,4}$	...
	Prime field	$p_1 > k_2$	$p_2 > k_3$	$p_3 > k_4$	$p_4 > k_5$	...
	Degree	k_0	k_1	k_2	k_3	...
	Threshold	(dk_0, k_2)	(dk_1, k_3)	(dk_2, k_4)	(dk_3, k_5)	...
Gen. 1: Server 1 to k_1		$P_{i,1}(t)$	$g_2(r_{i,t}, P_{i,1}(t))$	$g_3(r_{i,t}, P_{i,2}(t))$	$g_4(r_{i,t}, P_{i,3}(t))$	...
Gen. 2: Server $k_1 + 1$ to k_2		$P_{i,1}(t)$	$P_{i,2}(t)$	$g_3(r_{i,t}, P_{i,2}(t))$	$g_4(r_{i,t}, P_{i,3}(t))$	...
Gen. 3: Server $k_2 + 1$ to k_3			$P_{i,2}(t)$	$P_{i,3}(t)$	$g_4(r_{i,t}, P_{i,3}(t))$	...
Gen. 4: Server $k_3 + 1$ to k_4				$P_{i,3}(t)$	$P_{i,4}(t)$	...
... ...				...	...	

Reconstruction. According to Shamir's scheme [25], if the subset satisfies the access structure, Lagrange interpolation can be used to reconstruct the corresponding polynomial. The values in Table 3 will be used in the reconstruction process corresponding to the specified polynomial. For example, suppose $(k_0, k_1, k_2, k_3) = (1, 2, 5, 9)$. When we have information from server 1, 6, and 7, we can reconstruct $P_{i,2}$ using $P_{i,2}(1) = g_2(r_{i,1}, P_{i,1}(1))$, $P_{i,2}(6)$, and $P_{i,2}(7)$.

Evaluation. From the property of Shamir's scheme, to calculate a degree-d polynomial f of the secret inputs, each computing server can locally compute f on its given shares corresponding to the satisfied threshold level (see Table 3).

5.3 Properties

Similar to the previous section, the properties of the second scheme are summarized in the following theorem with a brief explanation.

Theorem 2. *The evolving homomorphic secret sharing scheme proposed in Sect. 5.2 is perfectly correct and computationally secure.*

Correctness. Each polynomial $P_{i,j}$ can be uniquely generated from pseudo-random value of the first $j - 1$ generations. According to Proposition 2, a set of computing servers satisfied the conditions in the defined access structure will be able to compute degree-d polynomials. The Eval algorithm can be performed by calculating the function f on the corresponding share of each secret input.

The correctness of scheme 2 should not be confusing with scheme 1. In scheme 1, the "input" of the polynomial may be collided from the use of hash function. Thus, the scheme is almost perfectly correct. However, in scheme 2, the "output" of the polynomial may be collided from the use of pseudo-random function, but this does not affect the perfect correctness of the scheme. That is because in the original Shamir's scheme, shares for different servers can have the same value.

Security. We prove the security of the scheme with a sequence of games. It starts from the first setting with values from pseudo-random functions, and ends with the final setting with totally random values.

Game 0. This game is based on the exact construction in Sect. 5.2. Assume that the adversary collects at most k_j shares for all level j, and $q \leq poly(\lambda)$ of them are shares from pseudo-random functions. The adversary tries to distinguish between shares of any two secrets.

Game 1. The setting is same as Game 0 except that one share from pseudo-random function is changed to random value.

We continue changing one pseudo-random share to random value for each game. In the final game, *Game q*, all shares are totally random values.

The security of the final game follows the security of the Shamir's scheme. The advantage of the adversary to distinguish the shares is $\varepsilon_q = 0$. Let us consider the following lemma.

Lemma 1. *Assume that there is an adversary with advantages ε_g and ε_{g+1} in Game g and Game $g + 1$, respectively. Then, we can construct an adversary against pseudo-random function with advantage $Adv_{PRF} = \frac{1}{2}(\varepsilon_g - \varepsilon_{g+1})$.*

Proof. We define Game g based on the secret sharing setting with the usage of $q - g$ pseudo-random functions. The difference between Game g and Game $g + 1$ is only at the g-th part of the share; the former comes from pseudo-random function while the latter comes from random function. The other parts of the shares are exactly the same. Assume that we have an adversary Ψ such that the advantage to distinguish shares in Game g and Game $g + 1$ are ε_g and ε_{g+1}, respectively. We will construct an adversary Φ against the security of pseudo-random function as follows.

The challenger flips coin $a \in \{0, 1\}$ which represents pseudo-random and random function, respectively. Adversary Φ wins if it can make a guess a' equals to a. Adversary Φ firstly let the adversary Ψ generate two secrets x_0 and x_1. Next, Φ flips coin $b \in \{0, 1\}$, and generates shares of x_b according to the scheme in Sect. 5.2, using one query to the challenger and its own $q - g - 1$ pseudo-random functions. Φ then forwards the shares to Ψ. After receiving b' in return from Ψ, if $b' = b$, Φ guesses $a' = 0$, and guesses $a' = 1$ otherwise.

If the challenger has $a = 0$, the setting is Game g, which Ψ has advantage of ε_g. On the other hand, if the challenger has $a = 1$, the setting is Game $g + 1$, which Ψ has advantage of ε_{g+1}. Hence by the definition, we have

$$Pr[b' = b \mid a = 0] - \frac{1}{2} = \varepsilon_g$$

$$Pr[b' = b \mid a = 1] - \frac{1}{2} = \varepsilon_{g+1}.$$

Let the advantage to break pseudo-random function is Adv_{PRF}. In the other words, $Pr[a' = a] - \frac{1}{2} = Adv_{PRF}$. And from the explanation above, $Pr[a' = 0] = Pr[b' = b]$ and $Pr[a' = 1] = 1 - Pr[b' = b]$. We will show that $\varepsilon_g - \varepsilon_{g+1} = 2Adv_{PRF}$. Consider the probability that $a' = a$ as follows.

$$\begin{aligned}
Pr[a' = a] &= Pr[a' = 0 \mid a = 0]Pr[a = 0] \\
&\quad + Pr[a' = 1 \mid a = 1]Pr[a = 1] \\
&= (\frac{1}{2} + \varepsilon_g)(\frac{1}{2}) + (\frac{1}{2} - \varepsilon_{g+1})(\frac{1}{2}) \\
&= \frac{1}{2} + \frac{1}{2}\varepsilon_g - \frac{1}{2}\varepsilon_{g+1}
\end{aligned}$$

Substitute this probability to the advantage of pseudo-random function, we have $Adv_{PRF} = \frac{1}{2}(\varepsilon_g - \varepsilon_{g+1})$. □

Put everything together, the advantage to break our scheme is $\varepsilon_0 = \varepsilon_0 - \varepsilon_q = (\varepsilon_0 - \varepsilon_1) + \cdots + (\varepsilon_{q-1} - \varepsilon_q) = 2q Adv_{PRF}$ which is negligible if Adv_{PRF} is negligible.

Share Size. Since the random values $r_{i,t}$ are not related to the secrets, these values can be distributed in the setup phase. The communication complexity here is $O(\lambda)$ for each pair of input client and server. After the secret inputs are determined in the online phase, the t-th computing server will get at most two shares per secret input. The share size depends on the value k_j in the access structure. One possible way is to choose $k_j \approx d^{(j+1)/2}$. If $t \approx d^j$, it will receive two field elements, where the size of the field is at most d^{j+1}. The share size is then approximately $2(j + 1) \log d$. Thus, the share size of the t-th server in the online phase is approximately $O(\log t)$.

5.4   Variant of the Scheme

The scheme in this section can be generalized so that each server receives at most α shares, where α is a positive integer. In this case, the combinations of computing servers that can compute degree-d polynomials are $(d \cdot k_m, k_{m+\alpha})$-threshold, for any $m \in \mathbb{N}$. Compare to Table 3, the parts with pseudo-random functions are the same, but more cells of bold shares will be added. It can be seen that these combinations are more generalized than the scheme in Sect. 5.2 when α is increased. This is a trade-off between the generality of the access structure and the share size.

6   Comparison to a Recent Scheme

In this section, we briefly compare communication costs of our schemes to Fluid MPC [9]. Note that the cost of our works is a result from Definition 10, and does not depend on the construction.

Assume that there are n input clients. For computing servers, at first we use m_1 servers. Later, we increase the number of servers to m_2, and then $m_3, \ldots, m_\ell$. In [9], there are nm_1 messages sent from n input clients to the first set of m_1 computing servers. Since resharing between servers is required, $m_i m_{i+1}$ messages are sent from the i-th set of servers to the $(i+1)$-th set. Thus, the total number of messages sent is $nm_1 + m_1 m_2 + \cdots + m_{\ell-1} m_\ell$. In contrast, our schemes do not use resharing, shares are only sent from the input clients to newly added servers. With some restrictions on computing functions, our schemes only require $nm_1 + n(m_2 - m_1) + \cdots + n(m_\ell - m_{\ell-1}) = nm_\ell$ communications. Furthermore, servers which already received shares do not have to be online when new servers are added.

7   Concluding Remarks

In this paper, we propose two evolving homomorphic secret sharing schemes. By relaxing the conditions to be almost perfectly correct or computationally secure, our schemes are simpler than the existing ones. Users can choose the appropriate schemes and trade-off between several parameters. We suggest some interesting issues that are left for future studies.

For the first scheme, the number of shares for each computing server is small, but the share size may be large, since the prime p has to be large. If we can increase the size of the prime field later during the protocol (similar to the second scheme), then the share size can be reduced. In order to do this, we may integrate the polynomial to a different prime field, and then solve multi-variable Chinese remainder theorem, which is studied in [19], instead of simple linear system. However, the multi-variable CRT is not thoroughly understood.

As the other issue, the paper [18] mentioned the access structure of type Q_d (union of any d sets in the access structure cannot cover all parties), but not the multiplicativity of d secret inputs when $d > 2$. This issue should be further investigated. The other work [27] can perform unlimited number of multiplications by using precomputed multiplicative triples. This requires some interactions between computing servers.

For the second scheme, the appropriate value of threshold k_m for all $m \in \mathbb{N}$ should be suggested, but these values may depend on the applications. We may try to extend the idea of this construction to more general class of access structures.

Acknowledgments. Nuttapong Attrapadung was partly supported by JST CREST Grant Number JPMJCR19F6, and by JSPS KAKENHI Kiban-A Grant Number 19H01109. Kanta Matsuura was partially supported by JSPS KAKENHI Grant Number 17KT0081.

References

1. Beimel, A., Othman, H.: Evolving ramp secret-sharing schemes. In: Catalano, D., De Prisco, R. (eds.) SCN 2018. LNCS, vol. 11035, pp. 313–332. Springer, Cham (2018). https://doi.org/10.1007/978-3-319-98113-0_17
2. Beimel, A., Othman, H.: Evolving ramp secret sharing with a small gap. In: Annual International Conference on the Theory and Applications of Cryptographic Techniques, pp. 529–555 (2020)
3. Ben-Or, M., Goldwasser, S., Wigderson, A.: Completeness theorems for noncryptographic fault-tolerant distributed computation. In: Proceedings of the Twentieth Annual ACM Symposium on Theory of Computing, pp. 1–10 (1988)
4. Benhamouda, F., et al.: Can a public blockchain keep a secret? In: Pass, R., Pietrzak, K. (eds.) TCC 2020. LNCS, vol. 12550, pp. 260–290. Springer, Cham (2020). https://doi.org/10.1007/978-3-030-64375-1_10
5. Boneh, D., Shoup, V.: A graduate course in applied cryptography (2020). https://toc.cryptobook.us/book.pdf
6. Boyle, E., Gilboa, N., Ishai, Y.: Breaking the circuit size barrier for secure computation under DDH. In: Robshaw, M., Katz, J. (eds.) CRYPTO 2016. LNCS, vol. 9814, pp. 509–539. Springer, Heidelberg (2016). https://doi.org/10.1007/978-3-662-53018-4_19
7. Boyle, E., Gilboa, N., Ishai, Y., Lin, H., Tessaro, S.: Foundations of homomorphic secret sharing. In: 9th Innovations in Theoretical Computer Science Conference (2018)
8. Boyle, E., Kohl, L., Scholl, P.: Homomorphic secret sharing from lattices without FHE. In: Ishai, Y., Rijmen, V. (eds.) EUROCRYPT 2019. LNCS, vol. 11477, pp. 3–33. Springer, Cham (2019). https://doi.org/10.1007/978-3-030-17656-3_1
9. Choudhuri, A.R., Goel, A., Green, M., Jain, A., Kaptchuk, G.: Fluid MPC: Secure multiparty computation with dynamic participants. IACR Cryptology ePrint Archive 2020/754 (2020)
10. Feige, U., Killian, J., Naor, M.: A minimal model for secure computation. In: Proceedings of the Twenty-Sixth Annual ACM Symposium on Theory of Computing, pp. 554–563 (1994)
11. Gentry, C.: Fully homomorphic encryption using ideal lattices. In: Proceedings of the Forty-First Annual ACM Symposium on Theory of Computing, pp. 169–178 (2009)
12. Goldreich, O., Goldwasser, S., Micali, S.: How to construct random functions. J. ACM (JACM) 33(4), 792–807 (1986)
13. Goldreich, O., Micali, S., Wigderson, A.: How to play any mental game, or a completeness theorem for protocols with honest majority. In: Proceedings of the Nineteenth Annual ACM Symposium on Theory of Computing, pp. 218–229 (1987)
14. Goyal, V., Kothapalli, A., Masserova, E., Parno, B., Song, Y.: Storing and retrieving secrets on a blockchain. IACR Cryptology ePrint Archive 2020/504 (2020)
15. Halevi, S., Lindell, Y., Pinkas, B.: Secure computation on the web: computing without simultaneous interaction. In: Rogaway, P. (ed.) CRYPTO 2011. LNCS, vol. 6841, pp. 132–150. Springer, Heidelberg (2011). https://doi.org/10.1007/978-3-642-22792-9_8
16. Kamara, S., Mohassel, P., Raykova, M.: Outsourcing multi-party computation. IACR Cryptology ePrint Archive (2011)
17. Kamara, S., Mohassel, P., Riva, B.: Salus: a system for server-aided secure function evaluation. In: Proceedings of the 2012 ACM Conference on Computer and Communications Security, pp. 797–808 (2012)

18. Käsper, E., Nikov, V., Nikova, S.: Strongly multiplicative hierarchical threshold secret sharing. In: Desmedt, Y. (ed.) ICITS 2007. LNCS, vol. 4883, pp. 148–168. Springer, Heidelberg (2009). https://doi.org/10.1007/978-3-642-10230-1_13

19. Knill, O.: A multivariable chinese remainder theorem. arXiv preprint arXiv:1206.5114 (2012)

20. Komargodski, I., Naor, M., Yogev, E.: How to share a secret, infinitely. In: Hirt, M., Smith, A. (eds.) TCC 2016. LNCS, vol. 9986, pp. 485–514. Springer, Heidelberg (2016). https://doi.org/10.1007/978-3-662-53644-5_19

21. Komargodski, I., Paskin-Cherniavsky, A.: Evolving secret sharing: dynamic thresholds and robustness. In: Kalai, Y., Reyzin, L. (eds.) TCC 2017. LNCS, vol. 10678, pp. 379–393. Springer, Cham (2017). https://doi.org/10.1007/978-3-319-70503-3_12

22. Lai, R.W.F., Malavolta, G., Schröder, D.: Homomorphic secret sharing for low degree polynomials. In: Peyrin, T., Galbraith, S. (eds.) ASIACRYPT 2018. LNCS, vol. 11274, pp. 279–309. Springer, Cham (2018). https://doi.org/10.1007/978-3-030-03332-3_11

23. NIST: SHA-3 standard: Permutation-based hash and extendable-output functions. Federal Information Processing Standards Publication 202 (2015)

24. Phalakarn, K., Suppakitpaisarn, V., Attrapadung, N., Matsuura, K.: Constructive t-secure homomorphic secret sharing for low degree polynomials. In: Bhargavan, K., Oswald, E., Prabhakaran, M. (eds.) INDOCRYPT 2020. LNCS, vol. 12578, pp. 763–785. Springer, Cham (2020). https://doi.org/10.1007/978-3-030-65277-7_34

25. Shamir, A.: How to share a secret. Commun. ACM **22**(11), 612–613 (1979)

26. Tassa, T.: Hierarchical threshold secret sharing. In: Naor, M. (ed.) TCC 2004. LNCS, vol. 2951, pp. 473–490. Springer, Heidelberg (2004). https://doi.org/10.1007/978-3-540-24638-1_26

27. Traverso, G., Demirel, D., Buchmann, J.: Performing computations on hierarchically shared secrets. In: Joux, A., Nitaj, A., Rachidi, T. (eds.) AFRICACRYPT 2018. LNCS, vol. 10831, pp. 141–161. Springer, Cham (2018). https://doi.org/10.1007/978-3-319-89339-6_9

28. Yao, A.C.: Protocols for secure computations. In: 23rd Annual Symposium on Foundations of Computer Science, pp. 160–164 (1982)

Machine Learning and Security

Understanding Update
of Machine-Learning-Based Malware
Detection by Clustering Changes
in Feature Attributions

Yun Fan[1], Toshiki Shibahara[2], Yuichi Ohsita[1(✉)], Daiki Chiba[2],
Mitsuaki Akiyama[2], and Masayuki Murata[1]

[1] Osaka University, Osaka, Japan
{h-un,y-ohsita,murata}@ist.osaka-u.ac.jp
[2] NTT, Tokyo, Japan
toshiki.shibahara.de@hco.ntt.co.jp, {daiki.chiba,akiyama}@ieee.org

Abstract. Machine learning (ML) models are often adopted in malware
detection systems. To ensure the detection performance in such ML-based
systems, updating ML models with new data is crucial for minimizing the
influence of data variation over time. After an update, validating the new
model is commonly done using the detection accuracy as a metric. However, the accuracy does not include detailed information, such as changes
in the features used for prediction. Such information is beneficial for avoiding unexpected updates, such as overfitting or noneffective updates. We,
therefore, propose a method for understanding ML model updates in malware detection systems by using a feature attribution method called Shapley additive explanations (SHAP), which interprets the output of an ML
model by assigning an importance value called a SHAP value to each feature. In our method, we identify patterns of feature attribution changes
that cause a change in the prediction. In this method, we first obtain the
feature attributions for each sample, which change before and after the
update. Then, we obtain the patterns of the changes in the feature attributions that are common for multiple samples by clustering the changes
in the feature attributions. In this study, we conduct experiments using an
open dataset of Android malware and demonstrate that our method can
identify the causes of performance changes, such as overfitting or noneffective updates.

Keywords: Malware detection · Machine learning · Feature
attribution

1 Introduction

Machine learning (ML) has been used to detect malware. Such ML-based malware detection systems adopt ML models trained on previously collected data
to perform predictions on new data. Owing to a phenomenon called concept
drift [22], the detection performance in an ML-based system gradually degrades

© Springer Nature Switzerland AG 2021
T. Nakanishi and R. Nojima (Eds.): IWSEC 2021, LNCS 12835, pp. 99–118, 2021.
https://doi.org/10.1007/978-3-030-85987-9_6

as the statistical characteristics of data change over time [10]. In this situation, updating the ML model using new data can effectively improve the detection performance of the systems.

After an update, the new model is validated using validation data in terms of detection performance [11]. Once the model is successfully validated, it can be deployed in a real detection system. Thus far, the detection accuracy of the validation data has been used as a metric to validate the model after an update. However, the accuracy does not reflect detailed information, such as changes in the features used for prediction. Such information is beneficial for avoiding unexpected updates, such as overfitting or noneffective updates.

To obtain detailed information about model updates, we propose a method for identifying patterns of feature attribution changes that cause a change in the prediction. Feature attributions represent the extent of contribution that features have made to model predictions in a system. When a model is retrained using a dataset updated with newly collected data, important features that were overlooked or did not appear before the update may be found. The attributes of such features change significantly. In other words, by analyzing significant changes in feature attributions, we can identify model changes in detail. In the proposed method, we first obtain the feature attributions for each sample that change before and after the update. Then, we obtain the patterns of the changes in the feature attributions, which are common for multiple samples, by clustering the changes of the feature attributions using the similarities of the features whose attributions changed significantly.

In our experiments, we use Android application samples and build models to detect malicious samples. We evaluate the effectiveness of the proposed method by analyzing model changes while the training dataset is updated with different biased data, and as time goes by, we demonstrate that our method can identify the unexpected model changes caused by the biased data. The experimental results show that updates with severely biased data can lead to an overfitting or noneffective update, causing the performance to deteriorate or remain unchanged. The results also indicate that our method can identify the important features relevant to the performance change, which are difficult to find by using a method that calculates only the feature attributions. Some important features found by our method cannot be found unless by checking more than 100 features if the features are checked in the order of the feature attributions.

The remainder of this paper is organized as follows: Sect. 2 introduces related works, especially the feature attribution method. Section 3 presents the proposed method. Section 4 introduces the experimental setup and Sect. 5 presents our experimental results. Finally, Sect. 6 discusses our observations and Sect. 7 concludes the paper.

2   Background and Related Work

We propose a method for analyzing updates to determine the cause of the performance changes. Before presenting our method, in this section, we introduce other methods to evaluate the appropriateness of models. We also introduce a method for determining features that contribute to classification.

2.1   Evaluation Methods

Model Evaluation Metric. There are several common metrics, such as accuracy, precision, recall, F-measure, true positive rate (TPR), and false positive rate (FPR), for evaluating the classification performance of ML models. These are used to calculate a value that indicates the model performance. In binary classification—distinguishing between positive and negative classes—samples are divided into four different categories based on their predicted and true classes: true positive (TP), true negative (TN), false positive (FP), and false negative (FN). TPs and TNs are samples *correctly* predicted as positive and negative, respectively. FPs and FNs are samples *incorrectly* predicted as positive and negative, respectively. In malware detection, positive and negative samples refer to malicious and benign samples, respectively. For example, the FPs are benign samples which are incorrectly predicted as malicious.

The accuracy metric simply computes the ratio of the correct prediction number to the total sample number, $\frac{TP+TN}{TP+TN+FP+FN}$. Precision is the ratio of the correct positive prediction number to the total positive prediction number, $\frac{TP}{TP+FP}$. The recall (also known as the TPR) is the ratio of the correct positive prediction number to the total positive sample number, $\frac{TP}{TP+FN}$. The FPR is the ratio of the incorrect positive prediction number to the total negative sample number, $\frac{FP}{FP+TN}$. The F-measure (or F1-score) is the harmonic mean of precision and recall: $2 \times \frac{precision \times recall}{precision+recall}$.

The model performance is also shown in the receiver operating characteristic (ROC) curves. ROC curves have true and false positive rates as the vertical and horizontal axes, respectively. ROC curves and the area under the curve (AUC) are commonly used to evaluate the performance of the ML model in cybersecurity.

In addition to these metrics, there are also some criteria to evaluate the model from other perspectives. Typically, the Akaike information criterion (AIC) [2] and the Bayesian information criterion (BIC) [20], are widely used to avoid overfitting. They are defined as

$$AIC = -2\ln(\mathcal{L}) + 2K, \qquad (1)$$
$$BIC = -2\ln(\mathcal{L}) + K\ln(n), \qquad (2)$$

where K is the number of learnable parameters in the model, $\mathcal{L}$ is the maximum likelihood of the model, and n is the number of samples.

Cross-Validation. Cross-validation evaluates ML models by dividing a dataset into several subsets. To estimate the model classification performance, one subset is used for validation and the others are used for training. In k-fold cross-validation, a dataset D is randomly split into k mutually exclusive subsets D_1, D_2, ..., D_k. The model is then trained and tested over k rounds. In each round $i \epsilon \{1, 2, ..., k\}$, training is performed on subset $D \setminus D_i$ and testing on subset D_i. In validation, evaluation metrics such as accuracy and AUC score are typically used to estimate the classification performance. To reduce variability, the validation results are combined or averaged over all rounds to obtain a final estimate of the classification performance. In stratified cross-validation, subsets are stratified such that they contain approximately the same proportions of labels as the original dataset.

Although these evaluation methods can compute indicators reflecting model performance, they cannot provide sufficient details of the model updates.

2.2   Feature Attribution Methods

To explain predictions by ML models, importance values are typically attributed to each feature to show its impact on predictions. The importance values of features can be output by some popular ML packages, such as scikit-learn [17], wherein permutation importance is frequently used. Permutation importance randomly permutes the values of a feature in the test dataset and observes a change in error. If a feature is important, then permuting it should significantly increase the model error [13].

Another method for interpreting ML models is the partial dependence plots (PDPs) [8]. A PDP can show how a feature affects model predictions by the relation between the target prediction and features (e.g., linear, monotonic, or more complex). However, a PDP can compute two features at most, and it assumes that these features are not correlated with other features. Thus, it is unrealistic to use PDP for models trained on data containing numerous features.

Another popular approach is the local interpretable model-agnostic explanations (LIME) [19]. LIME explains a given prediction by learning a model around that prediction. By computing the feature importance values of a single prediction, we can easily analyze what made the classifier output that prediction. Instead of explaining the whole model, LIME explains only a single sample prediction result. However, LIME still uses permutation to compute feature importance values, making LIME an inconsistent method.

Although these methods are intended to provide insight into how features affect model predictions, the feature attribution methods described above are all inconsistent, meaning that when the model has changed and a feature impact on the model's output has increased, the importance of that feature can actually be lower. Inconsistency makes comparison of attribution values across models meaningless because it implies that a feature with a large attribution value might be less important than another feature with a smaller attribution.

2.3   SHAP

The inconsistency of the methods in Sect. 2.2 makes it meaningless to compare feature attributions across models, which necessitates a consistent method for analyzing feature attribution changes in different models.

SHAP [14] is a method that explains individual predictions based on Shapley values from game theory. The Shapley value method is represented as an additive

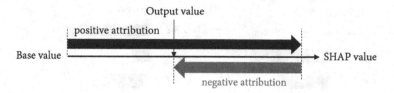

Fig. 1. SHAP values explaining model output as a sum of the attributions of each feature

feature–attribution method (demonstrated in Fig. 1) with a linear explanation model g, described as

$$g(z) = \phi_0 + \sum_{i=1}^{M} \phi_i z_i, \tag{3}$$

where $z \in (0,1)^M$, M is the number of input features, and $\phi_i \in \mathbb{R}$. z_i is a binary decision variable that represents a feature being observed or unknown and ϕ_i is the feature attribution value.

Currently, SHAP is the only consistent and locally accurate individualized feature attribution method. According to Ref. [14], SHAP has three desirable properties: local accuracy, missingness, and consistency. Local accuracy means that the sum of feature attributions equals the output of the model that we want to explain. Missingness means that missing features are assigned no importance, i.e., 0. Consistency means that the attribution assigned to a feature will not be decreased when we change a model such that the feature has a larger impact on the model. Consistency enables comparison of attribution values across models.

When explaining a model f, SHAP assigns ϕ_i values to each feature [13] as

$$\phi_i = \sum_{S \subseteq A \setminus \{i\}} \frac{|S|!(M - |S| - 1)!}{M!} [f_x(S \cup \{i\}) - f_x(S)], \tag{4}$$

where $f_x(S) = f(h_x(z)) = E[f(x)|x_S]$, $E[f(x)|x_S]$ is the expected value of a function conditioned on a subset S of the input features, S is the set of nonzero indices in z, and A is the set of all input features. h_x maps the relationship between the pattern of binary features z and the input vector space.

Because SHAP is the only consistent, locally accurate method for measuring missingness, there is a strong motivation to use SHAP values for feature attribution. However, there are two practical problems remaining to be solved, namely,

1. efficiently estimating $E[f(x)|x_S]$, and
2. the exponential complexity of Eq. (4).

When estimating the predictions of tree models, Lundberg and Lee [13] designed a fast SHAP value estimation algorithm specific to trees and tree ensembles. This algorithm runs in polynomial time instead of exponential time, reducing the computational complexity of exact SHAP value computations for trees and tree ensembles.

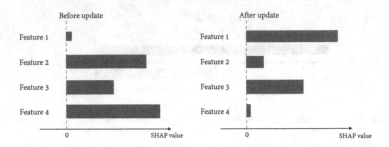

Fig. 2. Changes in SHAP values of features after update

3　Proposed Method

When updating an ML model for real-world deployment, detailed information about model updates is beneficial for preventing unexpected predictions. To obtain detailed information, we propose a method to identify common patterns of feature attribution changes that cause prediction changes. More precisely, the pattern is a combination of features whose attributions changed drastically after the update. Using such information, the operators of the ML model can understand common reasons for prediction changes. Our method consists of two steps. The first step is to calculate feature attribution changes based on SHAP. The second is to identify typical change patterns by clustering samples based on their features whose attributions have drastically changed.

3.1　Calculating Feature Attribution Changes

Because SHAP is a consistent attribution method—meaning that SHAP values are invariant regardless of models—we use SHAP values to measure the attribution changes of features across different models. We investigate changes in the models in detail by analyzing changes in the SHAP values of the features.

　Figure 2 shows an example of the changes in SHAP values before and after an update regarding predictions of the same sample. A SHAP value is assigned to each feature to show how important it is. A high SHAP value means that the corresponding feature has a large effect on the prediction and a SHAP value close to 0 means that the corresponding feature has almost no effect on the prediction. The SHAP values for Features 2 and 4 decreased to near 0, and the SHAP value of Feature 1 increased greatly from a value near 0 after the update, indicating that the model significantly changed with respect to these features. On the other hand, the SHAP values of Feature 3 showed no significant change, indicating that the model did not change with respect to this feature. By analyzing features whose SHAP values have significantly changed, we can infer the cause of model updates and their effect on classification performance.

　Our method defines an increasing rate that indicates the significance of changes in feature attributions after a model update. Specifically, we compute the SHAP values for different models and then calculate the significance of the increase in each feature's SHAP value due to the update. This increasing rate also indicates whether changes in SHAP values increase or decrease. As shown in Fig. 2, Feature 1 exhibits a significant increase, whereas Features 2 and 4 show significant decreases after updating. Unlike these features, the increasing rate of Feature 3 is close to 0 because its SHAP value has no significant change after the update.

The following describes our definition of the increasing rate. Let D_1 be the dataset on which the model was trained before the update and D_2 be the dataset after the update. Then, let the model be trained on D_1 and D_2 be f_1 and f_2, respectively. When predicting a label for data $\mathbf{x}$ with model f_m, we denote the SHAP value of the i-th feature x_i as v_{mx_i}.

We define the rate of increase I_{x_i} of a feature x_i as the ratio of the SHAP value increase to the smallest absolute SHAP value. Let v_{1x_i} be the SHAP value of feature x_i in the old model and let v_{2x_i} be the SHAP value of feature x_i in the new model. The rate of increase is high only if the absolute value of one SHAP value (v_{1x_i} or v_{2x_i}) is large and the other is close to zero. In other words, if the absolute values of both SHAP values are either large or small, the rate of increase is small. We add constant terms c_1 and c_2 to make the increasing rate small when both SHAP values are close to zero.

The increasing rate for feature x_i is defined as

$$I_{x_i} = \frac{v_{2x_i} - v_{1x_i} + c_1}{\min(|v_{1x_i}|, |v_{2x_i}|) + c_2},$$

$$where \ c_2 > 0, \ c_1 = \begin{cases} c_2, & when \ v_{2x_i} - v_{1x_i} \geq 0, \\ -c_2, & when \ v_{2x_i} - v_{1x_i} < 0. \end{cases} \tag{5}$$

In this paper, we set the constant term $c_2 = 0.01$.

The SHAP value of a sample $\mathbf{x}$ is an array of size N, where N is the number of features.

$$\mathbf{v}_{mx} = [v_{mx_1}, v_{mx_2}, ..., v_{mx_i}, ..., v_{mx_N}].$$

The increasing rate of a sample is also an array of size N:

$$\mathbf{I_x} = [I_{x_1}, I_{x_2}, ..., I_{x_i}, ..., I_{x_N}].$$

3.2   Clustering Based on Feature Attribution Changes

To make the output more concise and clearer for the operators, we divide the samples into clusters based on their feature attribution changes. By analyzing samples in each cluster in terms of prediction changes and feature attribution changes, the operators can understand common reasons for prediction changes and infer the performance change in real-world deployment.

We use Jaccard similarity [9] to measure the similarity based on feature attribution changes. Specifically, we define the set A as the set of features whose SHAP rate of increase exceeds k or under $-k$ in sample $\mathbf{x}_A$. In this way, we can represent the sample $\mathbf{x}_A$ based on features that significantly changed after the update. If A is empty, we do not use sample $\mathbf{x}_A$ for clustering. The Jaccard similarity between samples $\mathbf{x}_A$ and $\mathbf{x}_B$ is defined as the size of the intersection divided by the size of the union of sets A and B:

$$J(A, B) = \frac{|A \cap B|}{|A \cup B|} = \frac{|A \cap B|}{|A| + |B| - |A \cap B|}. \tag{6}$$

Note that $0 \leq J(A, B) \leq 1$.

Based on the Jaccard similarity matrix, we conducted clustering via density-based spatial clustering of applications with noise (DBSCAN) [17]. The maximum distance between two samples to be considered as the same cluster was 0.5. In other words, samples in which half of the significantly changed features are common are considered similar and assigned to the same cluster. We used the default set of the software for other parameters, which means the minimum number of samples in a neighborhood for a point to be considered as a core point was five.

After clustering, we calculated the average prediction of each cluster and selected the clusters whose average predictions changed after the update. Then, we calculated each feature's average rate of increase in each cluster and output the top 10 features in terms of the rate of increase (for the cluster having less than 10 features, output all). Based on the output, the operators can understand which features cause prediction changes and infer the performance change in real-world deployment.

4   Experimental Setup

In this section, we introduce the experimental setup for our evaluation using Android applications.

4.1   Dataset

We used samples from AndroZoo [3] to conduct the experiments. AndroZoo is a collection of Android applications from several sources, including the official Google Play app market and VirusShare. It contains over ten million Android application package (APK) files. Each file was analyzed by over 70 antivirus software packages, providing knowledge of malware. We selected files that were not detected as malware by any antivirus software for use as benign samples. For malicious samples, we selected files that were detected as malware using at least four antivirus software packages.

We collected over 1,000 samples per month from AndroZoo between 2016 and 2018. In total, we gathered 61,724 benign samples and 11,160 malicious samples. We used applications collected from 2016 to 2018 because Miller etal. [16] empirically showed that antivirus detection became stable after approximately one year. We followed Ref. [18] when adjusting the ratio of malicious samples to benign ones. Specifically, we set the percentage of malicious samples to 10% and benign samples to 90% in the dataset.

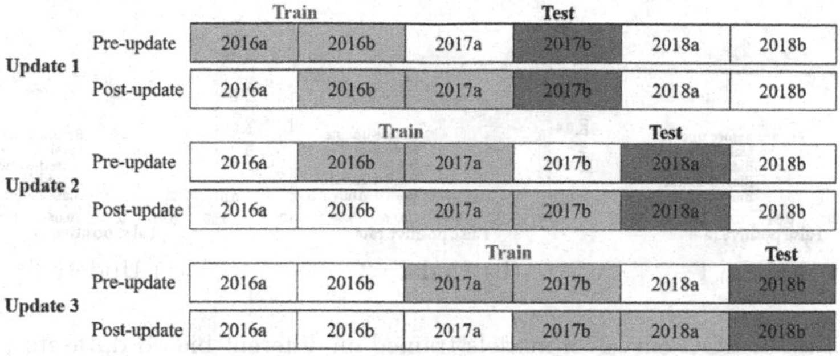

		Train			Test		
Update 1	Pre-update	2016a	2016b	2017a	2017b	2018a	2018b
	Post-update	2016a	2016b	2017a	2017b	2018a	2018b

		Train				Test	
Update 2	Pre-update	2016a	2016b	2017a	2017b	2018a	2018b
	Post-update	2016a	2016b	2017a	2017b	2018a	2018b

		Train					Test
Update 3	Pre-update	2016a	2016b	2017a	2017b	2018a	2018b
	Post-update	2016a	2016b	2017a	2017b	2018a	2018b

Fig. 3. Sliding window setup. a represents the first half of the year. b represents the second half of the year.

4.2 Model Update

In real-world applications, ML models are often updated based on a sliding window setup [5], which means that new data are added to the pre-update dataset, and old data are removed. Thus, we evaluated our method thrice under this setup, as shown in Fig. 3. In each update, the data from the next period of six months were added to the pre-update training dataset, and the older half in the pre-update training dataset was removed. Each training dataset had a similar size of approximately 3,800 benign samples and 420 malicious samples. The number of samples in each dataset is listed in Table 9 in Appendix A. We used the data from the following period of the post-update training dataset as the test dataset to evaluate the model ROC curve and AUC in real-world deployment. Each test dataset contained approximately 5,000 benign samples and 550 malicious samples. The number of samples is also shown in Table 9.

To simulate successful and failed updates, we used biased and unbiased post-update training datasets. For pre-update training datasets, we always used unbiased datasets because we assumed that the pre-update models are successfully trained and validated in real-world deployment. Consequently, post-update training datasets were composed of the first half of the unbiased dataset and the second half of the differently biased dataset. For example, the post-update training dataset of update 1 consisted of the *unbiased* dataset of 2016b and the *biased* dataset of 2017b. Using such datasets, the models updated differently depending on the bias. We evaluated whether operators can distinguish different updates based on the output of our method. The unbiased and biased datasets were prepared as follows:

1. *Unbiased:* We randomly selected an equal number of samples from every month.
2. *Biased-Time:* We randomly selected all samples from the latest month of the period.
3. *Biased-Family:* We randomly selected malicious samples from 3 major families; there were more than 40 small families in total. The benign samples were the same as those in the *unbiased dataset.*

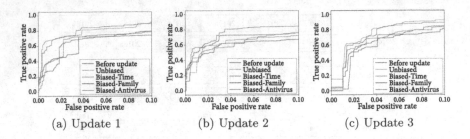

(a) Update 1   (b) Update 2   (c) Update 3

Fig. 4. ROC curves of models trained on different biased datasets

4. *Biased-Antivirus:* We randomly selected malicious samples from samples easily detected. Samples were determined as easily detected if they were detected by more than 20 antivirus software in VirusTotal [21]. The benign samples were the same as those in the *unbiased dataset*.

4.3 Features and Models

We use Drebin [4], which is a lightweight method for detecting malicious APK files based on broad static analyses, to extract features from APK files. Features were extracted from the manifest and disassembled dex codes of the APK file. From these, Drebin collected discriminative strings, such as permissions, API calls, and network addresses. To build a machine learning model, we used random forest [6], a method well known for its excellent classification performance and applicability to many tasks, including malware detection. For a detailed setup of the features, models, and hyper parameters, please refer to Appendix A.

5   Experimental Results

We conducted experiments with three updates using the four biased datasets described in Sect. 4. First, we show which models are successfully updated by using test datasets. Then we describe results of quantitative and qualitative evaluation. In these evaluations, we investigate whether the output of our method is beneficial to ML system operators in understanding model updates. As a quantitative evaluation, we investigate the extent to which our method can reduce the number of features that operators must consider to understand model updates. This evaluation shows that operators can easily understand model updates using our method. As a qualitative evaluation, we investigate whether operators can infer the classification performance of the updated models in real-world deployment by using the output of our method with a post-update training dataset. This evaluation shows how useful our method is.

Table 1. AUC in cross-validation and AUC on test dataset

			Update 1	Update 2	Update 3
Pre-update	Unbiased	CV	0.9673	0.9722	0.9522
		Test	0.9095	0.8932	0.9163
Post-update	Unbiased	CV	0.9722	0.9522	0.9573
		Test	0.9425	0.9273	0.9493
	Biased-Time	CV	0.9729	0.9538	0.9693
		Test	0.9509	0.9513	0.9439
	Biased-Family	CV	0.9809	0.9687	0.9739
		Test	0.9313	0.8976	0.9296
	Biased-Antivirus	CV	0.9812	0.9727	0.9696
		Test	0.9157	0.8731	0.9320

5.1 Classification Performance of Updated Models

We show which models are successfully updated by using test datasets. In addition, we show that inferring the classification performance on test datasets and understanding changes in models are difficult based on the conventional model validation method, i.e., cross-validation (CV) with post-update training datasets. We use AUCs and ROC curves to evaluate classification performance. The AUC on test datasets and in CV are shown in Table 1. The AUC in CV were much better than the AUC on test datasets, indicating that the cross-validation is inappropriate because its result may be over-optimistic under concept drift. Moreover, operators cannot understand why model updates cause prediction changes and infer whether the updates are reasonable.

To investigate the classification performance more precisely, we show the ROC curve of each model in each update in Fig. 4. In general, the performance improved after updates of "Unbiased" and "Biased-Time" datasets, and deteriorated or almost stayed unchanged after updates of "Biased-Family" and "Biased-Antivirus" datasets.

5.2 Quantitative Evaluation

We investigate the number of features that operators must analyze to understand model updates. The smaller the number, the less effort the operators need to make for the analysis. Without our method, operators analyze features important to classification. In other words, operators look into features in descending order of SHAP values, i.e., from the most important to the least important. For this reason, we investigate the maximum order of the SHAP value (the least important) in each cluster's features. Table 2 shows the number of clusters, the number of features in each cluster, and the maximum order of SHAP values. The number of features with our method is much smaller than that without our method.

More detailed results are shown in Table 3; it shows the output features of the two clusters when using the Unbias dataset in Update 1. In cluster 1, the

Table 2. Number of cluster/features and maximum order of SHAP

		# clusters	# features in each cluster	Max. order of SHAP
Update 1	Unbiased	5	7–10	39–487
	Biased-Time	4	1–10	39–142
	Biased-Family	3	2–8	22–110
	Biased-Antivirus	3	3–9	53–218
Update 2	Unbiased	1	6	64
	Biased-Time	6	3–8	24–190
	Biased-Family	3	4–10	24–428
	Biased-Antivirus	0	–	–
Update 3	Unbiased	5	2–10	31–371
	Biased-Time	6	3–10	55–371
	Biased-Family	2	3–10	371
	Biased-Antivirus	1	2	198

Table 3. Output features of two clusters using Unbiased dataset in Update 1

	Features	Order of increasing rate	Order of SHAP
Cluster 1	android.location.locationmanager.getproviders	1	49
	android.nfc.tech.ndefformatable.format	2	86
	android.nfc.tech.ndefformatable.connect	3	109
	android.nfc.tech.ndef.connect	4	81
	android.nfc.tech.ndef.writendefmessage	5	100
Cluster 2	android.permission.vibrate	1	30
	android.widget.videoview.setvideopath	2	7
	android.widget.videoview.pause	3	13
	android.widget.videoview.stopplayback	4	6
	android.widget.videoview.start	5	14

features causing prediction change are mainly relevant to `nfc.tech` because four out of five features are relevant to `nfc.tech`. Similarly, in cluster 2, the features relevant to `widget.videoview` mainly caused the prediction changes. However, these features are difficult to identify if only SHAP values are used because the maximum order of SHAP is 109.

5.3   Qualitative Evaluation

As shown above, the classification performance on the test dataset depends on the bias in the training dataset, and our method can reduce the number of features that operators must analyze to understand a model update. Here, we investigate whether operators can infer that a model update is successful or failed using the output of our method with a post-update training dataset. Specifically, the main cause of a failed model update is overfitting and noneffective update.

Table 4. Example of similar clusters

	Features	Mean rate
Cluster 1	android.permission.write_external_storage	4.77
	android.permission.read_external_storage	4.11
Cluster 2	android.intent.action.main	6.5
	android.permission.read_external_storage	4.81
	android.widget.videoview.setvideopath	4.76
	android.permission.internet	4.47
	android.permission.write_external_storage	4.12
	android.permission.internet	3.29
	android.permission.access_network_state	3.2

Overfitting involves learning the training dataset too much and not generalizing it to the test dataset. More precisely, an overfitted model learns only a few families or overlooks some families. The noneffective update is that a model update does not change predictions, even though a model update is expected to change some predictions under concept drift. The noneffective update is mainly caused by noninformative newly added data.

We describe how to analyze the output of our method from the aforementioned three perspectives: learning a few families, overlooking some families, and noneffective updates. Note that our method does not output any cluster of benign data, which means that the performance changes are mainly caused by malicious data. For this reason, we only show results of malicious data.

Learning a Few Families. To confirm whether a model learns only a few families, we focus on a variety of changes caused by the model update. Using our method, data with similar attribution changes are assigned to the same cluster. The number of clusters reflects the variety of changes. The lack of variety can result in an overfitting model because the model can only learn features related to some types of data, causing a performance degradation after the update. The number of clusters can be used to evaluate whether the model is overfitted.

Table 2 shows the number of clusters in each update. When the dataset is biased, for example, it only contains major families with a large number of malicious samples, and the lack of variety may cause the model to only learn features related to certain families, resulting in overfitting. As can be seen in Table 2, the cluster numbers of "Biased-Family" are always less than the results of other updates, and the results of "Biased-Antivirus" are also low in some cases, which indicates that the bias of the dataset causes a lack of variety and influences the update as a result.

We can more precisely identify the lack of variety by investigating the similarity of features between clusters. For example, Table 4 shows the features of two of the clusters using "Biased-Family" in Update 1. All features in Cluster 1 are included in Cluster 2, meaning that the variety of data is low.

Table 5. The number of clusters whose predictions become false

	Unbiased	Biased-Time	Biased-Family	Biase-Antivirus
Update 1	0	0	0	0
Update 2	0	0	1	0
Update 3	0	0	2	0

Table 6. Cluster with false prediction change in Update 2. "None" means SHAP value is 0 after update and ranked in the last.

Features	Mean rate	Order of SHAP
com.qihoo.util.appupdate.appupdateactivity	−25.66	None
com.qihoo.util.startactivity	−25.06	None
com.swityfpass.pay.activity.qqwappaywebview	−17.20	None
com.alipay.sdk.auth.authactivity	−15.54	None
blue.sky.vn.api	−14.66	None
landroid/telephony/smsmanager.sendtextmessage	−14.23	33
blue.sky.vn.mainactivity	−11.85	None
blue.sky.vn.webviewactivity	−10.42	None
blue.sky.vn.gamehdactivity	−10.33	None
com.qihoo.util.commonactivity	−8.09	None

Table 7. Difference values used to measure the extent of improvement

	Unbiased	Biased-Time	Biased-Family	Biased-Antivirus
Update 1	103	122	31	25
Update 2	70	104	−17	0
Update 3	78	131	−27	12

Overlooking Some Families. To confirm whether a model overlooks some families, we focus on clusters with predictions going false from true. For example, the shortage of certain data, such as minor malware families, can prevent the model from learning features related to those data. When the model is unable to learn some data after the update, the predictions of such data become false. Thus, we investigate the clusters with predictions changing from true to false.

Table 5 shows the number of clusters whose predictions change from true to false. As we can see, only the results of "Biased-Family" have such clusters. We can also obtain further information about the failure related to these clusters by showing their features of a high rate of increase. For example, Table 6 shows the cluster whose prediction changes from true to false in update 2. The false predictions are mainly caused by the lack of features `com.qihoo.util` and `blue.sky.vn`, because their SHAP values decreased to zero after the update.

Noneffective Update. To identify noneffective updates mainly caused by non-informative newly added data, we focus on cluster size, i.e., the number of samples in each cluster. The cluster size shows how many samples have a different prediction after the update. The more the prediction results change from false to true, the better the model performance will improve. If the performance does not improve sufficiently after the update, the update is ineffective. In a malware detection system, a change in the prediction results from false to true means that the prediction of malicious samples becomes positive, or the prediction of benign samples becomes negative. Therefore, the size of the output clusters indicates the extent of the performance change during the update. We use the number of samples whose prediction changes from false to true to evaluate whether the model has been updated effectively. Specifically, we measure the extent of performance improvement by the difference value between the number of samples whose predictions become true and the number of samples whose predictions become false. Table 7 presents the results for each difference value. The minus number in Table 7 indicates that the samples whose predictions change from true to false are more than those whose predictions change from false to true.

Table 7 indicates that for a dataset of approximately 220 samples, the performance of "Unbiased" and "Biased-Time" improve after update, whereas the performance of "Biased-Family" and "Biased-Antivirus" have very limited change or no change after update, which is consistent with the results of the ROC and AUC but more clear. When the difference value of the data becomes true and the data becoming false is large, we can conclude that the model performance has improved after the update, and the update is effective. When the difference value is relatively small, the performance remains almost unchanged, and the update is ineffective.

Summary. In our experiment, we used data with four different types of bias and three different periods of time to conduct 36 updates to demonstrate our method. Table 8 shows the evaluation result of each update. As we can see, in most cases, the results of "Biased-Family" and "Biased-Antivirus" appear to be overfitted or noneffective, which explains the performance not improving after updates by those dataset. All the results of "Biased-Time" are neither overfitted nor noneffective, explaining the performance improvement after updates by "Biased-Time," as shown in the ROC curves.

6 Discussion

Application of the Proposed Method. Although this study focuses mainly on malware detection systems, our method should be applied to all types of machine learning tasks. The SHAP method provides algorithms for estimating SHAP values for any ML model, i.e., our method can be applied to any ML model, regardless of the dataset or model. For example, our method can be applied to suspicious URL detection [15], malicious website detection [7],

Table 8. Summary of qualitative evaluation. ✓ represents that an undesirable update is observed, and × represents that an undesirable update is not observed.

		Learning a few families	Overlooking some families	Noneffective update
Update 1	Unbiased	×	×	×
	Biased-Time	×	×	×
	Biased-Family	✓	×	✓
	Biased-Antivirus	×	×	✓
Update 2	Unbiased	✓	×	×
	Biased-Time	×	×	×
	Biased-Family	✓	✓	✓
	Biased-Antivirus	✓	×	✓
Update 3	Unbiased	×	×	×
	Biased-Time	×	×	×
	Biased-Family	✓	✓	✓
	Biased-Antivirus	✓	×	✓

and malware family classification [1]. In multiclass classifications, we can identify changes in important features by analyzing feature attribution changes by focusing on each class.

Limitation. In this paper, we demonstrated that our method outputs detailed information about model updates, such as the important features that are relevant to the performance change during the update. Though we discussed the importance of the outputted information, we need a user study, which is one of our future works.

7   Conclusion

ML methods have been widely applied to many tasks. In practical use, it is necessary to regularly update the model to maintain its classification performance. AUC and accuracy are generally used to validate models to confirm their performance after updates. However, it is difficult to gain sufficiently detailed information for understanding model updates, such as what causes performance changes and the influence on a certain type of data.

Therefore, we propose a method for determining samples in which the features important for classification have significant changes. By selecting those samples and clustering them by feature attribution changes, we can know more about why performance changes or how an update influences a certain type of data. For the feature attribution computation, we used a consistent importance value called the SHAP value because SHAP values are comparable across different models. Our proposed method calculates the rates of increase in SHAP values after updates to reflect changes in feature importance, and clustering the samples by their feature attribution changes to generate the information given to the operator.

We conducted experiments using an open dataset of Android malware. We investigated model changes while the training dataset is updated with different biased data, and demonstrated that our method can identify the unexpected model changes such as overfitting or noneffective update caused by the biased data. The results also indicate that our method can identify the important features relevant to the performance change, which are difficult to find by using a method that calculates only the feature attributions.

Though we discussed the importance of the outputted information, we need a user study, which is one of our future works.

A   Detailed Experimental Setup

Dataset. Each training dataset had a similar size of approximately 3,800 benign samples and 420 malicious samples, and each test dataset contained approximately 5,000 benign samples and 550 malicious samples. The number of samples is shown in Table 9.

Feature. To extract features in our experiments, we used Drebin [4], a lightweight method for detecting malicious APK files based on broad static analyses. Features are extracted from the manifest and disassembled dex codes of the APK file. From these, Drebin collects discriminative strings, such as permissions, API calls, and network addresses. Drebin extracts eight sets of strings: four from manifests and four from dex code.

1. Hardware components
2. Requested permissions
3. App components
4. Filtered intents
5. Restricted API calls
6. Used permissions
7. Suspicious API calls
8. Network addresses

The features are embedded into an N-dimensional vector space, where each element is either 0 or 1. Each element corresponds to a string, with 1 representing the presence of the string and 0 representing its absence. The extracted feature vector $\mathbf{x}$ is denoted as

$$\mathbf{x} = (\cdots \; 0 \; 1 \; \cdots \; 0 \; 1 \; \cdots).$$

The feature vector can be used as input for a machine-learning model.

Classification Models. Our experiments use random forest [6], which is well known for its excellent classification performance and can be applied to many tasks, including malware detection. Random forest is an ensemble of decision trees. Each decision tree is built using a randomly sampled subset of data and features. By creating an ensemble of many decision trees, random forest achieves high classification performance even when the dimensions of feature vectors exceed the dataset size. Furthermore, the SHAP package [12] associated with Ref. [13] provides a high-speed algorithm called TreeExplainer for tree ensemble methods, including random forests.

Table 9. Number of samples in each dataset

			Malicious	Benign
Update 1	Pre-update	Unbiased	416	3,732
	Post-update	Unbiased	416	3,809
		Biased-Time	425	3,847
		Biased-Family	424	3,809
		Biased-Antivirus	417	3,841
	Test	Unbiased	595	5,322
Update 2	Pre-update	Unbiased	416	3,809
	Post-update	Unbiased	423	3,816
		Biased-Time	423	3,850
		Biased-Family	423	3,854
		Biased-Antivirus	421	3,837
	Test	Unbiased	598	5,302
Update 3	Pre-update	Unbiased	423	3,816
	Post-update	Unbiased	429	3,814
		Biased-Time	432	3,854
		Biased-Family	431	3,814
		Biased-Antivirus	431	3,843
	Test	Unbiased	532	4,628

Hyperparameter Optimization. When training random forest models, we conduct a grid search for each model to determine the best combination of parameters among the following candidates:

1. Number of trees: 10, 100, 200, 300, 400.
2. Maximum depth of each tree: 10, 100, 300, 500.
3. Ratio of features used for each tree: 0.02, 0.05, 0.07, 0.1, 0.2.
4. Minimum number of samples required at a leaf node: 5, 7, 10, 20.

Each candidate combination is validated using five-fold cross validation. Specifically, we calculated an average of five AUC scores for each combination and selected the best combination in terms of the average AUC score as the result of the grid search.

References

1. Ahmadi, M., Ulyanov, D., Semenov, S., Trofimov, M., Giacinto, G.: Novel feature extraction, selection and fusion for effective malware family classification. In: Proceedings of the 6th ACM Conference on Data and Application Security and Privacy, pp. 183–194 (2016)
2. Akaike, H.: Information theory and an extension of the maximum likelihood principle. In: Parzen, E., Tanabe, K., Kitagawa, G. (eds.) Selected Papers of Hirotugu Akaike, pp. 199–213. Springer, New York (1998). https://doi.org/10.1007/978-1-4612-1694-0_15
3. Allix, K., Bissyandé, T.F., Klein, J., Le Traon, Y.: Androzoo: collecting millions of android apps for the research community. In: Proceedings of the 13th IEEE/ACM Working Conference on Mining Software Repositories, pp. 468–471 (2016)
4. Arp, D., Spreitzenbarth, M., Hubner, M., Gascon, H., Rieck, K.: Drebin: effective and explainable detection of android malware in your pocket. In: Proceedings of the 2014 Network and Distributed System Security Symposium (2014)
5. Bouktif, S., Fiaz, A., Ouni, A., Serhani, M.A.: Single and multi-sequence deep learning models for short and medium term electric load forecasting. Energies 12(1), 149 (2019)
6. Breiman, L.: Random forests. Mach. Learn. 45(1), 5–32 (2001)
7. Canali, D., Cova, M., Vigna, G., Kruegel, C.: Prophiler: a fast filter for the large-scale detection of malicious web pages. In: Proceedings of the 20th International Conference on World Wide Web, pp. 197–206 (2011)
8. Friedman, J.H., Meulman, J.J.: Multiple additive regression trees with application in epidemiology. Stat. Med. 22(9), 1365–1381 (2003)
9. Jaccard, P.: The distribution of the flora in the alpine zone. 1. New Phytologist 11(2), 37–50 (1912)
10. Jordaney, R., et al.: Transcend: detecting concept drift in malware classification models. In: Proceedings of the 26th USENIX Security Symposium, pp. 625–642 (2017)
11. Karlaš, B., et al.: Building continuous integration services for machine learning. In: Proceedings of the 26th ACM SIGKDD International Conference on Knowledge Discovery & Data Mining, pp. 2407–2415 (2020)
12. Lundberg, S.M., et al.: From local explanations to global understanding with explainable AI for trees. Nat. Mach. Intell. 2(1), 2522–5839 (2020)
13. Lundberg, S.M., Erion, G.G., Lee, S.I.: Consistent individualized feature attribution for tree ensembles. arXiv preprint arXiv:1802.03888 (2018)
14. Lundberg, S.M., Lee, S.I.: A unified approach to interpreting model predictions. In: Proceedings of the 31st Advances in Neural Information Processing Systems, pp. 4765–4774 (2017)
15. Ma, J., Saul, L.K., Savage, S., Voelker, G.M.: Beyond blacklists: learning to detect malicious web sites from suspicious URLs. In: Proceedings of the 15th ACM SIGKDD International Conference on Knowledge Discovery and Data Mining, pp. 1245–1254 (2009)

16. Miller, B., et al.: Reviewer integration and performance measurement for malware detection. In: Proceedings of the 13th International Conference on Detection of Intrusions and Malware, and Vulnerability Assessment, pp. 122–141 (2016)
17. Pedregosa, F., et al.: Scikit-learn: machine learning in python. J. Mach. Learn. Res. **12**, 2825–2830 (2011)
18. Pendlebury, F., Pierazzi, F., Jordaney, R., Kinder, J., Cavallaro, L.: TESSERACT: eliminating experimental bias in malware classification across space and time. In: Proceedings of the 28th USENIX Security Symposium, pp. 729–746 (2019)
19. Ribeiro, M.T., Singh, S., Guestrin, C.: "Why should I trust you?": explaining the predictions of any classifier. In: Proceedings of the 22nd ACM SIGKDD International Conference on Knowledge Discovery and Data Mining, pp. 1135–1144 (2016)
20. Schwarz, G.: Estimating the dimension of a model. Ann. Stat. **6**(2), 461–464 (1978)
21. Sood, G.: virustotal: R Client for the virustotal API (2017). R package version 0.2.1
22. Tsymbal, A.: The problem of concept drift: definitions and related work. Computer Science Department, Trinity College Dublin, vol. 106, no. 2, p. 58 (2004)

Proposal of Jawi CAPTCHA Using Digraphia Feature of the Malay Language

Hisaaki Yamaba[1]([envelope]), Ahmad Saiful Aqmal Bin Ahmad Sohaimi[1],
Shotaro Usuzaki[1], Kentaro Aburada[1], Masayuki Mukunoki[1], Mirang Park[2],
and Naonobu Okazaki[1]

[1] University of Miyazaki, 1-1, Gakuen Kibanadai-nishi, Miyazaki 889-2192, Japan
yamaba@cs.miyazaki-u.ac.jp
[2] Kanagawa Institute of Technology, 1030, Shimo-Ogino,
Atsugi, Kanagawa 243-0292, Japan

Abstract. This paper proposes a new text-based CAPTCHA using Jawi script and Latin script, which are both used in the Malay language writing system. Many web sites have adopted CAPTCHA to prevent bots and other automated programs from malicious activities such as posting comment spam. Text-based CAPTCHA is the most common and earliest CAPTCHA. But as optical character recognition (OCR) technology has improved, the intensity of distortions that must be applied to a CAPTCHA for it to remain unrecognizable by OCR has increased. This has reached a point where humans are having difficulty recognizing CAPTCHA text. The idea of the proposed CAPTCHA is to generate two identical character strings, one written in Latin script and the other in Jawi script. Because some of the strings characters are hidden by obstacles, users need to combine both strings to solve this CAPTCHA. This idea uses the fact that most Jawi characters have one-to-one correspondence with Latin characters. A series of experiments was carried out to evaluated the performance of the proposed CAPTCHA. First, a computer program was developed with various software languages for the usability evaluation. The results showed that the average time to solve the CAPTCHA and the accuracy rates were acceptable compared with the indices reported in existing research. Next, two OCR programs were applied to the Jawi CAPTCHA, and it was demonstrated that they could not read the partially hidden Latin and Jawi strings. Lastly, we discussed the effectiveness of the proposed CAPTCHA by relating to the priming effect.

Keywords: CAPTCHA · Jawi script · Malay language · Digraphia · Priming effect

1 Introduction

CAPTCHA—Complete Automated Public Turing Test to Tell Computers and Humans Apart—has become quite common on websites and applications. CAPTCHA is a type of challenge-response test used to distinguish between

T. Nakanishi and R. Nojima (Eds.): IWSEC 2021, LNCS 12835, pp. 119–133, 2021.
https://doi.org/10.1007/978-3-030-85987-9_7

Fig. 1. Example of the proposed Jawi CAPTCHA

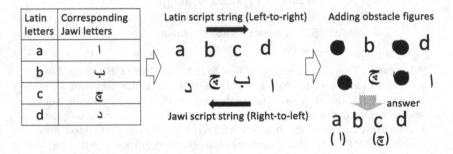

Fig. 2. Basic idea of the proposed CAPTCHA

human users and automated programs. It is used to prevent bots and other automated programs from signing up for email, posting comment spam, violating privacy, and making brute force login attacks on user accounts. CAPTCHA must be both highly secure and easy to use. To date, many versions of CAPTCHA have been proposed and developed so as to be not only difficult to solve by computer programs but also easy for humans to solve.

Text-based CAPTCHAs are the most common and earliest CAPTCHA. They request users to enter the string of characters that appears in a distorted form on the screen. It was easy for human beings to read the distorted strings, but this was difficult for computer programs when this CAPTCHA was introduced.

However, as optical character recognition (OCR) technology has improved, the amount of distortion that must be applied to CAPTCHA strings has also increased. This has reached a point where humans are having difficulty solving CAPTCHAs. Thus, there is a need to develop a new text-based CAPTCHA that does not use distortion of letters.

Based on the identified problem, this paper proposes a new CAPTCHA that uses digraphia (Fig. 1). We adopted Latin script and Jawi script, which is based on the Arabic script and used for writing the Malay language, on the assumption that the CAPTCHA system is used in nations using the Malay language, such as Malaysia. The same word is written in both scripts and some of the strings' characters are hidden by interference (Fig. 2). Users need to combine the two fragmented strings to solve this CAPTCHA.

Table 1. 29 Jawi characters similar to Arabic characters

Character	Final	Medial	Initial	Isolated
ا	ـا			ا
ب	ـب	ـبـ	بـ	ب
ت	ـت	ـتـ	تـ	ت
ث	ـث	ـثـ	ثـ	ث
ج	ـج	ـجـ	جـ	ج
ح	ـح	ـحـ	حـ	ح
خ	ـخ	ـخـ	خـ	خ
د	ـد			د
ذ	ـذ			ذ
ر	ـر			ر
ز	ـز			ز
س	ـس	ـسـ	سـ	س
ش	ـش	ـشـ	شـ	ش
ص	ـص	ـصـ	صـ	ص
ض	ـض	ـضـ	ضـ	ض
ط	ـط	ـطـ	طـ	ط
ظ	ـظ	ـظـ	ظـ	ظ
ع	ـع	ـعـ	عـ	ع
غ	ـغ	ـغـ	غـ	غ
ف	ـف	ـفـ	فـ	ف
ق	ـق	ـقـ	قـ	ق
ک	ـک	ـکـ	کـ	ک
ل	ـل	ـلـ	لـ	ل
م	ـم	ـمـ	مـ	م
ن	ـن	ـنـ	نـ	ن
و	ـو			و
ه	ـه	ـهـ	هـ	ه
ء	ء			ء
ی	ـی	ـیـ	یـ	ی

The rest of this paper is organized as follows: Sect. 2 discusses some related works. Section 3 deals with specific characteristics of Jawi script that are used for generating CAPTCHAs. The proposed CAPTCHA scheme is presented in Sect. 4. Next, Sect. 5 describes the usability evaluation experiment process and the results. The security evaluation experiment process and results are discussed in Sect. 6. Sections 7 and 8 provide discussion and conclusions, respectively.

2 Jawi Script: An Overview

This section explains the characteristics of Jawi script in terms of origin, writing direction, and shapes.

Digraphia refers to the use of more than one writing system for the same language [1]. The Malay language uses two scripts: Latin and Jawi. Historically, Jawi script, which is based on Arabic script, became one of the first scripts used among the Malaysians, Indonesians, and Bruneians. After the latter half of the 20th century, these countries introduced Latin scripts to write the Malay

Table 2. Six additional Jawi characters

Character	Final	Medial	Initial	Isolated
چ	ـچ	ـچـ	چـ	چ
غ	ـغ	ـغـ	غـ	غ
ڤ	ـڤ	ـڤـ	ڤـ	ڤ
ݢ	ـݢ	ـݢـ	ݢـ	ݢ
ژ	ـژ			ژ
ڽ	ـڽ	ـڽـ	ڽـ	ڽ

One-to-one character conversion

"ا"→"a"	"ب"→"b"	"ت"→"t"	"ث"→"s"
"ج"→"j"	"ح"→"h"	"د"→"d"	"ذ"→"z"
"ر"→"r"	"ز"→"z"	"س"→"s"	"ص"→"s"
"ض"→"d"	"ط"→"t"	"ظ"→"z"	"ع"→"a/i/u"
"ف"→"f"	"ق"→"q"	"ک"→"k"	"ل"→"l"
"م"→"m"	"ن"→"n"	"و"→"w/u/o"	"ه"→"h"
"ء"→"a"	"ي"→"y/i/e"	"چ"→"c"	"ڤ"→"p"
"ݢ"→"g"	"ژ"→"v"		

Others

"خ"→"kh"	"ش"→"sy"	"غ"→"gh"	"ڠ"→"ng"
"ڽ"→"ny"			

Fig. 3. Conversion of Jawi script to Latin script

language. Malay words spelled in Latin scripts, or the writing system, are called Rumi. However, Jawi script is still taught in the education system, specifically in Asian countries such as Malaysia, Indonesia, and Brunei.

Jawi script contains 35 letters, and they are written from right to left like Arabic script. Further, Jawi script is similar to Arabic script except for six letters that were added for spelling Malay-specific phonemes. The Jawi characters that are similar to those in Arabic script are listed in Table 1. The additional six unique letters of the Jawi alphabet are shown in Table 2. As shown in the tables, the Jawi letters have different shapes depending on their position in the word, that is, initial, middle, final, or isolated.

In spelling with the Malay language, almost Jawi characters have one-to-one correspondence with Latin characters, as shown in Fig. 3. Several characters in Jawi script represent more than one character in Latin script (underlined characters in Fig. 3). There are also several Jawi characters that represent the same Latin characters depending on the word, as shown in Fig. 4 (a)–(d).

This paper proposes an alternative identity verification solution by providing another text-based CAPTCHA using Jawi and Latin scripts in combination. Jawi script is expected to provide better security against OCR software due to its unique characteristics, because many Jawi characters share the same main

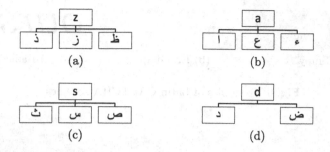

Fig. 4. Latin characters that can be converted to multiple Jawi characters

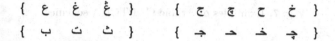

Fig. 5. Examples of Jawi characters that differ only in the number of dots

body and differ only in the number of dots, as shown in Fig. 5. In addition, OCR software supporting Jawi script has not yet been actively developed, making this script the best choice.

3 Related Work

This section highlights studies of both text-based Latin CAPTCHA and Arabic CAPTCHA schemes.

3.1 Latin CAPTCHA Schemes

Latin CAPTCHA, or CAPTCHA that consists of English letters, is the earliest and most prevalent CAPTCHA, and it typically asks users to correctly identify distorted words. The CAPTCHA idea was first implemented by Alta Vista to prevent automated bots from automatically registering web sites [2].

The mechanism behind the CAPTCHA idea was to generate a word with slightly distorted characters and present it to the user. There are many examples of Latin script used CAPTCHAs, such as Gimpy CAPTCHA, EZ-Gimpy CAPTCHA, and Baffle-Text CAPTCHA, as shown in Fig. 6. Gimpy CAPTCHA selects several words from the dictionary and displays all the distorted words to the users [3] while EZ-Gimpy only displays one distorted word [4]. Baffle-Text CAPTCHA [5] is a modified version of Gimpy that generates a random meaningless word as a CAPTCHA.

3.2 Arabic CAPTCHA Scheme

So far, no CAPTCHA has been implemented using Jawi script, but many studies have been done on Arabic CAPTCHAs. Because Jawi script has some resemblance to Arabic script, several Arabic CAPTCHA schemes are explained here.

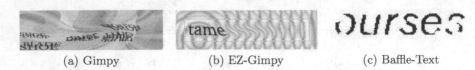

(a) Gimpy   (b) EZ-Gimpy   (c) Baffle-Text

Fig. 6. Examples of Latin CAPTCHA schemes

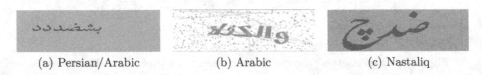

(a) Persian/Arabic   (b) Arabic   (c) Nastaliq

Fig. 7. Examples of Arabic CAPTCHA schemes

The first work that employed Arabic script as a CAPTCHA is presented in [6], where the authors generated random meaningless Arabic words as CAPTCHA. In particular, the work reported in [6] presents an application of Persian/Arabic CAPTCHA, while the work in [7] applies Arabic CAPTCHA for verifying spam SMS. Khan et al. [8] improved on the previous work on typed-text Arabic CAPTCHA. Specifically, they exploited the limitations of Arabic OCR in reading Arabic text by adding background noise and using specific Arabic font types for CAPTCHA generation. The study in [9] proposed advanced Nastaliq CAPTCHA to provide essentially random meaningless Persian words that are close to Arabic words in terms of script. Examples of Arabic CAPTCHA schemes are shown in Fig. 7.

4   Proposed Scheme

This section describes the basic idea of the proposed CAPTCHA, the answer text generation process, and the obstacle patterns.

4.1   Basic Concept

This paper proposes a new CAPTCHA that uses digraphia. The proposed CAPTCHA combines two different character scripts, Latin and Jawi, into one CAPTCHA, as shown in Fig. 1. The idea of this CAPTCHA is to generate the same word or character string spelled in both the Latin and Jawi scripts. To solve this CAPTCHA, the users need to combine both the Latin and Jawi strings because some of each string characters are hidden by obstacles.

It is not difficult to guess the answer word even if a few characters of the word are hidden, but it becomes harder when more characters are hidden. For example, although we can understand "ch rac er" may be "character", it is hard to guess "character" from "ch te". However, "rac r" is also given together with "ch te" the correct answer will come up to our mind because one of the fragment strings becomes the clue to finding the answer from the other fragment.

Fig. 8. Placement of text in CAPTCHA generation

id	latin	jawi	image	pattern
1	aduan	ادوان	aduan.png	1
2	amanah	امانه	amanah.png	2
3	akui	اکوي	akui.png	1
4	berurat	براورت	berurat.png	2
5	diurus	داوروس	diurus.png	1
6	berbuah	بربواه	berbuah.png	2
7	diusir	داوسير	diusir.png	1
8	berasas	براساس	berasas.png	2

Fig. 9. Example of database for storing Jawi CAPTCHAs

Guessing the answer from the two fragments is harder than the combined "ch racter" because composing "ch racter" from the two fragments is not easy. Even if OCR programs can read each character in the shown string, it is expected that they cannot understand the word like human beings.

In addition, we added another hurdle for bots to answer the CAPTCHA by adopting two scripts for spelling the two fragments. But it is not a barrier for people living in nations using Malay language because they are familiar with words spelled in Jawi and Latin scripts.

4.2   Answer Text Generation

The proposed scheme has two types of answer text generation methods: (1) A Malay word is randomly selected from a dictionary or (2) A random meaningless Latin/Jawi string is composed by a computer program.

For type (1), a database that contains pairs of string images is constructed. Words are selected from a Malay dictionary and two spellings are obtained, one in Latin script and the other in Jawi script, for each word. The selected strings are stored in the table for type (1) of the database.

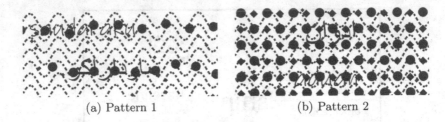

(a) Pattern 1   (b) Pattern 2

Fig. 10. Obstacle patterns

For type (2), strings four to eight characters long are randomly generated using Latin script. Then, the generated Latin string is converted to a Jawi string letter by letter according to the table shown in Fig. 3. In this case, Jawi characters that have one-to-one correspondence with Latin characters are used. All the generated strings are stored in the table for type (2) of the database.

To generate a CAPTCHA, one set of words/strings written in Latin and Jawi scripts is selected from the created database, converted to images using JavaScript programming language, and placed on a plain image. First, the Latin word image is placed at a random coordinate on the screen. Then, the equivalent Jawi word is placed outside the minimum and maximum heights of the Latin word, as shown in Fig. 8, to prevent the two words from overlapping. Lastly, a obstacle pattern explained in the next section is added to the image, and the image and the obstacle pattern type are stored in the database. A sample of the database is shown in Fig. 9.

4.3 Obstacle Patterns

In this CAPTCHA scheme, two geometric obstacle patterns are introduced, pattern 1 and pattern 2, as shown in Fig. 10. The primary purpose of obstacle pattern introduction is to protect the generated CAPTCHA from OCR attacks while keeping it readable to a human.

These patterns use dashed sine waves as the background because Jawi characters have a cursive shape. In addition, black dots are added to the CAPTCHA image, as many Jawi characters share the same main body and differ only in the number of dots, as shown in Fig. 5. It is expected that this kind of background can confuse OCR software and prevent it from recognizing characters. Specifically, 7 dashed sine waves and 20 square dots are generated on the image as a background. The sine waves are generated at a fixed coordinate, while the square dots are generated at random coordinates on the image.

Then, these obstacle patterns (1 or 2) are added to the image.

For pattern 1, black circles are used to hide different characters in Jawi and Latin words. This pattern was designed to avoid hiding the same character in both words, as shown in Fig. 10 (a). Since an answer text of type (2) is randomly generated string, each character in the answer has to be shown in one of the two lines to solve the problem. Then we introduced the method shown below and it

Latin script written from right to left

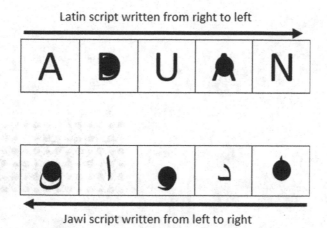

Jawi script written from left to right

Fig. 11. Placement of obstacle circles in pattern 1

was used for both type (1) and type (2) words in this experiment. First, each word's width is measured and then divided by the number of characters present in the word to obtain the average character width. Then, using the coordinates of the text position and the character's average width, black circles are added as shown in Fig. 11. Because this pattern depends on the word length, the text generation for type 1 only uses words that have the same number of characters in both Jawi and Latin scripts.

For pattern 2, black circles and squares are used to hide the characters in the image, as shown in Fig. 10 (b). This pattern implementation is more straightforward than that for pattern 1, as the black circles and squares are placed at fixed coordinates.

5   Usability Evaluation

This section describes a usability evaluation experiment of the proposed method and the results of the experiment.

5.1   Experimental System and Data

The experimental system was built using the HTML, CSS, and PHP programming languages. A screenshot of the start screen of the system is shown in Fig. 12 (a). MySQL was used as the database to organize and store the experiment's data.

The evaluation system was designed to display generated CAPTCHA images to the user. The user then entered an answer, either in Latin or Jawi script, into a text box and submitted it by clicking the "Submit" button (Fig. 12 (b)). The system then determined whether the answer was correct or incorrect by comparison with data in the database. The system was also designed to measure

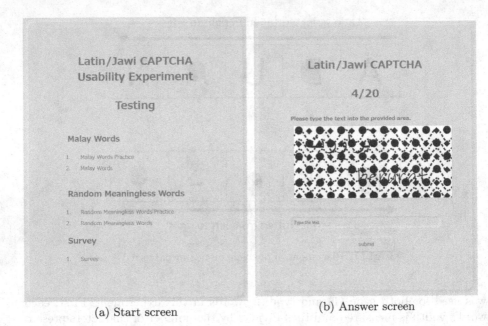

(a) Start screen   (b) Answer screen

Fig. 12. Screenshots of the experimental system

Table 3. CAPTCHA samples for experiment

Type	Pattern 1	Pattern 2
Malay words	10 images	10 images
Meaningless words	10 images	10 images

the time taken for the user to solve the CAPTCHA. Finally, all the data were retained in the database for further investigation.

20 Malay words and 20 random meaningless Latin/Jawi words with a length of four to eight characters were prepared for the experiments (Table 3). The text images and obstacle lines/figures were generated using the HTML canvas element via Javascript.

5.2   Purpose and Conditions

The experiments were divided into two parts, experiment 1 and experiment 2. Experiment 1 was conducted to check the users' accuracy in reading a character string written in only one script, whether Jawi or Latin. Since some characters are hidden by obstacle figures, it is supposed to be difficult to recognise correct answers. Experiment 2, which was the most important part of the experiment, was conducted to estimate the users' accuracy in reading the generated character strings presented in both scripts together. Though some characters are hidden

Table 4. Results of usability evaluation experiment 1

Metric	MW				RMW			
	P_1		P_2		P_1		P_2	
	Latin	Jawi	Latin	Jawi	Latin	Jawi	Latin	Jawi
Average time	7.5 s	17.9 s	7.0 s	14.8 s	12.0 s	27.3 s	10.0 s	21.2 s
Accuracy rate	91.4%	37.1%	85.7%	54.3%	68.6%	8.6%	65.7%	20.0%

Note: MW = Malay word, RMW = random meaningless word, P_1 = pattern 1, and P_2 = pattern 2.

by obstacle figures, it is expected that users can obtain the correct answer by combining the two fragmented strings.

There was a total of 7 participants for experiment 1 and a total of 13 participants for experiment 2. Participants for this experiment were all able to read Jawi script and speak Malay. The Malaysian co-author recruited overseas students whom he knew well for the experiment. They were all native-speakers of Malay language, could read and speak plain Japanese, and cooperated with the experiment earnestly without rewards. The number of the participants were quite small, but we could not hire unknown persons nor people who were not familiar with Malay language in order to ensure the reliability of the experiment.

The CAPTCHA images used for both experiments were generated using the scheme described in Sect. 4, with two obstacle patterns (1 and 2) and two types of strings (Malay words and random meaningless words). The CAPTCHA image samples are summarized in Table 3.

In the usability study, we measured the following two outcome metrics:

Time taken: The time (in seconds) elapsed between when the CAPTCHA image was shown to the user and when the "Submit" button was clicked.

Accuracy: The degree of conformity and correctness of typing the presented CAPTCHA.

Both experiments were carried out according to the following procedure. First, the general procedure was explained to each participant before starting the experiment. After that, participants completed a practice section to verify understanding of the whole experiment process. Then, the main experiment began, starting with Malay words and followed by random meaningless words.

During the experiments, participants were asked to recognize and type the words displayed on the screen into the text box and submit their answer by clicking on the "Submit" button. The system recorded the submitted answers and the time taken to solve the CAPTCHA. Each participant was also asked to complete a short survey about their experience, as shown in Fig. 13 (The questions are written in Japanese).

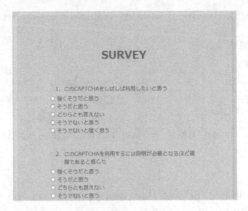

Fig. 13. A screenshot of the survey screen

Table 5. Results of usability evaluation experiment 2

Metric	MW		RMW	
	P_1	P_2	P_1	P_2
Average time	6.8 s	6.0 s	10.1 s	10.0 s
Accuracy rate	97.7%	96.9%	92.3%	88.5%

5.3   Results

For experiment 1, although we expected that it would be difficult to solve the proposed CAPTCHA by reading only one of the two scripts, the Latin strings could lead users to the correct answers in many cases. Table 4 shows the average time taken and accuracy data for each type of CAPTCHA pattern collected from experiment 1. The results for experiment 1 showed that the accuracy results for Latin strings were higher than 60.0% for all types of strings and patterns. The results were quite different from what we expected, that they would be lower when only one string could be read, and when combined with both strings, the accuracy rate would be better. The size of obstacle figures and the type of font used may be the reason for this result, and further studies should account for this to improve the proposed CAPTCHA. However, it was confirmed that the two obstacle patterns were both effective, according to the comments from many participants, especially for Jawi script.

For experiment 2, regardless of the type of string and pattern used for this experiment, the accuracy results seem promising for all types of strings and patterns. Table 5 shows the average time taken and accuracy data for each type of CAPTCHA pattern collected from experiment 2. The previous study in [10] stated that users' average time and accuracy rate in solving the current text-based CAPTCHA image are 9.8 s and 87.0%, respectively. Thus, the average time taken and accuracy rate to solve the proposed CAPTCHA is acceptable.

Table 6. Results of security evaluation

Program	MW		RMW	
	P_1	P_2	P_1	P_2
Tesseract OCR	0	0	0	0
ABBYY FineReader	0	0	0	0

Furthermore, the qualitative data collected in post-experiment surveys revealed interesting results. In experiment 1, many participants indicated that the dashed sine waves and black dots used as obstacles made the recognition of various Jawi characters difficult because Jawi characters have a curved shape, and many characters differ only in the number of dots. However, with the help of Latin characters in experiment 2, users could recognize the character correctly, as we expected.

6   Security Evaluation

This section describes a security evaluation experiment for the proposed method and the results of the experiment.

6.1   Purpose and Conditions

The purpose of security evaluation is to find how secure the method is against bot attacks. To prove that the proposed CAPTCHA is secure, a security experiment was conducted using two modern OCR software products: Tesseract and ABBYY FineReader. These software products can recognize both Latin and Arabic scripts but cannot recognize the six added Jawi characters. Tesseract has a Rumi dictionary, which includes Malay words spelled in Latin scripts. This dictionary supports the recognition of characters of Malay words spelled in Latin script.

The CAPTCHA samples for each type of string and each pattern were generated and tested, as shown in Table 3. For Malay word strings that used Latin script, the software was set to recognize Latin characters with the support of the Malay dictionary. In contrast, a random meaningless word written in Latin script was recognized without using the dictionary support. For words written in Jawi script, the software was set to recognize Arabic script because neither OCR program supports Jawi script. For this reason, the experiment was conducted to use only the 29 Jawi characters that correspond to Arabic characters (Table 1).

6.2   Results

The results for the word recognition accuracies for security evaluation are shown in Table 6. Both Tesseract OCR and ABBYY FineReader failed to detect words from the proposed CAPTCHA.

7   Discussion

It is supposed that the priming effect helps human beings recognize two partially hidden character strings. Priming is a phenomenon whereby exposure to one stimulus influences a response to a subsequent stimulus, without conscious guidance or intention [11–13]. Though two Malay strings are presented at the same time, because a user sees them one after the other, the stimulus of seeing the first one leads to recognition of the other string. It is expected that the same effect can be obtained with other languages that have the characteristic of digraphia, such as Japanese. The Japanese writing system uses several scripts, specifically hiragana, katakana, kanji (Chinese characters), and Latin (romaji). We can develop a similar CAPTCHA system for the Japanese language using hiragana and kanji. It is also expected that activation of the priming effect is not limited to two different scripts. For example, a CAPTCHA that pairs a picture and a word may work well. To improve the performance of CAPTCHAs, CAPTCHAs should be based on a more advanced human cognitive processing ability. Some studies proposed CAPTCHAs according to this approach: a CAPTCHA using the human ability to understand humor of four-panel cartoon [14], a CAPTCHA using phonetic punning riddles found on Knock-Knock Jokes [15], and a CAPTCHA using the ability of mathematical or logical thinking of human beings [16]. CAPTCHAs using priming are also expected to satisfy the condition.

To realize the proposed Jawi CHAPTCHA, some socio-political issues need to be addressed. For example, the Malaysian population includes people of Chinese and Indian descent who are not good at reading or writing Jawi script. To maintain fair access to web sites, an option to choose another CAPTCHA scheme should be provided. A CAPTCHA using Chinese characters or Tamil script together with Latin script may be a candidate for such an option. We have to devise a way to select words and obstacle patterns for the characters, but an excellent outcome similar to that with the proposed CAPTCHA is expected due to the effect of priming.

8   Conclusion

Because previous studies have shown that several existing Latin script-based CAPTCHAs have been defeated by bots, CAPTCHA's distortion intensity keeps increasing to strengthen its security, making CAPTCHA more difficult for a human to recognize.

This paper proposed a method using both Jawi and Latin scripts to generate CAPTCHA. By combining both scripts, we can keep the CAPTCHA easy for humans to recognize despite increasing the CAPTCHA distortion intensity to a level that cannot be recognized by a bot. To the best of our knowledge, this study is the first to combine Jawi script and Latin script as a CAPTCHA scheme.

The overall results show that the proposed CAPTCHA can be solved by human users with far better effectiveness compared with modern OCR software. The efficiency of solving the proposed CAPTCHA is also excellent.

In the future, we intend to modify the proposed method by increasing the distortion level for Latin script and reducing the distortion level for Jawi script to improve the performance of the CAPTCHA against bots while maintaining human usability with larger number of experimental subjects.

References

1. Ian, R.H.: Dale: digraphia. Int. J. Sociol. Lang. **26**, 5–13 (1980)
2. Lillibridge, M., Abadi, M., Bharat, K., Broder, A.: Method for Selectively Restricting Access to Computer Systems, United States Patent 6195698. Applied 1998 and Approved 2001
3. The CAPTCHA Project. Gimpy. http://www.captcha.net/captchas/gimpy. Accessed 6 Apr 2021
4. Mori, G., Malik, J.: Recognizing objects in adversarial clutter: breaking a visual CAPTCHA. In: IEEE Computer Society Conference on Computer Vision and Pattern Recognition, vol. 1, pp. 134–144 (2003)
5. Baird, H.S., Chew, M.: BaffleText: a human interactive proof. In: Proceedings of the 10th SPIE/IST Document Recognition and Retrieval Conference, Santa Clara, CA, pp. 305–316 (2003)
6. Shirali-Shahreza, M.H., Shirali-Shahreza, M.: Persian/Arabic Baffletext CAPTCHA. J. Univ. Comput. Sci. **12**(12), 1783–1796 (2006)
7. Shahreza, M.S.: Verifying spam SMS by Arabic CAPTCHA. In: 2nd IEEE International Conference on Information and Communication Technologies (ICTTA 2006), pp. 78–83 (2006)
8. Khan, B., Alghathbar, K., Khan, M.K., AlKelabi, A.M., Alajaji, A.: Cyber security using Arabic captcha scheme. Int. Arab J. Inf. Technol. **10**(1), 76–84 (2013)
9. Shirali-Shahreza, M.H., Shirali-Shahreza, M.: Advanced Nastaliq CAPTCHA. In: 7th IEEE International Conference on Cybernetic Intelligent Systems, London, pp. 1–3 (2008)
10. Bursztein, E., Bethard, S., Fabry, C., Mitchell, J.C., Jurafsky, D.: How good are humans at solving CAPTCHAs? A large scale evaluation. In: IEEE Symposium on Security and Privacy, Berkeley/Oakland, CA, pp. 399–413 (2010)
11. Meyer, D.E., Schvaneveldt, R.W.: Facilitation in recognizing pairs of words: evidence of a dependence between retrieval operations. J. Exp. Psychol. **90**(2), 399–413 (1971)
12. Collins, A.M., Loftus, E.F.: A spreading activation theory of semantic processing. Psychol. Rev. **82**(6), 407–428 (1975)
13. Tulving, E., Schacter, D.L., Stark, H.A.: Priming effects in word-fragment completion are independent of recognition memory. J. Exp. Psychol. Learn. Mem. Cogn. **8**(4), 336–342 (1982)
14. Kani, J., Suzuki, T., Uehara, A., Yamamoto, T., Nishigaki, M.: Four-panel Cartoon CAPTCHA. Inf. Process. Soc. Jpn. **54**(9), 2232–2243 (2013). (in Japanese)
15. Ximenes, P., dos Santos, A., Fernandez, M., Celestino, J.: A CAPTCHA in the text domain. In: Meersman, R., Tari, Z., Herrero, P. (eds.) OTM 2006. LNCS, vol. 4277, pp. 605–615. Springer, Heidelberg (2006). https://doi.org/10.1007/11915034_84
16. Kaur, R., Choudhary, P.: A novel CAPTCHA design approach using boolean algebra. Int. J. Comput. Appl. **127**(11), 13–18 (2015)

Post-Quantum Cryptography (1)

Solving the Problem of Blockwise Isomorphism of Polynomials with Circulant Matrices

Yasufumi Hashimoto[✉]

Department of Mathematical Science, University of the Ryukyus, Nishihara, Japan
hashimoto@math.u-ryukyu.ac.jp

Abstract. The problem of Isomorphism of Polynomials (IP problem) is
known to be important to study the security of multivariate public key
cryptosystems, one of major candidates of post-quantum cryptography,
against key recovery attacks. In these years, several schemes based on the
IP problem itself or its generalization have been proposed. At PQCrypto
2020, Santoso introduced a generalization of the problem of Isomorphism
of Polynomials, called the problem of Blockwise Isomorphism of Polynomials (BIP problem), and proposed a new Diffie-Hellman type encryption
scheme based on this problem with Circulant matrices (BIPC problem).
Quite recently, Ikematsu et al. proposed an attack called the linear stack
attack to recover an equivalent key of Santoso's encryption scheme. While
this attack reduced the security of the scheme, it does not contribute to
solve the BIPC problem itself. In the present paper, we describe how to
solve the BIPC problem directly by simplifying the BIPC problem due
to the conjugation property of circulant matrices. In fact, we experimentally solved the BIPC problem with the parameter, which has 256 bit
security by Santoso's security analysis and has 72.7 bit security against
the linear stack attack, by about 10 min.

Keywords: Isomorphism of polynomials · Blockwise isomorphism of
polynomials · Circulant matrix

1 Introduction

The problem of Isomorphism of Polynomials (IP problem) is the problem to
recover two affine maps S, T satisfying

$$\mathbf{g} = T \circ \mathbf{f} \circ S$$

for given polynomial maps $\mathbf{g}, \mathbf{f}$ over a finite field. This problem was introduced
by Patarin [8] and has been discussed mainly in the context of the security
analyses of multivariate public key cryptosystems, one of major candidates of
post-quantum cryptography [2,4,7], since the public key $\mathbf{g}$ of most such cryptosystems are generated by $\mathbf{g} = T \circ \mathbf{f} \circ S$ with a (not necessarily public) quadratic
map $\mathbf{f}$ inverted feasibly, and recovering S, T is enough to break the corresponding
schemes (e.g. [1,5]).

© Springer Nature Switzerland AG 2021
T. Nakanishi and R. Nojima (Eds.): IWSEC 2021, LNCS 12835, pp. 137–150, 2021.
https://doi.org/10.1007/978-3-030-85987-9_8

In these years, several schemes based on the IP problem or its generalization have been proposed. For example, Wang et al. [10] proposed a key exchange scheme and an encryption scheme based on the IP problem with S, T chosen in commutative rings of square matrices. While the commutativity for S, T was required for convenience of these schemes, it yields a vulnerability; in fact, it was broken by Chen et al. [3] since the numbers of unknowns of the IP problem in Wang's schemes is too small. Later, at PQCrypto 2020, Santoso [9] introduced a generalization of the IP problem, called the problem of Blockwise Isomorphism of Polynomials (BIP problem), and proposed a new Diffie-Hellman type encryption scheme based on the BIP problem with Circulant matrices (BIPC problem). It had been considered that the BIP problem was more difficult against analogues of known attacks on the original IP problem (see, e.g. [1]) and then it had been expected that Santoso's scheme was secure enough under suitable parameter selections. However, Ikematsu et al. [6] discovered that this scheme is less secure than expected against the linear stack attack, which is an attack to recover an equivalent key by studying a special version of sufficiently larger size BIPC problem than the original BIPC problem. Remark that, while this attack works to reduce the security of Santoso's scheme, it does not contribute to solve the BIPC problem itself.

In the present paper, we describe how to solve the BIPC problem directly. Since any circulant matrices can be diagonalized or block-diagonalized simultaneously, the BIPC problem can be simplified drastically after (block-) diagonalization. Our approach is quite effective; in fact, the BIPC problem with the parameter, which has 256 bit security by Santoso's security analysis and has 72.7 bit security against the linear stack attack, was experimentally solved by about 10 min.

2   Isomorphism of Polynomials

In this section, we describe the Isomorphism of Polynomials, the Blockwise Isomorphism of Polynomials and the encryption scheme proposed by Santoso [9].

2.1   Isomorphism of Polynomials

Let q be a power of prime and $\mathbf{F}_q$ a finite field of order q. For integers $n, m \geq 1$, denote by $\mathrm{MQ}(n, m)$ the set of m-tuples of homogeneous quadratic polynomials ${}^t(f_1(\mathbf{x})), \ldots, f_m(\mathbf{x}))$ of n variables $\mathbf{x} = {}^t(x_1, \ldots, x_n)$ over $\mathbf{F}_q$. We call that $\mathbf{f}, \mathbf{g} \in \mathrm{MQ}(n, m)$ are *isomorphic* if there exist two invertible linear maps $S : \mathbf{F}_q^n \to \mathbf{F}_q^n$, $T : \mathbf{F}_q^m \to \mathbf{F}_q^m$ such that

$$\mathbf{g} = T \circ \mathbf{f} \circ S, \tag{1}$$

i.e.

$$\begin{pmatrix} g_1(\mathbf{x}) \\ \vdots \\ g_m(\mathbf{x}) \end{pmatrix} = T \begin{pmatrix} f_1(S(\mathbf{x})) \\ \vdots \\ f_m(S(\mathbf{x})) \end{pmatrix},$$

where $\mathbf{f} = {}^t(f_1(\mathbf{x}), \ldots, f_m(\mathbf{x}))$ and $\mathbf{g} = {}^t(g_1(\mathbf{x}), \ldots, g_m(\mathbf{x}))$. The *problem of Isomorphism of Polynomials (IP problem)* is the problem to recover invertible linear maps $S : \mathbf{F}_q^n \to \mathbf{F}_q^n$, $T : \mathbf{F}_q^m \to \mathbf{F}_q^m$ satisfying (1) for given $\mathbf{f}, \mathbf{g} \in \mathrm{MQ}(n, m)$.

2.2   Blockwise Isomorphism of Polynomials

Santoso [9] introduce the blockwise isomorphism of polynomials as a generalization of isomorphism of polynomials.

For $n, m, k \geq 1$, let $\mathbf{f}, \mathbf{g} \in \mathrm{MQ}(n, mk)$ and divide $\mathbf{f}, \mathbf{g}$ by $\mathbf{f} = (\mathbf{f}_1, \ldots, \mathbf{f}_k)$, $\mathbf{g} = (\mathbf{g}_1, \ldots, \mathbf{g}_k)$ with $\mathbf{f}_1, \ldots, \mathbf{f}_k, \mathbf{g}_1, \ldots, \mathbf{g}_k \in \mathrm{MQ}(n, m)$. We call that $\mathbf{f}$ and $\mathbf{g}$ are *blockwise isomorphic* if there exist invertible or zero linear maps $S_1, \ldots, S_k : \mathbf{F}_q^n \to \mathbf{F}_q^n$, $T_1, \ldots, T_k : \mathbf{F}_q^m \to \mathbf{F}_q^m$ satisfying

$$\mathbf{g}_u = \sum_{1 \leq l \leq k} T_l \circ \mathbf{f}_{\overline{u+l-1}} \circ S_l \tag{2}$$

for $1 \leq u \leq k$, where $1 \leq \overline{a} \leq k$ is given by $\overline{a} \equiv a \bmod k$, i.e.

$$\mathbf{g}_1 = T_1 \circ \mathbf{f}_1 \circ S_1 + T_2 \circ \mathbf{f}_2 \circ S_2 + \cdots + T_k \circ \mathbf{f}_k \circ S_k,$$
$$\mathbf{g}_2 = T_1 \circ \mathbf{f}_2 \circ S_1 + T_2 \circ \mathbf{f}_3 \circ S_2 + \cdots + T_k \circ \mathbf{f}_1 \circ S_k,$$
$$\vdots$$
$$\mathbf{g}_k = T_1 \circ \mathbf{f}_k \circ S_1 + T_2 \circ \mathbf{f}_1 \circ S_2 + \cdots + T_k \circ \mathbf{f}_{k-1} \circ S_k.$$

Denote by $\mathbf{g} = \psi \boxtimes \mathbf{f}$ for $\mathbf{g}, \mathbf{f} \in \mathrm{MQ}(n, mk)$ and $\psi = (S_1, \ldots, S_k, T_1, \ldots, T_k)$, if (2) holds. Santoso [9] defined the following two problems: One is the *problem of blockwise isomorphism of polynomials (BIP problem)*. It is the problem to recover $\psi = (S_1, \ldots, S_k, T_1, \ldots, T_k)$ with $\mathbf{g} = \psi \boxtimes \mathbf{f}$ for given $\mathbf{f}, \mathbf{g} \in \mathrm{MQ}(n, mk)$. The other is *Computational Diffie-Hellman for BIP (CDH-BIP) problem* to recover $\mathbf{g}^{(2)} \in \mathrm{MQ}(n, mk)$ such that $\mathbf{g}^{(2)} = \psi \boxtimes \mathbf{f}^{(2)}$ for given $\mathbf{g}^{(1)}, \mathbf{f}^{(1)}, \mathbf{f}^{(2)} \in \mathrm{MQ}(n, mk)$ satisfying $\mathbf{g}^{(1)} = \psi \boxtimes \mathbf{f}^{(1)}$ for some $\psi = (S_1, \ldots, S_k, T_1, \ldots, T_k)$. It is clear that, if one can solve the BIP problem, he/she can solve also the CDH-BIP problem.

2.3   Blockwise Isomorphism of Polynomials with Circulant Matrices

Santoso's encryption scheme is based on BIP problem with circulant matrices.

Let I_n be the $n \times n$ identity matrix and $J_n := \begin{pmatrix} & & 1 \\ & \cdot^{\cdot^{\cdot}} & \\ 1 & & \end{pmatrix}$ the n-cyclic permutation matrix. A *circulant matrix* is a linear sum of $I_n, J_n, J_n^2, \ldots, J_n^{n-1}$, i.e. a circulant matrix is given by

$$a_0 I_n + a_1 J_n + a_2 J_n^2 + \cdots + a_{n-1} J_n^{n-1} = \begin{pmatrix} a_0 & a_1 & \cdots & a_{n-2} & a_{n-1} \\ a_{n-1} & a_0 & \cdot^{\cdot^{\cdot}} & a_{n-3} & a_{n-2} \\ \vdots & & \ddots & \ddots & \vdots \\ a_2 & a_3 & \cdot^{\cdot^{\cdot}} & a_0 & a_1 \\ a_1 & a_2 & \cdots & a_{n-1} & a_0 \end{pmatrix}$$

for some $a_0, \ldots, a_{n-1} \in \mathbf{F}_q$. Note that the multiplication between circulant matrices is commutative. Let $\mathrm{Circ}(n)$ be the set of $n \times n$ circulant matrices and

$$\Psi(n, m, k) := \left\{ (S_1, \ldots, S_k, T_1, \ldots, T_k) \,\middle|\, \begin{array}{l} S_1, \ldots, S_k \in \mathrm{Circ}(n), \\ T_1, \ldots, T_k \in \mathrm{Circ}(m), \end{array} \text{ invertible or } 0 \right\}.$$

Note that $\psi, \varphi \in \Psi(n, m, k)$ is commutative for the operator $\boxplus$, i.e. it holds

$$\varphi \boxplus (\psi \boxplus \mathbf{f}) = \psi \boxplus (\varphi \boxplus \mathbf{f})$$

for any $\mathbf{f} \in \mathrm{MQ}(n, mk)$ (see Lemma 1 in [9]).

2.4   Encryption Scheme Based on BIP with Circulant Matrices

Santoso's El-Gammal-like encryption scheme is constructed as follows [9].

Parameters. $n, m, k \geq 1$: integers.

Secret key. $\Upsilon \in \Psi(n, m, k)$.

Public key. $\mathbf{f}, \mathbf{g} \in \mathrm{MQ}(n, mk)$ with $\mathbf{g} = \Upsilon \boxplus \mathbf{f}$.

Encryption. For a plain-text $\nu \in \mathrm{MQ}(n, mk)$, choose $\psi \in \Psi(n, m, k)$ randomly and compute

$$\mathbf{c}_0 := \psi \boxplus \mathbf{g}, \qquad \mathbf{c}_1 := \nu + \psi \boxplus \mathbf{f}.$$

The cipher-text is $(\mathbf{c}_0, \mathbf{c}_1) \in \mathrm{MQ}(n, mk)^2$.

Decryption. The plain-text is recovered by

$$\nu = \mathbf{c}_1 - \Upsilon \boxplus \mathbf{c}_0.$$

Since the operations by ψ and Υ are commutative, the cipher-text can be decrypted correctly.

2.5   Previous Security Analyses and Parameter Selections

We first note that, if the BIP problem with Circulant matrices can be solved, the secret key Υ can be recovered from the public key $(\mathbf{f}, \mathbf{g})$. We also note that this scheme was proven to be secure against one way under chosen plain-text attack (OW-CPA) under the assumption that the CDH-BIP problem with Circulant matrices is hard [9]. Furthermore, it was pointed out that this scheme can be transformed into an IND-CCA secure encryption scheme by an approach of Fujisaki-Okamoto-like transformation. Until now, the following three attacks have been studied by Santoso himself [9] and Ikematsu et al. [6].

(1) Attack by Bouillagust et al. Bouillagust et al. [1] proposed an attack to solve the IP problem to recover S, T with $\mathbf{g} = T \circ \mathbf{f} \circ S$. The basic approach is to find a pair of vectors $\mathbf{a}, \mathbf{b} \in \mathbf{F}_q^n$ such that $\bar{S}^{-1}\mathbf{a} = \mathbf{b}$, where $\bar{S}$ is an linear map with $\mathbf{g} = \bar{T} \circ \mathbf{f} \circ \bar{S}$. Santoso [9] generalized this attack on the BIP problem with circulant matrices and estimated the complexity by $O\left(k^2 n^5 2^{n \frac{k}{k+1}}\right)$.

(2) The Gröbner basis attack. This is to solve the BIP problem with circulant matrices directly. The unknown parameters in $S_1, \ldots, S_k \in \mathrm{Circ}(n)$ and $T_1, \ldots, T_k \in \mathrm{Circ}(m)$ are $nk + mk$ in the total, and the coefficients of the quadratic polynomials in $\mathbf{g} = \Upsilon \boxtimes \mathbf{f}$ give a system of $\frac{1}{2}n(n+1)mk$ equations over $\mathbf{F}_q$, which are linear for the unknowns in T's, quadratic for the unknowns in S's and cubic in the total. The Gröbner basis attack is to solve such a system equations directly by the Gröbner basis algorithm. Santoso [9] estimated its complexity by $O\left(2^{k \log(nm)/4m}\right)$.

(3) Linear stack attack. The BIP problem with Circulant matrices is the problem to recover $\Upsilon \in \Psi(n, m, k)$ such that $\mathbf{g} = \Upsilon \boxtimes \mathbf{f}$. The linear stack attack [6] is not an attack to solve it but to recover $\Upsilon_1, \ldots, \Upsilon_N \in \Psi(n, m, k)$ such that $\mathbf{g} = \sum_{1 \le i \le N} \Upsilon_i \boxtimes \mathbf{f}$ for sufficiently large N. It is easy to check that, if such $\Upsilon_1, \ldots, \Upsilon_N$ are recovered, the cipher-text $(\mathbf{c}_0, \mathbf{c}_1)$ is decrypted by $\nu = \mathbf{c}_1 - \sum_{1 \le i \le N} \Upsilon_i \boxtimes \mathbf{c}_0$. The attacker chooses S's in $\Upsilon_1, \ldots, \Upsilon_N$ randomly to linearize the equations required in this attack, and reduce the problem of recovering $\Upsilon_1, \ldots, \Upsilon_N$ to that of recovering T's in $\Upsilon_1, \ldots, \Upsilon_N$. Although the existence of such T's is quite heuristic, the authors in [6] claimed that it is applicable if $N \gg \frac{1}{2}n^2 m$ and its complexity is $O\left(n^6 m^3 k^3\right)$.

Table 1 shows the parameter selections by Santoso [9] based on the security analyses (1), (2) above, and their security against the attack (3).

Table 1. Parameter selections of Santoso's encryption scheme and previous security analyses

(n, m, k)	(1), (2) [9]	(3) [6]
(84,2,140)	128 bit	62.7 bit
(206,2,236)	256 bit	72.7 bit
(16,2,205)	128 bit	50.0 bit
(16,2,410)	256 bit	53.0 bit

3 Solving the BIP Problem with Circulant Matrices

In this section, we describe how to solve the BIP problem with circulant matrices. Before it, we study the conjugations of circulant matrices to simplify the problem.

3.1 Conjugations of Circulant Matrices

Let $n \ge 1$ be an integer and p the characteristic of $\mathbf{F}_q$. When $p \nmid n$, denote by θ_n an n-th root of 1, i.e. θ_n is an element of $\mathbf{F}_q$ or its extension field satisfying $\theta_n^n = 1$ and $\theta_n^l \ne 1$ for $1 \le l \le n - 1$. Define the $n \times n$ matrix Θ_n by

$$\Theta_n := \left(\theta_n^{(i-1)(j-1)}\right)_{1 \le i,j \le n} = \begin{pmatrix} 1 & 1 & \cdots & 1 \\ 1 & \theta_n & \cdots & \theta_n^{n-1} \\ \vdots & \vdots & \ddots & \vdots \\ 1 & \theta_n^{n-1} & \cdots & \theta_n^{(n-1)^2} \end{pmatrix}.$$

We also define the $n \times n$ matrices B_n by the lower triangular matrix whose (i,j)-entries $(i \geq j)$ is $\binom{i-1}{j-1}$, and L_n by the upper triangular matrix whose $(i, i+1)$-entries are 1 $(1 \leq i \leq n)$ and others are 0, i.e.

$$B_n := \begin{pmatrix} 1 & & & & \\ 1 & 1 & & & \\ 1 & 2 & 1 & & \\ \vdots & \vdots & \vdots & \ddots & \\ 1 & n-1 & \binom{n-1}{2} & \cdots & 1 \end{pmatrix}, \quad L_n := \begin{pmatrix} 0 & 1 & & & \\ & 0 & 1 & & \\ & & \ddots & \ddots & \\ & & & 0 & 1 \\ & & & & 0 \end{pmatrix}.$$

Note that

$$L_n^2 := \begin{pmatrix} 0 & 0 & 1 & & \\ & \ddots & \ddots & \ddots & \\ & & 0 & 0 & 1 \\ & & & 0 & 0 \\ & & & & 0 \end{pmatrix}, \quad \cdots, \quad L_n^{n-1} := \begin{pmatrix} & & 1 \\ & & \\ & & \\ & & \end{pmatrix}$$

and $L_n^n = 0_n$. We also denote by

$$\mathrm{diag}(a_1, \ldots, a_n) := \begin{pmatrix} a_1 & & \\ & \ddots & \\ & & a_n \end{pmatrix}, \quad A \otimes B := \begin{pmatrix} a_{11}B & \cdots & a_{1n}B \\ \vdots & \ddots & \vdots \\ a_{n1}B & \cdots & a_{nn}B \end{pmatrix}$$

for scalars or matrices $a_1, \ldots, a_n$ and matrices $A = (a_{ij})_{i,j}$, B. Then the following lemmas hold.

Lemma 1. *Let n be an integer factored by $n = n_1 p^r$ with $p \nmid n_1$, $r \geq 0$. Then there exists an $n \times n$ permutation matrix K_n such that*

$$Q_n^{-1} J_n Q_n = \mathrm{diag}\left(1, \theta_{n_1}, \ldots, \theta_{n_1}^{n_1-1}\right) \otimes (I_{p^r} + L_{p^r}),$$

where $Q_n := K_n \cdot (\Theta_{n_1} \otimes B_{p^r})$.

Proof. (i) When $p \nmid n$ $(r = 0)$, the (i,j)-entries of $J_n \Theta_n$ and $\Theta_n \mathrm{diag}(1, \theta_n, \ldots, \theta_n^{n-1})$ are $\theta_n^{i(j-1)}$ for $1 \leq i \leq n-1$ and 1 for $i = n$ since $\theta_n^n = 1$. Then it holds

$$J_n \Theta_n = \Theta_n \mathrm{diag}\left(1, \theta_n, \ldots, \theta_n^{n-1}\right).$$

(ii) When $n = p^r$ $(n_1 = 1)$, the (i,j)-entries of $J_n B_n$ are $\binom{i}{j-1}$ for $j-1 \leq i \leq n-1$, 1 for $(i,j) = (n,1)$ and 0 otherwise. On the other hand, the (i,j)-entries of $B_n (I_n + L_n)$ is 1 for $j = 1$, $\binom{i-1}{j-2} + \binom{i-1}{j-1} = \binom{i}{j-1}$ for $2 \leq j \leq i+1$ and 0 otherwise. Since $\binom{p^r}{j-1} = 0$ in $\mathbf{F}_q$ for $2 \leq j \leq p^r$, we have

$$J_{p^r} B_{p^r} = B_{p^r} (I_{p^r} + L_{p^r}).$$

(iii) We finally study the general case. Since both J_n and $J_{n_1} \otimes J_{p^r}$ are of n-cyclic, these are conjugate to each other in the symmetric group $\mathfrak{S}_n$, i.e. there exists an $n \times n$ permutation matrix K_n such that

$$K_n^{-1} J_n K_n = J_{n_1} \otimes J_{p^r}.$$

We thus obtain

$$\begin{aligned}
Q_n^{-1} J_n Q_n &= (\Theta_{n_1} \otimes B_{p^r})^{-1} (J_{n_1} \otimes J_{p^r}) (\Theta_{n_1} \otimes B_{p^r}) \\
&= (\Theta_{n_1}^{-1} J_{n_1} \Theta_{n_1}) \otimes (B_{p^r}^{-1} J_{p^r} B_{p^r}) \\
&= \mathrm{diag}\left(1, \theta_{n_1}, \ldots, \theta_{n_1}^{n_1-1}\right) \otimes (I_{p^r} + L_{p^r}).
\end{aligned}$$

$\square$

Lemma 2. *Let n be an integer factored by $n = n_1 p^r$ with $p \nmid n_1$, $r \geq 0$ and $Q_n := K_n(\Theta_{n_1} \otimes B_{p^r})$. Then, for $S \in \mathrm{Circ}(n)$, there exist $s_{11}, \ldots, s_{1p^r} \in \mathbf{F}_q$ and $s_{21}, \ldots, s_{2p^r}, s_{31}, \ldots, \ldots, s_{n_1 p^r} \in \mathbf{F}_q(\theta_{n_1})$ such that*

$$Q_n^{-1} S Q_n = \mathrm{diag}\Big(s_{11} I_{p^r} + s_{12} L_{p^r} + \cdots + s_{1p^r} L_{p^r}^{p^r-1},$$

$$s_{21} I_{p^r} + s_{22} L_{p^r} + \cdots + s_{2p^r} L_{p^r}^{p^r-1},$$

$$\cdots, s_{n_1 1} I_{p^r} + s_{n_1 2} L_{p^r} + \cdots + s_{n_1 p^r} L_{p^r}^{p^r-1}\Big)$$

$$= \mathrm{diag}\left(\left(\begin{pmatrix} s_{11} & s_{12} & \cdots & s_{1p^r} \\ & \ddots & \ddots & \vdots \\ & & s_{11} & s_{12} \\ & & & s_{11} \end{pmatrix}\right), \ldots, \begin{pmatrix} s_{n_1 1} & s_{n_1 2} & \cdots & s_{n_1 p^r} \\ & \ddots & \ddots & \vdots \\ & & s_{n_1 1} & s_{n_1 2} \\ & & & s_{n_1 1} \end{pmatrix}\right)\right).$$

Proof. A circulant matrix S is written by

$$S = a_1 I_n + a_2 J_n + \cdots + a_n J_n^{n-1}$$

for some $a_1, \ldots, a_n \in \mathbf{F}_q$. Then, according to Lemma 1, we have

$$\begin{aligned}
Q_n^{-1} S Q_n =& a_1 I_n + a_2 \cdot \mathrm{diag}\left(1, \theta_{n_1}, \ldots, \theta_{n_1}^{n_1-1}\right) \otimes (I_{p^r} + L_{p^r}) \\
&+ a_3 \cdot \mathrm{diag}\left(1, \theta_{n_1}^2, \ldots, \theta_{n_1}^{2(n_1-1)}\right) \otimes (I_{p^r} + L_{p^r})^2 \\
&+ \cdots + a_n \cdot \mathrm{diag}\left(1, \theta_{n_1}^{n-1}, \ldots, \theta_{n_1}^{(n_1-1)(n-1)}\right) \otimes (I_{p^r} + L_{p^r})^{n-1}.
\end{aligned}$$

Since $L_{p^r}^{p^r} = 0$, the matrices $I_{p^r}, I_{p^r} + L_{p^r}, (I_{p^r} + L_{p^r})^2, \ldots, (I_{p^r} + L_{p^r})^{n-1}$ are linear sums of $I_{p^r}, L_{p^r}, L_{p^r}^2, \ldots, L_{p^r}^{p^r-1}$. Thus we can easily check that Lemma 2 holds.

$\square$

3.2 Equivalent Keys

Let $n, m \geq 1$ be integers factored by $n = n_1 p^a$, $m = m_1 p^b$ with $a, b \geq 0$, $p \nmid n_1, m_1$. For $1 \leq l \leq k$, define

$$\bar{f}_l := Q_m^{-1} \circ f_l \circ Q_n, \qquad \bar{g}_l := Q_m^{-1} \circ g_l \circ Q_n,$$
$$\bar{S}_l := Q_n^{-1} \circ S_l \circ Q_n, \qquad \bar{T}_l := Q_m^{-1} \circ T_l \circ Q_m.$$

Note that, due to Lemma 2, we see that $\bar{S}_l, \bar{T}_l$ are written by

$$
\bar{S}_l = \text{diag}\left(\begin{pmatrix} s_{11}^{(l)} & s_{12}^{(l)} & \cdots & s_{1p^a}^{(l)} \\ & \ddots & \ddots & \vdots \\ & & s_{11}^{(l)} & s_{12}^{(l)} \\ & & & s_{11}^{(l)} \end{pmatrix}, \ldots, \begin{pmatrix} s_{n_1 1}^{(l)} & s_{n_1 2}^{(l)} & \cdots & s_{n_1 p^a}^{(l)} \\ & \ddots & \ddots & \vdots \\ & & s_{n_1 1}^{(l)} & s_{n_1 2}^{(l)} \\ & & & s_{n_1 1}^{(l)} \end{pmatrix} \right),
$$
$$
\bar{T}_l = \text{diag}\left(\begin{pmatrix} t_{11}^{(l)} & t_{12}^{(l)} & \cdots & t_{1p^b}^{(l)} \\ & \ddots & \ddots & \vdots \\ & & t_{11}^{(l)} & t_{12}^{(l)} \\ & & & t_{11}^{(l)} \end{pmatrix}, \ldots, \begin{pmatrix} t_{m_1 1}^{(l)} & t_{m_1 2}^{(l)} & \cdots & t_{m_1 p^b}^{(l)} \\ & \ddots & \ddots & \vdots \\ & & t_{m_1 1}^{(l)} & t_{m_1 2}^{(l)} \\ & & & t_{m_1 1}^{(l)} \end{pmatrix} \right).
\tag{3}
$$

Since

$$Q_m^{-1} \circ (T_l \circ f_u \circ S_l) \circ Q_n = (Q_m^{-1} \circ T_l \circ Q_m) \circ (Q_m^{-1} \circ f_u \circ Q_n) \circ (Q_n^{-1} \circ S_l \circ Q_n)$$
$$= \bar{T}_l \circ \bar{f}_u \circ \bar{S}_l,$$

we have

$$\bar{g}_u = \sum_{1 \leq l \leq k} \bar{T}_l \circ \bar{f}_{\overline{u+l-1}} \circ \bar{S}_l. \tag{4}$$

This means that the BIP problem with Circulant matrices is reduced to the problem recovering $\bar{S}_1, \ldots, \bar{S}_k, \bar{T}_1, \ldots, \bar{T}_k$ in the forms (3) for given $\bar{f}$ and $\bar{g}$. Furthermore, since

$$(\alpha^2 \bar{T}_l) \circ \bar{f}_u \circ (\alpha^{-1} \bar{S}_l) = \bar{T}_l \circ \bar{f}_u \circ \bar{S}_l$$

for any $\alpha \in \mathbf{F}_q \backslash \{0\}$ and

$$0 \circ \bar{f}_u \circ \bar{S}_l = \bar{T}_l \circ \bar{f}_u \circ 0 = 0,$$

we can take $s_{11}^{(l)} = 1$ for $1 \leq l \leq k$ without loss generality. In the next subsection, we describe how to recover other parameters in $\bar{S}_l$ and $\bar{T}_l$.

3.3 Solving the BIP Problem with Circulant Matrices

For $1 \leq u \leq k$ and $1 \leq v \leq m$, denote by

$$\bar{f}_u(\mathbf{x}) = {}^t(\bar{f}_{u1}(\mathbf{x}), \ldots, \bar{f}_{um}(\mathbf{x})), \qquad \bar{f}_{uv}(\mathbf{x}) = \sum_{1 \leq i \leq j \leq n} \alpha_{ij}^{(uv)} x_i x_j,$$

$$\bar{g}_u(\mathbf{x}) = {}^t(\bar{g}_{u1}(\mathbf{x}), \ldots, \bar{g}_{um}(\mathbf{x})), \qquad \bar{g}_{uv}(\mathbf{x}) = \sum_{1 \leq i \leq j \leq n} \beta_{ij}^{(uv)} x_i x_j.$$

We can recover $\bar{S}_l$ and $\bar{T}_l$ as follows.

Recovering $\bar{T}_l$. We first study the polynomial $\bar{g}_{um}(\mathbf{x})$ for $1 \leq u \leq k$. Since $\bar{S}_l, \bar{T}_l$ are as in (3) and $s_{11}^{(l)} = 1$, we see that the coefficient of x_1^2 of $\bar{g}_{um}(\mathbf{x})$ in (4) gives the equation

$$\beta_{11}^{(um)} = \sum_{1 \leq l \leq k} \alpha_{11}^{\overline{(u+l-1,m)}} t_{m_1 1}^{(l)}. \tag{5}$$

Since the set of the Eq. (5) for $1 \leq u \leq k$ is a system of k linear equations of k variables $t_{m_1 1}^{(1)}, \ldots, t_{m_1 1}^{(k)}$, one can recover $t_{m_1 1}^{(1)}, \ldots, t_{m_1 1}^{(k)}$ by solving this system.

Next, the coefficient of x_1^2 of $\bar{g}_{u,m-1}(\mathbf{x})$ in (4) gives

$$\beta_{11}^{(u,m-1)} = \sum_{1 \leq l \leq k} \left(\alpha_{11}^{\overline{(u+l-1,m-1)}} t_{m_1 1}^{(l)} + \alpha_{11}^{\overline{(u+l-1,m)}} t_{m_1 2}^{(l)} \right).$$

Since $t_{m_1 1}^{(1)}, \ldots, t_{m_1 1}^{(k)}$ are already given, one can recover $t_{m_1 2}^{(1)}, \ldots, t_{m_1 2}^{(k)}$ by solving the equations above for $1 \leq u \leq k$. Other parameters in $\bar{T}$ can be recovered by the equations derived from the coefficients of x_1^2 in $\bar{g}_{u,m-2}(\mathbf{x}), \ldots, \bar{g}_{u,1}(\mathbf{x})$ recursively.

Recovering $\bar{S}_l$. Study $\bar{g}_{um}(\mathbf{x})$ again. Since $s_{11}^{(l)} = 1$, the coefficient of $x_1 x_2$ of $\bar{g}_{um}(\mathbf{x})$ gives the equation

$$\beta_{12}^{(um)} = \sum_{1 \leq l \leq k} \left(2\alpha_{11}^{\overline{(u+l-1,m)}} s_{12}^{(l)} + \alpha_{12}^{\overline{(u+l-1,m)}} \right) t_{m_1 1}^{(l)}. \tag{6}$$

Since $t_{m_1 1}^{(l)}$ is already given, one can recover $s_{12}^{(l)}$ by solving the system of k linear equations of k variables $s_{12}^{(1)}, \ldots, s_{12}^{(k)}$ derived from the equation (6) for $1 \leq u \leq k$.

Next, the coefficient of $x_1 x_3$ in $\bar{g}_{um}(\mathbf{x})$ is

$$\beta_{13}^{(um)} = \sum_{1 \leq l \leq k} \left(2\alpha_{11}^{\overline{(u+l-1,m)}} s_{13}^{(l)} + \alpha_{12}^{\overline{(u+l-1,m)}} s_{12}^{(l)} + \alpha_{13}^{\overline{(u+l-1,m)}} \right) t_{m_1 1}^{(l)}. \tag{7}$$

Since $t_{m_1 1}^{(l)}, s_{12}^{(l)}$ are already given, $s_{13}^{(l)}$ can be recovered from the equation above for $1 \leq l \leq k$. It is easy to see that one can recover other parameters $s_{14}^{(l)}, \ldots, s_{n_1 p^a}^{(l)}$ by the systems of linear equations derived from the coefficients of $x_1 x_4, \ldots, x_1 x_n$ in $\bar{g}_{um}(\mathbf{x})$ recursively.

Remark 1. If q is even, $s_{12}^{(l)}$ does not appear in the equation (6) and then $s_{12}^{(l)}$ cannot be recovered from the coefficient of $x_1 x_2$. On the other hand, the equation (7) derived from the coefficient of $x_1 x_3$ includes $s_{12}^{(l)}$ but not $s_{13}^{(l)}$. This means that $s_{12}^{(l)}$ is recovered from the coefficient of $x_1 x_3$ instead of $x_1 x_2$. Similarly, we can easily check that $s_{13}^{(l)}, \ldots, s_{1p^a}^{(l)}$ are recovered from the coefficients of $x_1 x_4, \ldots, x_1 x_{p^a}, x_2 x_{p^a}$ respectively instead of $x_1 x_3, \ldots, x_1 x_{p^a}$.

Remark 2. There is a possibility that the parameters in $(\bar{S}_1, \ldots, \bar{S}_k, \bar{T}_1, \ldots, \bar{T}_k)$ are not fixed uniquely from the linear equations derived from the coefficients of x_1^2 in $\bar{g}_{u1}(\mathbf{x}), \ldots, \bar{g}_{um}(\mathbf{x})$ and of $x_1 x_2, \ldots, x_1 x_n$ in $\bar{g}_{um}(\mathbf{x})$. If such a case occurs, recover the parameters in $(\bar{S}_1, \ldots, \bar{S}_k, \bar{T}_1, \ldots, \bar{T}_k)$ as possible, study the coefficients not used to recover such parameters and state the equations for the parameters not fixed uniquely yet. Then one can expect to fix them uniquely. For example, the coefficients of x_2^2 includes $s_{12}^{(l)}$ quadratically and then it helps to fix $s_{12}^{(l)}$.

Complexity. It is easy to see that, to compute $\bar{f}, \bar{g}$ totally, we need (at most) $O(n^3 m k)$ arithmetics on $\mathbf{F}_q(\theta_{n_1}, \theta_{m_1})$. However, we use only the coefficients of $x_1^2, x_1 x_2, \ldots, x_1 x_n$ and then the number of required arithmetics in this process is $O(n^2 m k)$. Furthermore, since the attacker solves the systems of k linear equations of k variables in m times for recovering $\bar{T}_l$ and in n times for recovering $\bar{S}_l$, the number of required arithmetics for recovering them is (at most) $O(k^3(n+m))$ over $\mathbf{F}_q(\theta_{n_1}, \theta_{m_1})$. We thus conclude that the total number of arithmetics on $\mathbf{F}_q(\theta_{n_1}, \theta_{m_1})$ of our approach is estimated by $O(kn^2 m + k^3 n + k^3 m)$.

Table 2. Parameter selections of the proposed encryption scheme

(n, m, k)	(1), (2) [9]	(3)	[6]	Our attack
(42,2,102)	—	—	4.8 days	9.9 s
(84,2,140)	128 bit	62.7 bit	—	34.5 s
(206,2,236)	256 bit	72.7 bit	—	619 s
(16,2,205)	128 bit	50.0 bit	10 h	15.5 s
(16,2,410)	256 bit	53.0 bit	—	150 s

Experiments. We implemented our attack on Magma ver.2.24-5 under macOS Mojave ver.10.14.16, Intel Core i5, 3 GHz. In Table 2, we describe the experimental results of our attack for the parameters selected in [9] and studied in [6]. This shows that our approach is quite effective to solve the BIP problem with Circulant matrices.

4   Conclusion

The present paper shows that solving the BIP problem with Circulant matrices directly is not difficult since the secret maps $S_1, \ldots, S_k, T_1, \ldots, T_k$ are known to be circulant. We consider that, while the original BIP problem is difficult enough at the present time, it will be solved similarly if the secret maps to be recovered have some kind of "special" structures. We thus consider that, to build a secure scheme based on the BIP problem, one should choose the secret maps as randomly as possible.

Acknowledgments. The author would like to thank the anonymous reviewers for reading the previous draft of this paper carefully and giving helpful comments. He was supported by JST CREST no. JPMJCR14D6 and JSPS Grant-in-Aid for Scientific Research (C) no. 17K05181.

A   Toy Example

We now demonstrate how to solve the BIPC problem for $(q, n, m, k) = (2, 6, 2, 2)$ as a toy example. The public keys $\mathbf{f} = (\mathbf{f}_1, \mathbf{f}_2) = (f_{11}, f_{12}, f_{21}, f_{22})$ and $\mathbf{g} = (\mathbf{g}_1, \mathbf{g}_2) = (g_{11}, g_{12}, g_{21}, g_{22})$ are as follows.

$$
f_{11}(\mathbf{x}) = {}^t\mathbf{x} \begin{pmatrix} 1 & 0 & 0 & 0 & 0 & 0 \\ & 1 & 0 & 0 & 0 & 1 \\ & & 0 & 0 & 0 & 0 \\ & & & 0 & 0 & 0 \\ & & & & 1 & 1 \\ & & & & & 0 \end{pmatrix} \mathbf{x}, \qquad
f_{12}(\mathbf{x}) = {}^t\mathbf{x} \begin{pmatrix} 0 & 0 & 0 & 1 & 1 & 1 \\ & 1 & 1 & 0 & 0 & 1 \\ & & 1 & 0 & 1 & 1 \\ & & & 0 & 0 & 0 \\ & & & & 1 & 1 \\ & & & & & 1 \end{pmatrix} \mathbf{x},
$$

$$
f_{21}(\mathbf{x}) = {}^t\mathbf{x} \begin{pmatrix} 0 & 0 & 1 & 1 & 1 & 0 \\ & 1 & 1 & 1 & 1 & 1 \\ & & 0 & 1 & 0 & 0 \\ & & & 0 & 1 & 1 \\ & & & & 0 & 0 \\ & & & & & 1 \end{pmatrix} \mathbf{x}, \qquad
f_{22}(\mathbf{x}) = {}^t\mathbf{x} \begin{pmatrix} 1 & 1 & 1 & 0 & 1 & 0 \\ & 0 & 0 & 1 & 1 & 1 \\ & & 0 & 1 & 0 & 0 \\ & & & 0 & 0 & 1 \\ & & & & 1 & 1 \\ & & & & & 1 \end{pmatrix} \mathbf{x},
$$

$$
g_{11}(\mathbf{x}) = {}^t\mathbf{x} \begin{pmatrix} 1 & 1 & 1 & 1 & 0 & 1 \\ & 0 & 1 & 0 & 0 & 0 \\ & & 1 & 0 & 0 & 1 \\ & & & 0 & 1 & 1 \\ & & & & 1 & 0 \\ & & & & & 1 \end{pmatrix} \mathbf{x}, \qquad
g_{12}(\mathbf{x}) = {}^t\mathbf{x} \begin{pmatrix} 1 & 0 & 0 & 0 & 0 & 0 \\ & 1 & 0 & 0 & 0 & 0 \\ & & 0 & 1 & 1 & 1 \\ & & & 1 & 1 & 1 \\ & & & & 0 & 0 \\ & & & & & 1 \end{pmatrix} \mathbf{x},
$$

$$
g_{21}(\mathbf{x}) = {}^t\mathbf{x} \begin{pmatrix} 1 & 0 & 1 & 0 & 0 & 0 \\ & 0 & 1 & 1 & 0 & 1 \\ & & 1 & 1 & 0 & 1 \\ & & & 0 & 0 & 1 \\ & & & & 1 & 0 \\ & & & & & 1 \end{pmatrix} \mathbf{x}, \qquad
g_{22}(\mathbf{x}) = {}^t\mathbf{x} \begin{pmatrix} 0 & 1 & 1 & 0 & 0 & 0 \\ & 1 & 1 & 1 & 1 & 0 \\ & & 0 & 0 & 0 & 1 \\ & & & 0 & 0 & 0 \\ & & & & 1 & 0 \\ & & & & & 0 \end{pmatrix} \mathbf{x},
$$

where the coefficient matrices are expressed by triangular matrices. Our aim is to recover $S_1, S_2 \in \mathrm{Circ}(6)$, $T_1, T_2 \in \mathrm{Circ}(2)$ satisfying

$$
\begin{aligned}
\begin{pmatrix} g_{11}(\mathbf{x}) \\ g_{12}(\mathbf{x}) \end{pmatrix} &= T_1 \begin{pmatrix} f_{11}(S_1(\mathbf{x})) \\ f_{12}(S_1(\mathbf{x})) \end{pmatrix} + T_2 \begin{pmatrix} f_{21}(S_2(\mathbf{x})) \\ f_{22}(S_2(\mathbf{x})) \end{pmatrix}, \\
\begin{pmatrix} g_{21}(\mathbf{x}) \\ g_{22}(\mathbf{x}) \end{pmatrix} &= T_1 \begin{pmatrix} f_{21}(S_1(\mathbf{x})) \\ f_{22}(S_1(\mathbf{x})) \end{pmatrix} + T_2 \begin{pmatrix} f_{11}(S_2(\mathbf{x})) \\ f_{12}(S_2(\mathbf{x})) \end{pmatrix}.
\end{aligned}
\tag{8}
$$

Let θ be a cubic root of 1 (i.e. $\theta^2 + \theta + 1 = 0$),

$$
K_6 := \begin{pmatrix} 1 & & & & \\ & & 1 & & \\ & & & & 1 \\ & 1 & & & \\ & & & 1 & \\ & & & & & 1 \end{pmatrix}, \qquad
\Theta_3 := \begin{pmatrix} 1 & 1 & 1 \\ 1 & \theta & \theta^2 \\ 1 & \theta^2 & \theta \end{pmatrix}, \qquad
Q_2 = B_2 := \begin{pmatrix} 1 & 0 \\ 1 & 1 \end{pmatrix}
$$

and $Q_6 := K_6 (\Theta_3 \otimes B_2)$. Then $\bar{\mathbf{f}}_1 = Q_2^{-1} \circ \mathbf{f}_1 \circ Q_6 = (\bar{f}_{11}, \bar{f}_{12})$, $\bar{\mathbf{f}}_2 = Q_2^{-1} \circ \mathbf{f}_2 \circ Q_6 = (\bar{f}_{21}, \bar{f}_{22})$, $\bar{\mathbf{g}}_1 = Q_2^{-1} \circ \mathbf{g}_1 \circ Q_6 = (\bar{g}_{11}, \bar{g}_{12})$, $\bar{\mathbf{g}}_2 = Q_2^{-1} \circ \mathbf{g}_2 \circ Q_6 = (\bar{g}_{21}, \bar{g}_{22})$ are as follows.

$$\bar{f}_{11}(\mathbf{x}) = {}^t\mathbf{x}\begin{pmatrix} 1 & 1 & 0 & \theta & 0 & \theta^2 \\ 0 & \theta^2 & 1 & \theta & 1 \\ & 1 & 1 & 0 & \theta \\ & & \theta & \theta^2 & 1 \\ & & & 1 & 1 \\ & & & & \theta^2 \end{pmatrix}\mathbf{x}, \qquad \bar{f}_{12}(\mathbf{x}) = {}^t\mathbf{x}\begin{pmatrix} 1 & 0 & 1 & \theta^2 & 1 & \theta \\ 1 & 0 & 0 & 0 & 0 \\ & \theta^2 & 1 & 0 & 0 \\ & & 0 & 0 & 0 \\ & & & \theta & 1 \\ & & & & \theta^2 \end{pmatrix}\mathbf{x},$$

$$\bar{f}_{21}(\mathbf{x}) = {}^t\mathbf{x}\begin{pmatrix} 0 & 1 & 1 & 1 & 1 & 1 \\ 1 & 1 & 0 & 1 & 0 \\ & \theta & \theta & 0 & \theta \\ & & 1 & \theta^2 & 1 \\ & & & \theta^2 & \theta^2 \\ & & & & 1 \end{pmatrix}\mathbf{x}, \qquad \bar{f}_{22}(\mathbf{x}) = {}^t\mathbf{x}\begin{pmatrix} 0 & 1 & 0 & \theta^2 & 0 & \theta \\ 1 & \theta^2 & 0 & 0 & 0 \\ & 0 & 1 & 0 & 1 \\ & & \theta^2 & 1 & 0 \\ & & & 0 & 1 \\ & & & & \theta 1 \end{pmatrix}\mathbf{x},$$

$$\bar{g}_{11}(\mathbf{x}) = {}^t\mathbf{x}\begin{pmatrix} 0 & 0 & \theta^2 & \theta & \theta & \theta^2 \\ 0 & 1 & \theta & 1 & \theta^2 \\ & \theta^2 & 1 & 0 & 0 \\ & & 1 & 0 & 1 \\ & & & \theta & 1 \\ & & & & 1 \end{pmatrix}\mathbf{x}, \qquad \bar{g}_{12}(\mathbf{x}) = {}^t\mathbf{x}\begin{pmatrix} 1 & 1 & 1 & \theta^2 & 1 & \theta \\ 0 & 1 & 0 & 1 & 0 \\ & \theta^2 & \theta & 0 & 1 \\ & & \theta & 1 & 0 \\ & & & \theta & \theta^2 \\ & & & & \theta^2 \end{pmatrix}\mathbf{x},$$

$$\bar{g}_{21}(\mathbf{x}) = {}^t\mathbf{x}\begin{pmatrix} 1 & 1 & 1 & 0 & 0 & 1 \\ 0 & \theta^2 & 0 & \theta & 0 \\ & 1 & 0 & 0 & 1 \\ & & \theta & 1 & 1 \\ & & & 1 & 0 \\ & & & & \theta^2 \end{pmatrix}\mathbf{x}, \qquad \bar{g}_{22}(\mathbf{x}) = {}^t\mathbf{x}\begin{pmatrix} 1 & 1 & \theta & \theta & \theta^2 & \theta^2 \\ 0 & \theta^2 & \theta^2 & \theta & \theta \\ & \theta & \theta & 0 & 1 \\ & & \theta^2 & 1 & 0 \\ & & & \theta^2 & \theta^2 \\ & & & & \theta \end{pmatrix}\mathbf{x}.$$

Then the problem of recovering S_1, S_2, T_1, T_2 with (8) is reduced to the problem of recovering $\bar{S}_1 = Q_6^{-1} \circ S_1 \circ Q_6$, $\bar{S}_2 = Q_6^{-1} \circ S_2 \circ Q_6$, $\bar{T}_1 = Q_2^{-1} \circ T_1 \circ Q_2$, $\bar{T}_2 = Q_2^{-1} \circ T_2 \circ Q_2$ satisfying

$$\begin{pmatrix} \bar{g}_{11}(\mathbf{x}) \\ \bar{g}_{12}(\mathbf{x}) \end{pmatrix} = \bar{T}_1 \begin{pmatrix} \bar{f}_{11}(\bar{S}_1(\mathbf{x})) \\ \bar{f}_{12}(\bar{S}_1(\mathbf{x})) \end{pmatrix} + \bar{T}_2 \begin{pmatrix} \bar{f}_{21}(\bar{S}_2(\mathbf{x})) \\ \bar{f}_{22}(\bar{S}_2(\mathbf{x})) \end{pmatrix},$$

$$\begin{pmatrix} \bar{g}_{21}(\mathbf{x}) \\ \bar{g}_{22}(\mathbf{x}) \end{pmatrix} = \bar{T}_1 \begin{pmatrix} \bar{f}_{21}(\bar{S}_1(\mathbf{x})) \\ \bar{f}_{22}(\bar{S}_1(\mathbf{x})) \end{pmatrix} + \bar{T}_2 \begin{pmatrix} \bar{f}_{11}(\bar{S}_2(\mathbf{x})) \\ \bar{f}_{12}(\bar{S}_2(\mathbf{x})) \end{pmatrix}. \tag{9}$$

Due to Lemma 2, we see that $\bar{S}_1, \bar{S}_2, \bar{T}_1, \bar{T}_2$ are written by

$$\bar{S}_1 = \mathrm{diag}\left(\begin{pmatrix} 1 & s_{12}^{(1)} \\ & 1 \end{pmatrix}, \begin{pmatrix} s_{21}^{(1)} & s_{22}^{(1)} \\ & s_{21}^{(1)} \end{pmatrix}, \begin{pmatrix} s_{31}^{(1)} & s_{32}^{(1)} \\ & s_{31}^{(1)} \end{pmatrix} \right),$$

$$\bar{S}_2 = \mathrm{diag}\left(\begin{pmatrix} 1 & s_{12}^{(2)} \\ & 1 \end{pmatrix}, \begin{pmatrix} s_{21}^{(2)} & s_{22}^{(2)} \\ & s_{21}^{(2)} \end{pmatrix}, \begin{pmatrix} s_{31}^{(2)} & s_{32}^{(2)} \\ & s_{31}^{(2)} \end{pmatrix} \right),$$

$$\bar{T}_1 = \begin{pmatrix} t_1^{(1)} & t_2^{(1)} \\ & t_1^{(1)} \end{pmatrix}, \qquad \bar{T}_2 = \begin{pmatrix} t_1^{(2)} & t_2^{(2)} \\ & t_1^{(2)} \end{pmatrix}.$$

We first study the coefficients of x_1^2 in $\bar{g}_{12}, \bar{g}_{22}$. The relation (9) gives the following equations.

$$\begin{pmatrix} 1 \\ 1 \end{pmatrix} = \begin{pmatrix} 1 & 0 \\ 0 & 1 \end{pmatrix} \begin{pmatrix} t_1^{(1)} \\ t_1^{(2)} \end{pmatrix}.$$

We then get $t_1^{(1)} = 1$ and $t_1^{(2)} = 1$. Similarly, from the coefficients of x_1^2 in $\bar{g}_{11}, \bar{g}_{21}$, we have

$$\begin{pmatrix} 0 \\ 1 \end{pmatrix} = \begin{pmatrix} 1 & 0 \\ 0 & 1 \end{pmatrix} \begin{pmatrix} t_2^{(1)} \\ t_2^{(2)} \end{pmatrix} + \begin{pmatrix} 1 & 0 \\ 0 & 1 \end{pmatrix} \begin{pmatrix} t_1^{(1)} \\ t_1^{(2)} \end{pmatrix}.$$

From the equations above, we obtain $t_2^{(1)} = 1$ and $t_2^{(2)} = 0$. We thus have T_1, T_2 as

$$T_1 = Q_2 \begin{pmatrix} 1 & 1 \\ & 1 \end{pmatrix} Q_2^{-1} = J_2, \qquad T_2 = Q_2 \begin{pmatrix} 1 & \\ & 1 \end{pmatrix} Q_2^{-1} = I_2. \tag{10}$$

Next, we study the coefficient of $x_1 x_3$ in $\bar{g}_{12}, \bar{g}_{22}$. From (9) and (10), we have

$$\begin{pmatrix} 1 \\ \theta \end{pmatrix} = \begin{pmatrix} 1 & 0 \\ 0 & 1 \end{pmatrix} \begin{pmatrix} s_{21}^{(1)} \\ s_{21}^{(2)} \end{pmatrix}.$$

We then get $s_{21}^{(1)} = 1$, $s_{21}^{(2)} = \theta$. Similarly, the following equations are derived from the coefficients of $x_1 x_4$, $x_1 x_5$ and $x_1 x_6$ in $\bar{g}_{12}, \bar{g}_{22}$.

$$\begin{pmatrix} \theta^2 \\ \theta \end{pmatrix} = \begin{pmatrix} \theta^2 & \theta^2 \\ \theta^2 & \theta^2 \end{pmatrix} \begin{pmatrix} s_{21}^{(1)} \\ s_{21}^{(2)} \end{pmatrix} + \begin{pmatrix} 1 & 0 \\ 0 & 1 \end{pmatrix} \begin{pmatrix} s_{22}^{(1)} \\ s_{22}^{(2)} \end{pmatrix},$$

$$\begin{pmatrix} 1 \\ \theta^2 \end{pmatrix} = \begin{pmatrix} 1 & 0 \\ 0 & 1 \end{pmatrix} \begin{pmatrix} s_{31}^{(1)} \\ s_{31}^{(2)} \end{pmatrix},$$

$$\begin{pmatrix} \theta \\ \theta^2 \end{pmatrix} = \begin{pmatrix} \theta & \theta \\ \theta & \theta \end{pmatrix} \begin{pmatrix} s_{31}^{(1)} \\ s_{31}^{(2)} \end{pmatrix} + \begin{pmatrix} 1 & 0 \\ 0 & 1 \end{pmatrix} \begin{pmatrix} s_{32}^{(1)} \\ s_{32}^{(2)} \end{pmatrix}.$$

Then we get $s_{22}^{(1)} = 1$, $s_{22}^{(2)} = 0$, $s_{31}^{(1)} = 1$, $s_{31}^{(2)} = \theta^2$, $s_{32}^{(1)} = 1$ and $s_{32}^{(2)} = 0$. To recover the remaining parameters $s_{12}^{(1)}, s_{12}^{(2)}$, we study the coefficients of x_2^2 in $\bar{g}_{12}, \bar{g}_{22}$ and have

$$0 = s_{12}^{(1)2} + s_{12}^{(2)}, \qquad 0 = s_{12}^{(1)} + s_{12}^{(2)2}.$$

Since $s_{12}^{(1)}, s_{12}^{(2)} \in \mathbf{F}_2$, the solution of the equations above is $s_{12}^{(1)} = s_{12}^{(2)}$. To fix $s_{12}^{(1)}, s_{12}^{(2)}$ uniquely, we further study the coefficients $x_2 x_3$ in $\bar{g}_{12}, \bar{g}_{22}$ and have the equations

$$1 = s_{12}^{(1)} s_{21}^{(1)} + \theta^2 s_{21}^{(2)}, \qquad \theta^2 = \theta^2 s_{21}^{(1)} + s_{12}^{(2)} s_{21}^{(2)}.$$

Since $s_{21}^{(1)} = 1$, $s_{21}^{(2)} = \theta$, we obtain $s_{12}^{(1)} = s_{12}^{(2)} = 0$. We thus conclude that

$$S_1 = Q_6 \cdot \mathrm{diag}\left(\begin{pmatrix} 1 & 0 \\ & 1 \end{pmatrix}, \begin{pmatrix} 1 & 1 \\ & 1 \end{pmatrix}, \begin{pmatrix} 1 & 1 \\ & 1 \end{pmatrix} \right) Q_6^{-1} = I_6 + J_6 + J_6^2 + J_6^4 + J_6^5,$$

$$S_2 = Q_6 \cdot \mathrm{diag}\left(\begin{pmatrix} 1 & 0 \\ & 1 \end{pmatrix}, \begin{pmatrix} \theta & 0 \\ & \theta \end{pmatrix}, \begin{pmatrix} \theta^2 & 0 \\ & \theta^2 \end{pmatrix} \right) Q_6^{-1} = J_6^4.$$

$$\tag{11}$$

The solution of this BIPC problem is given by (10) and (11). $\square$

References

1. Bouillaguet, C., Faugére, J.-C., Fouque, P.-A., Perret, L.: Isomorphism of Polynomials: New Results (2009). http://citeseerx.ist.psu.edu/viewdoc/download;jsessionid=20524EF65899B40DEE494630B0574F53?doi=10.1.1.156. 9570&rep=rep1&type=pdf
2. Casanova, A., Faugère, J.C., Macario-Rat, G., Patarin, J., Perret, L., Ryckeghem, J.: GeMSS: A Great Multivariate Short Signature. https://www-polsys.lip6.fr/Links/NIST/GeMSS.html
3. Chen, J., Tan, C.H., Li, X.: Practical cryptanalysis of a public key cryptosystem based on the morphism of polynomials problem. Tsinghua Sci. Technol. **23**, 671–679 (2018)
4. Chen, M.-S., et al.: Rainbow Signature. https://www.pqcrainbow.org/
5. Faugère, J.-C., Perret, L.: Polynomial equivalence problems: algorithmic and theoretical aspects. In: Vaudenay, S. (ed.) EUROCRYPT 2006. LNCS, vol. 4004, pp. 30–47. Springer, Heidelberg (2006). https://doi.org/10.1007/11761679_3
6. Ikematsu, Y., Nakamura, S., Santoso, B., Yasuda, T.: Security Analysis on an El-Gamal-like Multivariate Encryption Scheme Based on Isomorphism of Polynomials (2021). https://eprint.iacr.org/2021/169
7. NIST, Post-Quantum Cryptography, Round 3 submissions. https://csrc.nist.gov/projects/post-quantum-cryptography/round-3-submissions
8. Patarin, J.: Hidden fields equations (HFE) and isomorphisms of polynomials (IP): two new families of asymmetric algorithms. In: Maurer, U. (ed.) EUROCRYPT 1996. LNCS, vol. 1070, pp. 33–48. Springer, Heidelberg (1996). https://doi.org/10.1007/3-540-68339-9_4
9. Santoso, B.: Generalization of isomorphism of polynomials with two secrets and its application to public key encryption. In: Ding, J., Tillich, J.-P. (eds.) PQCrypto 2020. LNCS, vol. 12100, pp. 340–359. Springer, Cham (2020). https://doi.org/10.1007/978-3-030-44223-1_19
10. Wang, H., Zhang, H., Mao, S., Wu, W., Zhang, L.: New public-key cryptosystem based on the morphism of polynomials problem. Tsinghua Sci. Technol. **21**, 302–311 (2016)

FFT Program Generation for Ring LWE-Based Cryptography

Masahiro Masuda[✉] and Yukiyoshi Kameyama

University of Tsukuba, Tsukuba, Japan
masa@logic.cs.tsukuba.ac.jp, kameyama@acm.org

Abstract. Fast Fourier Transform (FFT) enables an efficient implementation of polynomial multiplication, which is at the core of any cryptographic constructions based on the hardness of the Ring learning with errors (RLWE) problem. Existing implementations of FFT for RLWE-based cryptography rely on hand-written assembly code for performance, making it difficult to understand, maintain, and extend for new architectures.

We present a novel framework to implement FFT for RLWE-based cryptography, based on a principled program-generation approach. We start with a high-level, abstract definition of an FFT program, and generate low-level code by interpreting high-level primitives and delegating low-level details to an architecture-specific module. Since low-level details concerning modular arithmetic and vectorization are separated from high-level logic, we can easily generate both AVX2- and AVX512-optimized low-level code from the same high-level description of the FFT program. Our generated code is highly competitive compared to expert-written assembly code: For AVX2 (and AVX512, resp) it runs 1.13x (and 1.39x, resp) faster than the AVX2-optimized assembly implementation in the NewHope key-exchange protocol.

1 Introduction

Lattice cryptography has been receiving increasing attention due to its widely believed resistance against quantum attacks while still allowing efficient implementations of important cryptographic protocols. A construction based on the hardness of Ring learning with errors (RLWE) problem [15] is particularly efficient, thanks to its algebraic structure. At the heart of all RLWE-based protocols is the multiplication of polynomials, whose coefficients are taken from integers modulo a certain prime. It is well known that the polynomial multiplication can be computed in $O(n \log n)$ time via Fast Fourier transform (FFT)[1] [6]. Since the computational cost for polynomial multiplication is dominated by FFT, there have been many work on optimized FFT implementations for RLWE-based cryptography [2,7,14,19].

However, we believe that existing implementations have some shortcomings, in terms of ease of understanding, maintainability, and reusability:

---

[1] FFT in which coefficients are taken from a finite field is often called NTT (Number Theoretic Transform), but we use the term FFT throughout this paper.

© Springer Nature Switzerland AG 2021
T. Nakanishi and R. Nojima (Eds.): IWSEC 2021, LNCS 12835, pp. 151–171, 2021.
https://doi.org/10.1007/978-3-030-85987-9_9

- They support either only one set of security parameters, or multiple sets of parameters by duplicating code. Duplication makes implementation and maintenance of code tedious and error prone.
- Precomputed constants are hardcoded in the source code. In the context of RLWE, the size and modulus parameters are always fixed, making it possible to precompute all the twiddle factors in an FFT implementation. In addition, it is common to pre-multiply the twiddle factors by other factors arising from Montgomery multiplication or negative wrapped convolution [2,14]. Since each implementation does precomputation in slightly different ways and often comes without explanation of how those constants are computed, it is difficult to precisely understand what each constant represents.
- Most likely, an optimized implementation is written in assembly. This makes it extremely difficult to understand the code and be confident in its correctness. Moreover, since an assembly program is hardcoded using a particular SIMD instruction set (e.g. AVX2), porting the implementation to new architectures requires writing another assembly program from scratch. We are not aware of any FFT implementation that leverages AVX512 instructions in the context of RLWE-based cryptography.

We address these problems by a principled program-generation approach. By adopting program-generation techniques developed in programming language research, it is possible to give an abstract description of an FFT algorithm, from which we can generate highly optimized low-level code for various instruction sets, including AVX2 and AVX512. Moreover, the program-generation approach makes it easy to combine optimization techniques developed in different studies, which allows us to generate more efficient code than the assembly program in NewHope[2], one of the recent FFT implementations.

Our framework is written in a functional programming language OCaml [12]. A user would write an FFT program in a specialized domain-specific language (DSL) embedded in OCaml. The DSL program can be evaluated in multiple ways. For example, we can generate an equivalent C program, including those optimized with SIMD intrinsics. Since our vectorized DSL programs are written in a way that is generic with respect to the vector length and not tied to a particular SIMD instruction set, we can easily generate both AVX2 and AVX512 code from the same high-level DSL program. Supporting a new ISA, such as ARM Neon, should be straightforward: We only need to provide the mapping between vectorized primitives in our DSL, such as `add`, `mullo` and `mulhi`, and corresponding SIMD instructions in the target ISA.

We demonstrate our framework by implementing vectorized FFT code for RLWE-based cryptography. We start with the reference implementation of NewHope [2], and incorporate an optimization technique introduced in Kyber FFT [19]. We demonstrate that our high-level framework allows expressing the low-level optimization in Kyber FFT that was the key to its performance. On a recent laptop with Intel Ice Lake CPU, our AVX2- and AVX512-optimized FFT are 1.13x and 1.39x faster than the NewHope AVX2 implementation respectively.

---

[2] https://github.com/newhopecrypto/newhope-usenix.

We would like to stress that obtaining one FFT implementation that outperforms an existing one is not our primary goal. Our goal is to build a program-generation framework which can be applied to *any* existing FFT algorithm, to improve code maintainability, reusability and modularity. To show the effectiveness of our framework, we chose to start with the NewHope reference implementation because of its relative simplicity compared to the state of the art implementation of Kyber [19], and compare and report our results with respect to the optimized counterpart.

2 Related Work

There is already a large body of work on optimizing FFT or polynomial multiplication as a whole for RLWE-based cryptography [1,2,7,13,14,18,19]. Here, we focus on the most relevant work whose optimized AVX2 implementations are publicly available [2,14,19].

The NewHope key-exchange protocol [2] introduced two implementations of FFT for RLWE-based key exchange: One is a reference C implementation, and the other is an AVX2 assembly implementation. The optimized one uses double-precision floating-point instructions to compute modular reduction by $a \bmod q = a - \left\lfloor a\frac{1}{q} \right\rfloor q$, since they found that the floating-point implementation is faster than their integer one when vectorization is applied.

The current fastest FFT implementation is the one used in Kyber KEM [4], described in detail in [19]. For the first time, it outperformed the floating-point implementation in NewHope using only integer SIMD instructions. It also incorporates the optimization used in [13,14] to remove the bit reversal step.

All of the existing work above implement FFT in assembly using AVX2 instructions. To the best of our knowledge, there is no AVX512 implementation, even though an AVX512-capable CPU is becoming widely available. This work presents an AVX512 implementation of FFT for RLWE-based cryptography. In particular, we generate both AVX2 and AVX512 code from the same FFT program.

3 Background

3.1 FFT in the RLWE Context

FFT is an $O(n\log n)$ time algorithm to compute Discrete Fourier Transform (DFT) for an input of size n. Given an input $a = (a_0, a_1, ..., a_{n-1}), a_i \in \mathbb{Z}_q$, its DFT $y = (y_0, y_1, ..., y_{n-1}), y_i \in \mathbb{Z}_q$ is defined by the following equation [6]:

$$y_k = \sum_{j=0}^{n-1} a_j\omega_n^{kj}$$

ω_n is the nth primitive root of unity modulo q, satisfying $\omega_n^n \equiv 1 \pmod{q}$. All addition and multiplication are done in $\bmod\, q$. In the context of RLWE-based cryptography, n is a power of two, and q must satisfy $q \equiv 1 \pmod{2n}$ for FFT to be valid[3]. For example, NewHope uses $n = 1024$ and $q = 12289$ [2], while Kyber uses $n = 256$ and $q = 7681$ [4].

All existing implementations of FFT in the context of RLWE-based cryptography compute FFT in an iterative, bottom-up manner [2,14,19]. Moreover, the output is computed in-place. Although in-place FFT generally requires a bit reverse step to make an output in the standard order, recent work showed a way to eliminate it entirely for the two transforms (forward and inverse FFT) used in polynomial multiplication [13,18]. However, for simplicity we do not implement the full polynomial multiplication and focus on a standard, self-contained forward FFT which uses the bit reverse step at the beginning.

Algorithm 1 shows the pseudocode of our FFT implementation. It uses the standard Cooley-Tukey algorithm [6] and all powers of ω_n, called twiddle factors, are precomputed and stored in an array. Each iteration of the outermost loop is often called *stage*, and the number of stages is $\log_2 n$. The innermost loop performs the Cooly-Tukey butterfly with modular arithmetic.

Algorithm 1. The pseudocode for the bottom-up, in-place FFT

```
1: procedure FFT
       Input: a = (a_0, a_1, ..., a_{n-1}) ∈ Z_q^n, precomputed constants table Ω ∈ Z_q^n
2: Output: y = DFT(a), in standard order
3:     bit-reverse(A)
4:     for (s = 1; s <= log_2(n); s = s + 1) do
5:         m = 2^s
6:         o = 2^{s-1} - 1
7:         for (k = 0; k < m; k = k + m) do
8:             for (j = 0; j < m/2; j = j + 1) do
9:                 u = a[k + j]
10:                t = (a[k + j + m/2] · Ω[o + j]) mod q
11:                a[k + j] = (u + t) mod q
12:                a[k + j + m/2] = (u - t) mod q
13:            end for
14:        end for
15:    end for
16: end procedure
```

An efficient implementation of the modular reduction is the most important component in FFT for RLWE-based cryptography. We follow existing work for the choice of algorithms [2,19]: We use Barrett reduction [3] to reduce the results of addition and subtraction, and Montgomery reduction [16] for multiplication.

3.2   Tagless-Final Style

The tagless-final style is an approach to embed a domain-specific language (DSL) in a general-purpose host language in a type-safe way. The DSL, embedded in our

---

[3] The requirement on q comes from the fact that in general multiplying two polynomials of degree n requires a transform of size $2n$. However, thanks to the property of negative wrapped convolution, it is enough to do a transform of size n in practice.

host language OCaml, allows high-level descriptions of algorithms independent of security parameters and target architectures. Here, we give its brief introduction to understand the rest of the paper. For more details, see [5,9].

The following OCaml program `vector_add` adds two vectors of integers:

```
let vector_add arr1 arr2 =
  for i = 0 to (n - 1) do
    arr1.(i) = arr1.(i) + arr2.(i)
  done
```

The variable n is the length of arrays and assumed to be a compile-time constant. The operator `.(i)` indexes array elements in OCaml.

In the tagless-final style, a DSL program is implemented using language primitives offered by a *signature*. In particular, the signature declares language primitives as abstract functions, whose implementations are yet to be defined.

It is easy to rewrite the above program into an abstract one; we only have to replace all constants and language syntactic constructs by new, abstract functions, for instance, `for` by `for_`, the integer constant 0 by `zero` or `int_ 0`, and `arr1.(i)` by `arr_get arr1 i`. We can write an abstract program equivalent to `vector_add` above in our DSL as follows:

```
func2 "vector_add" arg_ty arg_ty (fun arr1 arr2 ->
    (for_ zero (int_ n) (int_ 1) (fun i ->
        arr_set arr1 i (D.add (arr_get arr1 i) (arr_get arr2 i)))))
```

This is the signature of our C-like language:[4]

```
module type C_lang = sig
  type 'a expr type 'a stmt ...
  val zero : int expr
  val int_ : int -> int expr
  val for_ : int expr -> int expr -> int expr -> (int expr -> unit stmt)
           -> unit stmt
  val arr_set : int array expr -> int expr -> int expr -> unit stmt
  ...
end
```

The tagless-final style lets us implement the signature in various ways, and different implementations give different meanings to the same program.

For example, if we use MetaOCaml [10] for the implementation, the meaning of the above program would become "OCaml code that adds two arrays". The brackets `.<>.` surround the value representation of the generated OCaml code.

---

[4] It is similar to "interface" in other languages.

```
.<let vector_add arg0 arg1 =
  let num_iter_3 = (1024 - 0) / 1 in
  for i_4 = 0 to num_iter_3 - 1 do
    let index_5 = 0 + (1 * i_4) in
    let t_7 = Array.get arg0 index_5 in
    let t_6 = Array.get arg1 index_5 in
    Array.set arg0 index_5 ((t_7 + t_6) mod 12289)
  done in vector_add>.
```

Similarly, we can also obtain equivalent C code, using a different interpretation of the same program. Under this interpretation, a string representation of the C program is generated.

```
void vector_add(uint16_t *arg0, uint16_t *arg1) {
  for (int v_8 = 0; v_8 < ((1024 - 0) / 16); v_8 += 1) {
    arg0[v_8] = arg0[v_8] + arg1[v_8];
  }
}
```

Program transformation can be done by redefining the meaning of language primitives. For example, in this program the meaning of language primitives are overwritten to be a "vectorization mode" by Vectorize module (see Appendix A for more details). Under this new interpretation, integer addition, array access and assignment are reinterpreted as vector addition, vector load and store, respectively. The loop bound and index are also recalculated accordingly.

```
func2 "vector_add" (fun arr1 arr2->
  let open Vectorize(AVX2_UInt16(D)) in
  for_ (int_ 0) (int_ 1024) (int_ 1) (fun i ->
    arr_set arr1 i (D.add (arr_get arr1 i) (arr_get arr2 i))))
```

Here is the generated code using the AVX2 instruction set. By changing one line, we can also generate AVX512 code, without modifying the DSL program.

```
void vector_add(uint16_t *arg0, uint16_t *arg1) {
  for (int v_8 = 0; v_8 < ((1024 - 0) / 16); v_8 += 1) {
    _mm256_storeu_si256(
        (__m256i *)(arg0 + (0 + (v_8 * 16))),
        _mm256_add_epi16(
            _mm256_loadu_si256((__m256i *)(arg0 + (0 + (v_8 * 16)))),
            _mm256_loadu_si256((__m256i *)(arg1 + (0 + (v_8 * 16))))));
  }
}
```

This shows the strength of the tagless-final style: From a high-level, abstract description of a program, we can generate a variety of low-level code. Although the example above is trivial, the same technique can be applied to vectorize the innermost loop of FFT, as we will see next.

4 The Proposed Approach

We propose to apply program-generation techniques to an FFT implementation using the tagless-final style, to obtain highly optimized FFT implementations tailored to various security parameters and target architectures. The tagless-final style allows us to give different interpretations of the same abstract program, which makes it possible to generate both AVX2 and AVX512 vectorized FFT code from a single, abstract FFT program.

While the approach and the language used are both high-level, that does not mean we would lose low-level control necessary for the optimal performance. We show that it is possible to reason and program at very low-level, involving delicate arithmetic or vector shuffling, for example. A clean separation between high- and low-level layers is the key to the generality and reusability of our framework.

4.1 Abstract Definition of the FFT Innermost Loop

We begin by translating the pseudocode of bottom up, in-place FFT in Algorithm 1 into our DSL. This is a description of the innermost loop using primitives defined in our DSL.

```
for_ (int_ 0) m_half (int_ 1) (fun j ->
    let index = k %+ j in
    let omega = arr_get prim_root_powers (coeff_begin %+ j) in
    let2
      (D.mul (arr_get input (index %+ m_half)) omega)
      (arr_get input index)
      (fun t u ->
          seq
            (arr_set input index (D.add u t))
            (arr_set input (index %+ m_half) (D.sub u t))))
```

let2 V1 V2 (fun t u -> V3) is an syntax sugar for a doubly-nested let binding: let t = V1 in let u = V2 in V3. The variable prim_root_powers stores precomputed twiddle factors in an array. An array and operations on it are also abstracted using the following signature:

```
module type Array_lang = sig
  include C_lang
  type 'a arr = 'a array

  val arr_init: int -> (int -> 'a expr) -> 'a arr expr
  val arr_get: 'a arr expr -> int expr -> 'a expr
  val arr_set: 'a arr expr -> int expr -> 'a expr -> unit stmt
end
```

Unlike previous implementations where constants are precomputed offline and embedded in the source code without further information, we compute constants at the code-generation time, in OCaml (not shown). Therefore, our OCaml source code tells exactly how all constants are precomputed.

The domain our FFT will operate on, which in our case is always integers modulo q, is abstracted with the following signature. This is not strictly necessary in the context of this work, but this abstraction increases the reusability of our FFT program: For example, by implementing this signature for complex numbers, we would obtain a standard complex valued FFT implementation from the same FFT program.

```
module type Domain = sig
  type 'a expr    type t
  val lift: t -> t expr
  val add: t expr -> t expr -> t expr
  val sub: t expr -> t expr -> t expr
  val mul: t expr -> t expr -> t expr
end
```

4.2 Vectorizing Modular Reductions

Our goal is to vectorize the innermost loop. The first challenge we need to address is the vectorization of Barrett and Montgomery reductions [3,16]. Even though the FFT program itself is generic with respect to the choice of parameters and the data type of inputs and outputs, instantiating the implementation of modular reductions requires choosing them ahead of time. We follow the setting of NewHope reference implementation: The input size n is 1024, the modulus parameter q is 12289, and inputs and outputs are arrays of unsigned 16 bit integers whose values fit in 14 bits.

Below is the implementation of Barrett and Montgomery reductions from the NewHope reference implementation, modified slightly for our exposition. The code does not fully reduce modulo q: the output is correct as long as the output from reduction fits in 14 bits [2].

```
static const uint32_t rlog = 18;
static const uint32_t R = 1 << rlog;

uint16_t barrett_reduce(uint16_t a) {
  uint32_t u = ((uint32_t) a * 5) >> 16;
  return a - (uint16_t)(u * PARAM_Q);
}

uint16_t montgomery_multiply_reduce(uint16_t x, uint16_t twiddle) {
  uint32_t a = ((uint32_t)x * (uint32_t)twiddle) & (R - 1);
  uint32_t u = (a * PARAM_Q_INV) & (R - 1);
  return (a + u * PARAM_Q) >> rlog;
}
```

Suppose that the size of a vector register is 256 bit, so that we can pack 16 unsigned 16 bit integer into one vector register. Since the scalar code uses 32 bit arithmetic, a direct vectorization of these routines requires extracting 8 32 bit values from a 16 element vector, doing 8-way 32 bit integer arithmetic, and packing reduced 16 bit values back into an output 16 element register. This is highly inefficient, and not surprisingly the optimized assembly implementation of NewHope uses floating-point SIMD instructions to compute reduction by a mod $q = a - \left\lfloor a \frac{1}{q} \right\rfloor q$.

An idea for efficient vectorization of modular reduction using 16 bit integer SIMD instructions was introduced in [19]. The key observation is that 32 bit value is introduced as a result of multiplying two 16 bit integers, and the multiplication is always followed by division or modulo by a power of two. For example, the first multiplication in Barrett reduction is immediately followed by a right shift of 16. Since we immediately discard the lower 16 bits half of the product, we only have to compute the upper 16 bits half of it. AVX has the `mulhi` instruction for this purpose. Similarly, the second 32 bit multiplication can be replaced by `mullo` instruction, since the cast to 16 bit discards the upper 16 bits half of the product.

The case for Montgomery reduction is not as straightforward, since NewHope uses the constant $R = 2^{18}$ as the divisor. Naively replacing 18 by 16 leads to an incorrect result, because the result of reduction is not guaranteed to fit in 14 bits if we right shift a 32 bit value by 16. Fortunately, one conditional subtraction by q is enough to make the output of the reduction fit in 14 bits. Using $R = 2^{16}$, we can replace the two occurrences of the multiplication followed by modulo R (`& (R - 1)` in the code) by 16 bit `mullo` instruction.

The last multiplication by q is not followed by either division or modulo by R, so it seems we cannot replace this 32 bit multiplication by either 16 bit `mulhi` or `mullo` instructions. Here, we can exploit a property of Montgomery reduction: The result of the last addition is guaranteed to be divisible by R. Since we can make R to be 2^{16}, this means that low 16 bits half of the addition result is 0. This suggests the possibility to multiply only the high 16 bits half just before the addition, and do the addition of the high 16 bits. To realize this, we need to take care of a carry bit from the lower 16 bits half addition that we are going to omit. We can determine if a carry is necessary by examining the lower 16 bits half of the left hand side of the addition (a in the code). If it is zero, there is no carry. Otherwise, there must be a carry into the 17-th bit because of the requirement that lower 16 bits half is zero after addition. In the latter case, we need to explicitly add a carry bit after the last addition.

Based on the above reasoning, we declare a DSL signature necessary to implement vectorized reductions as follows:

```
module type SIMD_Instr = sig
  val broadcast: t -> (t, n) vec expr
  val add: (t, n) vec expr -> (t, n) vec expr -> (t, n) vec expr
  val sub: (t, n) vec expr -> (t, n) vec expr -> (t, n) vec expr
  val mullo: (t, n) vec expr -> (t, n) vec expr -> (t, n) vec expr
  val mulhi: (t, n) vec expr -> (t, n) vec expr -> (t, n) vec expr
  val bitwise_and: (t, n) vec expr -> (t, n) vec expr -> (t, n) vec expr
  val shift_right_a: (t, n) vec expr -> int -> (t, n) vec expr
  val not_zero: (t, n) vec expr -> (t, n) vec expr
  module Infix: sig
    val (%+): (t, n) vec expr -> (t, n) vec expr -> (t, n) vec expr
    val (%-): (t, n) vec expr -> (t, n) vec expr -> (t, n) vec expr
  end
end
```

(t, n) vec is the type of a length-n vector whose element type is t, but the details are not important. not_zero takes a vector and returns 0x0000 or 0x0001 for each element depending on whether or not the input element is not zero. shift_right_a does arithmetic right shift and it is used to implement the constant-time conditional subtraction csub (not shown) [19].

Using the primitives above, we can implement vectorized reductions as follows. The final line in vmul (for Montgomery modular multiplication) does the conditional subtraction, to ensure that the result of modular multiplication fits in 14 bits as required by our specification.

```
func "barrett_reduce" in_ty (fun v ->
    let vec_5 = broadcast 5 in
    let v_1 = mulhi v vec_5 in
    let vec_q = broadcast Param.q in
    return_ (v %- (mullo v_1 vec_q)))

func2 "vmul" in_ty in_ty (fun v1 v2 ->
    let_ (mullo v1 v2) (fun mlo ->
    let_ (mulhi v1 v2) (fun mhi ->
    let_ (broadcast Param.q) (fun vec_q ->
    let_ (broadcast Param.qinv) (fun vec_qinv ->
    let_ (mullo mlo vec_qinv) (fun mlo_qinv ->
    let_ (mulhi mlo_qinv vec_q) (fun t ->
    let_ (not_zero mlo) (fun carry ->
    let_ (mhi %+ t %+ carry) (fun res ->
    return_ (app csub res))))))))))
```

Here is the generated vectorized Barrett reduction and Montgomery modular multiplication, using the AVX2 instruction set.

```
__m256i barrett_reduce(__m256i arg0) {
  return _mm256_sub_epi16(
    arg0, _mm256_mullo_epi16(_mm256_mulhi_epu16(arg0,
                                        _mm256_set1_epi16(5)),
                            _mm256_set1_epi16(12289)));
}


__m256i vmul(__m256i arg0, __m256i arg1) {
  __m256i v_19 = _mm256_mullo_epi16(arg0, arg1);
  __m256i v_20 = _mm256_mulhi_epu16(arg0, arg1);
  __m256i v_21 = _mm256_set1_epi16(12289);
  __m256i v_22 = _mm256_set1_epi16(12287);
  __m256i v_23 = _mm256_mullo_epi16(v_19, v_22);
  __m256i v_24 = _mm256_mulhi_epu16(v_23, v_21);
  __m256i v_25 = _mm256_add_epi16(
      _mm256_cmpeq_epi16(v_19, _mm256_set1_epi16(0)),
      _mm256_set1_epi16(1));
  __m256i v_26 = _mm256_add_epi16(_mm256_add_epi16(v_20, v_24), v_25);
  return csub(v_26);
}
```

Note that the optimizations in this section is generic with respect to the choice of instruction sets. Indeed, we can generate AVX512 code by changing only the last part of code generation (see Sect. 4.6).

4.3   Subtraction

Since we use unsigned arithmetic following the reference implementation of NewHope, we need to be careful with the subtraction in the butterfly operation. To prevent an unsigned underflow, we need to add a sufficiently large multiple of q, which we call the bias, to the left hand side of the subtraction. The reference implementation of NewHope first casts the left-hand side to 32 bit and adds $3q$. However, we would like to avoid the cast to 32 bit, because we want to vectorize with 16 bit arithmetic. Since $3q = 36867 > 2^{15}$, and the left hand side of the subtraction can be 15 bit because of the lazy reduction explained later, naively adding $3q$, using 16 bit arithmetic, could lead to an overflow. Therefore, a more careful analysis is needed to allow 16 bit vectorized arithmetic without a concern for overflow or unsigned underflow.

The right hand side of the subtraction is always the result of a modular multiplication, which is guaranteed to fit in 14 bit. Therefore, the bias needs to be bigger than the maximum of a 14 bit unsigned integer, $2^{14} - 1$. Since the left hand side can be 15 bit, the bias needs to fit in 15 bits to avoid overflow in the addition using 16 bit arithmetic. The above considerations leads to the choice of $2q = 24578$ as the bias, since $2^{14} - 1 < 24578 < 2^{15} - 1$.

The result of the bias addition followed by subtraction in general requires 16 bits. However, the result of a modular subtraction needs to be either 14 or 15 bit, following the specification we adopted from NewHope. We have chosen to reduce the result of the subtraction to 14 bits via one Barrett reduction. This means that the lazy reduction will not be concerned with the result of the subtraction in the butterfly operation.

This is the implementation of the vectorized modular subtraction in our DSL. Generated AVX2 code is shown below.

```
func2 "vsub" in_ty in_ty (fun v1 v2 ->
    let bias = broadcast (Param.q * 2) in
    return_ (app barrett_reduce ((v1 %+ bias) %- v2)))
```

```
__m256i vsub(__m256i arg0, __m256i arg1) {
  return barrett_reduce(
      _mm256_sub_epi16(_mm256_add_epi16(arg0, _mm256_set1_epi16(24578)),
                       arg1));
}
```

We also define a vectorized addition vadd, whose implementation is omitted because it is simply a wrapper around add (%+ in the infix notation).

4.4   Vectorizing the Innermost Loop

Having decided all the ingredients necessary to vectorize the butterfly operation, we can now discuss how we vectorize the innermost loop.

Since the number of iterations in the innermost loop is different for each stage, vectorization needs to be done carefully. Suppose that the width of a vector is 16. When the input size is 1024, as in NewHope, the number of iterations becomes greater or equal to 16 after the fifth stage. Therefore, for stages after the fifth stage, vectorization can be done by just adding one line, thanks to Vectorize module introduced in the Sect. 3.2.

```
let open Vectorize(V_lang) in
for_ (int_ 0) m_half (int_ 1) (fun j ->
    ...
```

Here is an example of the generated AVX2 code, for the fifth stage. Note the use of vadd, vsub, and vmul introduced earlier.

```
for (int v_90 = 0; v_90 < ((16 - 0) / 16); v_90 += 1) {
  __m256i v_99 =
      vmul(_mm256_loadu_si256(
              (__m256i *)(arg0 + ((v_89 + (0 + (v_90 * 16))) + 16))),
          _mm256_loadu_si256((__m256i *)(v_9 + (64 + (0 + (v_90 * 16)))))));
  __m256i v_100 =
      _mm256_loadu_si256((__m256i *)(arg0 + (v_89 + (0 + (v_90 * 16)))));
  _mm256_storeu_si256((__m256i *)(arg0 + (v_89 + (0 + (v_90 * 16)))),
                      vadd(v_100, v_99));
  _mm256_storeu_si256((__m256i *)(arg0 + ((v_89 + (0 + (v_90 * 16))) + 16)),
                      vsub(v_100, v_99));
}
```

Vectorizing the earlier stages is more difficult, since the number of iterations of the loop we want to vectorize is less than the vector width. The situation and the idea for the solution are illustrated in Fig. 1, for the case where the vector width is 4. Two butterfly operations on four neighboring elements on the left correspond to one innermost loop. Since the top two and bottom two elements undergo different operations, we cannot apply vectorization to the four-element group. The key to enable vectorization is to operate on two neighboring four-element groups at the same time. By shuffling elements between two groups, we can group elements that undergo the same operations into one vector. For example, the blue elements (2, 3) are first multiplied by twiddle factors, and added and subtracted with the red elements. By applying the same shuffling to the result of vectorized butterfly operations, we recover the expected results.

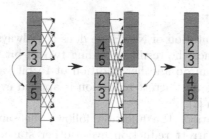

Fig. 1. Shuffling elements between neighboring two vectors enables vectorization

Based on the observation above, we introduce the `shuffle` primitive in our language. Since each stage requires different shuffling, this primitive takes an integer representing the stage as its arguments. Given two vectors, it shuffles elements between them and returns a new pair of vectors.

```
val shuffle: int -> t vec expr -> t vec expr -> (t vec expr * t vec expr)
```

Using the `shuffle` primitive, we can write the vectorized inner loop for earlier stages as follows. `vadd`, `vsub`, and `vmul` are vectorized modular arithmetic introduced earlier. `vload`, `vstore` are vector load and store respectively.

```
for_ zero (int_ n) (int_ (vec_len * 2)) (fun k ->
   let_ (vload input k) (fun v0 ->
   let_ (vload input (k %+ (int_ vec_len))) (fun v1 ->
   let2_ (shuffle s v0 v1) (fun v_lo v_hi ->
   let_ (vmul v_hi coeff) (fun v_mul ->
   let_ (vadd v_lo v_mul) (fun tmp_add ->
   let_ (vsub v_lo v_mul) (fun tmp_sub ->
   let2_ (shuffle s tmp_add tmp_sub) (fun v0_res v1_res ->
   seq
      (vstore input k v0_res)
      (vstore input (k %+ (int_ vec_len)) v1_res)))))))))))
```

By abstracting the details of different shuffling into the `shuffle` primitive, we are able to write a generic vectorized inner loop that can be specialized to each stage. Unlike the vectorization of the innermost loop for later stages where we do not have to change the original sequential FFT program, the vectorization for earlier stages required rewriting the innermost loop with explicit vectorized primitives. Although it is not ideal in terms of program reuse, we believe that the rewriting is necessary to enable low-level optimization involving shuffling. Our framework is flexible enough to accomodate both the trivial vectorization via **Vectorize** module and the explicit vectorization using vectorized primitives.

4.5 Lazy Reduction

The reference implementation of NewHope does not always reduce the result of addition to 14 bits. Since the result of adding two 14 bit values fits in 15 bits, in the next stage we can do another addition of 15 bit values without causing 16 bit overflow. Therefore, Barrett reduction is applied every other stage. This is called lazy reduction [2].

In our implementation, the addition follows the same lazy approach as NewHope, applying Barrett reduction every other stage. For subtraction, we always reduce the result to 14 bits as explained earlier. The implementation detail of our lazy reduction is in Appendix B.

4.6 SIMD Backend Implementation

We have shown "vectorized" programs without specifying which SIMD instruction sets we use. At the lowest layer of abstraction in our framework, we need a mapping between our primitives and concrete SIMD instructions.

For the AVX2 backend, we specify the mapping in the following way. The AVX512 backend is entirely similar, modulo the names of instructions and the vector length.

```
module AVX2_v16_Instr = struct
  let vec_len = 16
  let add = "_mm256_add_epi16"
  let mullo = "_mm256_mullo_epi16"
  let mulhi = "_mm256_mulhi_epi16"
  ...
end
```

We also need to specify the implementation of shuffle operations for earlier stages. For the AVX2 backend, for example, we need to implement different shuffle operations for the stages between 1 and 4. See Appendix C for more details.

5   Experiments

We benchmarked our generated code against the optimized AVX2 implementation of NewHope. We used Clang version 11 with -O3 to compile our code. Each implementation was run 100000 times on an input of size 1024 and we recorded average cycles spent using the **perf_event** feature in the Linux kernel. Furthermore, we take the median of 100 average cycles measurements, since we observed some variations in the average cycles count during our experiment.

The result on a desktop machine with Intel Coffee Lake CPU is shown in Table 1. The efficient vectorization using only 16 bit integer instructions is the only reason we were able to outperform NewHope: While we are able to pack four times more elements into a one vector register[5], NewHope uses more optimizations at the assembly level, such as merging multiple stages to compute as much as possible inside registers [7,19]. In contrast, we compute intermediate outputs stage by stage following the pseudocode in Algorithm 1 and overall our code is much simpler and more readable than the NewHope assembly implementation.

Table 1. Cycle counts on Core i7-8700K (Coffee Lake, AVX2)

	Cycle counts	Speedup over NewHope
NewHope	6903	
Our AVX2 result	6099	1.132

AVX512 is becoming widely available in consumer laptops. Since our framework can easily target AVX512 instructions from the same abstract definition of FFT, we were able to generate an optimized AVX512 FFT implementation without significant effort after we completed the AVX2 one[6]. Table 2 shows the

---

[5] Recall that NewHope uses double precision floating-point instructions to compute reductions.

[6] Both of our AVX2 and AVX512 support code are less than 90 lines of OCaml.

benchmark result on a laptop with AVX512-capable Intel Ice Lake CPU. AVX512 gave speedup of 23% over our AVX2 result.

Table 2. Cycle counts on Core i7-1065G7 (Ice Lake, AVX2 and AVX512)

	Cycle counts	Speedup over NewHope
NewHope	6082	
Our AVX2 result	5398	1.127
Our AVX512 result	4381	1.388

The work on Kyber showed that their AVX2 forward NTT implementation, tailored for the NewHope parameters ($n = 1024, q = 12289$), achieved 3.5x speedup against the NewHope AVX2 implementation [19]. Based on the results from Table 1 and 2, our AVX2 implementation are expected to be significantly slower than Kyber. A direct comparison is not possible at the moment since the Kyber implementation that works with the NewHope parameters is not publicly available and both we and Kyber implement optimizations that are specific to respective choice of parameters (for example, Kyber does not apply any Barrett reduction during the forward transform). It would be interesting to apply our program-generation framework to a Kyber-based implementation: To do so, we need to analyze the low-level optimizations of Kyber further and provide high-level descriptions for them, which is left for future work.

6   Conclusion

We have proposed implementing optimized FFT for RLWE-based cryptography via a program-generation approach. By separating the high-level description of the FFT program from low-level details concerning arithmetic and vectorization, we have achieved a reusable FFT program-generation framework. Generated code is also efficient, outperforming the NewHope assembly implementation by non-trivial factors using AVX2 and AVX512 instruction sets. Our implementation is available at https://github.com/masahi/iwsec21_ntt.

This work opens up several avenues for future work. For the code generation aspect, we believe further speedup is possible: For example, while both existing and our work use the simplest formulation of FFT using the radix-2 butterfly exclusively, we are also interested in exploring the radix-4 or the split-radix variants which involve fewer multiplications than the dominant radix-2 case [8, 11]. Instantiating the implementation of Kyber FFT [19] in our framework or adding new targets, such as ARM or RISC-V would also be interesting.

Finally, since the correctness of the code is of paramount importance in cryptography in general, we would like to offer some notion of correctness assurance. One way is to automatically prove that our implementation does not have the possibility of overflow: As we have shown in Sect. 4.2 and 4.3, making sure and be confident that our implementation of modular arithmetic is free from over-flow required very careful low-level reasoning. A promising direction has been demonstrated in the recent work of Navas et al. [17]. We believe starting from abstract high-level description of the program, as proposed in this work, opens up many possibilities for such verification effort.

Acknowledgement. We thank Tadanori Teruya for helpful discussion. Feedbacks from anonymous reviewers helped improve this paper and are greatly appreciated. The second author is supported in part by JSPS Grant-in-Aid for Scientific Research (B) 18H03218.

Appendix A   Vectorize Module

`Vectorize` module is used to generate vectorized code for trivially vectorizable loops. It simply redefines the meaning of language primitives used in a sequential program so that the same program can evaluated to vectorized loop code. It is implemented as a OCaml functor, which is often used in the tagless-final style to extend the meaning of existing DSL.

```
module Vectorize(Base_lang: Vector_lang): Vec
  ...
= struct

  module D = struct
    let add = Vec_D.vadd
    ...
  end

  let arr_get = Base_lang.vload
  let arr_set = Base_lang.vstore

  let vec_len = ...

  let for_ lo hi _ body =
    let num_loop = (hi %- lo) %/ (int_ vec_len) in
    Base_lang.for_ (int_ 0) num_loop (int_ 1) (fun i ->
        body (lo %+ (i %* (int_ vec_len))))
end
```

Appendix B   Lazy Reduction Implementation

We implement lazy reduction again as a OCaml functor, extending the original meanings of `vadd` and `vsub` to give semantics of lazy reduction. As explained in Sect. 4.3, we allow the result of addition to stay in 15 bits and apply Barrett reduction every other stage, while the result of subtraction is reduced to 14 bits in every stage by Barrett reduction. We can implement such specification for lazy reduction as follows:

```
module Lazy_reduction(V: Vector_lang)(Stage: sig val s: int end) : Vector_lang
  (* ... *)
struct
  include V
  module Vector_domain = struct
    let vadd v0 v1 =
      let res = V.Vector_domain.vadd v0 v1 in
      if Stage.s mod 2 == 0 then barrett_reduce res
      else res
    let vsub = V.Vector_domain.vsub
  end
end
```

This is used in our FFT code generator as follows. `Lazy_reduction` is instantiated for each stage s, and by simply wrapping the original meanings of vectorized primitives such as vadd and vsub defined in `V_lang`, the innermost loop now executes with the lazy reduction enabled. Note that we do not have to change the code of the innermost loop at all. The tagless-final style allows such an extension in a highly modular manner.

```
let fft n =
  ...
  let fft_stage s =
    ...
    let module V_lang_lazy = Lazy_reduction(V_lang)(struct let s = s end) in
    func fname input_ty (fun input ->
        ...
        let open V_lang_lazy in
        let open V_lang_lazy.Vector_domain in
        ...
```

Appendix C   Details on SIMD Backend Implementation

This is the full mapping between language primitives used in vectorized reductions of Sect. 4.2 and corresponding AVX2 instructions.

```
module AVX2_v16_Instr : SIMD_str = struct
  let add = "_mm256_add_epi16"
  let sub = "_mm256_sub_epi16"
  let mullo = "_mm256_mullo_epi16"
  let mulhi = "_mm256_mulhi_epu16"
  let broadcast = "_mm256_set1_epi16"
  let shift_right_a = "_mm256_srai_epi16"
  let bitwise_and = "_mm256_and_si256"
  let not_zero v =
    sprintf "_mm256_add_epi16(_mm256_cmpeq_epi16(%s, _mm256_set1_epi16(0)),
                              _mm256_set1_epi16(1))" v
end
```

`not_zero` primitive is implemented in a cumbersome way, since AVX instruction returns OxFFFF or Ox0000 for the result of comparison instructions, while we need Ox0001 or Ox0000 to represent the presence or absence of the carry bit. `not_zero` primitive hides such details specific to a particular ISA and provides a straightforward interface to a programmer.

Shuffle operations can be implemented by `shift`, `blend`, `unpack`, and `permute` instructions. The implementation using AVX2 is shown below. The AVX512 counterpart is entirely similar but uses different instruction combinations to realize desired permutations.

```
let shuffle1 v0 v1 =
  let v1_left_shift = sprintf "_mm256_slli_epi32(%s, 16)" v1 in
  let v0_right_shift = sprintf "_mm256_srli_epi32(%s, 16)" v0 in
  let v_lo = sprintf "_mm256_blend_epi16(%s, %s, 0xAA)" v0 v1_left_shift in
  let v_hi = sprintf "_mm256_blend_epi16(%s, %s, 0xAA)" v0_right_shift v1 in
  v_lo, v_hi

let shuffle2 v0 v1 =
  let v1_left_shift = sprintf "_mm256_slli_epi64(%s, 32)" v1 in
  let v0_right_shift = sprintf "_mm256_srli_epi64(%s, 32)" v0 in
  let v_lo = sprintf "_mm256_blend_epi32(%s, %s, 0xAA)" v0 v1_left_shift in
  let v_hi = sprintf "_mm256_blend_epi32(%s, %s, 0xAA)" v0_right_shift v1 in
  v_lo, v_hi

let shuffle3 v0 v1 =
  let v_lo = sprintf "_mm256_unpacklo_epi64(%s, %s)" v0 v1 in
  let v_hi = sprintf "_mm256_unpackhi_epi64(%s, %s)" v0 v1 in
  v_lo, v_hi

let shuffle4 v0 v1 =
  let v_lo = sprintf "_mm256_permute2x128_si256(%s, %s, 0x20)" v0 v1 in
  let v_hi = sprintf "_mm256_permute2x128_si256(%s, %s, 0x31)" v0 v1 in
  v_lo, v_hi

let shuffle n v0 v1 = match n with
  | 1 -> shuffle1 v0 v1
  | 2 -> shuffle2 v0 v1
  | 3 -> shuffle3 v0 v1
  | 4 -> shuffle4 v0 v1
  | _ -> assert false
```

References

1. Aguilar-Melchor, C., Barrier, J., Guelton, S., Guinet, A., Killijian, M.-O., Lepoint, T.: NFLLIB: NTT-based fast lattice library. In: Sako, K. (ed.) CT-RSA 2016. LNCS, vol. 9610, pp. 341–356. Springer, Cham (2016). https://doi.org/10.1007/978-3-319-29485-8_20

2. Alkim, E., Ducas, L., Pöppelmann, T., Schwabe, P.: Post-quantum key exchange: a new hope. In: Proceedings of the 25th USENIX Conference on Security Symposium, SEC 2016, pp. 327–343. USENIX Association, USA (2016)

3. Barrett, P.: Implementing the Rivest Shamir and Adleman Public key encryption algorithm on a standard digital signal processor. In: Odlyzko, A.M. (ed.) CRYPTO 1986. LNCS, vol. 263, pp. 311–323. Springer, Heidelberg (1987). https://doi.org/10.1007/3-540-47721-7_24

4. Bos, J., et al.: CRYSTALS - Kyber: a CCA-secure module-lattice-based KEM, pp. 353–367 (2018). https://doi.org/10.1109/EuroSP.2018.00032

5. Carette, J., Kiselyov, O., Shan, C.: Finally tagless, partially evaluated. In: Shao, Z. (ed.) APLAS 2007. LNCS, vol. 4807, pp. 222–238. Springer, Heidelberg (2007). https://doi.org/10.1007/978-3-540-76637-7_15

6. Cormen, T.H., Leiserson, C.E., Rivest, R.L., Stein, C.: Introduction to Algorithms, 3rd edn. The MIT Press, Cambridge (2009)

7. Güneysu, T., Oder, T., Pöppelmann, T., Schwabe, P.: Software speed records for lattice-based signatures. In: Gaborit, P. (ed.) PQCrypto 2013. LNCS, vol. 7932, pp. 67–82. Springer, Heidelberg (2013). https://doi.org/10.1007/978-3-642-38616-9_5

8. Johnson, S.G., Frigo, M.: A modified split-radix FFT with fewer arithmetic operations. Trans. Sig. Proc. 55(1), 111–119 (2007). https://doi.org/10.1109/TSP.2006.882087

9. Kiselyov, O.: Typed tagless final interpreters. In: Gibbons, J. (ed.) Generic and Indexed Programming. LNCS, vol. 7470, pp. 130–174. Springer, Heidelberg (2012). https://doi.org/10.1007/978-3-642-32202-0_3

10. Kiselyov, O.: Reconciling abstraction with high performance: a MetaOCaml approach. Found. Trends Program. Lang. 5(1), 1–101 (2018). https://doi.org/10.1561/2500000038

11. Kiselyov, O., Taha, W.: Relating FFTW and split-radix. In: Wu, Z., Chen, C., Guo, M., Bu, J. (eds.) ICESS 2004. LNCS, vol. 3605, pp. 488–493. Springer, Heidelberg (2005). https://doi.org/10.1007/11535409_71

12. Leroy, X., Doligez, D., Frisch, A., Garrigue, J., Rémy, D., Vouillon, J.: The OCaml system release 4.11 (2020). https://caml.inria.fr/pub/docs/manual-ocaml/

13. Liu, Z., et al.: High-performance ideal lattice-based cryptography on 8-bit AVR microcontrollers. ACM Trans. Embed. Comput. Syst. 16(4) (2017). https://doi.org/10.1145/3092951

14. Longa, P., Naehrig, M.: Speeding up the number theoretic transform for faster ideal lattice-based cryptography. In: Foresti, S., Persiano, G. (eds.) CANS 2016. LNCS, vol. 10052, pp. 124–139. Springer, Cham (2016). https://doi.org/10.1007/978-3-319-48965-0_8

15. Lyubashevsky, V., Peikert, C., Regev, O.: On ideal lattices and learning with errors over rings. In: Gilbert, H. (ed.) EUROCRYPT 2010. LNCS, vol. 6110, pp. 1–23. Springer, Heidelberg (2010). https://doi.org/10.1007/978-3-642-13190-5_1

16. Montgomery, P.L.: Modular multiplication without trial division. Math. Comput. 44, 519–521 (1985)

17. Navas, J.A., Dutertre, B., Mason, I.A.: Verification of an optimized NTT algorithm. In: Christakis, M., Polikarpova, N., Duggirala, P.S., Schrammel, P. (eds.) NSV/VSTTE -2020. LNCS, vol. 12549, pp. 144–160. Springer, Cham (2020). https://doi.org/10.1007/978-3-030-63618-0_9
18. Roy, S.S., Vercauteren, F., Mentens, N., Chen, D.D., Verbauwhede, I.: Compact ring-LWE cryptoprocessor. In: Batina, L., Robshaw, M. (eds.) CHES 2014. LNCS, vol. 8731, pp. 371–391. Springer, Heidelberg (2014). https://doi.org/10.1007/978-3-662-44709-3_21
19. Seiler, G.: Faster AVX2 optimized NTT multiplication for Ring-LWE lattice cryptography. IACR Cryptology ePrint Archive 2018/39 (2018)

Symmetric-Key Cryptography

Optimum Attack on 3-Round Feistel-2 Structure

Takanori Daiza[1] and Kaoru Kurosawa[2,3(⊠)]

[1] Ibaraki University, Hitachi, Japan
20nm713t@vc.ibaraki.ac.jp
[2] Research and Development Initiative, Chuo University, Tokyo, Japan
kaoru.kurosawa.kk@vc.ibaraki.ac.jp
[3] National Institute of Advanced Industrial Science and Technology, Tokyo, Japan

Abstract. Feistel-2 structure is a variant of Feistel structure such that the ith round function is given by $F_i(k_i \oplus x)$, where F_i is a public random function and k_i is a key of $n/2$ bits. Lampe and Seurin showed that 3-round Feistel-2 structure is secure if $D + T \ll 2^{n/4}$ (which is equivalent to $D \ll 2^{n/4}$ and $T \ll 2^{n/4}$), where D is the number of queries to the encryption oracle and T is the number of queries to each F_i oracle. On the other hand, only the meet-in-the-middle attack is known for 3-round Feistel-2 structure which works only for $(D, T) = (O(1), O(2^{n/2}))$ with $O(2^{n/2})$ amount of memory.

In this paper, we first show that 3-round Feistel-2 structure is broken by a key recovery attack if $DT \geq 2^{n/2}$ (which requires $O(D+T)$ amount of memory). Since it works for $D = T = O(2^{n/4})$, this attack proves that the security bound of Lampe and Seurin is tight at $D = T = O(2^{n/4})$. We next present a memoryless key recovery attack for $(D, T) = (O(1), O(2^{n/2}))$. We finally show a memoryless key recovery attack for $D = O(2^{n/4})$ and $T = O(2^{n/4})$.

Keywords: Feistel structure · Key recovery · 3-round

1 Introduction

1.1 Feistel Structure

Feistel structure is a popular design framework of block cipher, and hence it is important both in practice and theory. The r round Feistel structure takes a plaintext $P = (a_0, b_0)$ as an input, where $a_0, b_0 \in \{0,1\}^{n/2}$. Then it computes

$$(a_{i+1}, b_{i+1}) = (b_i \oplus R_i(a_i), a_i)$$

for $i = 0, 1, \dots, r-1$, where $R_i : \{0,1\}^{n/2} \mapsto \{0,1\}^{n/2}$ is a keyed round function. Finally it outputs a ciphertext $C = (a_r, b_r)$. See the left half of Fig. 1.

Luby and Rackoff [11] considered a construction such that each round function R_i is an independent random function. Then they showed that

© Springer Nature Switzerland AG 2021
T. Nakanishi and R. Nojima (Eds.): IWSEC 2021, LNCS 12835, pp. 175–192, 2021.
https://doi.org/10.1007/978-3-030-85987-9_10

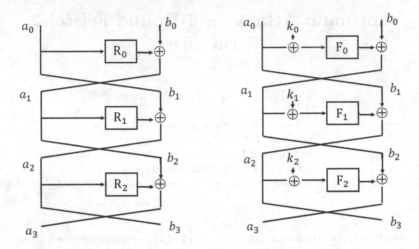

Fig. 1. Feistel Structure and Feistel-2 Structure

- 3-round construction is pseudo-random up to $2^{n/4}$ queries against chosen plaintext attack (CPA), and
- 4-round construction is super pseudo-random up to $2^{n/4}$ queries against chosen ciphertexttext attack (CCA).

This construction has been further studied by many researchers extensively [8,12,14–19].

1.2 Feistel-2 Structure

A problem of Luby-Rackoff construction is how to design R_i in such a way that it includes a key. Feistel-2 structure, which offers a solution, is a variant of Feistel structure such that each round function $R_i(x)$ is replaced by $F_i(k_i \oplus x)$, where $F_i : \{0,1\}^{n/2} \mapsto \{0,1\}^{n/2}$ is a public independent random function, and $k_i \in \{0,1\}^{n/2}$ is a round key. (It is also known as key-alternating Feistel cipher. This construction is closely related to Even-Mansour cipher [6] and its extension [1].) See the right half of Fig. 1.

Lampe and Seurin [13] proved the security of Feistel-2 structure as follows. Suppose that an adversary issues D queries to the encryption/decryption oracles and T queries to each F_i-oracle. Then it is pseudo-random if $D + T \ll 2^{tn/2(t+1)}$, where

- $t = \lfloor r/3 \rfloor$ for non-adaptive CPA, where an adversary can make encryption queries after issuing all F_i-oracle queries.
- $t = \lfloor r/6 \rfloor$ for CCA.

Their result means that 3-round Feistel-2 structure is pseudo-random against non-adaptive CPA if $D + T \ll 2^{n/4}$.

1.3 Our Contribution

Feistel-2 structure is equivalent to Feistel structure if $T = 0$. Therefore 3-round Feistel-2 structure is pseudo-random against CPA if $D \ll 2^{n/4}$ and $T = 0$ from the result of Luby and Rackoff [11]. (See Fig. 2.) Further, as mentioned in Sect. 1.2, Lampe and Seurin [13] showed that 3-round Feistel-2 structure is pseudo-random against non-adaptive CPA if

$$D + T \ll 2^{n/4} \tag{1}$$

which is equivalent to $D \ll 2^{n/4}$ and $T \ll 2^{n/4}$. (See Fig. 2.)

On the other hand, only the meet-in-the-middle attack is known for 3-round Feistel-2 structure which works only for $(D, T) = (O(1), O(2^{n/2}))$ [9]. It is a known plaintext attack (KPA) with memory size $O(2^{n/2})$ and the time complexity $O(2^{n/2})$.

In this paper, we first show that 3-round Feistel-2 structure is broken by a key recovery attack if $DT \geq 2^{n/2}$. (See Fig. 2.) Since it works for $D = T = O(2^{n/4})$, this attack proves that the security bound of Lampe and Seurin is tight at $D = T = O(2^{n/4})$. It is a non-adaptive chosen plaintext attack in the same sense as that of Lampe and Seurin. (See Sect. 1.2.) The required memory size is $O(D + T)$ and the time complexity is $O(D^2 + T^2)$.

We next present a memoryless key recovery attack for $(D, T) = (O(1), O(2^{n/2}))$. (See Fig. 3.) It is a known plaintext attack and the time complexity is $O(D + T) = O(2^{n/2})$. We finally show a memoryless key recovery attack for $(D, T) = (O(2^{n/4}), O(2^{n/4}))$. (See Fig. 3.) It is an adaptive chosen plaintext attack and the time complexity is $O(D + T) = O(2^{n/4})$.

See Table 1 for comparison. In what follows, M denotes the size of memory.

Table 1. Key recovery attack on 3-round Feistel-2 structure

	(D, T)	Memory	Time	Type
Previous [9]	$(D, T) = (O(1), O(2^{n/2}))$	$O(2^{n/2})$	$O(2^{n/2})$	KPA
Our 1st attack	$DT \geq 2^{n/2}$	$O(D + T)$	$O(D^2 + T^2)$	Non-adaptive CPA
Our 2nd attack	$(D, T) = (O(1), O(2^{n/2}))$	$O(1)$	$O(2^{n/2})$	KPA
Our 3rd attack	$(D, T) = (O(2^{n/4}), O(2^{n/4}))$	$O(1)$	$O(2^{n/4})$	CPA

1.4 Related Works

Several attacks on Feistel structure have been proposed for 4 or more rounds. For example, Isobe and Shibutani [10] extended the meet-in-the middle attack to 4 rounds. Dinur et al. showed a dissection attack [5] and a more memory efficient attack [4].

Even and Mansour [6] introduced Even-Mansour cipher such that

$$C = E(P) = \pi(P \oplus K_1) \oplus K_2,$$

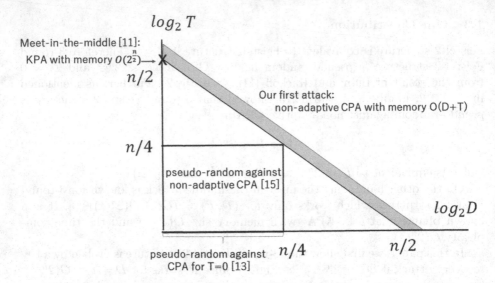

Fig. 2. Our first attack on 3-round Feistel-2 structure

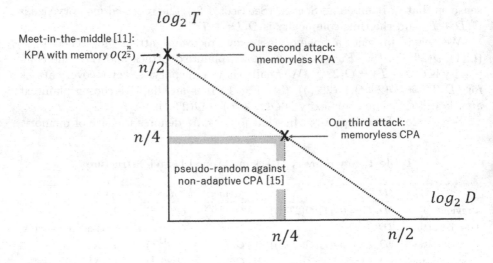

Fig. 3. Our second and third attacks

where π is a public random permutation, (K_1, K_2) is a key with $K_1 \in \{0,1\}^n$ and $K_2 \in \{0,1\}^n$, $P \in \{0,1\}^n$ is a plaintext and $C \in \{0,1\}^n$ is a ciphertext. They then proved that the probability that an attacker $\mathcal{A}$ outputs a new (P^*, C^*) such that $C^* = E(P^*)$ is $O(DT/2^n)$, where $\mathcal{A}$ makes D queries to E-oracle or E^{-1} oracle, and T queries to π-oracle or π^{-1} oracle.

Daemen [2] showed a chosen plaintext key recovery attack such that $DT = O(2^n)$ for any D. Dunkelman et al. [3] showed a known plaintext key recovery attack such that $DT = O(2^n)$ for any $D \le 2^{n/2}$. Dunkelman et al. [3] also showed a memoryless chosen plaintext key recovery attack such that $D = T = O(2^{n/2})$ by using Pollard rho algorithm [20][7, Sec.14.2.2].

2   Preliminaries

2.1   3-Round Feistel-2 Structure

Let $P = (a_0, b_0)$ be a plaintext. Then in 3-round Feistel-2 structure, the ciphertext $C = (a_3, b_3)$ is computed as follows.

$$(a_1,\ b_1) \leftarrow (b_0 \oplus F_0(k_0 \oplus a_0),\ a_0) \tag{2}$$
$$(a_2,\ b_2) \leftarrow (b_1 \oplus F_1(k_1 \oplus a_1),\ a_1) \tag{3}$$
$$(a_3,\ b_3) \leftarrow (b_2 \oplus F_2(k_2 \oplus a_2),\ a_2) \tag{4}$$

Therefore it holds that

$$\begin{aligned} b_3 &= a_2 \\ &= b_1 \oplus F_1(k_1 \oplus a_1) \\ &= a_0 \oplus F_1(k_1 \oplus b_0 \oplus F_0(k_0 \oplus a_0)) \end{aligned} \tag{5}$$

2.2   Meet in the Middle Attack [9]

Suppose that an attacker $\mathcal{A}$ is given two plaintext/ciphertext pairs of 3-round Feistel-2 structure, (P_1, C_1) and (P_2, C_2). Then the meet-in-the-middle attack works as follows [9]. Let $P_1 = (a_0, b_0)$ and $C_1 = (a_3, b_3)$.

1. For each $k_0 \in \{0,1\}^{n/2}$, an attacker $\mathcal{A}$ computes a_1 by querying $a_0 \oplus k_0$ to F_0-oracle.
2. For each $k_2 \in \{0,1\}^{n/2}$, $\mathcal{A}$ computes b_2 by querying $b_3 \oplus k_2$ to F_2-oracle.
3. $\mathcal{A}$ finds all (k_0, k_2) such that $a_1 = b_2$.
4. $\mathcal{A}$ selects one of them by using (P_2, C_2).
5. Finally $\mathcal{A}$ finds k_1 by exhaustive search.

(See Fig. 4.)

In this attack, $D = O(1)$ and $\mathcal{A}$ makes $T = O(2^{n/2})$ queries to each F_i-oracle. The memory size is $M = O(2^{n/2})$ and the time complexity is also $O(2^{n/2})$.

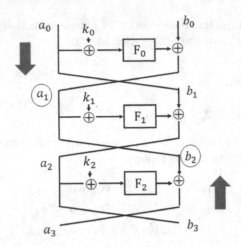

Fig. 4. Meet in the middle attack

3   Data-Time Tradeoff Attack on 3-Round Feistel-2 Structure

In this section, we show a key recovery attack on 3-round Feistel-2 structure which works for any (D, T) satisfying $DT = O(2^{n/2})$ while the previous meet-in-the middle attack [9] works only for $D = O(1)$ and $T = O(2^{n/2})$. Further our attack matches with the security bound given by Lampe and Seurin [13] at $D = T = O(2^{n/4})$. This proves that their security bound is tight at $D = T = O(2^{n/4})$.

Our attack is a non-adaptive chosen plaintext attack in the same sense as that of Lampe and Seurin. (See Sect. 1.2.) The required memory size is $O(D+T)$ and the time complexity is $O(D^2 + T^2)$.

In what follows, we consider any (D, T) such that $DT = O(2^{n/2})$.

3.1   Attack Outline

Let $(0^{n/2}, x)$ be a plaintext and (a_3, b_3) be the ciphertext of 3-round Feistel-2 structure. Then it holds that

$$b_3 = F_1(k_1 \oplus F_0(k_0) \oplus x) \tag{6}$$
$$a_3 = F_0(k_0) \oplus x \oplus F_2(k_2 \oplus b_3). \tag{7}$$

(See Fig. 5.)

1. In phase 1, we find $k_1 \oplus F_0(k_0)$ by applying a birthday attack to Eq. (6).
2. In phase 2, we find $F_0(k_0)$ and k_2 by applying a kind of differential attack to Eq. (7).
3. We compute k_1 from the above two results. Once we obtain k_1 and k_2, 3-round Feistel-2 structure is reduced to 1-round. In phase 3, we find k_0 by applying a birthday attack.

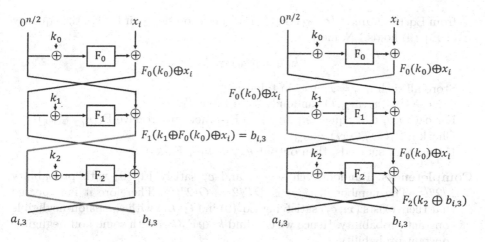

Fig. 5. Phase 1 and Phase 2

3.2 Offline Phase

For $i = 1, \ldots, T$, do:

1. Choose $c_i \in \{0,1\}^{n/2}$ randomly.
2. For $j = 0, 1, 2$, do:
   (a) Query c_i to F_j-oracle and receive $F_j(c_i)$.
   (b) Store $(F_j(c_i), c_i, i)$ in table L_j, sorted by the first coordinate.

   Namely

 - L_0 is a sorted list of $(F_0(c_1), c_1, 1), \ldots, (F_0(c_T), c_T, T)$.
 - L_1 is a sorted list of $(F_1(c_1), c_1, 1), \ldots, (F_1(c_T), c_T, T)$.
 - L_2 is a sorted list of $(F_2(c_1), c_1, 1), \ldots, (F_2(c_T), c_T, T)$.

3.3 How to Recover $k_1 \oplus F_0(k_0)$

Phase 1

1. For $i = 1, \ldots, D/2$, choose $x_i \in \{0,1\}^{n/2}$ randomly, and query a plaintext $(0^{n/2}, x_i)$ to the encryption oracle. Then receive the ciphertext $(a_{i,3}, b_{i,3})$ and store $(b_{i,3}, x_i, a_{i,3}, i)$ in table T_1, sorted by the first coordinate.
2. Find all $(b_{i,3}, F_1(c_j))$ such that

$$b_{i,3} = F_1(c_j). \tag{8}$$

by using T_1 and L_1. Such a tuple suggests

$$c_j = k_1 \oplus F_0(k_0) \oplus x_i \tag{9}$$

because

$$b_{i,3} = F_1(k_1 \oplus F_0(k_0) \oplus x_i)$$

from Eq. (6). (Unless $(c_j, k_1 \oplus F_0(k_0) \oplus x_i)$ is a collision pair for F_1, the equality of Eq. (9) holds.) Namely

$$k_1 \oplus F_0(k_0) = x_i \oplus c_j.$$

Store all such $\kappa_{i,j} = x_i \oplus c_j$ in table K.

3. Choose $(b_{\ell,3}, x_\ell, a_{\ell,3}, \ell)$ randomly from table T_1.
   For each $\kappa_{i,j} \in K$, query $\kappa_{i,j} \oplus x_\ell$ to F_1-oracle and receive $F_1(\kappa_{i,j} \oplus x_\ell)$.
   Check if $F_1(\kappa_{i,j} \oplus x_\ell) = b_{\ell,3}$.
   If the check succeeds, then output $\kappa_{i,j}$ as $k_1 \oplus F_0(k_0)$.

Completeness. Randomly chosen x_i and c_j satisfy Eq. (9) with probability $1/2^{n/2}$. The number of (i,j) is $DT/2 = O(2^{n/2})$. Therefore it is expected that there exists (x_i, c_j) satisfying Eq. (9) in (T_1, L_1) with some non-negligible constant probability. Hence we can find $k_1 \oplus F_0(k_0)$ with some non-negligible constant probability.

Soundness. The number of (i,j) is $DT/2 = O(2^{n/2})$, and Eq. (8) holds with probability $1/2^{n/2}$ because F_1 is a random function. Therefore it is expected that the number of (i,j) which satisfies Eq. (8) is small. Hence the number of queries to F_1-oracle at step 3 is small.

3.4   How to Recover k_2 and $F_0(k_0)$

A pair of plaintext/ciphertext satisfies

$$a_{i,3} = F_0(k_0) \oplus x_i \oplus F_2(k_2 \oplus b_{i,3}). \tag{10}$$

(See the right half of Fig. 5.) Therefore

$$x_i \oplus a_{i,3} = F_0(k_0) \oplus F_2(k_2 \oplus b_{i,3}).$$

Hence we have

$$x_{i_1} \oplus x_{i_2} \oplus a_{i_1,3} \oplus a_{i_2,3} = F_2(c_{i_1}) \oplus F_2(c_{i_2}), \tag{11}$$

where

$$c_i = k_2 \oplus b_{i,3}.$$

From the above equation, it holds that

$$b_{i_1,3} \oplus b_{i_2,3} = c_{i_1} \oplus c_{i_2} \tag{12}$$

We find k_2 by using Eq. (11) and Eq. (12).
We then find $F_0(k_0)$ by using Eq. (10).

Phase 2

1. For each distinct $i_1, i_2 \in \{1, \ldots, D/2\}$, compute

$$w_{i_1,i_2} = x_{i_1} \oplus x_{i_2} \oplus a_{i_1,3} \oplus a_{i_2,3}$$

   from table T_1 and store (w_{i_1,i_2}, i_1, i_2) in table T_2, sorted by the first coordinate.

2. For each distinct $j_1, j_2 \in \{1, \ldots, T\}$, compute

$$F_2(c_{j_1}) \oplus F_2(c_{j_2})$$

from table L_2 and store $(F_2(c_{j_1}) \oplus F_2(c_{j_2}), j_1, j_2)$ in table L_2', sorted by the first coordinate.

3. Find all (i_1, i_2, j_1, j_2) such that

$$w_{i_1, i_2} = F_2(c_{j_1}) \oplus F_2(c_{j_2}). \tag{13}$$

4. For each such (i_1, i_2, j_1, j_2), check if

$$b_{i_1, 3} \oplus b_{i_2, 3} = c_{j_1} \oplus c_{j_2}. \tag{14}$$

5. Each (i_1, i_2, j_1, j_2) which satisfies Eq. (13) and Eq. (14) suggests

$$k_2 = c_{i_1} \oplus b_{i_1, 3}$$
$$F_0(k_0) = a_{i_1, 3} \oplus x_{i_1} \oplus F_2(c_{j_1})$$

from Eq. (10). Store all such

$$(\kappa_{i_1} = c_{i_1} \oplus b_{i_1, 3}, \Gamma_{i_1} = a_{i_1, 3} \oplus x_{i_1} \oplus F_2(c_{j_1}))$$

in table K'.

6. Choose $\ell_1, \ell_2 \in \{1, \ldots, D/2\}$ randomly.
   For each $\kappa_i \in K'$, query $\kappa_i \oplus b_{\ell_1, 3}$ and $\kappa_i \oplus b_{\ell_2, 3}$ to F_2-oracle and receive $F_2(\kappa_i \oplus b_{\ell_1, 3})$ and $F_2(\kappa_i \oplus b_{\ell_2, 3})$.
   Check if

$$x_{\ell_1} \oplus x_{\ell_2} \oplus a_{\ell_1, 3} \oplus a_{\ell_2, 3} = F_2(\kappa_i \oplus b_{\ell_1, 3}) \oplus F_2(\kappa_i \oplus b_{\ell_2, 3}).$$

If the check succeeds, then output $k_2 = \kappa_i$ and $F_0(k_0) = \Gamma_i$.

Completeness. Random $(b_{i_1, 3}, b_{i_2, 3})$ and (c_{j_1}, c_{j_2}) satisfies

$$c_{j_1} = k_2 \oplus b_{i_1, 3}$$
$$c_{j_2} = k_2 \oplus b_{i_2, 3}$$

with probability $(1/2^{n/2})^2 = 1/2^n$. The number of (i_1, i_2, j_1, j_2) is

$$\binom{D/2}{2} \times \binom{T}{2} \approx \frac{D^2 T^2}{16} = O(2^n).$$

Therefore it is expected that there exists such $(b_{i_1, 3}, b_{i_2, 3})$ and (c_{j_1}, c_{j_2}) in our data with some non-negligible constant probability. Hence we can find k_2 and $F_0(k_0)$ with some non-negligible constant probability.

Soundness. Eq. (13) and Eq. (14) are satisfied with probability $1/2^n$. The number of (i_1, i_2, j_1, j_2) is $O(2^n)$ as shown above. Therefore it is expected that the number of (i_1, i_2, j_1, j_2) which satisfies Eq. (13) and Eq. (14) is small. Hence the number of queries to F_2-oracle at step 6 is small.

3.5 How to Recover k_0

We compute k_1 from $k_1 \oplus F_0(k_0)$ (which is obtained by phase 1) and $F_0(k_0)$ (which is obtained by phase 2). Then since we know k_1 and k_2, 3-round Feistel-2 structure is reduced to 1-round. Then it is easy to recover k_0 by using a birthday attack. See Fig. 6.

Phase 3
For $i = 1, \ldots, D/2$, choose $x_i \in \{0,1\}^{n/2}$ randomly, query $(x_i, 0^{n/2})$ to the encryption and receive $F_0(k_0 \oplus x_i)$. By using table L_0, find (x_i, c_j) such that $F_0(k_0 \oplus x_i) = F_0(c_j)$.

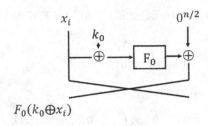

Fig. 6. Phase 3

3.6 Complexity

- In the offline phase, the number of queries to each F_i-oracle is T.
- In phase 1, the number of queries to the encryption oracle is $D/2$, and the number of queries F_1-oracle is *small*.
- In phase 2, the number of queries F_2-oracle is *small*.
- In phase 3, the number of queries to the encryption oracle is $D/2$, and the number of queries F_0-oracle is *small*.

Therefore the total number of queries to the encryption oracle is

$$D/2 \times 2 = D$$

and the total number of queries to each F_i-oracle is

$$T + small \approx T.$$

Hence

$$D \times (T + small) \approx DT = O(2^{n/2}).$$

as desired.

The required memory size is $M = O(D + T)$ and the time complexity is $O(D^2 + T^2)$.

4   Memoryless Attack for $D = 3$ and $T = O(2^{n/2})$

In this section, we show a memoryless key-recovery attack on 3-round Feistel-2 structure for $D = 3$ and $T = O(2^{n/2})$. It is a known plaintext attack and the time complexity is $O(D + T) = O(2^{n/2})$.

The previous meet-in-the-middle attack, on the other hand, needs $M = O(2^n)$ size of memory.

4.1   Attack Outline

Suppose that we are given three plaintext/ciphertext pairs, (P_1, C_1), (P_2, C_2) and (P_3, C_3). In our attack, (P_1, C_1) and (P_2, C_2) are used to compute candidates of $(k_0, k_1.k_2)$, and (P_3, C_3) is used to check their validity.

Let $P_i = (a_{i,0}, b_{i,0})$ and $C_i = (a_{i,3}, b_{i,3})$ for $i = 1, 2$.

1. We derive an equation such that $k_1 \oplus F_0(k_0 \oplus a_{i,0})$ is found by exhaustive search.
2. We derive an equation such that k_0 is found by exhaustive search.
3. We compute k_1 from the above two results. Then k_2 is found by exhaustive search.

Each step is executed with no memory because exhaustive search needs no memory.

4.2   Details

For $i = 1, 2$, it holds that

$$a_{i,0} \oplus b_{i,3} = F_1(k_1 \oplus F_0(k_0 \oplus a_{i,0}) \oplus b_{i,0}).$$

from Eq. (5). (See the left half of Fig. 5.)

Let

$$\beta_i = k_1 \oplus F_0(k_0 \oplus a_{i,0}). \tag{15}$$

Then we have

$$a_{i,0} \oplus b_{i,3} = F_1(\beta_i \oplus b_{i,0}).$$

We find β_i which satisfies the above equation by exhaustive search as follows.

1. For each $\beta_1 \in \{0,1\}^{n/2}$, we query $\beta_1 \oplus b_{1,0}$ to F_1-oracle and check if the answer is equal to $a_{1,0} \oplus b_{1,3}$.
2. For each $\beta_2 \in \{0,1\}^{n/2}$, we query $\beta_2 \oplus b_{2,0}$ to F_1-oracle and check if the answer is equal to $a_{2,0} \oplus b_{2,3}$.

Once such (β_1, β_2) are found, we have

$$\beta_1 \oplus \beta_2 = F_0(k_0 \oplus a_{1,0}) \oplus F_0(k_0 \oplus a_{2,0}). \tag{16}$$

1. We find k_0 which satisfies the above equation by exhaustive search.
2. We compute k_1 by using Eq. (15).
3. Then k_2 is found by exhaustive search.
4. If some candidates of (k_0, k_1, k_2) are found, we check their validity by using (P_3, C_3).

Since each F_i is a random function, it is expected that there are only a few candidates at each step. Therefore we need negligible amount of memory. Also it is easy to see that we make $O(2^{n/2})$ queries to each F_i-oracle in exhaustive search. Therefore it holds that $DT = O(2^{n/2})$ because $D = 3$.

The required memory size is $M = O(1)$ and the time complexity is $O(2^{n/2})$.

5   Memoryless Attack For $D = O(2^{n/4})$ and $T = O(2^{n/4})$

In this section, we show a memoryless key-recovery attack on 3-round Feistel-2 structure for $D = O(2^{n/4})$ and $T = O(2^{n/4})$. It is a chosen plaintext attack and the time complexity is $O(D + T) = O(2^{n/4})$.

We first derive a function $f(x)$ which satisfies

$$f(x) = f(k_0 \oplus x)$$

where an attacker $\mathcal{A}$ can compute $f(x)$ from a plaintext $P = (x, F_0(x))$ and its ciphertext C. $\mathcal{A}$ can find k_0 by applying a birthday attack to the above equation. Finally we apply Pollard's rho algorithm to

$$x_{i+1} = f(x_i)$$

together with Floyd's two finger cycle finding algorithm [7, Sec.14.2.2][20]. This algorithm uses negligible amount of memory.

5.1   Our Idea

Our idea is to choose $P = (a_0, b_0)$ such that

$$(a_0, b_0) = (x, F_0(x)).$$

Let the ciphertext be $C = (a_3, b_3)$. Then from Sect. 2, we have

$$
\begin{aligned}
a_1 &= F_0(x) \oplus F_0(x \oplus k_0) \\
b_3 &= a_2 \\
&= F_1(k_1 \oplus a_1) \oplus x \\
&= F_1(k_1 \oplus F_0(x) \oplus F_0(x \oplus k_0)) \oplus x
\end{aligned}
$$

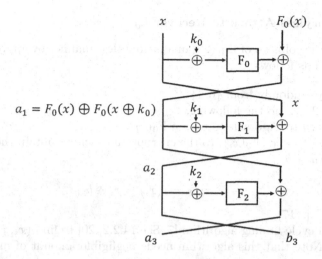

Fig. 7. Our idea

See Fig. 7. Let

$$f(x) = x \oplus b_3. \qquad (17)$$

Then we have

$$f(x) = F_1(k_1 \oplus F_0(x) \oplus F_0(k_0 \oplus x)). \qquad (18)$$

Now we can see that

$$f(x \oplus k_0) = f(x). \qquad (19)$$

This relation allows mounting the following attack.

1. For $i = 1, \ldots, 2^{n/4}$, choose x_i randomly. Query x_i to F_0-oracle to obtain $F_0(x_i)$. Query $P_i = (x_i, F_0(x_i))$ to the encryption oracle to obtain $C_i = (a_{i,3}, b_{i,3})$. Then compute

$$w_i = f(x_i) = x_i \oplus b_{i,3}$$

and store (w_i, x_i) in a table.
2. Then there exists a collision (w_i, w_j) such that

$$w_i = w_j$$

with high probability from the birthday paradox.
3. In the above case, we find a collision such that

$$f(x_i) = f(x_j). \qquad (20)$$

This collision suggests k_0 such that

$$k_0 = x_i \oplus x_j \qquad (21)$$

from Eq. (19).

In this attack, $D = O(2^{n/4})$, $T = O(2^{n/4})$, $M = O(2^{n/4})$ and the time complexity is $O(2^{n/4})$.

5.2   Memoryless Attack to Recover k_0

We can find the collision of Eq. (20) in a memoryless manner by applying Pollard rho algorithm as follows.

1. Choose x_1 randomly from $\{0,1\}^{n/2}$.
2. For $i = 1, 2, \ldots$, do the following.
   (a) Query x_i to F_0-oracle to obtain $F_0(x_i)$.
   (b) Query $P_i = (x_i, F_0(x_i))$ to the encryption oracle to obtain the ciphertext $C_i = (a_{i,3}, b_{i,3})$.
   (c) Let

   $$x_{i+1} = f(x_i) = x_i \oplus b_{i,3} \tag{22}$$

   from Eq. (17),
3. Use Floyd cycle finding algorithm [7, Sec.14.2.2][20] to find (x_i, x_j) such that $x_i = x_j$. Note that this algorithm needs negligible amount of memory. (See Fig. 8.)

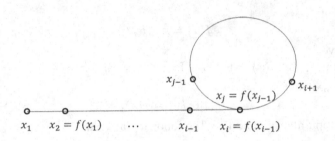

Fig. 8. Pollard rho algorithm

If $x_i = x_j$, then $f(x_{i-1}) = f(x_{j-1})$. This collision suggests k_0 such that

$$k_0 = x_{i-1} \oplus x_{j-1}$$

from Eq. (21).

$x_1, x_2, \ldots$ can be considered as a random sequence because F_i are random functions in Eq. (18). Therefore we can find a collision in time $O(2^{n/4})$ with high probability by the birthday paradox. This means that $D = O(2^{n/4})$, $T = O(2^{n/4})$ and $M = O(1)$. The time complexity is $O(2^{n/4})$.

5.3   Memoryless Attack to Recover k_1

We can similarly recover k_1 as in Sect. 5.2. This time, we choose $P = (a_0, b_0)$ such that

$$(a_0, b_0) = (0^{n/2}, x).$$

Let $C = (a_3, b_3)$. We have

$$a_1 = x \oplus F_0(k_0)$$
$$b_3 = a_2$$
$$= F_1(k_1 \oplus a_1) \oplus a_0$$
$$= F_1(k_1 \oplus F_0(k_0) \oplus x)$$

from Sect. 2. Then, let

$$f(x) = F_1(x) \oplus b_3 \tag{23}$$
$$= F_1(k_1 \oplus F_0(k_0) \oplus x) \oplus F_1(x)$$

and let

$$s = k_1 \oplus F_0(k_0). \tag{24}$$

We can see that

$$f(x \oplus s) = f(x).$$

The procedure is as follows.

1. Choose x_1 randomly from $\{0,1\}^{n/2}$.
2. For $i = 1, 2, \ldots$, do the following.
   (a) Query x_i to F_1-oracle to obtain $F_1(x_i)$.
   (b) Query $P_i = (0^n, x_i)$ to the encryption oracle to obtain the ciphertext $C_i = (a_{i,3}, b_{i,3})$.
   (c) Let
   $$x_{i+1} = f(x_i) = F_1(x_i) \oplus b_{i,3}$$
   from above Eq. (23),
3. Use Floyd cycle finding algorithm [7, Sec.14.2.2][20] to find (x_i, x_j) such that $x_i = x_j$.
   If $x_i = x_j$, then $f(x_{i-1}) = f(x_{j-1})$. This collision suggests $s = k_1 \oplus F_0(k_0)$ such that
   $$k_1 \oplus F_0(k_0) = x_{i-1} \oplus x_{j-1}$$
4. Compute k_1 by using k_0 which is previously obtained.

In this attack, $D = O(2^{n/4})$, $T = O(2^{n/4})$ and $M = O(1)$. The time complexity is $O(2^{n/4})$.

5.4 Memoryless Attack to Recover k_2

We can recover k_2 similarly. This time, we choose $P = (a_0, b_0)$ such that

$$(a_0, b_0) = (x, F_0(k_0 \oplus x)).$$

Let $C = (a_3, b_3)$. Then we have

$$a_1 = F_0(k_0 \oplus x) \oplus F_0(k_0 \oplus x) = 0^n$$
$$b_1 = x$$
$$a_3 = b_2 \oplus F_2(k_2 \oplus a_2)$$
$$= a_1 \oplus F_2(k_2 \oplus b_1 \oplus F_1(k_1 \oplus a_1))$$
$$= F_2(k_2 \oplus F_1(k_1) \oplus x)$$

from Sect. 2. Let

$$f(x) = F_2(x) \oplus a_3 \tag{25}$$
$$= F_2(k_2 \oplus F_1(k_1) \oplus x) \oplus F_2(x)$$

and let

$$s = k_2 \oplus F_1(k_1). \tag{26}$$

Then we see that

$$f(x \oplus s) = f(x)$$

The procedure is as follows.

1. Choose x_1 randomly from $\{0, 1\}^{n/2}$.
2. For $i = 1, 2, \ldots$, do the following.
   (a) Query $k_0 \oplus x_i$ to F_0-oracle to obtain $F_0(k_0 \oplus x_i)$.
   (b) Query x_i to F_2-oracle to obtain $F_2(x_i)$.
   (c) Query $P_i = (x_i, F_0(k_0 \oplus x_i))$ to the encryption oracle to obtain the cipher-text $C_i = (a_{i,3}, b_{i,3})$.
   (d) Let
   $$x_{i+1} = f(x_i) = F_2(x_i) \oplus a_{i,3}$$
   from above Eq. (25),
3. Use Floyd cycle finding algorithm [7, Sec.14.2.2][20] to find (x_i, x_j) such that $x_i = x_j$.
   If $x_i = x_j$, then $f(x_{i-1}) = f(x_{j-1})$. This collision suggests $s = k_2 \oplus F_1(k_1)$ such that
   $$k_2 \oplus F_1(k_1) = x_{i-1} \oplus x_{j-1}.$$
4. Compute k_2 by using k_1 which is previously obtained.

In this attack, $D = O(2^{n/4})$, $T = O(2^{n/4})$ and $M = O(1)$. The time complexity is $O(2^{n/4})$.

References

1. Bogdanov, A., Knudsen, L.R., Leander, G., Standaert, F.-X., Steinberger, J., Tischhauser, E.: Key-alternating ciphers in a provable setting: encryption using a small number of public permutations. In: Pointcheval, D., Johansson, T. (eds.) EUROCRYPT 2012. LNCS, vol. 7237, pp. 45–62. Springer, Heidelberg (2012). https://doi.org/10.1007/978-3-642-29011-4_5

2. Daemen, J.: Limitations of the Even-Mansour construction. In: Imai, H., Rivest, R.L., Matsumoto, T. (eds.) ASIACRYPT 1991. LNCS, vol. 739, pp. 495–498. Springer, Heidelberg (1993). https://doi.org/10.1007/3-540-57332-1_46
3. Dunkelman, O., Keller, N., Shamir, A.: Slidex attacks on the Even-Mansour encryption scheme. J. Cryptol. 28(1), 1–28 (2015)
4. Dinur, I., Dunkelman, O., Keller, N., Shamir, A.: New attacks on Feistel structures with improved memory complexities. In: Gennaro, R., Robshaw, M. (eds.) CRYPTO 2015. LNCS, vol. 9215, pp. 433–454. Springer, Heidelberg (2015). https://doi.org/10.1007/978-3-662-47989-6_21
5. Dinur, I., Dunkelman, O., Keller, N., Shamir, A.: Efficient dissection of bicomposite problems with cryptanalytic applications. J. Cryptol. 32(4), 1448–1490 (2019)
6. Even, S., Mansour, Y.: A construction of a cipher from a single pseudorandom permutation. In: Imai, H., Rivest, R.L., Matsumoto, T. (eds.) ASIACRYPT 1991. LNCS, vol. 739, pp. 210–224. Springer, Heidelberg (1993). https://doi.org/10.1007/3-540-57332-1_17
7. Galbraith, S.D.: Mathematics of Public Key Cryptography. Cambridge University Press, Cambridge (2012)
8. Hoang, V.T., Rogaway, P.: On generalized Feistel networks. In: Rabin, T. (ed.) CRYPTO 2010. LNCS, vol. 6223, pp. 613–630. Springer, Heidelberg (2010). https://doi.org/10.1007/978-3-642-14623-7_33
9. Isobe, T., Shibutani, K.: All subkeys recovery attack on block ciphers: extending meet-in-the-middle approach. In: Knudsen, L.R., Wu, H. (eds.) SAC 2012. LNCS, vol. 7707, pp. 202–221. Springer, Heidelberg (2013). https://doi.org/10.1007/978-3-642-35999-6_14
10. Isobe, T., Shibutani, K.: Generic key recovery attack on Feistel scheme. In: Sako, K., Sarkar, P. (eds.) ASIACRYPT 2013. LNCS, vol. 8269, pp. 464–485. Springer, Heidelberg (2013). https://doi.org/10.1007/978-3-642-42033-7_24
11. Luby, M., Rackoff, C.: How to construct pseudorandom permutations from pseudorandom functions. SIAM J. Comput. 17(2), 373–386 (1988)
12. Lucks, S.: Faster Luby-Rackoff ciphers. In: Gollmann, D. (ed.) FSE 1996. LNCS, vol. 1039, pp. 189–203. Springer, Heidelberg (1996). https://doi.org/10.1007/3-540-60865-6_53
13. Lampe, R., Seurin, Y.: Security analysis of key-alternating Feistel ciphers. In: Cid, C., Rechberger, C. (eds.) FSE 2014. LNCS, vol. 8540, pp. 243–264. Springer, Heidelberg (2015). https://doi.org/10.1007/978-3-662-46706-0_13
14. Maurer, U.M.: A simplified and generalized treatment of Luby-Rackoff pseudorandom permutation generators. In: Rueppel, R.A. (ed.) EUROCRYPT 1992. LNCS, vol. 658, pp. 239–255. Springer, Heidelberg (1993). https://doi.org/10.1007/3-540-47555-9_21
15. Maurer, U., Pietrzak, K.: The security of many-round Luby-Rackoff pseudorandom permutations. In: Biham, E. (ed.) EUROCRYPT 2003. LNCS, vol. 2656, pp. 544–561. Springer, Heidelberg (2003). https://doi.org/10.1007/3-540-39200-9_34
16. Maurer, U., Oswald, Y.A., Pietrzak, K., Sjödin, J.: Luby-Rackoff ciphers from weak round functions? In: Vaudenay, S. (ed.) EUROCRYPT 2006. LNCS, vol. 4004, pp. 391–408. Springer, Heidelberg (2006). https://doi.org/10.1007/11761679_24
17. Naor, M., Reingold, O.: On the construction of pseudorandom permutations: Luby-Rackoff revisited. J. Cryptol. 12(1), 29–66 (1999)
18. Patarin, J.: Security of random Feistel schemes with 5 or more rounds. In: Franklin, M. (ed.) CRYPTO 2004. LNCS, vol. 3152, pp. 106–122. Springer, Heidelberg (2004). https://doi.org/10.1007/978-3-540-28628-8_7

19. Ramzan, Z., Reyzin, L.: On the round security of symmetric-key cryptographic primitives. In: Bellare, M. (ed.) CRYPTO 2000. LNCS, vol. 1880, pp. 376–393. Springer, Heidelberg (2000). https://doi.org/10.1007/3-540-44598-6_24
20. Pollard, J.M.: Monte Carlo methods for index computation (mod p). Math. Comput. **32**(143), 918–924 (1978)

Post-Quantum Cryptography (2)

An Intermediate Secret-Guessing Attack on Hash-Based Signatures

Roland Booth[1]($\boxtimes$), Yanhong Xu[1]($\boxtimes$), Sabyasachi Karati[2],
and Reihaneh Safavi-Naini[1]

[1] Department of Computer Science, University of Calgary, Calgary, Canada
{roland.booth,yanhong.xu1}@ucalgary.ca
[2] Cryptology and Security Research Unit, Indian Statistical Institute, Kolkata, India

Abstract. Digital signature schemes form the basis of trust in Internet communication. Shor (FOCS 1994) proposed quantum algorithms that can be used by a quantum computer to break the security of today's widely used digital signature schemes, and this has fuelled intensive research on the design and implementation of post-quantum digital signatures. Hash-based digital signatures base their security on one-way functions that in practice are instantiated by hash functions. Hash-based signatures are widely studied and are part of NIST's post-quantum standardization effort.

In this paper we present a multi-target attack that we call Intermediate Secret-Guessing attack on two hash-based signatures: XMSS^{MT} (Draft SP 800-208 that was considered by NIST for standardization), and K2SN-MSS (AsiaCCS 2019). The attack allows an adversary to forge a signature on an arbitrary message. We describe the intuition behind the attack and give details of its application on the attacked schemes together with corresponding theoretical analysis. The attack implies that the effective security levels of XMSS (a special case of XMSS^{MT}), XMSS^{MT}, and K2SN-MSS are 10, 39 and 12 bits lower than their designed security levels given access to 2^{20}, 2^{60}, and 2^{20} signatures, respectively.

We implement the attack for each scheme, and give our results for reduced security parameters that validate our theoretical analysis. We also show that the attack can be avoided by modifying the application of a pseudorandom function for key generation. Our work shows the subtleties of replacing randomness with pseudo-randomness in the key generation of hash-based signatures, and the need for careful analysis of such designs.

Keywords: Post-quantum cryptography · Hash-based signatures · Multi-target attacks · XMSS^{MT} · K2SN-MSS · Implementation

1 Introduction

HASH-BASED SIGNATURES. Digital signature schemes [21] are used to authenticate the origin of a message and form the basis of trust establishment for

© Springer Nature Switzerland AG 2021
T. Nakanishi and R. Nojima (Eds.): IWSEC 2021, LNCS 12835, pp. 195–215, 2021.
https://doi.org/10.1007/978-3-030-85987-9_11

interactions on the Internet. The security of today's digital signature schemes relies on the hardness of mathematical problems that have efficient solutions if a quantum computer exists [41] and so post-quantum digital signatures must use new computational problems that stay hard when a quantum computer of sufficient scale is built.

The idea of hash-based signatures (HBS) dates back to the pioneering work of Lamport [32]. A number of improvements have been proposed by Diffie, Merkle, and Winternitz [37,38]. All these schemes are one-time, and become insecure if two messages are signed. To use the signature scheme many-times (2^h), a direct approach is to generate 2^h one-time signature (OTS) schemes. However, this would require 2^h public key and secret key pairs, which will be highly impractical for large h. To construct a many-time signature scheme with short public key, Merkle [37] proposed what we know as Merkle signature scheme (MSS). The MSS uses 2^h instances of OTS, each with a public and secret key pair $(\mathsf{opk}_i, \mathsf{osk}_i)$, and builds a Merkle (binary) tree whose leaves are the hashes of the public keys of the OTS instances, and each internal node is computed as the hash of its two child nodes. The public key consists of the root of the Merkle tree, and the secret key contains the secret keys of all the 2^h OTS instances. The signature of a message M consists of an index i that specifies an OTS instance $(\mathsf{opk}_i, \mathsf{osk}_i)$, the one-time signature σ_{OTS} on M under the key opk_i, the key opk_i, and an authentication path AUTH_i that is used to verify the validity of opk_i. Since the pioneering work of Merkle [37,38], a large number of works, e.g. [10–13,17,19], have been proposed to improve various aspects of MSS.

In 2011, Buchmann et al. [10] proposed an extended MSS (XMSS) together with a forward-secure [2,6] variant. To reduce the size of the secret key that consists of the secret keys of 2^h OTS instances, a pseudorandom function (PRF) is used with an n-bit master seed to generate an n-bit OTS seed for each OTS instance, which is in turn used to generate the secret key of that instance. There have been a number of variants of XMSS [7,8,16,23–26,30,36] that provide higher security and efficiency. Prominently, Hülsing et al. [24] proposed a multi-tree variant of XMSS, known as XMSS^{MT}, which greatly improves the key generation time and can sign virtually unlimited number of messages. This variant was later selected by NIST as the standard algorithm for stateful HBS [16]. Karati and Safavi-Naini [30] proposed K2SN-MSS scheme, that extends KSN-OTS [28] to sign multiple messages, and proved its security in the same security model used by XMSS. The authors gave an implementation of the scheme that has comparable, and in some cases superior, performance compared to XMSS^{MT}. KSN-OTS and K2SN-MSS both use SWIFFT [34] as the hash function.

The security of modern digital signature schemes is proved against Existential Unforgeability against Chosen Message Attack (EU-CMA) where the attacker must generate a valid signature on some message of their choice, after *querying* a signing oracle to obtain q message-signature pairs. The security proof of HBS assumes truly random keys for OTS, and then shows that replacing truly random keys with pseudorandom keys, which are obtained by using a PRF with a random seed, will only reduce the security by a negligible amount. The actual generation of the pseudorandom keys, however, is considered an implementation detail and is not part of the security model and proof. The goal of this paper is to show that an improper application of PRF can significantly reduce the designed security of the scheme.

OUR CONTRIBUTIONS AND TECHNIQUES. We propose an Intermediate Secret-Guessing (ISG) attack, which is a multi-target attack, on two many-time signature schemes: an earlier version of $XMSS^{MT}$ and K2SN-MSS. The attack on $XMSS^{MT}$ applies to SP 800-208 draft [15,23] but not the final version [16].

The attack breaks the EU-CMA security of the two schemes by outputting a forgery on an arbitrary message. It exploits a weakness in the way the secret key of an OTS is generated from its associated seed, without using any other information unique to this instance such as its index. Concretely, the OTS secret keys in [15,23,30] are generated as follows. Let SEED be a master seed and $\mathcal{F}$ be a secure PRF. The key generation algorithm first generates seeds for OTS instances as $SEED_{OTS,i} = \mathcal{F}(SEED, i)$ for $i \in [0, 2^h - 1]$, and then generates OTS secret keys as $osk_i = (\mathcal{F}(SEED_{OTS,i}, 1), \ldots, \mathcal{F}(SEED_{OTS,i}, \ell))$. Note that both SEED and $SEED_{OTS,i}$ are n bits, with n being the designed security level of the scheme. For concreteness, we outline the attack below.

Attack in a Nutshell. The attack has two phases. In the first *Query* Phase, the attacker collects $q \in [1, 2^h]$ signatures by querying the 2^h-time $XMSS^{MT}$/K2SN-MSS as a signing oracle[1]. Next, in the *Secret-Guessing* Phase, the attacker repeatedly guesses the value of an n-bit OTS seed.

For each guess the attacker evaluates the PRF and detects if the guessed value is the seed used for generating one of the OTS signatures. If, for example, the guess is the seed of the i-th OTS signature, then the secret key of the i-th OTS instance is revealed. The seed, together with the i-th queried signature, enables a forgery on an arbitrary message of the attacker's choice. Since there are in total q OTS signatures and the probability that the guess will match one of the q targets is $q/(2^n)$, we expect to recover one of the OTS seeds after $2^n/q$ guesses.

How a Guessed Seed is Matched for $XMSS^{MT}$. A crucial detail missing from the aforementioned outline is how to match a guessed seed and the seed used in the i-th OTS signature. We note that evaluating the PRF on an OTS seed produces the OTS secret key, which consists of ℓ n-bit strings. In addition, a signature of the Winternitz OTS scheme (WOTS+) [22] that is employed in the $XMSS^{MT}$ reveals some of these ℓ strings directly. A straightforward method is then to compare the j-th n-bit string generated from the guessed seed, with the one generated from the authentic one. If they are equal, then one considers the guess to be correct. This seed guess-verification strategy was also proposed by ETSI CyberSupport[2] in the public comment [1] on SP 800-208 draft. They

---

[1] Note that $XMSS^{MT}$ is slightly more complicated since we have more than q OTS signatures from q queried signatures. See Sect. 3 for more detail.

[2] ETSI CyberSupport only outlined the idea of matching a guessed seed with the real seed but did not develop the idea into a full attack.

further estimated that on average there are q/w WOTS+ signatures that will reveal the j-th n-bit string. Here, w is the Winternitz parameter. Therefore, the attack can only have q/w targets to compare with, and will be expected to succeed after $(2^n w)/q$ guesses.

Our attack, that is independently discovered, starts with the same guessing strategy. However we observe that when the j-th strings derived from the two seeds match, with a probability around $1/2$, the seed may not be the real seed. This reduces the success chance of the attack by a factor of $1/2$. To improve the success probability of guessing the correct seed, we compare two strings computed from the guessed seed (instead of one) with those computed from the real one. We then show that with this tweak, that is when two strings match, the guess is correct with overwhelming probability. We further show that at least 91% WOTS+ signatures will reveal at least two strings of its secret key. This improves the expected number of guesses to $2^n/(0.91q)$ by increasing the number of targets to $0.91q$.

How a Guessed Seed is Matched for K2SN-MSS. Verifying a guessed seed in K2SN-MSS is not as straightforward as in XMSS^{MT}. This is because a KSN-OTS signature does not directly reveal the strings of the secret key. Rather, the signature is the sum of a subset of strings in the secret key that is determined by the message. We therefore go a step further and evaluate the PRF on a guessed seed, compute a KSN-OTS signature and then compare the computed signature with q extracted KSN-OTS signatures. If the q messages are distinct, then one computed KSN-OTS signature can be matched against only 1 target, rendering the success probability of the ISG attack almost the same as that of a brute-force attack. However, the success probability increases significantly if the same message is used for all queries.

Analysis, Implementation and Experiments. We analyze our attack theoretically. We derive the success probability and estimate the runtime of the attack when the number of queries and guesses are q and g, respectively, and then provide an estimation of the effective security levels[3] of the two attacked schemes. The analysis shows that the ISG attack implies the effective security levels of XMSS, XMSS^{MT}, and K2SN-MSS are 10, 39, and 12 bits lower than their designed security levels given access to $q = 2^{20}$, $q = 2^{60}$, and $q = 2^{20}$ signatures, respectively.

To verify our analytical results, we implement the ISG attack on XMSS^{MT} and K2SN-MSS, that have bit security of 256 and 512 bits, respectively. Even though the attack diminishes their security levels, the experiment is still infeasible in practice. We thus perform our experiments on reduced security parameter of 16 bits for both schemes that result in feasible computation, allowing us to verify our theoretical results.

Discussion. The security implications of bad randomness in cryptosystems is widely recognized. Numerous cryptographic algorithms that use the output of a

---

[3] Security level is calculated as $\log_2(\tau/\epsilon)$, where τ is the runtime and ϵ is the success probability of ISG attack.

PRF that expands a truly random seed have been broken by adversarial control of the random seed [33,42,43]. There have also been reported weaknesses in the design of PRF algorithms that have led to predictable outputs [20,40]. Our work indicates that bad application of a PRF for generating structured randomness can compromise the security of schemes with proven properties. Modeling and proving the full security of hash based signatures, including generating randomness using a PRF, is an interesting direction for future research.

RELATED WORK. Shor's algorithm [41] and the prospect of building quantum computers at scale have fueled research on cryptographic schemes with post-quantum security. HBS is an attractive approach to construct digital signature schemes with post-quantum security because OWFs can be instantiated with hash functions that have been intensively studied in recent years, and avoid using new and less studied hardness assumptions. The security of HBS schemes was initially reduced to the collision resistance of the hash functions, and later to the second preimage resistance using a Merkle-like tree structure that used random bitmasks for intermediate tree nodes. The schemes, however, become vulnerable to a new type of attack called a multi-target attack that has been more recently proposed by Hülsing et al. [26]. To protect against this attack, Hülsing et al. proposed a new HBS scheme, called XMSS-T (XMSS with tight security), in which each hash function call is keyed with a different key and uses a different bitmask.

Leighton-Micali signature (LMS) and its hierarchical system (HSS) for multiple messages [36] use WOTS [32,37,38] as the underlying OTS scheme. Both LMS and HSS were also selected as the standard algorithms for stateful HBS [16]. Katz [31] showed that earlier versions [35] of LMS and IISS can be subjected to a multi-target attack. To strengthen the security of the schemes, any hash computation within LMS and HSS prepends a different prefix to the value that will be hashed. These prefixes can be seen to have the same role as using different keys and bitmasks in [26].

All above schemes are stateful and require the signer to maintain a state and update it after each signature. The security of stateful schemes critically depends on the correctness of the state update. Bernstein et al. proposed the first practical stateless HBS scheme SPHINCS [7], which was later improved in followup works [3–5,8,25]. All versions submitted to the NIST post-quantum competition[4] employ the same addressing scheme as in [26] and are immune to multi-target attacks.

Stateless signatures have also been constructed based on symmetric key primitives. Picnic [14] is an example of such a scheme and uses efficient zero-knowledge protocols based on the "MPC-in-the-head" paradigm [27]. Picnic 1.0 was shown [18] to be vulnerable to multi-target attacks. The more recent version of Picnic, however, is secure against these attacks.

ORGANIZATION. The rest of the paper is organized as follows. In Sect. 2 we briefly describe XMSS^{MT} and K2SN-MSS. Section 3 presents our ISG attack on

---

[4] https://csrc.nist.gov/projects/post-quantum-cryptography.

XMSS^{MT} and shows its impact on the security level of XMSS^{MT} and Sect. 4 outlines the attack and its impact on K2SN-MSS. We then present our implementation results in Sect. 5. Finally, we propose countermeasures for the attack and conclude the paper in Sect. 6 and Sect. 7, respectively.

2   Preliminaries

In this section, we briefly describe XMSS^{MT}and K2SN-MSS.

2.1   Description of XMSS^{MT}

XMSS^{MT} uses a variant of WOTS+ [22] as the underlying OTS scheme. Let w be the Winternitz parameter, n be the security parameter. The secret key is $\mathsf{osk} = (\mathbf{x}_1, \dots, \mathbf{x}_\ell)$ that contains ℓ strings of bit size n. The public key is $\mathsf{opk} = (\mathbf{y}_1, \dots, \mathbf{y}_\ell)$ where each $\mathbf{y}_i$ is computed from $\mathbf{x}_i$ by applying a PRF $w - 1$ times. To sign a message $M \in \{0,1\}^n$, one first computes its base-w representation $B_M = (b_1, \dots, b_\ell)$ and output a signature $\sigma = (\mathbf{z}_1, \dots, \mathbf{z}_\ell)$ where $\mathbf{z}_i$ is computed from $\mathbf{x}_i$ by applying the PRF b_i times. Specifically, if $b_i = 0$, then $\mathbf{z}_i = \mathbf{x}_i$. The signature is considered valid if one is able to obtain opk by applying the PRF $w - 1 - b_i$ times on $\mathbf{z}_i$ for all $i \in [1, \ell]$. More details can be found in Appendix A or [23, 26].

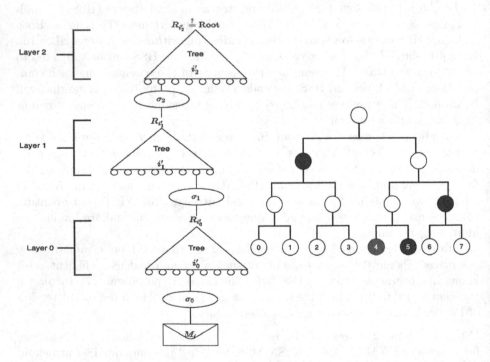

Fig. 1. A schematic representation of an XMSS^{MT} instance with $d = 3$ layers (Left) and the authentication path (yellow nodes) for the leaf 4 in a Merkle Tree of height 3 (Right). (Color figure online)

An XMSS instance is a Merkle tree whose leaves are the WOTS+ instances. An XMSS^{MT} instance is essentially a tree of XMSS instances, called a *hyper tree*, where the XMSS trees on the lowest layer sign the actual messages, and the XMSS trees on the upper layers sign the roots of the XMSS trees below them. In Fig. 1, we give a representation of an XMSS^{MT} instance with 3 layers. Consider an XMSS^{MT} tree of the total height h that has d layers of XMSS trees of height $h' = h/d$. Let the root value of the sole XMSS tree on layer $d - 1$ be ROOT. The public key consists of ROOT and some other public information, while the secret key contains SEED$_{RAND}$ and a master SEED $\in \{0,1\}^n$. The former is used to compute a randomness R whenever we need to sign a message while the latter is to compute all the secret keys of the WOTS+ instances. Concretely, to compute the secret key of an OTS instance, the algorithm first generates seeds of all XMSS trees as SEED$_{XMSS} = \mathcal{F}(SEED, s\|t)$, where s is the layer of the XMSS tree and t is the index of the tree within that layer. Next, it generates seeds for all OTS instances within a specific XMSS tree as SEED$_{OTS,i} = \mathcal{F}(SEED_{XMSS}, i)$ for $i \in [0, 2^{h'} - 1]$. Finally, the secret strings of the i-th OTS instance computed as $\mathbf{x}_{i,j} = \mathcal{F}(SEED_{OTS,i}, j)$ for $j \in [1, \ell]$. We note that the input to the generation of $\mathbf{x}_{i,j}$ does not depend on the index i and this fact is exploited in our ISG attack.

An XMSS^{MT} signature of a message M is of the form

$$\Sigma = (i, R, \sigma_0, \text{AUTH}_0, \ldots, \sigma_{d-1}, \text{AUTH}_{d-1}),$$

where $i \in [0, 2^h - 1]$ is the index that specifies the i_j-th WOTS+ instance within the i'_j-th XMSS tree on the layer j for all $j \in [0, d - 1]$ (see Fig. 1), $R = \mathcal{F}(SEED_{RAND}, i)$, σ_0 is the one-time signature on the message digest $D = \mathcal{H}_{msg}(R\|\text{ROOT}\|i, M) \in \{0,1\}^n$ with $\mathcal{H}_{msg}$ being a hash function, and σ_j is the one-time signature on the root value $R_{i'_j}$ for $j \in [1, d - 1]$. To verify a signature Σ on M, one first computes D as described above, and proceeds as follows. It computes the i_0-th WOTS+ public key opk_{i_0} from the message-signature pair (D, σ_0). Then root $R_{i'_0}$ of the i'_0-th XMSS tree on the layer 0 is computed from opk_{i_0} and AUTH$_0$. This procedure is then repeated for layers 1 to $d-1$ until root $R_{i'_{d-1}}$ of the i'_{d-1}-th XMSS tree on the layer $d - 1$ is obtained. The signature Σ is valid if $R_{i'_{d-1}} = \text{ROOT}$.

2.2 Description of K2SN-MSS

We now give a very brief overview of the K2SN-MSS protocol [30]. It is a single tree MSS where the underlying OTS is the KSN-OTS scheme [28]. The latter is an OTS scheme that employs an additive homomorphic hash function family SWIFFT [34]. The secret key is $\text{osk} = (\mathbf{x}_1, \ldots, \mathbf{x}_t)$ that consists of t binary strings of size $\hat{n}\hat{m}$ while the public key is $\text{opk} = (\mathbf{y}_1, \ldots, \mathbf{y}_t)$ where $\mathbf{y}_i = \text{SWIFFT}_{\mathbf{k}}(\mathbf{x}_i)$ for some key $\mathbf{k}$ specifying the SWIFFT function. To sign a message $M \in \{0,1\}^m$, one first derives a subset B_M of $\{1, 2, \ldots, t\}$ from M and then computes the signature as $\sigma = \sum_{j \in B_M}(\mathbf{x}_j)$. Here $|B_M| = t/2$. The signature is considered valid if $\text{SWIFFT}_{\mathbf{k}}(\sigma) = \sum_{j \in B_M}(\mathbf{y}_j) \bmod p$ and σ has small entries. More details can be found in [28].

In order to sign 2^h messages, K2SN-MSS builds a Merkle tree on top of 2^h KSN-OTS instances. The public key consists of the root of the tree and some other public information while secret key is a master SEED $\in \{0,1\}^n$. The seed is used to generate secret keys of those 2^h KSN-OTS instances as in XMSS^{MT}. Specifically, it first generates seeds for all OTS instances as SEED$_{OTS,i} = \mathcal{F}(\text{SEED}, i)$ for all $i \in [0, 2^h - 1]$. Next, it computes the secret strings of the i-th OTS instance as $\mathbf{x}_{i,j} = \mathcal{F}(\text{SEED}_{OTS,i}, j)$ for all $j \in [1, t]$. The fact that $\mathbf{x}_{i,j}$ does not depend on the index i is exploited in our ISG attack.

A K2SN-MSS signature of a message M is of the form $\Sigma = (i, \sigma_i, \text{opk}_i, \text{AUTH}_i)$, where i is the index of the used OTS instance, σ_i is the one-time signature on M under the public key opk_i of the i-th OTS instance, and AUTH_i is the authentication path. The signature is valid if σ_i is a valid signature on M and that opk_i is authenticated against AUTH_i. We observe that the signing algorithm here is not randomized as in XMSS^{MT}, which makes forging a signature quite straightforward once we guess correctly the seed of a KSN-OTS instance.

3   ISG Attack on XMSS^{MT}

We first give an overview of our ISG attack on XMSS^{MT}. We assume that the attacker has access to $q \in [1, 2^h]$ signatures on the same message M_Q[5] and repeatedly guess WOTS+ seeds for at most $g \in [1, 2^n]$ times. The goal of the attack is to output a forgery Σ_F on a message M_F of the attacker's choice with the condition that $M_F \neq M_Q$. Note that in Step 1, $q' > q$ since there are WOTS+ instances on higher layers other than layer 0. In Step 2, we only store pairs that reveal at least two strings (out of ℓ) of their secret keys. In Step 3, we simply guess the seed as an n-bit representation of 0 up to $g - 1$.

1. From the q queried signatures, extract q' WOTS+ message-signature pairs.
2. Out of q' pairs, filter out those that contain less data (about their underlying secret keys) than some threshold. For the remaining pairs, store the data in some tables for efficient match in the next step.
3. For each guess SEED$' \in [0, g - 1]$, derive a corresponding PRF output and compare with the stored data.
4. If a match is found for SEED$'$, output a forgery Σ_F on M_F using SEED$'$.

In the following, we show in Sect. 3.1 how to verify the legitimacy of a guessed seed. Section 3.2 describes how to forge a signature if the guessed seed is legitimate and Sect. 3.3 gives the detailed description of the attack. Lastly, we analyze the runtime and success probability of the attack in Sect. 3.4.

---

[5] This is not compulsory in our attack on XMSS^{MT}, which randomizes the message before signing it.

3.1 Verifying a WOTS+ Seed Guess for XMSS^{MT}

Consider an XMSS tree within an XMSS^{MT} hyper tree. Let $\text{SEED}_{\text{OTS},i}$ and osk_i be the seed and the secret key of the i-th WOTS+ instance in this XMSS tree, and let σ_i be a signature on a message M computed from osk_i. Given only the pair (M, σ_i), we want to determine if a guessed SEED' is equal to the legitimate seed $\text{SEED}_{\text{OTS},i}$. Recall that the secret key of the i-th WOTS+ instance is computed as

$$\text{osk}_i = (\mathbf{x}_{i,1}, \dots, \mathbf{x}_{i,\ell}) = (\mathcal{F}(\text{SEED}_{\text{OTS},i}, 1), \dots, \mathcal{F}(\text{SEED}_{\text{OTS},i}, \ell)),$$

To sign a message M, one first computes $B_M = (b_1, \dots, b_\ell)$ and outputs the signature $\sigma_i = (\mathbf{z}_1, \dots, \mathbf{z}_\ell)$ such that $\mathbf{z}_j = \mathbf{x}_{i,j}$ if $b_j = 0$ for some $j \in [1, \ell]$.

Verifying a Guess Against one WOTS+ Signature. Given a signature $\sigma_i = (\mathbf{z}_1, \dots, \mathbf{z}_\ell)$ and its corresponding message M, find two indices k_1 and k_2 such that b_{k_1} and b_{k_2} are zero. Then $\mathbf{z}_{k_1}$ and $\mathbf{z}_{k_2}$ are the k_1-th and the k_2-th elements of osk_i. If there are no such indices, then this test is inconclusive. Next, we compute $\text{osk}' = (\mathbf{x}'_1, \dots, \mathbf{x}'_\ell)$ from SEED' by evaluating PRF $\mathcal{F}$, and check if $\mathbf{x}'_{k_1} = \mathbf{z}_{k_1}$ and $\mathbf{x}'_{k_2} = \mathbf{z}_{k_2}$. If they are equal, we claim that $\text{SEED}' = \text{SEED}_{\text{OTS},i}$ with all but negligible probability. Fix a WOTS+ signature as above and let $\text{SEED}_{\text{OTS},i}$ be the real seed. Then

$$\Pr[\text{SEED}' = \text{SEED}_{\text{OTS},i} | (\mathbf{x}'_{k_1} = \mathbf{x}_{k_1}) \wedge (\mathbf{x}'_{k_2} = \mathbf{x}_{k_2})]$$
$$= \frac{\Pr[(\text{SEED}' = \text{SEED}_{\text{OTS},i}) \wedge (\mathbf{x}'_{k_1} = \mathbf{x}_{k_1}) \wedge (\mathbf{x}'_{k_2} = \mathbf{x}_{k_2})]}{\Pr[(\mathbf{x}'_{k_1} = \mathbf{x}_{k_1}) \wedge (\mathbf{x}'_{k_2} = \mathbf{x}_{k_2})]}$$
$$= \frac{E_1}{E_1 + E_2},$$

where $E_1 = \Pr[(\text{SEED}' = \text{SEED}_{\text{OTS},i}) \wedge (\mathbf{x}'_{k_1} = \mathbf{x}_{k_1}) \wedge (\mathbf{x}'_{k_2} = \mathbf{x}_{k_2})] = \frac{1}{2^n}$, $E_2 = \Pr[(\text{SEED}' \neq \text{SEED}_{\text{OTS},i}) \wedge (\mathbf{x}'_{k_1} = \mathbf{x}_{k_1}) \wedge (\mathbf{x}'_{k_2} = \mathbf{x}_{k_2})] = (1 - \frac{1}{2^n})\frac{1}{2^{2n}}$, and the probability is taken over $\text{SEED}' \in \{0, 1\}^n$. Note that conditioned on $\text{SEED}' \neq \text{SEED}_{\text{OTS},i}$, distributions of $\mathbf{x}'_{k_1}, \mathbf{x}'_{k_2}$ are indistinguishable from random distribution over $\{0, 1\}^n$ due to the security of $\mathcal{F}$. One then sees that $E_1/(E_1 + E_2)$ is all but negligible.

The reason to compare two elements instead of just one is because a similar argument shows that $\Pr[\text{SEED}' = \text{SEED}_{\text{OTS},i} | \mathbf{x}'_{k_1} = \mathbf{x}_{k_1}] \approx \frac{1}{2}$. In other words, SEED' is not $\text{SEED}_{\text{OTS},i}$ with probability around $1/2$ if the k_1-th strings derived from the guessed seed and the real seed match only.

Verifying a Guess Against Multiple WOTS+ Signatures. Given q message-signature pairs $(M_0, \sigma_0), \dots, (M_{q-1}, \sigma_{q-1})$ from q WOTS+ instances, the goal is to determine efficiently if a guess SEED' is the seed of one of these instances. For each pair (M_i, σ_i), we discard those whose signatures do not reveal at least two strings of their secret keys. For the remaining ones, we extract exactly two strings and then construct a tuple that contains these strings and the index i so we know which pair these strings are extracted from. The tuples will be sorted into tables that can be efficiently searched.

To this end, we build $\ell-1$ tables $T_1, \ldots, T_{\ell-1}$. For $k_1 \in [1, \ell-1]$, T_{k_1} contains tuples of the form $(\mathbf{x}_{k_1}, k_2, \mathbf{x}_{k_2}, i)$ indexed by $\mathbf{x}_{k_1}$. Here $\mathbf{x}_{k_1}, \mathbf{x}_{k_2}$ are two strings of the secret key revealed in σ_i.

Next, compute $\mathsf{osk}' = (\mathbf{x}'_1, \ldots, \mathbf{x}'_\ell)$ from a guessed SEED' as before. Then for every $k_1 \in [1, \ell-1]$, use a binary search algorithm to search T_{k_1}, checking whether it contains a tuple indexed by $\mathbf{x}'_{k_1}$. Suppose that, for some index k_1, we find a tuple $(\mathbf{x}'_{k_1}, k_2, \mathbf{x}_{k_2}, i)$ in T_{k_1}. Using the index k_2, we further compare $\mathbf{x}'_{k_2}$ with $\mathbf{x}_{k_2}$. If equal, we conclude that SEED' is the underlying seed for computing σ_i, as shown in Sect. 3.1.

Note that to uniquely identify the location of a WOTS+ signature σ in an XMSS^{MT} tree, one must know the index i of the XMSS^{MT} signature that σ is extracted from and the hyper tree layer j that σ belongs to. To this end, we store tuples of the form $(\mathbf{x}_{k_1}, k_2, \mathbf{x}_{k_2}, i, j)$ instead.

3.2   Using a WOTS+ Seed to Forge a Signature

Let us now describe how to forge an XMSS^{MT} signature once we guess correctly the underlying seed of a WOTS+ instance. Let an XMSS^{MT} signature on message M_i be

$$\Sigma_i = (i, R, \sigma_0, \mathrm{AUTH}_0, \ldots, \sigma_{d-1}, \mathrm{AUTH}_{d-1}).$$

Suppose we have guessed the seed SEED' of σ_j from Σ_i, and now want to forge an XMSS^{MT} signature on an arbitrary message M_F. We proceed as follows. Recall that the index i specifies that σ_j is from the i_j-th WOTS+ instance in the i'_j-th XMSS tree on layer j of the hyper tree.

Case 1: $j = 0$. It implies that SEED' is the seed of the i_0-th WOTS+ instance which is used to sign $D_i = \mathcal{H}_{\mathrm{msg}}(R\|\mathrm{ROOT}\|i, M_i)$. To compute a forged signature Σ_F on M_F, we first compute a WOTS+ signature on the digest of M_F and then replace σ_0 in Σ_i with the new signature. (Recall that σ_0 is a signature on D_i.) Concretely, compute $\widehat{D}_i = \mathcal{H}_{\mathrm{msg}}(R\|\mathrm{ROOT}\|i, M_F)$ and a WOTS+ signature $\sigma_{0,F}$ of $\widehat{D}_i$ using the SEED'. Let $\Sigma_F = (i, R, \sigma_{0,F}, \mathrm{AUTH}_0, \ldots, \sigma_{d-1}, \mathrm{AUTH}_{d-1})$ be obtained by substituting σ_0 with $\sigma_{0,F}$. It is straightforward to verify the validity of Σ_F.

Case 2: $0 < j \leq d-1$. It implies that SEED' is the seed of the i_j-th WOTS+ instance that is used to sign the root $R_{i'_{j-1}}$ of the i'_{j-1}-th XMSS tree on layer $j-1$. Recall that during the verification process of the pair (M_i, Σ_i), one computes WOTS+ public keys and XMSS roots $\mathsf{opk}_{i_0}, R_{i'_0}, \mathsf{opk}_{i_1}, R_{i'_1}, \ldots, \mathsf{opk}_{i_{d-1}}, R_{i'_{d-1}}$ sequentially and then compares $R_{i'_{d-1}}$ with ROOT. Since M_i is legitimately signed, the computed values are the real ones and in particular $R_{i'_{d-1}} = \mathrm{ROOT}$.

To compute a forged signature Σ_F, our strategy is to run the verification algorithm on (M_F, Σ_i) up to the point that the (fake) root value of i'_{j-1}-th XMSS tree is computed. Then we compute a WOTS+ signature on this (fake) root value using the SEED', and replace σ_j in Σ_i with the new signature. Since the new WOTS+ signature is legitimately signed, one is able to compute the real WOTS+ public key opk_{i_j}. In fact, from this point on, all the computed WOTS+ public keys and XMSS roots are the real ones and thus the signature is considered valid. Concretely, we perform the following steps.

To begin with, compute $\widehat{D}_i = \mathcal{H}_{\mathrm{msg}}(R\|\mathrm{ROOT}\|i, M_F)$. Next, compute a fake i_0-th WOTS+ public key $\widehat{\mathsf{opk}}_{i_0}$ from the pair $(\widehat{D}_i, \sigma_0)$, and a fake root $\widehat{R}_{i'_0}$ from $\widehat{\mathsf{opk}}_{i_0}$ and AUTH_0 as in the verification process of XMSS^{MT} described in Sect. 2.1. This procedure is repeated for layers 1 to $j-1$ until a fake root $\widehat{R}_{i'_{j-1}}$ is obtained. Then compute the signature $\sigma_{j,F}$ of the root $\widehat{R}_{i'_{j-1}}$ using SEED$'$. Finally, replace σ_j in Σ_i with $\sigma_{j,F}$, we obtain

$$\Sigma_F = (i, R, \sigma_0, \mathrm{AUTH}_0, \ldots, \sigma_{j,F}, \mathrm{AUTH}_j, \ldots, \sigma_{d-1}, \mathrm{AUTH}_{d-1}).$$

3.3 ISG Attack on XMSS^{MT}

Putting everything together, we are ready to describe our ISG attack on XMSS^{MT}. The inputs of the attack are the number of signature queries $q \in [1, 2^h]$ and the number of seed guesses $g \in [1, 2^n]$, and the output is a forgery (M_F, Σ_F) if successful, or empty otherwise.

The attack initializes a set S_{MSS} to store the response from the signing oracle, and $\ell - 1$ tables $T_1, \ldots, T_{\ell-1}$ as described in Sect. 3.1 to store the data extracted from WOTS+ signatures. It operates in two phases.

In the Query Phase, the attacker queries the signing oracle with an arbitrarily chosen M_Q for q times. On the i-th query, an XMSS^{MT} signature $\Sigma_i = (i, R, \sigma_0, \mathrm{AUTH}_0, \ldots, \sigma_{d-1}, \mathrm{AUTH}_{d-1})$ is obtained and then stored in S_{MSS}. From Σ_i, d WOTS+ message-signature pairs

$$(D_i, \sigma_0), (R_{i'_0}, \sigma_1), \ldots, (R_{i'_{d-2}}, \sigma_{d-1})$$

are computed. This can be done by running the XMSS^{MT} verification algorithm. For each $\sigma_j = (\mathbf{z}_{j,1}, \ldots, \mathbf{z}_{j,\ell})$ with $j \in [0, d-1]$, let $\mathbf{z}_{j,k_1}, \mathbf{z}_{j,k_2}$ be two strings of secret key revealed and then insert $(\mathbf{z}_{j,k_1}, k_2, \mathbf{z}_{j,k_2}, i, j)$ to table T_{k_1}. If no two such strings exists, discard σ_j. Note that the WOTS+ signatures on layers 1 to $d-1$ may be repeated and thus are ignored once they appear again.

In the Secret-Guessing Phase, the attacker repeatedly guesses WOTS+ seeds until it succeeds, or runs out of the g guesses. Let SEED$'$ be the j-th guess. It first computes $\mathsf{osk}' = (\mathbf{x}'_1, \ldots, \mathbf{x}'_\ell)$ from SEED$'$ and then searches tables $T_1, \ldots, T_{\ell-1}$. If there exists a tuple $(\mathbf{z}_{k_1}, k_2, \mathbf{z}_{k_2}, i, j)$ such that $\mathbf{z}_{k_1} = \mathbf{x}'_{k_1}$, $\mathbf{z}_{k_2} = \mathbf{x}'_{k_2}$, we know that SEED$'$ is the underlying seed of the j-th WOTS+ instance from the i-th queried signature with all but negligible probability. Thus, a forged signature Σ_F on the message M_F of the attacker's choice can be computed (as long as $M_F \neq M_Q$) as described in Sect. 3.2. Otherwise, we move to the next guess. If no forgery is computed after g guesses, return $\perp$.

3.4   Analysis of ISG Attack on XMSS^{MT}

Number of Targets. To calculate the success probability of our attack, it is crucial to find out the number of targets $N_{TARGETS}$. Recall that we have q' WOTS+ message-signature pairs. However, not all of them are valid targets to be matched against. Let P be the probability that a WOTS+ signature on a random message reveals at least two strings of its secret key. Then $N_{TARGETS} = q' \cdot P$. It is not hard to verify that $q' = \sum_{i=0}^{d-1} \lceil \frac{q}{2^{h' \cdot i}} \rceil$, where $h' = \frac{h}{d}$. Furthermore, P is lower bounded by $1 - (1 - \frac{1}{w})^{\ell_1} - \frac{\ell_1}{w}(1 - \frac{1}{w})^{\ell_1 - 1}$. (See Appendix B for details.) Given parameters $w = 16$, $n = 256$, $\ell_1 = 64$ for WOTS+, $P \geq 0.9153$.

Success Probability of the ISG Attack. The success probability of the ISG attack on XMSS^{MT} and inputs $q \in [1, 2^h]$, $g \in [1, 2^n]$ is:

$$\mathrm{Succ}^{\mathrm{EU\text{-}CMA}}_{\mathrm{XMSS}^{MT}, \mathcal{A}(q, g)}(1^n) = 1 - \left(\frac{2^n - g}{2^n}\right)^{N_{TARGETS}}.$$

The attack outputs a forgery if and only if a guessed SEED' equals one of the $N_{TARGETS}$ seeds, or equivalently, at least one of the $N_{TARGETS}$ seeds is in the set $[0, g-1]$. Note that these seeds are the outputs of a pseudorandom function whose output distribution over $\{0, 1\}^n$ is indistinguishable from random. Therefore, the probability that none of these seeds is in the set $[0, g - 1]$ can be approximated as $\left(\frac{2^n - g}{2^n}\right)^{N_{TARGETS}}$, and the success probability is thus $1 - \left(\frac{2^n - g}{2^n}\right)^{N_{TARGETS}}$.

How the Runtime is Measured. We measure the algorithmic time as the number of hash function evaluations, PRF evaluations, and the comparisons of $\mathcal{O}(n)$-bit strings. Denote these atomic operations as C_{HASH}, C_{PRF} and C_{COMP}.

Runtime of the ISG Attack. The runtime of the ISG attack on an instance of XMSS^{MT} with the inputs $q \in [1, 2^h]$ and $g \in [1, 2^n]$ is

$$\tau_{\mathrm{XMSS}^{MT}}(q, g) \leq q \cdot \tau_{\mathrm{MsgDigest}} + (q' - q) \cdot \tau_{\mathrm{XMSSRootAvg}} \tag{1}$$

$$+ N_{TARGETS} \cdot \log\left(\frac{N_{TARGETS}}{\ell - 1}\right) \cdot C_{COMP} \tag{2}$$

$$+ g \cdot \left(\ell \cdot C_{PRF} + (\ell - 1) \cdot \log\left(\frac{N_{TARGETS}}{\ell - 1}\right) \cdot C_{COMP}\right) \tag{3}$$

$$+ \tau_{\mathrm{ComputeForgeryIS}}. \tag{4}$$

The time complexity of the attack is dominated by, (1) the time to compute the q' WOTS+ message-signature pairs, (2) the time to sort $N_{TARGETS}$ targets, (3) the time to search against the $\ell - 1$ tables, and (4) the time to compute the forgery. Details are in the full version of this paper.

Effective Security Level of XMSS^{MT}. Following [17], the bit security of a digital signature scheme (DSS) is estimated as $\log_2\left(\tau_{DSS}(q, g)/\mathrm{Succ}^{\mathrm{EU\text{-}CMA}}_{DSS, \mathcal{A}(q, g)}(1^n)\right)$. Using the above formulas, we evaluate the effective security levels of XMSS and XMSS^{MT} in Table 1. In the calculations, we assume $C_{HASH} = C_{PRF} = C_{COMP} = 1$.

Table 1. Effective security level of XMSS and $XMSS^{MT}$ on concrete parameter sets.

Scheme	Designed security level	Scheme parameters	Attack parameters	Effective security level
XMSS	$n = 256$	$w = 16, \ell = 67, h = 20$	$q = 2^{20}, g = 2^{205}$	246.06
$XMSS^{MT}$	$n = 256$	$w = 16, \ell = 67, h = 60\ d = 12$	$q = 2^{60}, g = 2^{205}$	216.84

From the table, we see that the effective security levels of XMSS and $XMSS^{MT}$ are 10 and 39 bits lower than their designed security levels. These results demonstrate the significant effect of our attack. It is worth noting that our attack is more effective on $XMSS^{MT}$ due to significantly more target values.

4   ISG Attack on K2SN-MSS

We now give an outline of the ISG attack on K2SN-MSS. Assume that the attacker has access to $q \in [1, 2^h]$ signatures on the same message M_Q, and guesses KSN-OTS seeds for at most $g \in [1, 2^n]$ times. The aim of the attack is to output a forged signature Σ_F on an arbitrary message M_F where $M_F \neq M_Q$. It is crucial that all queries use the same message M_Q. This is because, unlike WOTS+, a KSN-OTS signature does not reveal strings of the secret key directly. Instead, a KSN-OTS signature reveals a sum of $t/2$ strings of its secret keys where the choice of the strings used for the sum depends on the message being signed.

1. From the q queried signatures, simply extract q KSN-OTS signatures.
2. Sort the q KSN-OTS signatures by interpreting the signatures as bit strings.
3. For each guess SEED$' \in [0, g-1]$, evaluate the PRF on $t/2$ inputs determined by B_{M_Q} and sums the $t/2$ outputs. (This is equivalent to signing M_Q using the secret key derived from SEED$'$.) Compare the sum with the stored signatures using a binary search algorithm.
4. If a match is found for SEED$'$, output a forgery Σ_F on M_F using SEED$'$.

We show how to verify the correctness of a guessed seed in Sect. 4.1, and how to forge a signature if we guess the seed correctly in Sect. 4.2. Section 4.3 describes our attack on K2SN-MSS and its runtime and success probability.

4.1   Verifying a KSN-OTS Seed Guess for K2SN-MSS

Let σ_i be a signature of the message M_Q derived from SEED$_{OTS,i}$ for some i. To test if SEED$'$ is SEED$_{OTS,i}$, it is tempting to simply evaluate PRF on two inputs using SEED$'$ and then compare with the extracted data as the attack on $XMSS^{MT}$. As we observe, however, this is impossible since KSN-OTS signature does not reveal strings of its secret key directly. To solve this issue, we compute a KSN-OTS signature on M_Q as $\sigma' = \sum_{j \in B_{M_Q}} \mathcal{F}(\text{SEED}', j)$ and then compare it with σ_i. If $\sigma' = \sigma_i$, we claim that $\text{SEED}' = \text{SEED}_{\text{OTS},i}$ with overwhelming probability.

Let

$$\Pr[\text{SEED}' = \text{SEED}_{\text{OTS},i} | \sigma' = \sigma_i] = \frac{\Pr[(\text{SEED}' = \text{SEED}_{\text{OTS},i}) \wedge (\sigma' = \sigma_i)]}{\Pr[\sigma' = \sigma_i]}$$

$$= \frac{E_1}{E_1 + E_2},$$

where $E_1 = \Pr[(\sigma' = \sigma_i) \wedge (\text{SEED}' = \text{SEED}_{\text{OTS},i})] = \frac{1}{2^n}$, $E_2 = \Pr[(\sigma' = \sigma_i) \wedge (\text{SEED}' \neq \text{SEED}_{\text{OTS},i})] \leq (1 - \frac{1}{2^n}) \frac{1}{2^{\hat{n}\hat{m}}}$, and the probability is taken over $\text{SEED}' \in \{0,1\}^n$. Note that conditioned on $\text{SEED}' \neq \text{SEED}_{\text{OTS},i}$, σ' is the addition of $t/2$ pseudorandom elements over $\{0,1\}^n$. Therefore, $\Pr[\sigma' = \sigma_i | \text{SEED}' \neq \text{SEED}_{\text{OTS},i}] \leq \left(\max_j \binom{t/2}{j} \frac{1}{2^{t/2}} \right)^{\hat{n}\hat{m}} \leq \frac{1}{2^{\hat{n}\hat{m}}}$. Since $t = 262$, $\hat{n}\hat{m} = 2n$ in [30], the probability $E_1/(E_1 + E_2) = 1 - E_2/(E_1 + E_2)$ is all but negligible. This proves our claim.

4.2 Using a KSN-OTS Seed to Forge a Signature

It is quite easy to forge a signature on M_F once we guess $\text{SEED}_{\text{OTS},i}$. Let the i-th queried signature be $\Sigma_i = (i, \sigma_i, \text{opk}_i, \text{AUTH}_i)$. We simply compute the KSN-OTS signature σ_F on M_F using $\text{SEED}_{\text{OTS},i}$, and output $\Sigma_F = (i, \sigma_F, \text{opk}_i, \text{AUTH}_i)$. It is straightforward to verify the validity of Σ_F on M_F.

4.3 ISG Attack on K2SN-MSS and Its Analysis

ISG Attack on K2SN-MSS. The inputs of the attack are $q \in [1, 2^h]$ and $g \in [1, 2^n]$ as in Sect. 3.3, and the goal is to output a forgery (M_F, Σ_F). The attack initializes a set S_{MSS} to store the received signatures from the signing oracle, and a table T_{OTS} to store the extracted KSN-OTS signatures. It operates in two phases.

In the Query Phase, the attacker queries the signing oracle with an arbitrary message M_Q for q times. On the i-th query, a signature $\Sigma_i = (i, \sigma_i, \text{opk}_i, \text{AUTH}_i)$ is received and stored in S_{MSS}. From Σ_i, we extract σ_i and insert (σ_i, i) in T_{OTS} that is indexed by σ_i. Note that for all i, σ_i is a signature on M_Q.

In the Secret-Guessing Phase, the attacker guesses the KSN-OTS seeds until it succeeds, or runs out of the g guesses. Let SEED' be the j-th guess. The attacker first computes $\sigma' = \sum_{j \in B_{M_Q}} \mathcal{F}(\text{SEED}', j)$, and then searches in T_{OTS}. If there is a tuple (σ_i, i) such that $\sigma_i = \sigma'$, then the attacker knows SEED' is the underlying seed with overwhelming probability as shown in Sect. 4.1. Thus, a forged signature Σ_F on M_F can be computed as described in Sect. 4.2. If it did not return any forgery after g guesses, abort.

Success Probability of the ISG Attack. Note that unlike $\mathrm{XMSS^{MT}}$, the attack on K2SN-MSS has exactly q valid targets from the q queried signatures. Thus, following Sect. 3.4, the success probability of the ISG attack on K2SN-MSS using the inputs $q \in [1, 2^h]$, $g \in [1, 2^n]$ is:

$$\mathrm{Succ}_{\mathrm{K2SN\text{-}MSS},\mathcal{A}(q,\,g)}^{\mathrm{EU\text{-}CMA}}(1^n) = 1 - \left(\frac{2^n - g}{2^n}\right)^q.$$

Runtime of the ISG Attack. The runtime of the ISG attack on an instance of K2SN-MSS with the inputs $q \in [1, 2^h]$ and $g \in [1, 2^n]$ is given as:

$$\tau_{\mathrm{K2SN}}(q,\,g) \le q \cdot \log q \cdot \mathrm{C_{COMP}} + g \cdot \left(\frac{t}{2} \cdot \mathrm{C_{PRF}} + \log q \cdot \mathrm{C_{COMP}}\right) + \frac{t}{2} \cdot \mathrm{C_{PRF}}.$$

The runtime is dominated by (1) the time to sort the q KSN-OTS signatures, (2) the time to compute a KSN-OTS signature from a guessed seed and compare it with the sorted signatures, and (3) the time to compute a forgery if the attack succeeds. In the worst case, we have to run the guesses g times.

Effective Security Level of K2SN-MSS. We estimate the new security level of K2SN-MSS as $\log_2\left(\tau_{\mathrm{K2SN\text{-}MSS}}(q, g)/\mathrm{Succ}_{\mathrm{K2SN\text{-}MSS},\mathcal{A}(q,\,g)}^{\mathrm{EU\text{-}CMA}}(1^n)\right)$. As in Sect. 3.4, we choose $\mathrm{C_{HASH}} = \mathrm{C_{PRF}} = \mathrm{C_{COMP}} = 1$. For parameters $n = 512$, $\hat{n} = 64$, $\hat{m} = 16$, $t = 262$, $h = 20$, the effective security level of K2SN-MSS is 500.15 for $q = 2^{20}$ and $g = 2^{250}$. This is 12 bits lower than the designed security level 512.

5   Implementation and Experiments

We implemented the ISG attacks on $\mathrm{XMSS^{MT}}$ and K2SN-MSS utilizing implementations from [39][6] and [29] as the signing oracles. Our implementation can be found in [9]. In order to make the attack feasible and obtain a meaningful performance estimate, we reduce the search space of the attack by fixing all but the least significant $n' = 16$ bits of OTS seeds. No other changes are made to the attacked schemes.

Description of the Experiments. Our two experiments are performed on **Skylake** Intel®Core™i7-6700 4-core CPU @ 3.40 GHz running. The system has 8GB RAM and the timing experiments are performed on a single core. The OS is 64-bit Ubuntu-18.04 LTS and C codes are compiled by GCC version 7.5.0. During the experiments, the turbo boost and hyper-threading are turned off

For each experiment, we performed 1000 trials on each of the possible input pairs (q, g) where $q \in \{1, 2^2, 2^4, 2^6, 2^8\}$ and $g \in \{1, 2^2, 2^4, \ldots, 2^{14}, 2^{16}\}$. From these trials we obtain an average runtime and success probability of the attack.

Results of the Experiments. Figure 2 and Fig. 3 show some of our experimental results. Figure 2 shows that the theoretical and actual success probabilities of the ISG attack on $\mathrm{XMSS^{MT}}$ and K2SN-MSS are well matched.

---

[6] For $\mathrm{XMSS^{MT}}$, we use the commit "fb7e3f8edce8d412a707f522d597ab3546863202" that is published on Apr 24, 2019 as the weakness was fixed in later commits.

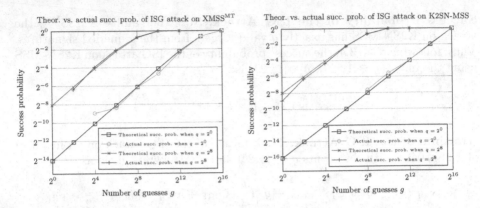

Fig. 2. Theoretical and actual success probability of ISG attack on XMSS^{MT} (Left) and K2SN-MSS (Right).

We note that the theoretical runtime is a count of the atomic operations while the actual runtime is in milliseconds. Figure 3 shows that both the theoretical and the actual runtimes increase at a similar rate as the number of guesses increase. Also note that the actual runtime begins to grow more slowly as g gets close to its maximum value due to that our actual attack terminates before making all the g guesses.

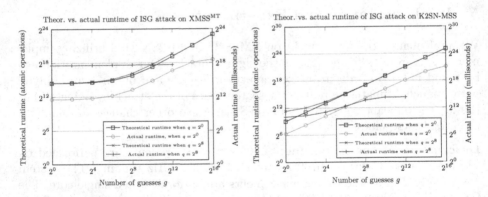

Fig. 3. Theoretical and actual runtime of ISG attack on XMSS^{MT} (Left) and K2SN-MSS (Right).

6 Mitigations Against the ISG Attack

To protect against the ISG attack, the generation of the pseudorandom keys for OTSs must be revised. Recall that in XMSS^{MT}, osk_i is generated as

$$\mathsf{osk}_i = (\mathbf{x}_{i,1}, \dots, \mathbf{x}_{i,\ell}) = (\mathcal{F}(\mathrm{SEED}_{\mathrm{OTS},i}, 1), \dots, \mathcal{F}(\mathrm{SEED}_{\mathrm{OTS},i}, \ell)).$$

To prevent the attack, it suffices to generate osk_i by having the input to $\mathcal{F}$ dependent on the position of the OTS instance. Specifically, one computes the secret key of the i-th WOTS+ instance within an XMSS tree as

$$\mathsf{osk}_i = \big(\mathcal{F}(\text{SEED}_{\text{OTS},i}, s\|t\|i\|1),\ldots,\mathcal{F}(\text{SEED}_{\text{OTS},i}, s\|t\|i\|\ell)\big),$$

where s is the layer of the XMSS tree and t is the index of that tree within layer s.

The same strategy can also be used for K2SN-MSS. Specifically, one can generate osk_i in the following manner:

$$\mathsf{osk}_i = (\mathbf{x}_{i,1},\ldots,\mathbf{x}_{i,t}) = (\mathcal{F}(\text{SEED}_{\text{OTS},i}, i\|1),\ldots,\mathcal{F}(\text{SEED}_{\text{OTS},i}, i\|t)).$$

ETSI CyberSupport [1] also proposed a fix to prevent the attack by generating each secret string as

$$\mathbf{x}_{i,j} = \mathcal{F}(\text{SEED}_{\text{XMSS}}, \text{ADDRES}),$$

where $\text{SEED}_{\text{XMSS}}$ is the seed of an XMSS tree and ADDRES is the unique address of $\mathbf{x}_{i,j}$ within the hyper tree.

7   Concluding Remarks

We proposed a multi-target attack called the ISG attack on XMSS^{MT} and K2SN-MSS, two hash-based signature schemes with provable security. The attacks, however, do not contradict the security proofs of the two schemes because the pseudorandom generation of secret keys is outside the security model and proofs of these schemes, and is considered an implementation detail of the algorithms. Thus our attack can be seen as an attack on the implementation. As discussed above, preventing the attack is straightforward. However, proving the soundness of using a secure PRF in an MSS structure remains a non-trivial open question. Our results show once again the importance of detailed specifications of cryptographic systems, and not leaving out important details that are needed in practice.

Acknowledgment. The works of Roland Booth, Yanhong Xu and Reihaneh Safavi-Naini were supported in part by Alberta Innovates Strategic Chair in Information Security Grant and Natural Sciences and Engineering Research Council of Canada Discovery Grant. Roland Booth was also supported by the Natural Sciences and Engineering Research Council of Canada (NSERC), [funding reference number 551629 - 2020]. (Roland Booth a été financé par le Conseil de recherches en sciences naturelles et en génie du Canada (CRSNG), [numéro de référence 551629 - 2020].)

A   Description of WOTS+

We now describe the WOTS+ used in [23, 26]. Let w be the Winternitz parameter, n be the security parameter, and $F : \{0,1\}^n \times \{0,1\}^n \to \{0,1\}^n$ be a secure hash function. Define $\ell_1 = \left\lceil \frac{n}{\log_2(w)} \right\rceil$ and $\ell_2 = \left\lfloor \frac{\log_2(\ell_1(w-1))}{\log_2(w)} \right\rfloor + 1$, and $\ell = \ell_1 + \ell_2$. The secret key of WOTS+ is $\mathrm{osk} = (\mathbf{x}_1, \ldots, \mathbf{x}_\ell) \in (\{0,1\}^n)^\ell$ and the public key is $\mathrm{opk} = (\mathbf{y}_1, \ldots, \mathbf{y}_\ell)$ where $\mathbf{y}_i = c^{w-1,0}(\mathbf{x}_i, \mathbf{a}_{c_i}, \text{PUBSEED})$. Here $\mathbf{a}_{c_i}$ is the address of the i-th chain within the OTS instance, PUBSEED is a public seed, and $c^{i,j}(\mathbf{x}, \mathbf{a}_c, \text{PUBSEED}) = F(k_{i,j}, c^{i-1,j}(\mathbf{x}, \mathbf{a}_c, \text{PUBSEED}) \oplus r_{i,j})$ and $c^{0,j}(\mathbf{x}, \mathbf{a}_c, \text{PUBSEED}) = \mathbf{x}$ for all $j \in \mathbb{Z}^+$, where $k_{i,j}, r_{i,j}$ are pseudorandomly computed. To sign a message M, one first computes a base-w representation $M = (M_1, \ldots, M_{\ell_1})$, then computes the checksum $C = \sum_{j=1}^{\ell_1}(w - 1 - M_j)$ and its base-w representation $C = (C_1, \ldots, C_{\ell_2})$. Set $B = (b_1, \ldots, b_\ell) = M \| C$. The signature of M is

$$\sigma = (\mathbf{z}_1, \ldots, \mathbf{z}_\ell) = (c^{b_1,0}(\mathbf{x}_1, \mathbf{a}_{c_1}, \text{PUBSEED}), \ldots, c^{b_\ell,0}(\mathbf{x}_\ell, \mathbf{a}_{c_\ell}, \text{PUBSEED})).$$

The signature $\sigma = (\mathbf{z}_1, \ldots, \mathbf{z}_\ell)$ is considered valid if for all $j \in [1, \ell]$: $\mathbf{y}_j = c^{w-1-b_j, b_j}(\mathbf{z}_j, \mathbf{a}_{c_j}, \text{PUBSEED})$.

B   Deferred Details of the ISG Attack on XMSS^{MT}

Lower Bound on P. Consider a WOTS+ signature σ on a random message M, let $B = (b_1, \ldots, b_\ell)$ be its base-w representation. The number of secret strings revealed in σ is the same as the number of b_i such that $b_i = 0$. Given a random message M, the probability that $b_i = 0$ for $i \in [1, \ell_1]$ is $\frac{1}{w}$. Unfortunately, there is no easy way to calculate the probability that $b_i = 0$ for $i \in [\ell_1 + 1, \ell]$. To this end, we provide a lower bound for P. Denote E as the number of b_i such that $b_i = 0$ for $i \in [1, \ell]$ and F as the number of b_i such that $b_i = 0$ for $i \in [1, \ell_1]$, then we obtain the following:

$$P = \Pr[E \geq 2] \geq \Pr[F \geq 2] = 1 - \Pr[F = 0] - \Pr[F = 1]$$
$$= 1 - (1 - \frac{1}{w})^{\ell_1} - \frac{\ell_1}{w}(1 - \frac{1}{w})^{\ell_1 - 1}.$$

References

1. Public comments on draft sp 800–208. https://csrc.nist.gov/CSRC/media/Publica tions/sp/800-208/draft/documents/sp800-208-draft-comments-received.pdf. Accessed 12 Oct 2020

2. Anderson, R.: Two remarks on public key cryptology. Unpublished (1997). http:// www.cl.cam.ac.uk/users/rja14

3. Aumasson, J.P., et al.: Sphincs (2020). round 3 Submisstion to NIST Post Quantum Project

4. Aumasson, J., Endignoux, G.: Clarifying the subset-resilience problem. IACR Cryptol. ePrint Arch. **2017**, 909 (2017)

5. Aumasson, J.-P., Endignoux, G.: Improving stateless hash-based signatures. In: Smart, N.P. (ed.) CT-RSA 2018. LNCS, vol. 10808, pp. 219–242. Springer, Cham (2018). https://doi.org/10.1007/978-3-319-76953-0_12

6. Bellare, M., Miner, S.K.: A forward-secure digital signature scheme. In: Wiener, M. (ed.) CRYPTO 1999. LNCS, vol. 1666, pp. 431–448. Springer, Heidelberg (1999). https://doi.org/10.1007/3-540-48405-1_28

7. Bernstein, D.J., et al.: SPHINCS: practical stateless hash-based signatures. In: Oswald, E., Fischlin, M. (eds.) EUROCRYPT 2015. LNCS, vol. 9056, pp. 368–397. Springer, Heidelberg (2015). https://doi.org/10.1007/978-3-662-46800-5_15

8. Bernstein, D.J., Hülsing, A., Kölbl, S., Niederhagen, R., Rijneveld, J., Schwabe, P.: The sphincs+ signature framework. In: Cavallaro, L., Kinder, J., Wang, X., Katz, J. (eds.) CCS 2019, pp. 2129–2146. ACM (2019)

9. Booth, R., Karati, S.: Isg attack, December 2020. https://github.com/rmbooth2/isg-attack. Accessed 16 Jun 2021

10. Buchmann, J., Dahmen, E., Hülsing, A.: XMSS - a practical forward secure signature scheme based on minimal security assumptions. In: Yang, B.-Y. (ed.) PQCrypto 2011. LNCS, vol. 7071, pp. 117–129. Springer, Heidelberg (2011). https://doi.org/10.1007/978-3-642-25405-5_8

11. Buchmann, J., Dahmen, E., Klintsevich, E., Okeya, K., Vuillaume, C.: Merkle signatures with virtually unlimited signature capacity. In: Katz, J., Yung, M. (eds.) ACNS 2007. LNCS, vol. 4521, pp. 31–45. Springer, Heidelberg (2007). https://doi.org/10.1007/978-3-540-72738-5_3

12. Buchmann, J., Dahmen, E., Schneider, M.: Merkle tree traversal revisited. In: Buchmann, J., Ding, J. (eds.) PQCrypto 2008. LNCS, vol. 5299, pp. 63–78. Springer, Heidelberg (2008). https://doi.org/10.1007/978-3-540-88403-3_5

13. Buchmann, J., García, L.C.C., Dahmen, E., Döring, M., Klintsevich, E.: CMSS – an improved Merkle signature scheme. In: Barua, R., Lange, T. (eds.) INDOCRYPT 2006. LNCS, vol. 4329, pp. 349–363. Springer, Heidelberg (2006). https://doi.org/10.1007/11941378_25

14. Chase, M., et al.: Picnic: A family of post-quantum secure digital signature algorithms. https://microsoft.github.io/Picnic/

15. Cooper, D.A., Apon, D.C., Dang, Q.H., Davidson, M.S., Dworkin, M.J., Miller, C.A.: Recommendation for stateful hash-based signature schemes. NIST Special Publication (SP) 800–208 draft (2019). https://doi.org/10.6028/NIST.SP.800-208-draft

16. Cooper, D.A., Apon, D.C., Dang, Q.H., Davidson, M.S., Dworkin, M.J., Miller, C.A.: Recommendation for stateful hash-based signature schemes. NIST Special Publication (SP) 800–208 (2020). https://doi.org/10.6028/NIST.SP.800-208

17. Dahmen, E., Okeya, K., Takagi, T., Vuillaume, C.: Digital signatures out of second-preimage resistant hash functions. In: Buchmann, J., Ding, J. (eds.) PQCrypto 2008. LNCS, vol. 5299, pp. 109–123. Springer, Heidelberg (2008). https://doi.org/10.1007/978-3-540-88403-3_8

18. Dinur, I., Nadler, N.: Multi-target attacks on the picnic signature scheme and related protocols. In: Ishai, Y., Rijmen, V. (eds.) EUROCRYPT 2010. LNCS, vol. 11478, pp. 699–727. Springer, Cham (2010). https://doi.org/10.1007/978-3-030-17659-4_24

19. Dods, C., Smart, N.P., Stam, M.: Hash based digital signature schemes. In: Smart, N.P. (ed.) Cryptography and Coding 2005. LNCS, vol. 3796, pp. 96–115. Springer, Heidelberg (2005). https://doi.org/10.1007/11586821_8

20. Gjøsteen, K.: Comments on dual-ec-drbg/nist sp 800–90, draft December 2005, April 2006

21. Goldwasser, S., Micali, S., Rivest, R.L.: A digital signature scheme secure against adaptive chosen-message attacks. SIAM J. Comput. 17(2), 281–308 (1988)

22. Hülsing, A.: W-OTS+ – shorter signatures for hash-based signature schemes. In: Youssef, A., Nitaj, A., Hassanien, A.E. (eds.) AFRICACRYPT 2013. LNCS, vol. 7918, pp. 173–188. Springer, Heidelberg (2013). https://doi.org/10.1007/978-3-642-38553-7_10

23. Hülsing, A., Butin, D., Gazdag, S.L., Rijneveld, J., Mohaisen, A.: XMSS: extended Merkle signature scheme. Technical report, RFC 8391 (2018)

24. Hülsing, A., Rausch, L., Buchmann, J.: Optimal parameters for $XMSS^{MT}$. In: Cuzzocrea, A., Kittl, C., Simos, D.E., Weippl, E., Xu, L. (eds.) CD-ARES 2013. LNCS, vol. 8128, pp. 194–208. Springer, Heidelberg (2013). https://doi.org/10.1007/978-3-642-40588-4_14

25. Hülsing, A., Rijneveld, J., Schwabe, P.: ARMed SPHINCS - computing a 41 KB signature in 16 KB of RAM. In: Cheng, C.-M., Chung, K.-M., Persiano, G., Yang, B.-Y. (eds.) PKC 2016. LNCS, vol. 9614, pp. 446–470. Springer, Heidelberg (2016). https://doi.org/10.1007/978-3-662-49384-7_17

26. Hülsing, A., Rijneveld, J., Song, F.: Mitigating multi-target attacks in hash-based signatures. In: Cheng, C.-M., Chung, K.-M., Persiano, G., Yang, B.-Y. (eds.) PKC 2016. LNCS, vol. 9614, pp. 387–416. Springer, Heidelberg (2016). https://doi.org/10.1007/978-3-662-49384-7_15

27. Ishai, Y., Kushilevitz, E., Ostrovsky, R., Sahai, A.: Zero-knowledge proofs from secure multiparty computation. SIAM J. Comput. **39**(3), 1121–1152 (2009)

28. Kalach, K., Safavi-Naini, R.: An efficient post-quantum one-time signature scheme. In: Dunkelman, O., Keliher, L. (eds.) SAC 2015. LNCS, vol. 9566, pp. 331–351. Springer, Cham (2016). https://doi.org/10.1007/978-3-319-31301-6_20

29. Karati, S.: K2sn-mss, June 2019. https://github.com/skarati/K2SN-MSS. Accessed 21 Jan 2020

30. Karati, S., Safavi-Naini, R.: K2SN-MSS: an efficient post-quantum signature. In: Galbraith, S.D., Russello, G., Susilo, W., Gollmann, D., Kirda, E., Liang, Z. (eds.) AsiaCCS 2019, pp. 501–514. ACM (2019)

31. Katz, J.: Analysis of a proposed hash-based signature standard. In: Chen, L., McGrew, D., Mitchell, C. (eds.) SSR 2016. LNCS, vol. 10074, pp. 261–273. Springer, Cham (2016). https://doi.org/10.1007/978-3-319-49100-4_12

32. Lamport, L.: Constructing digital signatures from a one way function. Technical report CSL-98, October 1979. this paper was published by IEEE in the Proceedings of HICSS-43 in January 2010 (2010)

33. Lenstra, A.K., Hughes, J.P., Augier, M., Bos, J.W., Kleinjung, T., Wachter, C.: Ron was wrong, whit is right. IACR Cryptol. ePrint Arch. **2012**, 64 (2012)

34. Lyubashevsky, V., Micciancio, D., Peikert, C., Rosen, A.: SWIFFT: a modest proposal for FFT hashing. In: Nyberg, K. (ed.) FSE 2008. LNCS, vol. 5086, pp. 54–72. Springer, Heidelberg (2008). https://doi.org/10.1007/978-3-540-71039-4_4

35. McGrew, D., Curcio, M.: Hash-based signatures. Internet-Draft draft-mcgrew-hash-sigs-02 (2014). https://datatracker.ietf.org/doc/html/draft-mcgrew-hash-sigs-02

36. McGrew, D., Curcio, M., Fluhrer, S.: Leighton-Micali hash-based signatures. Technical report, RFC 8554 (2019). https://doi.org/10.17487/RFC8554

37. Merkle, R.C.: A certified digital signature. In: Brassard, G. (ed.) CRYPTO 1989. LNCS, vol. 435, pp. 218–238. Springer, New York (1990). https://doi.org/10.1007/0-387-34805-0_21

38. Merkle, R.C.: Secrecy, authentication, and public key systems. Ph.D. thesis, Stanford University (1979)

39. Rijneveld, J., Hülsing, A., Cooper, D., Westerbaan, B.: XMSS-reference, April 2019. https://github.com/XMSS/xmss-reference/commit/fb7e3f8edce8d412a707f5 22d597ab3546863202
40. Schoenmakers, B., Sidorenko, A.: Cryptanalysis of the dual elliptic curve pseudo-random generator. IACR Cryptol. ePrint Arch. **2006**, 190 (2006)
41. Shor, P.W.: Algorithms for quantum computation: discrete logarithms and factoring. In: FOCS 1994, pp. 124–134. IEEE Computer Society (1994)
42. Strenzke, F.: An analysis of OpenSSL's random number generator. In: Fischlin, M., Coron, J.-S. (eds.) EUROCRYPT 2016. LNCS, vol. 9665, pp. 644–669. Springer, Heidelberg (2016). https://doi.org/10.1007/978-3-662-49890-3_25
43. Yang, G., Duan, S., Wong, D.S., Tan, C.H., Wang, H.: Authenticated key exchange under bad randomness. In: Danezis, G. (ed.) FC 2011. LNCS, vol. 7035, pp. 113–126. Springer, Heidelberg (2012). https://doi.org/10.1007/978-3-642-27576-0_10

(Short Paper) Analysis of a Strong Fault Attack on Static/Ephemeral CSIDH

Jason T. LeGrow[1]($\boxtimes$) and Aaron Hutchinson[2]

[1] Department of Mathematics, University of Auckland, Auckland, New Zealand
jason.legrow@auckland.ac.nz
[2] Institute for Quantum Computing and Department of Combinatorics and Optimization, University of Waterloo, Waterloo, ON, Canada

Abstract. CSIDH is an isogeny-based post-quantum key establishment protocol proposed in 2018. In this work we analyze attacking implementations of CSIDH which use dummy isogeny operations using fault injections from a mathematical perspective. We detail an attack (implicit in prior works on implementations of CSIDH) by which a static private key can be learned (up to sign) by the attacker with certainty using $\sum \lceil \log_2(b_i) + 1 \rceil$ faults using a binary search approach, where $\mathbf{b}$ is the bound vector defining the keyspace. A natural idea for a countermeasure to this attack is to randomly mix the real degree ℓ_j isogenies together with the dummy ones, so that binary search becomes ineffective. In this work we evaluate the efficacy of this idea as a fault attack countermeasure; in particular, we give bounds (as a function of the bound vector entries) on the number of fault injections (of a particular relatively strong, hypothetical type) required for an attacker to have a given success probability for guessing an unknown key, and present the results of simulated attacks on keys sampled from 6 keyspaces found in the literature. We find that the number of faults required to reach any constant success probability in guessing a static key is quadratic in the bound vector entries, rather than logarithmic as in the "real-then-dummy" setting— concretely, the number of faults required increases from a few hundred to tens of thousands. Broadly, this behaviour is reflected in our simulations.

Keywords: Isogeny-based cryptography · CSIDH · Fault attacks · Key exchange

1 Introduction

Commutative Supersingular Isogeny Diffie-Hellman (CSIDH) is a post-quantum key establishment protocol by Castryck *et al.* [3]. CSIDH uses isogenies of supersingular elliptic curves to perform key establishment *à la* Diffie-Hellman. Specifically, let $p = 4\ell_1 \cdots \ell_n - 1$ be prime, with $\ell_1, \ldots, \ell_n$ small odd primes (typically taken as the first $n - 1$ odd primes followed by the smallest ℓ_n which makes p prime). The value n depends on the targeted security level. The supersingular

© Springer Nature Switzerland AG 2021
T. Nakanishi and R. Nojima (Eds.): IWSEC 2021, LNCS 12835, pp. 216–226, 2021.
https://doi.org/10.1007/978-3-030-85987-9_12

Montgomery curve $E_0/\mathbb{F}_p : y^2 = x^3 + x$ has the property that the ideal generated by $[\ell_j]$ in the endomorphism ring $\mathcal{O}$ of E_0 splits as $\ell_i\mathcal{O} = \mathfrak{l}_j\bar{\mathfrak{l}}_j$ where $\mathfrak{l}_j := ([\ell_j], \pi - 1)$ and $\bar{\mathfrak{l}}_j := ([\ell_j], \pi + 1)$, where π is the Frobenius endomorphism of E_0; thus in the ideal class group we have $[\mathfrak{l}_j]^{-1} = [\bar{\mathfrak{l}}_j]$. For a vector of integers $\mathbf{e} = (e_1, \ldots, e_n)$ and an elliptic curve E with $\mathbb{F}_p$-endomorphism ring isomorphic to that of E_0, we define $\mathbf{e}*E := [\mathfrak{l}_1]^{e_1} \cdots [\mathfrak{l}_n]^{e_n}*E$, where $*$ in the latter expression denotes the class group action. CSIDH key establishment proceeds as follows. Alice and Bob choose their private keys $\mathbf{e}^A$ and $\mathbf{e}^B$ from $\prod_{j=1}^{n}[-b_j, b_j] \cap \mathbb{Z}$, respectively (here $\mathbf{b}$ is the *bound vector*: the system parameter which defines the keyspace). More recent works [7,9] on CSIDH choose private keys from the non-negative intervals $\prod_{j=1}^{n}[0, b_j] \cap \mathbb{Z}$; we distinguish these two scenarios as the *signed* and *unsigned* settings, respectively. Then, Alice computes her public key as $E_A := \mathbf{e}^A * E_0$ and similarly Bob computes his as $E_B := \mathbf{e}^B * E_0$. Alice sends E_A to Bob, and Bob sends E_B to Alice. To construct the shared secret, Alice computes $E_{BA} := \mathbf{e}^A * E_B$, while Bob computes $E_{AB} := \mathbf{e}^B * E_A$. By the commutativity of the ideal class group, we have $E_{BA} \cong E_{AB}$; the shared key is then (derived from) the $\mathbb{F}_p$-isomorphism class of this final curve.

CSIDH has been the subject of many works aimed at optimizing its performance [2,7,9–12]. Most works implement constant-time algorithms using dummy isogeny constructions; that is, for each $1 \leq j \leq n$, exactly b_j isogenies of degree ℓ_j are constructed regardless of the key e_j, with $|e_j|$ real and $b_j - |e_j|$ dummy. Nearly all constant-time implementations of CSIDH so far have used dummy isogeny constructions in this manner, with the exception of the slower "no-dummy" algorithm of [4]. Dummy operations often leave cryptosystems vulnerable to attack by means of fault injections, and these constant time implementations of CSIDH which use dummy isogenies are no exception.

Our contributions in this work can be summarized as follows:

1. We describe a fault attack in a natural model (with a relatively strong attacker) in which an attacker can achieve a complete break of the system under ideal conditions by recovering the private key using $\sum_{j=1}^{n}\lceil\log_2(b_j)+1\rceil$ faults using binary search.
2. As a potential countermeasure, for a fixed key $\mathbf{e}$ we propose randomly mixing the constructions of the $|e_j|$ degree ℓ_j real isogenies with the $b_j - |e_j|$ dummy isogenies at the time of evaluation of the group action. Working with this countermeasure in mind, we:
   (a) Formalize fault injections targeted at the ith isogeny of degree ℓ_j in a given group action computation as revealing an entry x_i^j of the *decision vector* $\mathbf{x}^j$ which is 1 if that isogeny is real, and 0 if it is dummy;
   (b) Analyze a naïve attack on the randomized protocol; in particular, we derive formulas for the distribution on the magnitude $|e_j|$ of the key given a string of outputs x_i^j from pairwise different group action evaluations under the same key $\mathbf{e}$. We present upper and lower bound on the number of faults required to achieve any desired error threshold ϵ;
   (c) Introduce an optimized approach based on Gray codes to determine the key signs given their magnitudes (recovered from a fault attack), and;

(d) Present the results of simulated fault attacks for static secret keys from keyspaces defined by bound vectors present in the literature [3,7,9,12].

This paper is organized as follows. Section 2 introduces decision vectors and describes the fault attacks we consider concretely and mathematically. In Sect. 3 we derive a probability distribution on the magnitude of the private key given a sequence of oracle outputs from each index j, and detail an algorithm which most effectively attacks CSIDH using this distribution. Furthermore Sect. 3 derives theoretical bounds on the number of attacks needed to reach a desired certainty threshold about the value of the key, and shows how Gray codes can be used to efficiently learn the sign of the key given its magnitude. Finally Sect. 4 reports the results of simulating these ideas on 6 different bound vectors.

2   Preliminaries

Let $p = 4\ell_1 \cdots \ell_n - 1$ be prime with $\ell_1, \ldots, \ell_n$ pairwise distinct small odd primes. For each prime ℓ_j we encode the choice of constructing the ith degree ℓ_j isogeny $\varphi_{i,j}$ as either a real or dummy into a binary *decision vector* $\mathbf{x}^j = (x_1^j, \ldots, x_{b_j}^j)$, in which $x_i^j = 1$ denotes that the ith degree ℓ_j isogeny shall be real, and $x_i^j = 0$ denotes that the ith degree ℓ_j isogeny shall be dummy. For correctness of the algorithm the Hamming weight $H(\mathbf{x}^j)$ of $\mathbf{x}^j$ must be equal to $|e_j|$. This vector $\mathbf{x}^j$ represents only the choice of the type of isogeny constructed and may be explicitly or implicitly stored in memory for a given implementation of the group action, and it is this vector which our attacks target. As an example, Algorithm 1 depicts the constant time algorithm given by Onuki *et al.* [12]. Line 12 of Algorithm 1 computes the boolean value "$e_i \neq 0$" which is used as a mask bit to determine the type of isogeny to be constructed. We consider this boolean as one of the values in the decision vector $\mathbf{x}^j$. The decision vector for other dummy-based constant time algorithms for CSIDH are defined similarly.

2.1   General Structure of the Attack

Our attacks target the second round of the key establishment, when one party is computing the action of their private key on the curve they received from the other party. Our attacker is an enhanced form of [1, Attacker 3]; in particular, our attacker who can introduce faults into isogenies of chosen degree in a chosen "round" of computation. We note that an attacker who can determine (but not choose) the degree of the isogeny they disrupt (like Attacker 3) can simply introduce $O(n)$ faults (in expectation) to obtain the result of a fault introduced at a chosen index with constant probability; thus our analysis can be applied (with some modifications) to the setting of [1, Attacker 3].

For simplicity we consider the scenario that the attacker introduces exactly one fault per group action evaluation targeting the ith isogeny of degree ℓ_j, for i, j of the attacker's choice.

Algorithm 1: Constant time version of CSIDH group action evaluation.

Input : $A \in \mathbb{F}_p, b \in \mathbb{N}$, a list of integers $(e_1, \ldots, e_n)$ s.t. $-b \le e_i \le b$ for
$i = 1, \ldots, n$, and distinct odd primes $\ell_1, \ldots, \ell_n$ s.t. $p = 4\prod_i \ell_i - 1$.
Output: $B \in \mathbb{F}_p$ s.t. $E_B = (\mathfrak{l}_1^{e_1} \cdots \mathfrak{l}_n^{e_n}) * E_A$, where $\mathfrak{l}_i = (\ell_i, \pi - 1)$ for
$i = 1, \ldots, n$, and π is the p-th power Frobenius endomorphism of E_A.

1   Set $e_i' = b - |e_i|$.
2   **while** some $e_i \ne 0$ or some $e_i' \ne 0$ **do**
3   Set $S = \{i \mid e_i \ne 0 \text{ or } e_i' \ne 0\}$.
4   Set $k = \prod_{i \in S} \ell_i$.
5   Generate $P_0 \in E_A[\pi - 1]$ and $P_1 \in E_A[\pi + 1]$ by Elligator [9, Section 5.3].
6   Let $P_0 = [(p+1)/k]P_0$ and $P_1 = [(p+1)/k]P_1$.
7   **for** $i \in S$ **do**
8   Set s be the sign bit of e_i.
9   Set $Q = [k/\ell_i]P_s$.
10   Let $P_{1-s} = [\ell_i]P_{1-s}$.
11   **if** $Q \ne \infty$ **then**
12   **if** $e_i \ne 0$ **then**
13   Compute an isogeny $\varphi : E_A \to E_B$ with $\ker(\varphi) = \langle Q \rangle$.
14   Let $A \leftarrow B$, $P_0 \leftarrow \varphi(P_0)$, $P_1 \leftarrow \varphi(P_1)$, and $e_i \leftarrow e_i - 1 + 2s$.
15   **else**
16   Dummy computation.
17   Let $A \leftarrow A$, $P_s \leftarrow [\ell_i]P_s$, and $e_i' \leftarrow e_i' - 1$.
18   **end**
19   **end**
20   **end**
21   Let $k \leftarrow k/\ell_i$.
22 **end**
23 **Return** A

---

3   Attack Analysis

Here we analyze how attacks from Sect. 2 which target particular isogenies $\varphi_{i,j}$ can be performed together for varying i and j to gain information about the private key **e**. Going forward, we use $\mathcal{O}$ to refer to an oracle which, on input (j, i), reveals x_i^j for a given group action computation.

Section 3.1 examines the setting in which all real degree ℓ_j isogenies are constructed first, followed by any remaining degree ℓ_j dummy isogenies. The remainder of the section analyzes when each $\mathbf{x}^j$ is chosen uniformly at random at the time of the group action evaluation with the correct Hamming weight.

3.1   "Real-then-Dummy" Decision Vector

Here we briefly consider the "real-then-dummy" method, which every instantiation of CSIDH in the literature has used so far at the time of this writing. Here, $\mathbf{x}^j$ has exactly the form $\mathbf{x}^j = (1, 1, \ldots, 1, 0, 0 \ldots, 0)$, where there are $|e_j|$ many 1's. For this scenario the attack is extremely simple: the magnitude of the private key $|e_j|$ corresponds exactly with the position in which the last 1 appears, and so a simple binary search can determine $|e_j|$ with absolute certainty in exactly $\lceil \log_2(b_j) \rceil + 1$ queries to the oracle $\mathcal{O}(j, \cdot)$. It follows that the entire key $\mathbf{e}$ can be determined exactly up to sign using $\sum_{j=1}^{n}(\lceil \log_2(b_j) \rceil + 1)$ calls to $\mathcal{O}$. As the above shows, the real-then-dummy case is susceptible to a very simple attack. The most obvious change to make to attempt to counter the binary search attack is to randomize the value of each $\mathbf{x}^j$. In Sect. 3.2, we consider the case when $\mathbf{x}^j$ is drawn from the set $X_j := \{\mathbf{x}^j \in \{0,1\}^{b_j} : H(\mathbf{x}^j) = |e_j|\}$ uniformly at random, where H denotes Hamming weight.

3.2 Dynamic Uniformly Random Decision Vector

We consider the setting where the decision vector $\mathbf{x}^j$ is chosen from $X_j = \{\mathbf{x}^j \in \{0,1\}^{b_j} : H(\mathbf{x}^j) = |e_j|\}$ uniformly at random during every evaluation $(\mathbf{e}, E) \mapsto \mathbf{e} * E$ of the group action. We refer to this setting as having a *dynamic* decision vector. If one views the decision vector $\mathbf{x}^j$ as a means of permuting the constructions of the real and dummy isogenies, then the oracle calls $\mathcal{O}(j, i_1)$ and $\mathcal{O}(j, i_2)$ for $i_1 \neq i_2$ on different computations of the group action may actually correspond to the construction of the "same" isogeny, and so multiple calls to $\mathcal{O}(j, \cdot)$ informally "yield less information" than in the previous settings.

We require formulas for the probability of a given key (magnitude) value given oracle outputs. For brevity we will only explicitly give the result in the unsigned setting. Fix an index $1 \leq j \leq n$ to analyze. For $\ell \in \mathbb{N}$, let $\boldsymbol{\beta}^{(\ell)} = (\beta_1^{(\ell)}, \ldots, \beta_\ell^{(\ell)})$ (depending on j) denote the string of outputs of the first ℓ queries of $\mathcal{O}(j, \cdot)$, and let $\mathbf{q}_j^{(\boldsymbol{\beta}^{(\ell)})}$ denote the adversary's *a posteriori* distribution on e_j, having seen $\boldsymbol{\beta}^{(\ell)}$. That is, $q_{j,k}^{(\boldsymbol{\beta}^{(\ell)})} := \mathbb{P}[e_j = k | \boldsymbol{\beta}^{(\ell)}]$ for $0 \leq k \leq b_j$. We compute the value of this probability explicitly:

Theorem 1. *In the setting of unsigned exponents and dynamic decision vectors, for every $1 \leq j \leq n$, $0 \leq k \leq b_j$, and binary string $\boldsymbol{\beta}^{(\ell)}$ of length $\ell \geq 1$ we have*

$$q_{j,k}^{(\boldsymbol{\beta}^{(\ell)})} = \frac{(b_j - k)^{\ell - H(\boldsymbol{\beta}^{(\ell)})} k^{H(\boldsymbol{\beta}^{(\ell)})}}{\sum_{t=0}^{b_j}(b_j - t)^{\ell - H(\boldsymbol{\beta}^{(\ell)})} t^{H(\boldsymbol{\beta}^{(\ell)})}}, \tag{1}$$

where $\boldsymbol{\beta}^{(0)}$ is the empty string and $q_{j,k}^{(0)} := \mathbb{P}[e_j = k] = 1/(b_j + 1)$ for every k.

Proof Idea. Apply Bayes' Theorem, the Law of Total Probability, and the fact that the e_j are chosen uniformly to get a recursive formula. Then use induction.

Attack Model. Here we detail an attack on CSIDH in the setting of dynamic decision vectors in both the signed and unsigned settings which makes use of the probabilities previously computed in this section. In the attack, referred to as *least certainty*, the attacker chooses a key index $1 \leq j^* \leq n$ in which to inject a fault on each iteration, where in the unsigned setting the index j^* is chosen as

$j^* = \arg\min_{1 \le j \le n} \{\max_{0 \le k \le b_j} q_{j,k}^{\beta_j^{(\ell)}}\}$. where $\beta_j^{(\ell)}$ is the string of oracle outputs for the index j (with ℓ also depending on j). That is, the attacker targets the index for which they are least certain about the value of the key. The variables q_j are initialized as the uniform distribution on $b_j + 1$ elements (in the unsigned setting) or $q_{j,0} = \frac{1}{2b_j+1}$, $q_{j,k} = \frac{2}{2b_j+1}$ for $k \ne 0$ (in the signed setting).

In both settings, the attacker performs some desired number of iterations, with each iteration choosing the index j^* to attack based on the index of least certainty. Once these iterations are complete, the attacker is left with a probability distribution on the (absolute value of the) key, in which the most likely value for $|e_j|$ is given by $\arg\max_{0 \le k \le b_j} q_{j,k}^{\beta_j^{(\ell)}}$.

The attacker's probability of correctly guessing the key (magnitudes) is given by $\prod_{j=1}^n \max_{0 \le k \le b_j} q_{j,k}^{(\beta^{(\ell_j)})}$; the attacker stops once this quantity is large enough.

Bounds on Naïve Attacks. Here we seek to determine bounds on the number of faults required to guarantee a given success rate $1 - \epsilon$ in a fault attack. For an upper bound, it suffices to consider any particular attack; we consider the attack we call the "naïve" method (we will also find a lower bound for this attack). This attack is as follows: choose a vector $\mathbf{m} \in \mathbb{N}^n$, and for $1 \le j \le n$, apply m_j fault attacks on isogenies of degree ℓ_j. This yields a sequence $\beta^{(m_j)}$ of outputs in which (say) w_j such isogenies are revealed to be real; we then guess that $e_j = e_j^* := \lceil b_j w_j / m_j \rfloor$. This value of e_j is what we would obtain by rounding the maximum likelihood estimate for e_j, *if the* a priori *distribution of e_j were uniform on $[0, b_j]$ rather than $[0, b_j] \cap \mathbb{Z}$*. Our guess at the entire key $\mathbf{e}$ is then $\mathbf{e} = (e_1^*, e_2^*, \ldots, e_n^*)^T$. We obtain the following bounds:

Theorem 2. *Let $\mathbf{b}$ be a bound vector. For any $\epsilon \subset (0,1)$, in order to guarantee success probability at least $1 - \epsilon$ in a naïve attack on a key chosen from the keyspace defined by $\mathbf{b}$, it suffices to inject*

$$\min\left\{\sum_{j=1}^n \left\lceil 2b_j^2 \log_e \frac{2}{1 - \sqrt[n]{1-\epsilon}} \right\rceil, \sum_{j=1}^n \left\lceil 2b_j^2 \log_e \left(2 + \frac{\frac{2}{\epsilon}\|\mathbf{b}\|^2 - 2\min_k\{b_k\}^2}{b_j^2}\right) \right\rceil\right\}$$

individual faults.

Proof Idea. Apply a Hoeffding bound [6] to obtain the number of faults required to get a given success probability for one key entry. For the first bound, consider an attack which achieves success probability $\sqrt[n]{1-\epsilon}$ for each key entry. For the second bound, compute the Lagrangian $\mathcal{L}(\mathbf{m}; \lambda)$ of

$$\min \sum_{j=1}^n m_j \quad \text{s.t.} \quad \sum_{j=1}^n \log_e\left(1 - 2e^{-m_j/2b_j^2}\right) \ge \log_e(1-\epsilon) \tag{P}$$

and solve $\nabla_{\mathbf{m}}\mathcal{L}(\mathbf{m}^*; \lambda^*) = \mathbf{0}$ for $\mathbf{m}^*$ in terms of λ^*. To complete the proof, note that $\lambda^* = \frac{2}{\epsilon}\|\mathbf{b}\|^2 - 2\min_k\{b_k\}$ is sufficient to satisfy the constraint. □

Theorem 3. *Let $\mathbf{b}$ be a bound vector and let $e_j \in \{1, 2, \ldots, b_j - 1\}$. Let $\hat{e}_j = \min\{e_j, b_j - e_j\}$, and $0 \le \epsilon \le \frac{\hat{e}_j}{8(b_j - \hat{e}_j)}$. Then for a naïve attack which targets m_j*

faults at the jth key entry and which correctly recovers its value with probability at least $1 - \epsilon$ when it is equal to e_j, we have $m_j \geq \frac{1}{2}\hat{e}_j^2 \left(1 - 2\sqrt{\frac{2(b_j - \hat{e}_j)}{\hat{e}_j}\epsilon}\right)^2$.

Proof Idea. Use the Marcinkiewicz-Zygmund inequality [5,8] to bound the expected value of $|w_j - m_j|e_j|/b_j|$, and the Payley-Zygmund inequality [13] to bound the probability that it is too large. The rest is straightforward.

As a particular consequence of Theorem 3, a naïve attack which succeeds with probability at least $1 - \epsilon$ (for ϵ small enough) for *every* possible key must satisfy

$$\sum_{j=1}^{n} m_j \geq \sum_{j=1}^{n} \frac{1}{2}\left(\frac{b_j - 1}{2}\right)^2 \left(1 - 2\sqrt{\frac{2(b_j + 1)}{b_j - 1}\epsilon}\right)^2. \tag{2}$$

For fixed ϵ, this lower bound has the same asymptotic behaviour as the upper bound of Theorem 2, up to logarithmic factors.

3.3 Determining the Signs of the Key

Given key magnitudes $|e_1^*|, \ldots, |e_n^*|$, the standard meet-in-the-middle approach to find the signs is to split $\ell_1, \ldots, \ell_n$ into two batches—say $B_L = \{\ell_1, \ell_2, \ldots, \ell_k\}$ and $B_R = \{\ell_{k+1}, \ell_{k+2}, \ldots, \ell_n\}$ where $k = \lceil \frac{n}{2} \rceil$. Define the sets

$$T_L = \left\{ [\ell_1^{(-1)^{s_1}|e_1^*|} \cdots \ell_k^{(-1)^{s_k}|e_k^*|}] * E_0 : s_i \in \{0, 1\} \right\},$$

$$T_R = \left\{ [\ell_{k+1}^{-(-1)^{s_{k+1}}|e_{k+1}^*|} \cdots \ell_n^{-(-1)^{s_n}|e_n^*|}] * E_A : s_i \in \{0, 1\} \right\},$$

where E_0 is the initial curve and E_A is the public key. All curves in T_L are computed and stored in a table, and curves in T_R are iterated through (but not stored) until a collision with T_L is found. When a match between the sets is found at $s_1^*, s_2^*, \ldots, s_n^*$, the correct key is $\mathbf{e}^* = ((-1)^{s_j^*}|e_j^*|)_{j=1}^n$.

Naïvely, computing all curves in the above sets T_L and T_R requires evaluating the class group action $2^k + 2^{n-k}$ times, using ideals whose product decomposition contains $\sum_{i=1}^{k}|e_i^*|$ terms (for T_L) or $\sum_{i=k+1}^{n}|e_i^*|$ terms (for T_R). However, this can be made more efficient by constructing the curves in a particular order. In the following we optimize computing all curves in T_L, and iteration through T_R can be optimized analogously.

Note that iterating through T_L corresponds with iterating through $\{0, 1\}^k$. If the tuples $(s_1, \ldots, s_k)$ are ordered according to a length-k binary Gray code C, we need only apply the class group element $\mathfrak{l}_j^{\pm 2|e_j^*|}$ to the previously computed curve, where j is the index which changes between the previous tuple and the current one. This reduces the cost to $\sum_{i=1}^{k} 2\tau_i|e_i^*|\kappa_i$ where τ are the *transition numbers* of C—that is, τ_i is the number of times that the ith bit flips in C—and κ_i is the cost of evaluating $(E, \ell_i) \mapsto [\mathfrak{l}_i] * E$.

To get a better performing partition of the ℓ_j, we define the permutation σ which satisfies $|e^*_{\sigma(1)}|\kappa_{\sigma(1)} \leq |e^*_{\sigma(2)}|\kappa_{\sigma(2)} \leq \cdots \leq |e^*_{\sigma(n)}|\kappa_{\sigma(n)}$, order the ℓ_j according to σ, and then alternately assign the $\ell_{\sigma(j)}$ to B_L and B_R so that

$$B_L = \{\ell_{\sigma(j)} : j \equiv 1 \pmod 2 \text{ and } 1 \leq j \leq n\},$$
$$B_R = \{\ell_{\sigma(j)} : j \equiv 0 \pmod 2 \text{ and } 1 \leq j \leq n\}.$$

To iterate through T_L and T_R, we order the sign vectors $\mathbf{s}$ according to the binary reflected Gray code, whose transition numbers are $\boldsymbol{\tau} = (2^{k-1}, 2^{k-2}, \ldots, 1)$. Iterating via σ and the reflected binary Gray code (RBGC) is optimal over all binary Gray codes. In T_L (all of whose curves are stored), one can use *any* curve already computed to determine the next curve rather than being limited to only the previously computed curve; such a method of iteration would correspond to a spanning tree in the hypercube graph Q_n. Even allowing such algorithms the RBGC method is still optimal. We estimate that for the bound vector of [7] the RBGC method would be approximately 88% faster than the naïve method.

4   Simulation Results

We simulated fault injection attacks on CSIDH-512, using the least certainty method and various values for the bound vector $\mathbf{b}$. For the unsigned dynamic setting, we used three bound vectors from previous works: (1) the uniform vector $(10, 10, \ldots, 10)$ given by Castryck *et al.* in [3], referred to as UD-Uniform; (2) the vector given by Meyer *et al.* in [9], labeled UD-MCR; (3) the vector given by Hutchinson *et al.* in [7], labeled UD-HLKA. In the signed dynamic setting, we also used three different vectors: (1) the uniform vector $(5, 5, \ldots, 5)$ given by Castryck *et al.* in [3], labeled SD-Uniform; (2) the vector of Onuki *et al.* in [12], labeled SD-OAYT; (3) the vector given by Hutchinson *et al.* in [7], labeled SD-HLKA. We recorded the number of trials required to reach certainty y for 990 values of y between 0.1% and 99.9%, across 1000 randomly-sampled private keys for each of the six bound vectors we considered. Table 1 reports the mean number of attacks used in our simulations for each vector to reach a certainty level of 1%, 50%, 99%, and 99.9%. The number of faults required increased by a

Table 1. Mean number of attacks used to reach specified certainty thresholds for various bound vectors over 1000 randomly generated private keys.

	Certainty:	1%	50%	90%	99.9%	$\sum \lceil \log(b_j) + 1 \rceil$
Unsigned setting	HLKA	15921	28865	45561	52062	356
	MCR	12067	21872	34855	39738	342
	Uniform	10584	19387	30760	35129	370
Signed setting	HLKA	3039	5708	9272	10734	263
	OAYT	3552	6574	10741	12447	266
	Uniform	2484	4667	7686	8890	296

factor between 8 (for 1% certainty for SD-Uniform) and 146 (for 99.9% certainty for UD-HLKA) over the real-then-dummy setting. The increase is greater in the unsigned setting than the signed setting since the bound vector entries are larger in the unsigned setting. Figure 1 gives more detailed experimental results.

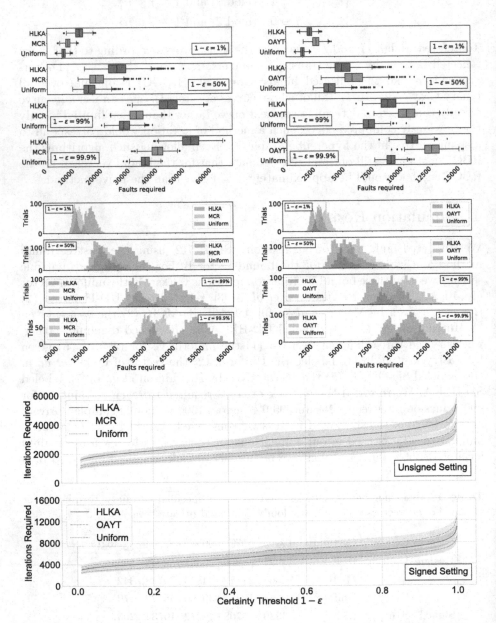

Fig. 1. Plots depicting the distribution of the number of faults required to achieve a given level of certainty in simulated fault attacks for six bound vectors: three in the unsigned setting and three in the signed setting.

5   Conclusions

Based on our analysis and simulated fault attacks, randomizing the order of isogenies in CSIDH does dramatically increase the number of faults required to learn a static secret key; however, this increase is likely not sufficient to thwart a fault attack of the (relatively strong) kind we consider.

Acknowledgements. Jason T. LeGrow was funded in part by MBIE fund UOAX1933.

References

1. Campos, F., Kannwischer, M.J., Meyer, M., Onuki, H., Stöttinger, M.: Trouble at the CSIDH: protecting CSIDH with dummy-operations against fault injection attacks. In: 2020 Workshop on Fault Detection and Tolerance in Cryptography (FDTC), pages 57–65, Los Alamitos, CA, USA, September 2020. IEEE Computer Society (2020)
2. Castryck, W., Decru, T.: CSIDH on the Surface. In: Ding, J., Tillich, J.-P. (eds.) PQCrypto 2020. LNCS, vol. 12100, pp. 111–129. Springer, Cham (2020). https://doi.org/10.1007/978-3-030-44223-1_7
3. Castryck, W., Lange, T., Martindale, C., Panny, L., Renes, J.: CSIDH: an efficient post-quantum commutative group action. In: Peyrin, T., Galbraith, S. (eds.) ASIACRYPT 2018. LNCS, vol. 11274, pp. 395–427. Springer, Cham (2018). https://doi.org/10.1007/978-3-030-03332-3_15
4. Cervantes-Vázquez, D., Chenu, M., Chi-Domínguez, J.-J., De Feo, L., Rodríguez-Henríquez, F., Smith, B.: Stronger and Faster Side-Channel Protections for CSIDH. In: Schwabe, P., Thériault, N. (eds.) LATINCRYPT 2019. LNCS, vol. 11774, pp. 173–193. Springer, Cham (2019). https://doi.org/10.1007/978-3-030-30530-7_9
5. Chow, Y., Teicher, H.: Probability Theory: Independence, Interchangeability, Martingales. Springer, New York (1997)
6. Hoeffding, W.: Probability inequalities for sums of bounded random variables. J. Am. Stat. Assoc. **58**(301), 13–30 (1963)
7. Hutchinson, A., LeGrow, J., Koziel, B., Azarderakhsh, R.: Further optimizations of CSIDH: a systematic approach to efficient strategies, permutations, and bound vectors. In: Conti, M., Zhou, J., Casalicchio, E., Spognardi, A. (eds.) ACNS 2020. LNCS, vol. 12146, pp. 481–501. Springer, Cham (2020). https://doi.org/10.1007/978-3-030-57808-4_24
8. Marcinkiewicz, J., Zygmund, A.: Sur les fonctions indépendantes. Fundam. Math. **29**(1), 60–90 (1937)
9. Meyer, M., Campos, F., Reith, S.: On lions and elligators: an efficient constant time implementation of CSIDH. In: Ding, J., Steinwandt, R. (eds.) PQCrypto 2019. LNCS, vol. 11505, pp. 307–325. Springer, Cham (2019). https://doi.org/10.1007/978-3-030-25510-7_17
10. Meyer, M., Reith, S.: A faster way to the CSIDH. In: Chakraborty, D., Iwata, T. (eds.) INDOCRYPT 2018. LNCS, vol. 11356, pp. 137–152. Springer, Cham (2018). https://doi.org/10.1007/978-3-030-05378-9_8
11. Moriya, T., Onuki, H., Takagi, T.: How to construct CSIDH on edwards curves. Cryptology ePrint Archive, Report 2019/843 (2019)

12. Onuki, H., Aikawa, Y., Yamazaki, T., Takagi, T.: (Short Paper) A Faster constant-time algorithm of CSIDH keeping two points. In: Attrapadung, N., Yagi, T. (eds.) IWSEC 2019. LNCS, vol. 11689, pp. 23–33. Springer, Cham (2019). https://doi.org/10.1007/978-3-030-26834-3_2
13. Paley, R.E.A.C., Zygmund, A.: On some series of functions, (3). Math. Proc. Cambridge Philos. Soc. **28**(2), 190–205 (1932)

(Short Paper) Simple Matrix Signature Scheme

Changze Yin[✉], Yacheng Wang, and Tsuyoshi Takagi

Department of Mathematical Informatics, University of Tokyo, Tokyo, Japan
{yin-changze,wang-yacheng,takagi}@g.ecc.u-tokyo.ac.jp

Abstract. Multivariate cryptography plays an important role in post-quantum cryptography. Many signature schemes, such as Rainbow remain secure despite the development of several attempted attack algorithms. However, most multivariate signature schemes use relatively large public keys compared with those of other post-quantum signature schemes. In this paper, we present an approach for constructing a multivariate signature scheme based on matrix multiplication. At the same security level, our proposed signature scheme has smaller public key and signature sizes compared with the Rainbow signature scheme.

Keywords: Post-quantum cryptography · Multivariate cryptography · UOV · Security

1 Introduction

The field of cryptography is critical for scientific development in general, especially in emerging social communication technologies. Traditionally, many standard cryptosystems, such as RSA, ECC, and Diffie-Hellman key exchange have been widely used in commercial production. Unfortunately, since Shor's [16] algorithm was proposed in 1994, existing cryptosystems are expected to encounter significant challenges as quantum computers will be brought into service in the near future. Therefore, more secure and robust cryptosystems need to be developed to protect the devices and systems begin used currently. This new type of cryptosystems has been widely referred to in the recent literature as post-quantum cryptography.

Among the most popular subjects in post-quantum cryptography, multivariate public key cryptography (MPKC) is based on the difficulty of solving a multivariate quadratic (MQ) problem. MQ problems are defined by the computation of solutions to a quadratic polynomial system with n unknowns and m equations over a finite field $\mathbb{F}_q$. Studies have shown that MQ problems are NP-complete [11]. This promising result is expected to be beneficial for the creation of secure cryptosystems such as encryption schemes and signature schemes.

Supported by JST CREST Grant Number JPMJCR14D6, Japan.

T. Nakanishi and R. Nojima (Eds.): IWSEC 2021, LNCS 12835, pp. 227–237, 2021.
https://doi.org/10.1007/978-3-030-85987-9_13

Until now, several effective MPKC encryption schemes and signature schemes have been proposed and have demonstrated good performance. For instance, Rainbow [8] is an MPKC signature scheme that survived in the 3rd round of NIST [3] standardization. Other signature schemes such as the unbalanced oil and vinegar scheme (UOV) [12] and HFEv- [15] are well-known for their groundbreaking and original trapdoor designs. Moreover, many MPKC encryption schemes, including hidden field equations (HFE) [15] and simple matrix encryption scheme (ABC) [18] have been explored recently.

Although numerous MPKC signature schemes and encryption schemes have been proposed, most of them have been proven to be insecure under various types of attacks, such as algebraic attacks, rank attacks, differential attacks, and equivalent key attacks, among others. Most MPKC cryptosystems are also limited in that the size of their public keys is too large to be utilized in practice. Considering these developments, some further improvements in such methods appear to be necessary to decrease the key size without loss of security.

Public keys that are too large to apply to small or low-capacity devices are among the most significant remaining problems in multivariable cryptosystems. The fundamental reason behind this is that cryptographers commonly use polynomials with numerous variables as public keys to ensure the security of their designed schemes. Therefore, the development of a secure signature scheme with low storage requirements remains an important and meaningful challenge in this field.

Contributions: We proposed a new method that is inspired by UOV and ABC for constructing an MPKC signature scheme. The key point of this construction method is to set some linear and quadratic terms as masks, and simply solve the remainder with the given mask values.

Furthermore, we selected some basic attacks, namely algebraic attack and MinRank attack, conducted experiments to test the security of our proposed scheme, and presented their results. Fortunately, we found that special attacks such as equivalent key attacks and invariant attacks [14] were ineffective in breaking our scheme, which is consistent with theoretical expectations. Based on these experiments, we propose some parameters that satisfy the requirements of different security levels. Compared with the Rainbow signature scheme, for the same security level, the sizes of the public key and signature used in our proposed method are smaller. In particular, for 256-bit security, the size of the public key of our signature scheme was reduced by 63.4%.

This paper is organized as follows. In Sect. 2, the general MPKC structure is introduced and some popular schemes are described. In Sect. 3, we focus on the basic outline of our proposed scheme. Then, we test some basic attack algorithms against our signature scheme in Sect. 4. By applying the computational results presented in Sect. 4, we will propose some parameters for the different security levels of our scheme in Sect. 5.

2   Trapdoor Designs for Multivariate Public Key Cryptosystems

In this section, we describe the construction of multivariate public key cryptosystems (MPKCs). In particular, some popular schemes are introduced as follows.

2.1   Constructions of MPKC

In general, an MPKC scheme has features of the following structure. Given parameters $q, n, m > 0$, the public key $P : \mathbb{F}_q^n \to \mathbb{F}_q^m$ of this MPKC scheme is defined as the composites of a tuple (T, F, S) over the polynomial ring $\mathbb{F}_q[x_1, \ldots, x_n]$ with unknowns $(x_1, \ldots, x_n)$ such that

$$P := T \circ F \circ S.$$

Especially, $T : \mathbb{F}_q^m \to \mathbb{F}_q^m, S : \mathbb{F}_q^n \to \mathbb{F}_q^n$ are invertible affine transformations and $F : \mathbb{F}_q^n \to \mathbb{F}_q^m$ which is called the central map, is a set of quadratic polynomials. For different scenarios, this structure can be used to design encryption schemes and signature schemes.

Clearly, F is the most essential part of an MPKC signature scheme. Several excellent encryption and signature schemes have been proposed, with various unique trapdoor designs. Among these, several schemes such as UOV [12], Rainbow [8] and HFEv - [15] stand out as excellent signature schemes. Considering encryption schemes, ABC [18] and EFC [17] are the representative methods. These schemes involve some very interesting and unique constructions; in the following, we focus on several of these schemes to clarify the theoretical foundation of the proposed approach.

2.2   UOV and Rainbow

In the construction of UOV[12], let o, v be positive integers and $n = o + v$. Then, the central map $F : \mathbb{F}_q^n \to \mathbb{F}_q^o$ has the following structure.

$$F = (f_1, \ldots, f_o),$$

in which

$$f_k = \sum_{i=1}^{v} \sum_{j=1}^{n} \alpha_{ij}^{(k)} x_i x_j + \sum_{i=1}^{n} \beta_i^{(k)} x_i + \gamma^{(k)}, \alpha_{ij}^{(k)}, \beta_i^{(k)}, \gamma^{(k)} \in \mathbb{F}_q, k \in \{1, \ldots, o\}.$$

For convenience, we mark the first v variables as vinegar variables, and the remainder are oil variables. Obviously, we can easily obtain exact values of the oil variables for given values of the vinegar variables.

In terms of security, except solving the quadratic system of public key directly, one possible approach is to find an inherent space $O = \{\mathbf{x} \in \mathbb{F}_q^n | x_1 = \cdots = x_v = 0\}$ that $P(O) = \mathbf{0}$. Many special attacks have been designed based on this particular property, for example, reconciliation attacks [4], Kipnis-Shamir attacks [13], and intersection attacks [1], among others.

Similarly, Rainbow [8] was designed using a multilayer oil and a vinegar structure. To generate a Rainbow signature scheme with l layers and n unknowns $\mathbf{x} = (x_1, \ldots, x_n)$, we first find an increasing sequence $(v_1, \ldots, v_{l+1})$ of $l+1$ integers with $0 < v_1 < \cdots < v_l < v_{l+1} = n$. The central map of the Rainbow scheme $F : \mathbb{F}_q^n \to \mathbb{F}_q^{n-v_1}$ is constructed of l layers. In the k-th layer, a set of functions are created in the range $\{f_{v_k - v_1 + 1}, \ldots, f_{v_{k+1} - v_1}\}$, and each contained function has the form

$$f_s = \sum_{i=1}^{v_{k+1}} \sum_{j=1}^{v_k} \alpha_{ij}^{(s)} x_i x_j + \sum_{i=1}^{v_{k+1}} \beta_i^{(s)} x_i + \gamma^{(s)}, \ s \in \{v_k - v_1 + 1, \ldots, v_{k+1} - v_1\}.$$

To generate a signature with a given message $\mathbf{m} \in \mathbb{F}_q^{n-v_1}$, we follow the property of UOV in each layer to obtain the values of new variables every stage and a signature can be generated after $l - 1$ times iterations. Similar to the UOV approach, some special attacks have been developed aiming to break the multilayer structure, including the MinRank and band separation attacks [4], among others.

2.3 Simple Matrix Encryption

In the construction of a simple matrix encryption scheme [18], given a positive integer s, $n = s^2, m = 2s^2$, we first define three matrices $A, B, C \in \mathbb{F}_q[x_1, \ldots, x_n]^{s \times s}$ in $A := \mathrm{Mat}_s(x_i), B := \mathrm{Mat}_s(b_i), C := \mathrm{Mat}_s(c_i)$ where the symbol

$$\mathrm{Mat}_s : \mathbb{F}_q^{s^2} \to \mathbb{F}_q^{s \times s}, \mathrm{Mat}_s(x_i) := \begin{pmatrix} x_1 & \cdots & x_s \\ \vdots & \ddots & \vdots \\ x_{s^2 - s + 1} & \cdots & x_{s^2} \end{pmatrix}$$

and for $\forall i \in \{1, \ldots, s^2\}, b_i, c_i$ are linear combinations of $(x_1, \ldots, x_n)$. The central map F is an enumeration of matrices E_1 and E_2 where $E_1 := AB, E_2 := AC$. Through decryption, the central map can be transformed into a linear system of $A^{-1}E_1 = B, A^{-1}E_2 = C$ when A is invertible. In contrast, decryption failure occurs with probability $1/q$. In addition to applying an algebraic attack to solve the polynomial system $P(\mathbf{x}) = \mathbf{m}$ in variables $\mathbf{x}$ with a given message $\mathbf{m} \in \mathbb{F}_q^m$, more subtle or sophisticated attacks such as invariant [14] and HOLE attacks [7] attempt to utilize the trapdoor structure.

3   Proposed Simple Matrix Signature Scheme

In this section, the outline of our proposed scheme is described in detail. Inspired by UOV and ABC, we present the following recommend structure as our proposed simple matrix signature scheme. Let $\mathbb{F}_q$ be a finite field with q elements, u, v be positive integers, $n = u^2 + uv, m = u^2$, and $l = \lceil \frac{v}{2} \rceil$. All the polynomials in the following are defined over the polynomial ring $\mathbb{F}_q[x_1, \ldots, x_n]$ with variables $\mathbf{x} = (x_1, \ldots, x_n)$.

- **Key Generation**: Generate matrices $A(\mathbf{x})$ of size $u \times v$, $C(\mathbf{x})$ of size $v \times u$ and $E(\mathbf{x})$ of size $u \times u$, such that

$$A(\mathbf{x}) = (A_1 \ A_2), \ A_1 = A_{1,0} + \sum_{i=1}^{n} A_{1,i} x_i, A_{1,i} \in \mathbb{F}_q^{u \times (v-l)}, \ A_2 \in \mathbb{F}_q^{u \times l},$$

$$C(\mathbf{x}) = \begin{pmatrix} C_1 \\ C_2 \end{pmatrix}, \ C_1 = C_{1,0} + \sum_{i=1}^{n} C_{1,i} x_i, C_{1,i} \in \mathbb{F}_q^{(v-l) \times u}, \ C_2 \in \mathbb{F}_q^{l \times u},$$

$$E(\mathbf{x}) = E_0 + \sum_{i=1}^{n} E_i x_i; E_i \in \mathbb{F}_q^{u \times u},$$

where $i \in \{0, \dots, n\}$. Then, we generate a tame-like map $h : \mathbb{F}_q^{ul} \to \mathbb{F}_q^{ul}$ such that

$$\begin{cases} h_1(\mathbf{x}) = x_1, \\ h_i(\mathbf{x}) = x_i + \sum_{j,k=1}^{i-1} h_{jk}^{(i)} x_j x_k, i = 2, \dots, ul, \end{cases}$$

where $h_{jk}^i \in \mathbb{F}_q$. The matrix $B(\mathbf{x})$ of size $v \times u$ is defined as

$$B(\mathbf{x}) = \begin{pmatrix} B_1 \\ B_2 \end{pmatrix}, \ B_1 = B_{1,0} + \sum_{i=1}^{n} B_{1,i} x_i, B_{1,i} \in \mathbb{F}_q^{(v-l) \times u},$$

$$B_2 = \begin{pmatrix} h_1(\mathbf{x}) & \cdots & h_u(\mathbf{x}) \\ \vdots & \ddots & \vdots \\ h_{ul-u+1}(\mathbf{x}) & \cdots & h_{ul}(\mathbf{x}) \end{pmatrix}.$$

Finally, we randomly choose a constant matrix $Q \in \mathbb{F}_q^{u \times u}$ with full rank, and two invertible affine transformations $T : \mathbb{F}_q^m \to \mathbb{F}_q^m$ and $S : \mathbb{F}_q^n \to \mathbb{F}_q^n$.
- **Secret Key**:
  - The maps S and T.
  - The coefficients $(A_{1,i}, A_2, C_{1,i}, C_2, E_i, B_{1,i}, h_{jk}^{(i)})$ of $A(\mathbf{x}), C(\mathbf{x}), E(\mathbf{x}), B(\mathbf{x})$ and a constant matrix Q.
- **Public Key**: Let the matrix $\bar{F}(\mathbf{x}) \in \mathbb{F}_q[x_1, \dots, x_n]$ be

$$\bar{F}(\mathbf{x}) = A(\mathbf{x})B(\mathbf{x}) + QB(\mathbf{x})^T C(\mathbf{x}) + E(\mathbf{x}).$$

The map $F = (f_1, \dots, f_{u^2})$ is an enumeration of $\bar{F}(\mathbf{x}) = \mathrm{Mat}_u(f_i)$. The public key is a quadratic map $P : \mathbb{F}_q^n \to \mathbb{F}_q^m$, in which $P = T \circ F \circ S$.
- **Signature Generation**: For a given message $\mathbf{m} \in \mathbb{F}_q^m$, we generate a signature via the following steps.
  - Step 1: Compute $\mathbf{y} = T^{-1}(\mathbf{m})$ and rewrite $\mathbf{y} = (y_1, \dots, y_m) \in \mathbb{F}_q^m$ as a matrix form $Y \in \mathbb{F}_q^{u \times u} = \mathrm{Mat}_u(y_i)$.
  - Step 2: Randomly choose a constant matrix $D \in \mathbb{F}_q^{v \times u}$ and solve the equations

$$\begin{cases} B(\mathbf{x}) = D \\ A(\mathbf{x})D + QD^T C(\mathbf{x}) + E(\mathbf{x}) = Y \end{cases} \tag{1}$$

If Eq. (1) has no solution, we repeat Step 2 until we find a solution. The probability that the equation can be solved successfully is $1 - \frac{1}{q}$ because it depends on whether the linear equations are independent.

- Step 3: The solution in Step 2 is denoted by $\mathbf{z} \in \mathbb{F}_q^m$; compute $\mathbf{s} = S^{-1}(\mathbf{z})$ as a signature.

- **Verification**: For a given message $\mathbf{m}' \in \mathbb{F}_q^n$ and a signature $\mathbf{s}' \in \mathbb{F}_q^m$, check whether the equation $P(\mathbf{s}') = \mathbf{m}'$ holds.

Remark 1. The reason for choosing matrix B with such block a matrix form instead of using a linear system is that attackers can transform the simple matrix signature scheme into a well-known broken balanced oil and vinegar system if B is linear. In this case, because B_2 is generated by a set of quadratic polynomials, it becomes difficult to separate oil variables and vinegar variables by finding an affine transformation.

4   Security Analysis

In this section, we will discuss various attacks against the simple matrix signature scheme such as algebraic attack, minrank attack and some special attacks.

4.1   Algebraic Attack

To solve the polynomial system $P(\mathbf{x}) = \mathbf{y}$ with n variables and m equations, a natural approach might be to perform reduction, such as a Gaussian elimination method, in solving linear systems. Presently, many algorithms such as Buchberger's algorithm [2] and the XL algorithm [5] have improved the computation process compared to direct guessing. In our experiments, we used the F_4 algorithm [9], which is a variant of computing a Gröbner basis. The complexity of the F_4 algorithm depends on an important parameter representing the degree of regularity d_{reg}. In F_4, d_{reg} is given by the index of the first non-positive coefficients of the Hilbert series $S_{m,n}(z) = \frac{\prod_{i=1}^{m}(1-z^{d_i})}{(1-z)^n}$ where d_i is the degree of the i-th polynomial. Therefore, the complexity of F_4 is bounded by

$$O\left(\left(m\binom{n + d_{reg} - 1}{d_{reg}}\right)^{\omega}\right),$$

where the constant ω is in range $2 \leq \omega < 3$. Considering the method of solving underdetermined systems [19], the problem of a quadratic system with n variables and m equations can be transformed into the problem of a quadratic system with $m - \lfloor \frac{n}{m} \rfloor + 1$ variables and $m - \lfloor \frac{n}{m} \rfloor + 1$ equations.

In this case, we performed the F_4 algorithm against the rectangular version of our proposed simple matrix signature scheme. The experiments were all conducted on MAGMA V2.24-8 using a system with an Intel(R) Xeon(R) Gold 6130 2.10 GHz CPU.

From the results presented in Table 1, the parameter d_{reg} is always equal to $m + 1$ in different experiment groups and the central map can be assumed to

Table 1. Algebraic attack(F_4 algorithm) against simple matrix signature scheme

(q,u,v,n,m,l)	d_{reg}	Cpu time(s)	(q,u,v,n,m,l)	d_{reg}	Cpu time(s)
(31,2,2,8,4,1)	5	0.010	(31,3,3,18,9,2)	10	1.350
(31,2,3,10,4,2)	5	≤0.010	(31,3,4,21,9,2)	10	1.600
(31,2,4,12,4,2)	5	≤0.010	(31,3,5,24,9,3)	10	1.710
(31,2,5,14,4,3)	5	≤0.010	(31,3,6,27,9,3)	10	1.840
(31,2,6,16,4,3)	5	≤0.010	(31,4,4,32,16,2)	17	29143.877

be semi-regular. From Fröberg's conjecture, a random polynomial system can be assumed to be semi-regular. Therefore, the complexity of the F_4 algorithm against the simple matrix signature scheme is bounded by the following formula:

$$O\left(\left((u^2-1)\binom{2u^2-2}{u^2-1}\right)^{\omega}\right).$$

4.2 MinRank Attack

The MinRank problem is known to be inherent in almost every MPKC scheme, and its definition is defined as follows.

Definition 1. *Given a finite field $\mathbb{F}_q$ and a sequence of n matrices $\{M_i \in \mathbb{F}_q^{m \times m}\}$, for a positive integer r where $1 \leq r \leq m$, the MinRank problem seeks to determine a vector $(x_1, \ldots, x_n)$ s.t.*

$$Rank\left(\sum_{i=1}^{n} x_i M_i\right) < r.$$

To find a linear combination with the minimum rank r, one simple approach is to guess its kernel by solving $(\sum_{i=1}^{n} x_i M_i)\mathbf{v} = \mathbf{0}$ with random vector $\mathbf{v} \in \mathbb{F}_q^m$. This method, called linear algebraic search, is expected to cost around $\mathcal{O}(q^{\lceil \frac{m}{n} \rceil} r m^3)$. Moreover, there are several other methods for solving MinRank problems, such as the Kipnis-Shamir method [13], Minors method [10] and Support Minors method [1]. Regardless of which method is selected, the efficiency of MinRank attack depends on the parameter r, given by the rank sequence of the central map.

Specifically, each element in the central map contains $2(v-l)$ terms of the multiplication of linear functions and one term of linear combinations of elements in B_2. Each term of the first part contributes at most rank 2 and the rank of the quadratic term bounds by the maximum rank in B_2. Therefore, the rank of the central map is bounded by $4(v-l)+ul-1$, and the complexity of the linear algebraic search method is approximately

$$O(q^{\lceil \frac{m}{n} \rceil r} m^3) = O(q^{4(v-l)+ul-1} u^3).$$

Table 2. Computational complexity of algebraic attack (alg.) and several MinRank attack (MR.) s under different parameters(q, u, v, n, m, l)

Parameters(q, u, v, n, m, l)	alg.	MR. (linear search)	MR. (minors)
$(2^8, 5, 5, 50, 25, 3)$	$2^{112.2}$	$2^{182.9}$	$2^{121.0}$
$(2^8, 6, 6, 72, 36, 3)$	$2^{164.9}$	$2^{239.7}$	$2^{168.1}$
$(2^8, 6, 8, 84, 36, 4)$		$2^{319.7}$	$2^{195.4}$
$(2^8, 7, 7, 98, 49, 4)$	2^{227}	$2^{320.4}$	$2^{228.9}$
$(2^8, 8, 8, 128, 64, 4)$	$2^{299.2}$	$2^{385.0}$	$2^{287.9}$

4.3 Other Attacks

In addition, we considered some other special attacks against the proposed simple matrix signature scheme.

Equivalent Key Attack: The main idea of this attack is to forge secret key pairs by using another secret key tuple (T', F', S') with $P = T \circ F \circ S = T' \circ F' \circ S'$. If the attacker can find some invertible transformations that allow the central map to be solved easily, the security level would accordingly decrease significantly. However, in our construction, matrices A and C are linear matrices that cannot be changed by adding linear transformations. Moreover, the matrix B consists of both linear and quadratic terms; thus, it is impossible to find an exact linear transformation to separate.

Invariant Attack: In the simple matrix encryption scheme, a central map is generated by the multiplication of two matrices. More precisely, matrices A, B, and C are square matrices of linear polynomial entries. The central map is an enumeration of matrices E_1, E_2, where $E_1 = AB, E_2 = AC$. In the invariant attack [14], polynomials selected from the same column in E_1 and E_2 have the same components. By computing the space generated from these polynomials, attackers can restore the coefficients in matrix A. In our simple matrix signature scheme, it becomes difficult to obtain a subspace from some set of particular rows or columns.

5 Parameters

In this section, we present some parameters for different security levels based on the analyses discussed in earlier sections. We chose a moderate setting of the finite field with a size of 2^8 from Table 2. Because the complexity formula in these attacks only involves u and $v \geq u$, the square matrix form would be the best choice.

For the given fixed parameters (q, u, v, n, m), the public key size len is calculated as

$$len = m \times \left(\frac{n(n+1)}{2} + n + 1 \right) \times \log_2 q \text{ bits.}$$

According to this formula, we calculated the public key size and signature size and compared them with those obtained in case of the Rainbow signature scheme [6].

Table 3. Comparison of public key size and signature size of Rainbow(q, v, o_1, o_2) and simple matrix signature scheme(q, u, v, n, m, l)

Level	Parameters	Pk. size (kB)	Sig. size (bit)
I	SM$(2^8, 6, 6, 72, 36, 3)$	93.7	576
	Rainbow$(2^4, 36, 32, 32)$	157.8	528
III	SM$(2^8, 7, 7, 98, 49, 4)$	234.5	784
	Rainbow$(2^8, 68, 32, 48)$	861.4	1,312
V	SM$(2^8, 8, 8, 128, 64, 4)$	520.0	1,056
	Rainbow$(2^8, 96, 36, 64)$	1885.0	1,632

From Table 3, it may be observed that with the exception of the signature size in 128-bit security, each number in the simple matrix scheme was smaller than that in the Rainbow scheme. For example, in 128-bit security, the public key size was smaller by 40.7%. The reduction range can reach approximately 63.4% in 256-bit security.

6 Conclusion

In this paper, we propose a new method for constructing an MPKC signature by matrix multiplication. The most notable part of our simple matrix signature scheme is the construction of its central map, which has both high randomness and expansibility. In addition, we chose several conventional attack algorithms to analyze the security of the proposed approach. The experimental results showed that our signature scheme demonstrated high resistance against algebraic attacks and rank attacks. Other attacks, such as invariant attacks, are expected to be ineffective because all multiplication of the entries is mingled together. By calculating the computational complexity formulas for different attacks, we presented some secure parameters at different levels. Compared to the Rainbow signature scheme, our proposed signature scheme requires approximately 40% to 60% smaller public key sizes. In further steps, we can use some special parameters to compress the public key size. We have considered some common attacks against our signature scheme. It should be noted that whether there exists a particular attack that may prove effective in breaking this signature scheme remains an open question.

References

1. Beullens, W.: Improved cryptanalysis of UOV and rainbow, Cryptology ePrint Archive, Report 2020/1343 (2020). https://eprint.iacr.org/2020/1343

236   C. Yin et al.

2. Buchberger, B.: Ein Algorithmus zum Auffinden der Basiselemente des Restklassenringes nach einem nulldimensionalen Polynomideal, Ph.D. thesis, Universität Innsbruck (1965)
3. Chen, L., et al.: Report on Post-quantum Cryptography, NIST Interagency Report 8105 (2016). https://www.nist.gov/publications/report-post-quantum-cryptography
4. Ding, J., Yang, B.-Y., Chen, C.-H.O., Chen, M.-S., Cheng, C.-M.: New differential-algebraic attacks and reparametrization of rainbow. In: Bellovin, S.M., Gennaro, R., Keromytis, A., Yung, M. (eds.) ACNS 2008. LNCS, vol. 5037, pp. 242–257. Springer, Heidelberg (2008). https://doi.org/10.1007/978-3-540-68914-0_15
5. Courtois, N., Klimov, A., Patarin, J., Shamir, A.: Efficient algorithms for solving overdefined systems of multivariate polynomial equations. In: Preneel, B. (ed.) EUROCRYPT 2000. LNCS, vol. 1807, pp. 392–407. Springer, Heidelberg (2000). https://doi.org/10.1007/3-540-45539-6_27
6. Ding, J., et al.: Rainbow, NIST PQC Project. https://csrc.nist.gov/projects/post-quantum-cryptography/
7. Ding, J., Hu, L., Nie, X., Li, J., Wagner, J.: High order linearization equation (HOLE) attack on multivariate public key cryptosystems. In: Okamoto, T., Wang, X. (eds.) PKC 2007. LNCS, vol. 4450, pp. 233–248. Springer, Heidelberg (2007). https://doi.org/10.1007/978-3-540-71677-8_16
8. Ding, J., Schmidt, D.: Rainbow, a new multivariable polynomial signature scheme. In: Ioannidis, J., Keromytis, A., Yung, M. (eds.) ACNS 2005. LNCS, vol. 3531, pp. 164–175. Springer, Heidelberg (2005). https://doi.org/10.1007/11496137_12
9. Faugère, J.-C.: A New Efficient Algorithm for Computing Gröbner Bases (F4). J. Pure Appl. Algebra 139(1), 61–88 (1999)
10. Faugère, J.-C., Din, M., Spaenlehauer, P.-J.: Computing loci of rank defects of linear matrices using Gröbner bases and applications to cryptology. In: ISSAC 2010, pp. 257–264 (2010)
11. Garey, M., Johnson, D.: Computers and Intractability: A Guide to the Theory of NP-Completeness. W. H. Freeman and Company, San Francisco (1979)
12. Kipnis, A., Patarin, J., Goubin, L.: Unbalanced oil and vinegar signature schemes. In: Stern, J. (ed.) EUROCRYPT 1999. LNCS, vol. 1592, pp. 206–222. Springer, Heidelberg (1999). https://doi.org/10.1007/3-540-48910-X_15
13. Kipnis, A., Shamir, A.: Cryptanalysis of the oil and vinegar signature scheme. In: Krawczyk, H. (ed.) CRYPTO 1998. LNCS, vol. 1462, pp. 257–266. Springer, Heidelberg (1998). https://doi.org/10.1007/BFb0055733
14. Moody, D., Perlner, R., Smith-Tone, D.: An asymptotically optimal structural attack on the ABC multivariate encryption scheme. In: Mosca, M. (ed.) PQCrypto 2014. LNCS, vol. 8772, pp. 180–196. Springer, Cham (2014). https://doi.org/10.1007/978-3-319-11659-4_11
15. Patarin, J.: Hidden fields equations (HFE) and isomorphisms of polynomials (IP): two new families of asymmetric algorithms. In: Maurer, U. (ed.) EUROCRYPT 1996. LNCS, vol. 1070, pp. 33–48. Springer, Heidelberg (1996). https://doi.org/10.1007/3-540-68339-9_4
16. Shor, P.: Polynomial-time algorithms for prime factorization and discrete logarithms on a quantum computer. SIAM J. Comput. 26(5), 1484–1509 (1997)
17. Szepieniec, A., Ding, J., Preneel, B.: Extension field cancellation: a new central trapdoor for multivariate quadratic systems. In: Takagi, T. (ed.) PQCrypto 2016. LNCS, vol. 9606, pp. 182–196. Springer, Cham (2016). https://doi.org/10.1007/978-3-319-29360-8_12

18. Tao, C., Xiang, H., Petzoldt, A., Ding, J.: Simple matrix - a multivariate public key cryptosystem (MPKC) for encryption. Finite Fields Appl. **35**, 352–368 (2015)
19. Thomae, E., Wolf, C.: Solving underdetermined systems of multivariate quadratic equations revisited. In: Fischlin, M., Buchmann, J., Manulis, M. (eds.) PKC 2012. LNCS, vol. 7293, pp. 156–171. Springer, Heidelberg (2012). https://doi.org/10.1007/978-3-642-30057-8_10

Game Theory and Security

Moving Target Defense for the CloudControl Game

Koji Hamasaki(✉) and Hitoshi Hohjo

Osaka Prefecture University, Osaka, Japan

Abstract. The recent global spread of cloud computing has streamlined all kinds of tasks by allowing people to go online and get the services they need, when they need them. The cloud is a revolutionary system that saves time, effort, and money. On the other hand, devices connected to the cloud pose the risk of cyber-attacks. One example is Advanced Persistent Threats (APTs), which analyze a target over a long period of time and expose it to danger. The increase in this threat has led to the need for robustness against stealthy attacks. In this paper, we propose Moving Target Defense (MTD) as a defense strategy in the CloudControl game model, which models the interaction between the cloud-connected devices, the defender and the attacker struggling for control of the cloud. We also prove the convergence of this strategy against a static attacker by numerical experiments. Our results contribute to cyber insurance, commercial investment, and corporate policy.

Keywords: Cloud computing · Game theory · Moving Target Defense

1 Introduction

These days the term IoT, which describes physical objects—"things"—connected to the Internet, is often used. At the same time Cyber-Physical Systems (CPS) [1, 2], which is closely related to the IoT, is also getting a lot of attention. CPS is about attaching many sensors to objects to be controlled in the real world, such as people and cars, and analyzing the data collected by these devices in cyberspace and feeding it back to the objects for more optimal control. These technologies will enable a variety of services that have never been available before.

In order to realize CPS/IoT society, a secure and safe networked relationship is needed to communicate. However, with new technology comes the risk of new cyber-attacks, for example, Advanced Persistent Threats (APTs) [3]. They target a specific individual or organization and continuously attack it with a combination of suitable attacks. Because they require a large amount of resources, these attacks are often carried out by huge organizations and have a significant impact on society. Since new technologies such as IoT and CPS have only been created for a short period of time, the vulnerabilities are undiscovered and the risk of a zero-day attacks to exploit them before a fix or countermeasure patch is made is high. APTs are often a combination of these zero-day

© Springer Nature Switzerland AG 2021
T. Nakanishi and R. Nojima (Eds.): IWSEC 2021, LNCS 12835, pp. 241–251, 2021.
https://doi.org/10.1007/978-3-030-85987-9_14

attacks and are highly dangerous. This attack could allow the attacker to take ownership of the cloud to send signals to the device.

In this paper, we propose Moving Target Defense (MTD) [4] as a strategy for the administrator of the cloud which is vulnerable to APT and may be controlled by the attacker. Furthermore, we model a situation in which the device decides whether to trust a command from the cloud controlled by the defender using MTD or the static attacker, and find a Gestalt Nash equilibrium (GNE) through game-theoretic analysis. We clarify that MTD is an effective strategy in this situation. We created a proposed model using the CloudControl game [5, 6]. This game consists of the signaling game and the FlipIt game. The signaling game is a typical incomplete information dynamics game, which have been developed based on the study of two-player language game [7]. Many studies have utilized this game to model various security situations [8–11]. The Flipit game is a recently created game in response to the development of cloud systems [12]. This game is suited for studying systems attacked by APTs [13–19].

Because APTs persistently attack the system, we believe that the defenders can count backwards the time that the defenders have moved since the system's IDs and passwords are no longer available. The attacker should use this information to conduct a dynamic attack. However, the proposed models in [5, 6] used simple and static attacker and defender strategies in the FlipIt game. Van Dijk proposed LM Attacker (LMA) and Defender playing with Exponential Distribution (DED) as dynamic strategies for attackers and defenders in the FlipIt game, respectively [12]. And Hyodo proposed the CloudControl game model that uses the above dynamic strategies in the FlipIt game and proved that GNE exists in the proposed model [20].

In this paper, we show that there is an effective strategy called Moving Target Defense (MTD) in addition to the defender's strategy in the FlipIt game proposed in [12], and we propose the CloudControl game model using that strategy. We also show that GNE is present in that model as well. This can guide the optimal action of defenders and IoT devices against attackers (APTs) who launch advanced attacks. The results of this study will be useful for cyber-insurance, commercial investment and corporate policies.

The remainder of this paper is organized as follows. We proposes the CloudControl game with a defender using MTD in Sect. 2. Then we presents the results of the simulations performed to reveal the presence of GNE in the above proposed model in Sect. 3. We conclude the paper in Sect. 4.

2   Our Model

We model a cloud-based system in which the cloud is the target of APTs. In this model, an attacker capable of APTs can pay the cost and compromise the cloud. The defender, or the cloud administrator, can pay the cost and regain control of the cloud. The cloud sends a message to the device, denoted by r. The device can follow this message, but has an on-board control system to operate autonomously. So it is also possible to use the autonomous motion system without following the message from the cloud.

In this scenario, we uses the CloudControl game that combines two games, the FlipIt game and the signaling game. The FlipIt game takes place between the attacker and the defender, while the signaling game takes place between the possibly compromised cloud and the device. Specifically, the player who controls the resource in the FlipIt game will be the sender of the signaling game.

The model proposed in this study is the CloudControl game model played by a static attacker and a defender using Moving Target Defense (MTD), described below. We investigated whether MTD is an effective strategy against the static attacker (Fig. 1).

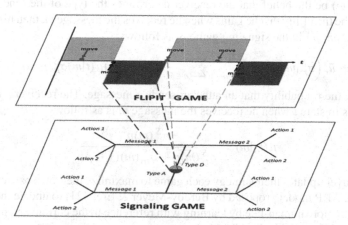

Fig. 1. The CloudControl game. The FlipIt game models the interaction between an attacker and a defender, or a cloud administrator, who compete for ownership of the cloud. The signaling game is played in which the player, who controls the cloud in the FlipIt game, sends a message to a device. The device then decides whether to trust or not to trust the message. (Hyodo, T., Hohjo, H., 2019)

2.1 The Signaling Game in the Proposed Game Model

We describe the symbols used in this study.

- Player: Sender (Cloud(t)), Receiver (Device(r))
- Type of the sender: $T = \{t | t_A, t_D\}$
- Message: $M = \{m | m_L, m_H\}$
- Action: $A = \{a | a_Y, a_N\}$

Player t_A is the attacker and t_D is the defender. In the CloudControl game, the type of the sender is determined by the equilibrium of the FlipIt game. Let m_L and m_H denote low and high risk messages, respectively. After receiving the message, the device chooses an action. Action a_Y represents trusting the message from the cloud, and a_N represents not trusting it.

Let $\sigma_{t_A}^S(m)$, $\sigma_{t_D}^S(m)$ be the strategy in which player t_A, t_D sends a message m, and $\sigma_r^S(a|m)$ be the strategy in which the device r takes an action a when it receives a message m. Also let $u_{t_A}^S(m, a)$, $u_{t_D}^S(m, a)$ be the utilities players t_A, t_D gain. Then the expected utilities $\bar{u}_{t_A}^S(\sigma_{t_A}^S, \sigma_r^S)$, $\bar{u}_{t_D}^S(\sigma_{t_D}^S, \sigma_r^S)$ in the signaling game of the attacker and defender is as follows.

$$\bar{u}_{t_A}^S\left(\sigma_{t_A}^S, \sigma_r^S\right) = \sum_{a \in A} \sum_{m \in M} u_{t_A}^S(m, a)\sigma_r^S(a|m)\sigma_{t_A}^S(m) \tag{1}$$

$$\bar{u}_{t_D}^S\left(\sigma_{t_D}^S, \sigma_r^S\right) = \sum_{a \in A} \sum_{m \in M} u_{t_D}^S(m, a)\sigma_r^S(a|m)\sigma_{t_D}^S(m) \tag{2}$$

Let $\mu(t|m)$ be the belief that the receiver determines the type of the sender is t and $\sigma_r^S(t, m, a)$ be the utility that he gains when he receives the message m, then his expected utility $\bar{u}_r^S\left(\sigma_r^S|m, \mu\right)$ in the signaling game is as follows.

$$\bar{u}_r^S\left(\sigma_r^S|m, \mu\right) = \sum_{a \in A} \sum_{m \in M} u_r^S(t, m, a)\mu(t|m)\sigma_r^S(a|m) \tag{3}$$

Let p be the probability that an attacker sends a message. The receiver's belief that the sender is in state t when he receives the message m is as follows.

$$\mu(t_A|m) = \frac{\sigma_{t_A}^S(m)p}{\sigma_{t_A}^S(m)p + \sigma_{t_D}^S(m)(1-p)} \tag{4}$$

Each player updates their strategy each game to maximize their own expected utility. We used the ARP model proposed by Bereby-Meyer & Erev [21] to update the strategy. This model is more human-like by learning with reference to the current and past reward values. The ARP model is described below.

The probability $Q_n(time)$ of taking a move n at time is given by

$$Q_n(time) = \frac{q_n(time)}{\sum q_n(time)} \tag{5}$$

$q_n(time)$ is the pure value at the move n and is updated with each passing $time$. Let g_j be the reward for choosing a move j at $time$, then the renewal formula is given by

$$q_n(time + 1) = \max\{v, (1 - \phi)q_n(time) + E_j(n, L_{time}(g_j))\}, \tag{6}$$

where φ is the forgetting rate and v is the guaranteed value. Also the functions E_j and L_{time} are given by

$$E_j(n, L_{time}(g_j)) = \begin{cases} L_{time}(g_j)(1 - \varepsilon) & (j = n) \\ L_{time}(g_j)\varepsilon & (otherwise) \end{cases} \tag{7}$$

$$L_{time}(g_j) = g_j - \rho(time), \tag{8}$$

where the parameter ε is the weight of the reward. The $\rho(time)$ in Eq. (8) is an important function in the ARP model. As mentioned above, the ARP model learns rewards and the function $\rho(time)$ plays the role. It is given by

$$\rho(time + 1) = \begin{cases} (1 - c^+)\rho(time) + (c^+)g_j & (g_j \geq \rho(time)) \\ (1 - c^-)\rho(time) + (c^-)g_j & (g_j < \rho(time)) \end{cases} \tag{9}$$

c^+ and c^- are parameters representing the impact of the next reward when the reward g_j was better and worse than the evaluation function $\rho(time)$, respectively.

2.2 The FlipIt Game in the Proposed Game Model

The FlipIt game in the original CloudControl game is a two-player game in which the attacker and the defender compete for one shared resource along a timeline. In this paper, we envision a system in which a defender can prevent an attack by moving the resource through the network. In the next subsection, we describe the defender's strategy in the proposed game model.

Moving Target Defense (MTD). MTD is a defender's strategy to migrate resources to node i through a fully connected network of $n(n \geq 2)$ nodes with a probability of $p(i)$. Defenders can use this strategy to prevent attackers from discovering vulnerabilities and critical resources in their systems. In other words, this model assumes a situation where the target resource is not visible to the attacker. For simplicity, we assume that the MTD in this study randomly migrates resources to all nodes (Fig. 2).

$$p(i) = \frac{1}{n}, i = 1, \ldots, n \tag{10}$$

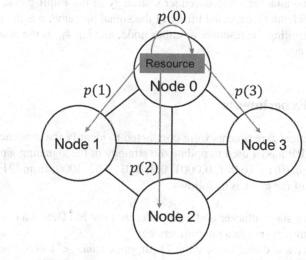

Fig. 2. Moving Target Defense (MTD) when the number of nodes is 3. The defender can migrate a resource to other node, through a fully connected network. $p(0) = p(1) = p(2) = p(3) = 1/4$.

The FlipIt Game with MTD. Let the number of nodes be n. The rules of the FlipIt game in this case are as follows.

- The game begins with the defender in control of the resource on *node* 0 (*time* = 1).
- Both players follow their own strategies at a certain *time* and determine whether to pay the moving cost.
- When the defender moves, he takes the ownership of the resource and may or may not migrate it to another node.

- When the attacker moves, he selects one node at random to attack. The attacker takes the ownership of the resource only if he attacks a node where the resource actually exists.
- When both players move at the same time, the defender takes the ownership of the resource.

For each FlipIt game, the player who controls the resource becomes the sender and plays multiple signaling games with the device (the receiver).

The expected utilities $\overline{u}_{t_A}^F(\alpha_{t_A}, \alpha_{t_D})$, $\overline{u}_{t_D}^F(\alpha_{t_A}, \alpha_{t_D})$ of the FlipIt game for the attacker and defender in the proposed model is as follows.

$$\overline{u}_{t_A}^S(\alpha_{t_A}, \alpha_{t_D}) = \overline{u}_{t_A}^S \frac{p}{n} - k_{t_A} \alpha_{t_A} \tag{11}$$

$$\overline{u}_{t_D}^S(\alpha_{t_A}, \alpha_{t_D}) = \overline{u}_{t_D}^S \left(1 - \frac{p}{n}\right) - k_{t_D} \alpha_{t_D} \tag{12}$$

where $\alpha_{t_A}, \alpha_{t_D}$ is the attacker's and defender's strategy in the FlipIt game, $\overline{u}_{t_A}^S, \overline{u}_{t_D}^S$ is the attacker's and defender's expected utility in the signaling game, p is the probability of the attacker controlling the resource at either node, and k_{t_A}, k_{t_D} is the attacker's and defender's moving cost.

3   Numerical Experiments

In this study, numerical experiments were conducted to identify the existence of GNE. The value of the ARP model used to update the strategy of the signaling game was set to $(\phi, \upsilon, \varepsilon, c^+, c^-, q_n(0)) = (0.001, 0.0001, 0.2, 0.01, 0.02, 1000)$ from [21].

The procedure of the game is as follows.

Step 1. Players are a static attacker and a defender that use MTD, and a device. At the start of the game, all players use a random strategy.
Step 2. The attacker and defender play the FlipIt game (*time* < 4000). Each time the player controlling the resource plays the signaling game with the device, and updates the signaling game strategy.
Step 3. From the expected utility of the signaling game, attackers and defenders find the FlipIt game strategy that maximizes the expected utility of the FlipIt game.
Step 4. The attacker and the defender reset the signaling game strategy and return to a random state.

We repeated Step 2 to Step 4 above 100 times to examine the variability of the expected utilities of attacker and defender in the signaling game and the strategies of both players in the FlipIt game. Also the signaling game was played enough times to reach equilibrium.

Table 1. The gain of the attacker, the defender and the device in the signaling game.

(Sender, Receiver)		Device	
		a_Y	a_N
Attacker	m_L	(12, -1)	(-40, 10)
	m_H	(30, -40)	(-40, 10)
Defender	m_L	(16, 20)	(-10, -5)
	m_H	(3, 3)	(-10, -5)

The gain in the signalling game was set up as shown in the Table 1. The number on the left is the sender's (attacker or defender) gain and the number on the right is the receiver's (device) gain.

We first experimented with fixed $n = 3$ and not fixed k_{t_A}, k_{t_D}. Figure 3 shows the result of the experiment for $k_{t_A} = 20, k_{t_D} = 15$. In the top graph, the red dots represent the attacker's expected utility $\bar{u}_{t_A}^S$ in the signaling game, and the blue dots represent the defender's expected utility $\bar{u}_{t_D}^S$ in the signaling game, with the vertical axis representing the expected utility and the horizontal axis representing the number of sets. In the bottom graph, the red dots represent the attacker's strategy α_{t_A} in the FlipIt game, and the blue dots represent the defender's strategy α_{t_D} in the FlipIt game, with the vertical axis representing the strategy and the horizontal axis representing the number of sets. In this situation, the expected utilities of the attacker and defender in the signaling game and their strategies in the FlipIt game converged to a certain value, respectively. This indicates a convergence to GNE. The converged values were $\bar{u}_{t_A}^S = 12, \bar{u}_{t_D}^S = 16, \alpha_{t_A} = 0.12$, and $\alpha_{t_D} = 0.15$.

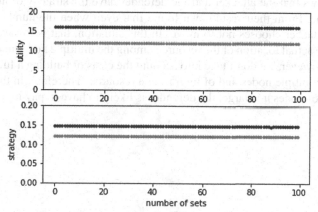

Fig. 3. The changes in the expected utilities $\bar{u}_{t_A}^S, \bar{u}_{t_D}^S$ and strategies $\alpha_{t_A}, \alpha_{t_D}$ with $n = 3, k_{t_A} = 20, k_{t_D} = 15$.

Figure 4 shows the result of the experiment for $k_{t_A} = 40$, $k_{t_D} = 30$. In this situation, $\alpha_{t_A} = \alpha_{t_D} = 0.00$. This shows that the attacker and the defender have the strategy of not moving in the FlipIt game even if the signaling game's utility conditions of Table 1. were met. From Eq. (11), (12), the expected utility of the FlipIt game is smaller as the moving cost increases. If they don't benefit from attacking, they won't bother attacking because they won't have to.

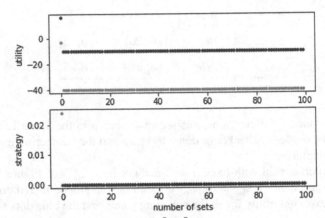

Fig. 4. The changes in the expected utilities $\overline{u}_{t_A}^S$, $\overline{u}_{t_D}^S$ and strategies α_{t_A}, α_{t_D} with $n = 3$, $k_{t_A} = 40$, $k_{t_D} = 30$.

Next, we experimented with fixed $k_{t_A} = 20$, $k_{t_D} = 15$ and not fixed n. Figure 5 shows the result of the experiment for $n = 5$. In this situation, the expected utilities of the attacker and defender in the signaling game and their strategies in the FlipIt game converged to a certain value, respectively. This indicates a convergence to GNE. The converged values were $\overline{u}_{t_A}^S = 12$, $\overline{u}_{t_D}^S = 16$, $\alpha_{t_A} = 0.09$, and $\alpha_{t_D} = 0.07$.

Figure 6 shows the result of the experiment for $n = 10$. In this situation, $\alpha_{t_A} = \alpha_{t_D} = 0.00$. This shows that the attacker and the defender have the strategy of not moving in the FlipIt game. From their results, we found that even when the number of nodes n is large, the attacker chooses not to move. In this situation, that is to say, the attacker cannot find the actual location of the resource among the multiple nodes and gives up on attacking it. However, we don't take into account the costs of building a fully connected network with multiple nodes and of migrating a resource. Therefore, in the real world, if the number of nodes n is large, the defender is likely to have to pay more costs.

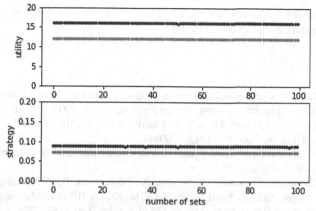

Fig. 5. The changes in expected utilities $\bar{u}^S_{t_A}, \bar{u}^S_{t_D}$ and strategies $\alpha_{t_A}, \alpha_{t_D}$ with $n = 5, k_{t_A} = 20, k_{t_D} = 15$.

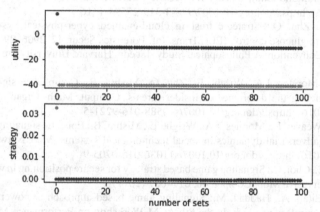

Fig. 6. The changes in the expected utilities $\bar{u}^S_{t_A}, \bar{u}^S_{t_D}$ and strategies $\alpha_{t_A}, \alpha_{t_D}$ with $n = 10, k_{t_A} = 20, k_{t_D} = 15$.

4 Conclusion and Future Work

In this paper, we proposed the cloud control game with a static attacker and a defender using MTD and showed that GNE exists in the proposed model. This equilibrium will help protect cloud-connected CPSs by revealing the frequency of attacks by attackers launching APTs in the future IoT/CPS society and the optimal strategies for MTD and IoT devices against these attackers.

However, the only thing revealed in this study is the presence of GNE in the proposed model. Its equilibrium equation is not clear.

In future work, it is important to find the equilibrium equation in the proposed model. We would also like to revisit a model that takes into account the cost of building the network and of migrating a resource. Furthermore, APTs in the real world are likely to launch more sophisticated attacks. Therefore, we want to clarify whether MTD is an effective strategy for defenders even against advanced and dynamic attackers, and whether GNE exists even in such a model.

References

1. Baheti, R., Gill, H.: Cyber-physical systems. Impact Control Technol. **12**, 161–166 (2011)
2. Lee, E.A.: Cyber physical systems: design challenges. In: 2008 11th IEEE International Symposium on Object Oriented Real-Time Distributed Computing (ISORC) on Proceedings, Orlando, FL, USA, pp. 363–369. IEEE (2008)
3. Tankard, C.: Advanced persistent threats and how to monitor and deter them. Netw. Secur. **2011**(8), 16–19 (2011)
4. Feng, X., Zheng, Z., Cansever, D., Swami, A., Mohapatra, P.: A signaling game model for moving target defense. In: IEEE INFOCOM 2017 - IEEE Conference on Computer Communications on Proceedings, Atlanta, GA, USA, pp. 1–9. IEEE (2017)
5. Pawlick, J., Farhang, S., Zhu, Q.: Flip the cloud: cyber-physical signaling games in the presence of advanced persistent threats. In: Khouzani, M., Panaousis, E., Theodorakopoulos, G. (eds.) Decision and Game Theory for Security. LNCS, vol. 9406, pp. 289–308. Springer, Cham (2015). https://doi.org/10.1007/978-3-319-25594-1_16
6. Pawlick, J., Zhu, Q.: Strategic trust in cloud-enabled cyber-physical systems with an application to glucose control. IEEE Trans. Inf. Forensics Secur. **12**, 2906–2919 (2017)
7. Lewis, D.: Convention: A Philosophical Study, 1st edn. Harvard University Press, Cambridge (1969)
8. Casey, W., Morales, J.A., Wright, E., Zhu, Q., Mishra, B.: Compliance signaling games: toward modeling the deterrence of insider threats. Comput. Math. Organ. Theory **22**(3), 318–349 (2016). https://doi.org/10.1007/s10588-016-9221-5
9. Casey, W., Weaver, R., Morales, J.A., Wright, E., Mishra, B.: Epistatic signaling and minority games, the adversarial dynamics in social technological systems. Mob. Netw. Appl. **21**(1), 161–174 (2016). https://doi.org/10.1007/s11036-016-0705-9
10. Christian, E., Choi, C.: Signaling game based strategy for secure positioning in wireless sensor network. Pervasive Mob. Comput. **40**, 611–627 (2017)
11. Khalil, I., Eitan, A., Haddad, M.: Signaling game based approach to power control management in wireless network. In the 8th ACM Workshop on Performance Monitoring and Measurement of Heterogeneous Wireless and Wired Networks on Proceedings, pp. 139–144. Association for Computing Machinery, New York (2013)
12. van Dijk, M., Juels, A., Oprea, A., Riveat, R.L.: Flipit: the game of "stealthy takecover." J. Cryptol. **26**, 655–713 (2013). https://doi.org/10.1007/s00145-012-9134-5
13. Laszka, A., Horvath, G., Felegyhazi, M., Buttyan, L.: FlipThem: modeling targeted attacks with FlipIt for multiple resources. In: Poovendran, R., Saad, W. (eds.) Decision and Game Theory for Security. LNCS, vol. 8840, pp. 175–194. Springer, Cham (2014). https://doi.org/10.1007/978-3-319-12601-2_10
14. Zhang, R., Zhu, Q.: FlipIn: a game-theoretic cyber insurance framework for incentive-compatible cyber risk management of internet of things. IEEE Trans. Inf. Forensics Secur. **15**, 2026–2041 (2019)
15. Feng, X., Zheng, Z., Hu, P., Cansever, D., Mohapatra, P.: Stealthy attacks meets insider threats: a three-player game model. In: MILCOM 2015 - 2015 IEEE Military Communications Conference on Proceedings, Tampa, FL, USA, pp. 25–30. IEEE (2015)
16. Oakley, L., Oprea, A.: QFlip: an adaptive reinforcement learning strategy for the FlipIt security game. In: Alpcan, T., Vorobeychik, Y., Baras, J.S., Dán, G. (eds.) Decision and Game Theory for Security. LNCS, vol. 11836, pp. 364–384. Springer, Cham (2019). https://doi.org/10.1007/978-3-030-32430-8_22

17. Bowers, K.D., et al.: Defending against the unknown enemy: applying FLIPIT to system security. In: Grossklags, J., Walrand, J. (eds.) Decision and Game Theory for Security. LNCS, vol. 7638, pp. 248–263. Springer, Cham (2012). https://doi.org/10.1007/978-3-642-34266-0_15

18. Greige, L., Chin, S.: Reinforcement learning in FlipIt. arXiv preprint arXiv: 2002.12909 (2020)

19. Feng, X., Zheng, Z., Hu, P., Cansever, D., Mohapatra, P.: Stealthy attacks with insider information: a game theoretic model with asymmetric feedback. In: MILCOM 2016 - 2016 IEEE Military Communications Conference on Proceedings, Baltimore, MD, USA, pp. 277–282. IEEE (2015)

20. Hyodo, T., Hohjo, H.: The Gestalt Nash equilibrium analysis in cyber security. In: RIMS Kokyuroku 2126, pp. 9–18. Kyoto University, Kyoto (2019). (in Japanese)

21. Bereby-Meyer, Y., Erev, I.: On learning to become a successful loser: a comparison of alternative abstractions of learning processes in the loss domain. J. Math. Psychol. 42, 266–286 (1998)

Author Index

Aburada, Kentaro   119
Akiyama, Mitsuaki   99
Attrapadung, Nuttapong   77

Booth, Roland   195

Chiba, Daiki   99

Daiza, Takanori   175

Fan, Yun   99
Fukushima, Kazuhide   23

Hamasaki, Koji   241
Hashimoto, Yasufumi   137
Hohjo, Hitoshi   241
Hutchinson, Aaron   216

Ikematsu, Yasuhiko   3
Ito, Hiroshi   64

Kameyama, Yukiyoshi   151
Karati, Sabyasachi   195
Kiyomoto, Shinsaku   23, 64
Kudo, Momonari   23
Kurosawa, Kaoru   175
Kuzuno, Hiroki   45

LeGrow, Jason T.   216

Masuda, Masahiro   151
Matsuura, Kanta   77

Mukunoki, Masayuki   119
Murata, Masayuki   99

Nakamura, Satoshi   3
Nakamura, Toru   64

Ohsita, Yuichi   99
Okazaki, Naonobu   119

Park, Mirang   119
Phalakarn, Kittiphop   77

Safavi-Naini, Reihaneh   195
Shibahara, Toshiki   99
Sohaimi, Ahmad Saiful Aqmal Bin Ahmad
      119
Suppakitpaisarn, Vorapong   77

Takagi, Tsuyoshi   23, 227

Uemura, Shusaku   23
Usuzaki, Shotaro   119

Wang, Yacheng   227

Xu, Yanhong   195

Yamaba, Hisaaki   119
Yamauchi, Toshihiro   45, 64
Yasuda, Masaya   3
Yin, Changze   227

Printed in the United States
by Baker & Taylor Publisher Services